D1232741

Land Filled with Flies

Land Filled with Flies

A Political Economy of the Kalahari

Edwin N. Wilmsen

The University of Chicago Press · Chicago and London

The University of Chicago Press, Chicago 60637
The University of Chicago Press, Ltd., London

© 1989 by The University of Chicago
All rights reserved. Published 1989
Printed in the United States of America

98 97 96 95 94 93 92   5432

Library of Congress Cataloging-in-Publication Data
Wilmsen, Edwin N.
  Land filled with flies : a political economy of the Kalahari /
Edwin N. Wilmsen.
     p. cm.
  Bibliography: p.
  Includes index.
  ISBN 0-226-90014-2. — ISBN 0-226-90015-0 (pbk.)
  1. San (African people)—Economic conditions. 2. Kalahari Desert—
Economic conditions. 3. Hunting and gathering societies.
4. Economic anthropology. I. Title.
DT764.B8W56   1989
330.968'0089961—dc19   89-30724
                                                      CIP

⊗ The paper used in this publication meets the minimum re-
quirements of the American National Standard for Information
Sciences—Permanence of Paper for Printed Library Materials,
ANSI Z39.48-1984.

For my children
Richard
David
Nancy
Carl
Lisa

Contents

Acknowledgments

Many people and organizations in a variety of ways great and small helped bring this book to fruition. Rather than single them out for specific contributions, I want to thank them all equally: Feriale Abdullah, Arthur Albert, Erika Albert, Kirsten Alnaes, Victor Alzamora, Debba Andree, Michael Asch, Alan Barnard, Mary Beaudry, Sara Berry, Sven Peter Birkerts, Allison Brooks, Robert Camby, Alec Campbell, Judy Campbell, Alvaro de Castro e Lima, Claudia Chang, Jean Comaroff, John Comaroff, Katherine Demuth, James Denbow, Jocelyn Denbow, Janis Diring, Patricia Draper, Ireneus Eibl-Eibesfeldt, Ed February, Ralph Fields, Lynn Focht, Richard Ford, Bennett Fuller, Jr., John Galaty, Tcuka Gcau, Irene Genzier, Halengisi Gomoseye, Richard Goodbody, Robert Gordon, Mary Greene, Anne Griffiths, Karen Harbeck, Henry Harpending, Jennifer Harris, Joanne Hart, Alice Hausman, Jean Hay, Ann Alfhild Hendrickson, Robert Hitchcock, Jenny Hochstadt, Nancy Howell, Trefor Jenkins, Gregory Johnson, Tcinxau Kao, Haruvesa Keharera, Varipaka Keirorere, Brian Kensley, Carol Kerven, Roy Larick, Flemming Larson, Brigetta Lau, Richard Lee, Sheila Letswiti, Sheila Mackenzie, John Marenga, Manuel Marenga, Isaac Marks, Shula Marks, Lorna Marshall, Alex Matseka, Paul Mattick, Jr., Nikolas van der Merwe, Bashile Mhapa, Mpho Molomo, Lisa Wilmsen Monahan, Fred Morton, Pnina Motzafi-Haller, Fred Myers, Katjateri Nderico, Manuel Nguvauva, Gabriella von Oettingen, Jack Parson, Neil Parsons, Pauline Peters, Salalena G. G. Phaladi, Dam Qam, Kao Qam, Leonard Ramatokwane, Jeff Ramsey, Sekgabo Ramsey, Dwight Reed, Janet Rodney, Franz Rottland, Beatrice Sandelowsky, Warren Schapiro, Harold Scheffler, Jill Schennum, Johanna Schoss, Carmel Schrire, Alina Segobye, Marjorie Shostak, Nancy Soyring, Louise Sperling, Wendy-Elizabeth Stauss, Nathaniel Tarn, Madeleine Taylor, Tcoma Tcashe, Kao Tcishe, Qam Tcishe, Qu Tcishe, Nqai Tcoma, Thomas Tlou, Phillip Tobias, Felicia Touhey, Anthony Traill, Kahae Tuvare, Makademe Tuvare, Simon Tuvare, Tohoperi Tuvare, Helga Vierich, Rainer Vossen, Martin West, Sonia White, Polly Wiessner, Carl Wilmsen, Martin Wobst, Eric Wolf, Henry Wright, Diana Wylie, Ssao Xau, John Yellen, Mindy Zeder.

African Studies Library—Boston University (Vicky Evalds, Gretchen Walsh), Cape Town Archives—Cape Town, William Cullen Library—University of the Witwatersrand (Elizabeth Dey), Melville Herskovits Library—Northwestern University, National Archives—Gaborone (Gilbert Mpholokeng), National Museum and Art Gallery—Gaborone (Teri Madondo, Doreen Nteta), Public Records Office—London, School of Oriental and African Studies—University of London, State Archive Service—Windhoek (Christel Stern), Alfred Tozzer Library—Harvard University (John Hansen), Universidade Eduardo Mondlane Repositoria Archiva—Maputo, Vereinigen Evangelisches Mission—Wupperthal (Sigfried Groth).

National Endowment for the Humanities, National Science Foundation, National Geographic Society, Max Planck Institut—Seewiesen, Rackham Graduate School—University of Michigan, Social Science Research Council, Sonderforschungsbereich—Universität Bayreuth, Wenner-Gren Foundation for Anthropological Research.

The government of Botswana.

Introduction

When rains descend on southern Africa, especially on those parts where cattle are kept, flies regenerate in numbers intolerable to Western sensibilities. Photographs of these winged invaders of eyes and nostrils, of milk pails and teacups, found in dozens of coffee-table books and television documentaries, faithfully depict this reality of rural African life. In stark contrast, the modern pesticides, drainage projects, and absentee ownership that keep cattle at a respectable rural distance have reduced the fly population of urban centers to insignificance. But the wealth and comfort of the capital metropole and its town satellites have been bought at the price of rural poverty and degradation. The process is centuries old. Colonial emissaries—preceded by merchants and missionaries—and their current independent replacements seem like metaphorical descendants of those flies sucking sustenance from rural lives.

As if in counterpoint, the supernatural being in Zhu cosmology responsible for life and death on earth, for rain and drought, for all that happens to people and plants and animals, eats flies. This being, Gxanwa, smears honey around his lips to attract the flies, but he does not eat the honey, which is an attribute of the creator, Kqho. Gxanwa, whom I call the administrator diety, eats flies when there is a shortage of his primary food, human corpses—people he has caused to die in order to feed himself. Herein lies the rationale for human death, which otherwise would be inexplicable; herein too lies the inverted wisdom of incontestable control—Gxanwa kwarra ncin : Gxanwa has no sense. For unlike animals, whose death is proper because they are food for people and carnivores, people are not earthly food. But they are consumed by their superior in the cosmic order of things, hence they die. This too became for me a metaphor for the outward flow of wealth from the locus of its production in the Kalahari to its consumption, and sometimes accumulation as private fortunes, in the world beyond.

The image is surely unfair to the many opponents, colonial and contemporary, of the one-sided process of rural dispossession. But it is true in its essentials and brings into sharp focus the artificially created polar nodes—rural and urban—of what is and has always been, in its operation, an integrated system. Beyond that, for my purpose, this image allows me to stress that no peoples—no matter how far they may seem removed from the rest of the world—have been so remote as to have escaped participation in the economic forces swirling around them. In keeping with their dichotomized creation, these nodes have all too often been examined in isolation from each other. City and town, village and cattlepost—the so-called centers and peripheries of the Kalahari—have been treated in ethnographies as if they had only tenuous ties to each other. Those whom anthropologists have labeled hunter-gatherer or forager ("Bushman" or San in the southern African context) have been even further removed in administrative and academic placement, assigned to a subperipheral sphere barely visible from any center.

My association has been primarily with Zhu and Mbanderu peoples in Ngamiland, but I have ranged far beyond that small corner of the Kalahari in order to incorporate essential details about the other peoples of this larger region into my account of the lives of those I know best. I have found it necessary to do this because my Zhu and Mbanderu colleagues constantly speak in terms of this wider social geography and its history; in doing so, they give voice to perceptions common among people in the region. The term "political economy" in the title of the book signals my intention to restore this context to Euroamerican awareness.

This book is thus not an ethnography. One of its major premises is that the ethnographic era of anthropology, an era marked by the excision of societies from their historical contexts, is behind us—we may hope never to return. If San-speaking peoples, those southern African peoples still thought of as "Bushmen," are more prominently featured in some parts of the text than are their Bantu-speaking coresidents in the Kalahari, it is because they have been more thoroughly ethnogracized—made "anthropological" in Clammer's (1978:3) apt term— in both academic thought and popular imagination, more thoroughly cut from the political and economic context they share with other southern African peoples. Cut, that is, from a social formation that San-speakers have constructed in concert with Bantu-speakers during their centuries-long history of association, a history that heretofore has received scant attention. In spirit, the book follows Asad (1986: 163) in asking how power has entered into the "cultural translation" of a people.

To speak thus presupposes the no longer exceptional understanding that anthropology is an intensely ideological practice. To suggest, as I do, that a category as deeply entrenched in anthropological dogma and the public imagination as is "Bushmen" (or any of its currently fashionable pseudonyms) may be—ought to be—abandoned is to recognize that this category, like all others of its kind, is continually recreated in the engagement of anthropology with both a subjectivized and an objectivized world. Subjectively, there is the initial fact that the category itself was adopted with few modifications from divisions encoded at the end of the nineteenth century for purposes of colonial administration. These divisions, in turn, first became strongly marked at the beginning of the eighteenth century when long-standing power struggles among indigenous groups were intensified by competition for advantage in the burgeoning European trade.

Then there are the contentions surrounding the reproduction of anthropology's own agenda and the production of its claims to knowledge for consumption by its practitioners and the public. To carry these knowledge claims to its recipients in Euroamerican society, anthropology's first product is ethnography. As such, ethnography is a rhetorical form that not only allows but, in its role as an agent in Euroamerican moral philosophy (theology, historiography, and the so-called classics are others), authenticates the creation of a "primitive" opposition to our "civilized" world.

Ethnographic practice thus provides empirical support for the theoretical justification of ideologies that tolerate—while claiming not to advocate—segregation of that "other" world. This is accomplished through ethnography's prefigured finding that "other" peoples lie at some point several degrees removed from a Euroamerican standard. This ethnographic distance, always on a retrogressive vector, has evolutionary, political, economic, social, and moral dimensions—dimensions that are measured on a scale anchored in our own conceptions of ourselves. In the resultant genre of presentation the ethnographer's voice is heard for the native's voice as well, thus establishing what Clifford (1983) and Sperber (1985) call the "ethnographic authority" needed to warrant control of the portrayal of other subjectivities by the anthropological author. Wagner (1981:4) goes further, finding the ethnographer "inventing" "the culture he believes himself to be studying . . . [the relation becoming] . . . more 'real' for being his particular acts and experiences than the thing it relates." The rhetorical discourse that emerges is consequently confined to Euroamerican society, which employs ethnography in this manner to authenticate its own form of existence. My critique of ethnographic texts, the forager mode of production models, and the history of anthropological attention to Kalahari peoples addresses these dimensions.

The engagement of anthropology with an objectified world rests on its imposing its claims to knowledge on the recipients of its attention, both those who are objects of study and those who are objects of pedagogy. My discoursive argument confronts this imposition. I have introduced a polyphonic valence into the text, so that voices of real persons from the past and the present are heard in an uninterrupted flow with my own. I have done this not to disperse the authority of the text among those voices, but to bring them to the fore. Without diluting my responsibility for orchestrating them, these voices are here for reasons far deeper than harmonic color or evocation of atmosphere (although stage settings have value and I do design them). They are meant to provide the basis upon which readers must decide how closely my quite radical revision of the received view of the Kalahari corresponds with reality. We are dealing, after all, with something well beyond that distant savanna, namely, the way anthropology founds its knowledge claims.

A third ideological dimension shapes any anthropological work; this is Althusser's (1969) notion of the "interpellation" of individuals as subjects. There are two prongs to this dimension. The first pertains to the perceptions that individuals have about their conditions of existence within their own society and culture. Traditionally, ethnographers have tried to insert themselves into another society at this juncture, hoping thereby to capture a "true" portrait of it. For this purpose it is essential to fix some limits to the society under study, limits that are invariably chosen to suit the immediate needs of the investigator. Ethnographers thus devalue the second prong of interpellation, the one that brought them to their locus of study in the first place.

This second prong concerns the fact that the persons and the society isolated for study are actively enmeshed in a wider system of social relations. In these wider relations, separate practices (such as anthropology, just as surely as market forces) interpellate persons and societies in terms dictated by the practices themselves. This has ramifications that resonate with those of anthropology's claims to knowledge based on ethnographic divisions. Since this is perhaps the most misperceived aspect of the history of the Kalahari region and contributes to further misperceptions of Kalahari peoples, especially San-speakers, I devote a great deal of the text to its clarification. In doing so, I draw heavily from archaeologies, ethnographies, and historiographies of Bantu-speaking peoples, primarily Batswana and Ovaherero, as well as from those of various Nama-speaking peoples; I need hardly point out that these have been written in the same segregating mold. Reading them, one does not see San peoples sitting on Tswana doorsteps, entering Herero houses without specific permission, supplying labor for domes-

tic and commodity production for everyone around regardless of what
they are called, finding themselves forgotten by ethnographers who are
not looking for them.

Ethnographies thus construct alien cultures. Few of the world's
peoples have been so thoroughly alienated both from their historical
context and from their contemporary condition by such constructions
as have those who are still too often called "Bushmen." It is true that
the term "San" instead of Bushman has gained favor since the 1970s;
this is, however, merely a substitution, applied to avoid using an offen-
sive word. In concept and practice, the components of the category to
which San is applied and the peoples assigned to that category have
changed little from those that defined Bushman. The ethnography of a
category rather than of a people has arisen, one that has become
prominent in anthropological claims to knowledge about the human
condition and its ancestry. These knowledge claims in turn have been
incorporated as central features in Euroamerican moral philosophy,
particularly in separating "primitive" from "civilized" society. As
such, these claims are important elements in what must become one of
the most momentous projects of the second half of this century, re-
structuring relations between Euroamerica and the rest of the world.
Ethnographic depictions of foragers enter the debate at many points:
they serve as the threshold in scientific, philosophical, and journalistic
thought over which all subsequent human development has stepped
and thus anchor an ordinal scale on which social accomplishment is
gauged; they dictate the scripts of modern morality plays such as *Clan
of the Cave Bear* and *Iceman* and thus dramatize public fantasies;
they inform serious artistic critiques of public notions of social justice
such as Peter Wier's film *The Last Wave* and thus raise questions of
ethics; they influence land-rights legislation and shape land-claims litigation in Australia, Canada, and the United States and thus become
elements of policy; and they are called upon in parliamentary debates
concerning the fate of San-speaking peoples in modern Botswana and
Namibia.

My motivations, goals, and strategies for writing this book lie in
this awareness that anthropological claims to knowledge do intervene
in the public arena. The consequences of these interventions are not
trivial, even if anthropologists are often wont to belittle them. But my
motivations, goals, and strategies for going to the Kalahari in the first
place were very different. Their genesis lies in my graduate student
days at the University of Arizona, where—as much at Ed Dozier's
kitchen table as in class—I became convinced that anthropological
study, whether of the past or the present, must examine both the past

and the present. At the University of Michigan a couple of years later, I became convinced of the need for an ecological component in this study.

So I went to the Kalahari in 1973 to do something that fell under the vague heading "ethnoarchaeology"—although I insisted that I was doing anthropology, not some segment of it. But I was searching for models with which to reconstruct the past and thereby understand the present. It was a pursuit of the pure Paleolithic, not noticeably unlike the quest of a host of others. I chose to work at CaeCae because the extensive research conducted by a group of Harvard students who worked with Richard Lee at and around this tiny place provided a baseline of information on which to build further knowledge.

But like Weiner in the Trobriand Islands, from the first day it was apparent to me that something had been overlooked. Perhaps my intention to include Ovaherero and Batswana in a comparative study with "Bushmen" precluded inattentiveness to those people all jumbled together. I was thoroughly discouraged rather than disillusioned— clearly my program needed to be redefined and expanded. I had no idea how I might do that, or even if I wanted to try. Polly Wiessner also noticed that things were not as they ethnographically seemed and encouraged me to continue; when she decided to concentrate on exchange networks, she turned her archaeological project over to me. I integrated this with my investigations into local history, which were intended to shed light on relations of production during the past couple of centuries or so; in those days I thought this would be enough to get me back to the pristine past. The very first excavations and interviews made me think I must have been wrong about that, but it was more than two years later—after much work—that I began to tell people that I had evidence for a very long history of complex social and economic relations at CaeCae and that this must imply a similar history for the region as a whole. In 1976 only Alec Campbell and Jim Denbow wanted to hear—or believe—the news; together we have since made it difficult for anyone not to listen. Meanwhile I continued to amass data on animal ecology, food acquisition and distribution, nutrition, physiology, fertility, kinship, labor relations, and land tenure (which I no longer thought of as territoriality); but though I could identify a number of significant correlations, I was dissatisfied with the way the data hung, or didn't hang, together.

Fortunately, in 1975–76 I was asked to survey part of the Western State Lands for the then-called Bushman Development Office and in those same years to act as consultant for the Rural Income Distribution Survey. Then in 1980 I participated in the Botswana Society Symposium on Settlement, and in 1981 I wrote the remote areas sec-

tion for the National Migration Study of Botswana. These activities
vastly increased my awareness of the political-economic structure of
the region; it was clear that San peoples were as thoroughly enmeshed
in that structure as everybody else who lived there. Carol Kerven and
Neil Parsons, to whom it came as no surprise, were willing to discuss
this proposition with equanimity and pointed out some of its deeper
implications. Ssao Xau, Simon Tuvare, Dam Qam, and John Marenga,
my constant companions wherever I went in Botswana, began to explain to me the sorts of things I should look for. Finally, Jack Parson
framed the key question in unambiguous terms: What accounts for the
presence of "Bushmen" in a modern state? By then I knew the answer
must lie in the colonial era and its aftermath—so, belatedly, I turned
my attention to archives (where I had been browsing aimlessly in odd
moments for years), and the fragments began to coalesce.

The principal results are found in this book. The place and the
peoples presented here are very different from the Kalahari depicted
by Marshall, Lee, Silberbauer, Tanaka, and others. To claim, as I do,
that my presentation is more complete—insofar as it explicitly addresses the interpellation of an anthropological object and examines
the trajectory of that interpellation and in this sense is also more
"true"—is not to belittle the work of those who went before. It is
simply to recognize that all of us who have attempted ethnographic
description have interpellated a place and its peoples in terms that have
more to do with Euroamerica's rationalization of its intervention in the
rest of the world than with those "other" parts of the world themselves. The premises and predicates of that rationalization have altered
radically in the thirty-five-year interval between Lorna Marshall's first
visit to the Kalahari and the writing of this book; of necessity, the
terms of its discourse have undergone a parallel transformation.

I shall close these prefatory remarks by adopting an important observation made by Frankenberg (1967), who was speaking about economic anthropology but whose words apply equally to our present
concern: the whole history of our subject up to now is a history not of
errors, but of legitimate attempts to grapple with issues generated by a
particular problematic. As Meillassoux (1973:188) remarks, "For a
long time, reference to their own society led anthropologists to consider the primitive societies as an antithesis . . . in negative and irrelevant terms [since positive categories seemed] more difficult to tease
out." But through their work we have learned much. Where Euroamerican thought and anthropological practice have gone astray is in
transferring much of the burden of our own search for authentication
of our conceptions of ourselves onto other peoples categorized for this

purpose as primitive—primitive in a dual sense: prior and protean, that is, superior, while at the same time residual and atavistic, that is, inferior. Before we can meet the peoples stigmatized in this way on anything approaching an equal footing, we must remove that burden from them. The first step is to discover how the subjects of our present discourse were historically constructed.

1

The Evolution of Illusion

The world of humankind constitutes a manifold, a totality of interconnected processes, and inquiries that disassemble this totality into bits and then fail to reassemble it falsify reality. Concepts like "nation," "society," and "culture" name bits and threaten to turn names into things. Only by understanding these names as bundles of relationships, and by placing them back into the field from which they were abstracted, can we hope to avoid misleading inferences and increase our share of understanding.

Eric Wolf, *Europe and the People without History*, 1982

Man the Hunter: A Nineteenth-Century Legacy

In company with many others called foragers in faraway corners of the earth, the San-speaking peoples of southern Africa have been relegated to an existential remoteness in time and space and being (fig. 1.1). This remoteness, as it is conceived to exist for the Kalahari, is represented as having been bridged only in recent decades, and that bridging itself is said to have been accomplished as often as not by social scientists seeking the wellspring of human existence. There is a basis for this perspective: unlike all other native peoples of southern Africa, among those called "Bushman" (most, but not all, of whom speak San languages) none have been able, in this century, to accumulate sufficient capital to maintain significant cattle herds of their own.[1] Why is this so? What accounts for the existence in modern southern African states of peoples who appear to many outside observers to have practiced until recently an aboriginal foraging economy? Why are there peoples in the twentieth century who could conceivably be labeled "Bushmen"?

At the same time, in this century in Botswana and Namibia, an overwhelming majority of peoples so labeled have pursued a substantially pastoralist way of life in symbiosis with, employed by, or enserfed to Bantu-speaking cattle owners, primarily Batswana and Ovaherero. As we shall see, this is equally true of earlier centuries, with the modification that some proportion of San-speakers them-

1

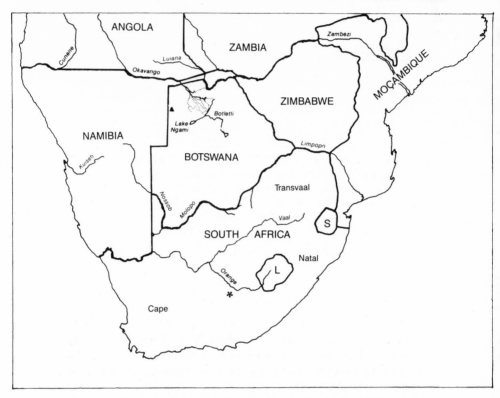

Figure 1.1. Map of southern Africa showing the countries mentioned in the text; L is Lesotho, S is Swaziland. In colonial times Botswana was known as the Bechuanaland Protectorate or simply the Protectorate; Namibia was South-West Africa to the British and Südwestafrika to Germans. Ngamiland is the part of northwestern Botswana west of the Okavango Delta and north of Lake Ngami, in which the location of CaeCae is marked by a triangle; the asterisk marks the location of Barrow's 1797 observations.

selves then owned herds of respectable size. And all "Bushmen foragers," no matter how far out into the Kalahari they may have been found at any particular moment, were in those previous centuries—and remain now—enmeshed in the dominant pastoralist economies of the region through kinship and material production networks. Despite this, during this century few contemporary San-speaking herders have been able to establish livestock-based domestic economies independent of Bantu-speaking pastoralists until this decade, when some are managing to do so. None have yet been able to enter into commodity production of cattle for readily available commercial markets now dominated by Tswana and Herero producers. What are the reasons for this state of affairs?

As we shall see, the current status of San-speaking peoples on the rural fringe of African economies can be accounted for only in terms of the social policies and economies of the colonial era and its aftermath. Their appearance as foragers is a function of their relegation to an underclass in the playing out of historical processes that began before the current millennium and culminated in the early decades of this century. The isolation in which they are said to have been found is a creation of our view of them, not of their history as they lived it. This is as true of their indigenous material-social systems as it is of their incorporation in wider spheres of political economy in southern Africa.

A false dichotomy has crept in, a line drawn between those who produce their means of existence and those who supposedly do not, between those who live on nature and those who live in it, between those whose social life is motivated primarily by self-interest and those guided by respect for reciprocal consensus. Both ecologists and materialists locate foragers in an evolutionarily prior history; we still hear contemporary forager societies spoken of as living in nature, bound together in prepolitical community.[2] An endless, aboriginal continuity of social relations is envisioned, its alterations wrenched from resistance by external impositions in the form of drastic changes in a fickle environment or of imperative direction—usually technological or economic at base—from a hostile outside world. Foragers, in this scenario, are assigned the role of passive receptor and become the testing laboratory for our own ideological preoccupations regarding historical transformations of social forms.

In the prevailing paradigm of anthropology applied to the Kalahari, that of evolutionary ecology, the questions posed above have been nonquestions, never asked, without answers. This is because a distinction drawn by Lévi-Strauss (1967:47) has fundamentally informed all anthropological approaches to San-speaking "foragers"; that distinction is between "societies, which we might define as 'cold' in that their internal environment neighbours on the zero of historical temperature, [and] are, by their limited total manpower and their mechanical mode of functioning, distinguished from the 'hot' societies which appeared in different parts of the world following the Neolithic revolution." In fact, Lee (1979:6) goes so far as to believe that it is the very act of ethnographic fieldwork itself that "can begin to place this 'ahistorical' society into history." Ethnographers of San-speakers have assumed that these peoples were quintessential aboriginal hunters and gatherers

whose way of life had changed little for millennia—those "cold" societies of Lévi-Strauss (1966:233–34), "'peoples without history' . . .
seeking, by the institutions they give themselves, to annul the possible
effects of historical factors on their equilibrium and continuity."

Both geographic isolation and cultural conservatism were invoked
to account for this static condition. It was asserted, without investigation, that neither African agropastoralists nor any other external influence had impinged significantly on their isolation until the middle
third of this century. As a consequence, San-speakers were declared to
be socially and culturally uninterested in and unprepared for participation in independent pastoral economies. Oddly, at the same time
they were acknowledged to be seasoned herdsmen for others. We shall
discover the reasons for this discordance.

These reasons lie in the epistemological discourse of Euroamerica's
representation of its own past. Once established in scholarly and scientific—and of parallel importance, popular—lexicons, the events,
peoples, and categories that become the objects of this discourse are
transmuted into "indexical signs which perpetually point to their status
as realities constituted independently of the process of re-presentation
itself" (Alonso 1988:36). The categories "Bushman," "San," "hunter-
gatherer," "forager," and so forth are products of just such transmu-
tation; they become objects and function to illuminate and legitimize
a crucial area in Euroamerica's symbolic reconstruction of its own
ontology.

It was just this discourse, Pratt (1985) tells us, that formed "what
Mr. Barrow saw in the land of the Bushmen" in 1797 (fig. 1.1). In
what follows, I shall trace the form that this discourse continues to dictate for modern ethnographies of "Bushmen." These ethnographies
serve to authenticate our own subjective ontology by fitting an iconic
"Bushman" into a prefigured category labeled "primitive." By displaying objectified peoples as examples of this category who exist "in a
timeless present tense . . . not as a particular historical event but as an
instance of a pregiven custom or trait" (Pratt 1985:120), ethnography
validates the epistemological program. Consequently, the intrinsic realities of these objects are, as themselves, of little or no interest to this
program. What is important is that its objects conform to a discoursive narrative; while any of the parts may be questioned at any time,
the ontological reconstruction itself becomes increasingly unchallenge-
able as a whole.

Since about 1960, most students of "forager" social formations have
self-consciously espoused either some form of ecological or Marxian
model or some combination of such models as the foundation of their

work. This may be especially true of those whose attention is on African "foragers" and their relation to "food producers"; the general
formulations of Meillassoux, Terray, Dupré and Rey, and Godelier in
France, of Hindess and Hirst in England, and of Sahlins in the United
States along with the particular field studies of Lee, Silberbauer, and
Tanaka in the Kalahari come readily to mind and will be examined in
the course of our discussion. It is true that tenets of Marxian theory
figure prominently in the presentations of the first five of these authors
and infiltrate in decreasing degree those of the others. It is equally true
that ecological parameters are recognized as important by all (at least
to the extent that they are among the forces of production defined by
Marx) and are invoked as primary explanatory factors by the last four
of these writers. But the intellectual basis upon which they all construct their theoretical foundations has a far more ancient pedigree
and is to be found in two corollary trajectories of nineteenth-century
European thought. The first of these was an antiquarian and ethnological interest aroused by the realization that the biblical account of
history could no longer accommodate accumulating empirical observations of geological, biological, and social processes made both at
home and in exotic parts of the hitherto unknown world. The second
was an idealist sociology that in part arose to answer questions about
human society thus exposed.

It has often been remarked that these trajectories have long histories
in Western thought (see, for example, Worsaae 1849:138; Sorokin
1957:vii–viii; Leacock 1972:8; Stocking 1987:9–10, passim), and
this is true, with the proviso that neither their referents nor the problematic engagement with those referents has remained constant. It is
nevertheless worth quoting briefly from Hesiod (Athanassakis 1983:
70–71), whose words on the subject resonate in many rationalizations
of the study of "primitive foragers" today:

At first the immortals who dwell on Olympos
created a golden race of mortal men.
That was when Kronos was king of the sky,
and they lived like gods, carefree in their hearts,
. . . .
            They knew no constraint
and lived in peace and abundance as lords of their land.

Then, after recounting the second, silver, and third, bronze, races and
the fourth, "divine race of heroes," Hesiod continues:

I wish I were not counted among the fifth race of men,
but rather had died before, or been born after it.

This is the race of iron. Neither day nor night
will give them rest as they waste away with toil
and pain.
  (*Works and Days*, lines 110–13, 119–20, 174–78)

These themes, of an early era of ease and equality contrasted with an
ever more baneful present existence, recur regularly again in post–
World War II ethnographies of African foragers, as they did in the
eighteenth century. Leslie White, who helped inspire a renewed anthropological quest for human authenticity in the evolutionarily "primitive" cultures, gave voice to a common feeling when he declared that
these cultures—crude and limited as they may be—were infinitely superior in meeting human needs to any other ever realized, including
our own (p. 23).

In the nineteenth century, especially after about 1860, the same bi-
polar eras were identified, but their attributes were reversed by evolutionists of that time, for whom foragers lived as savage brutes (Guenther
1980 assembles many of the more lurid details), a condition from
which the peak of Euroamerican civilization had long ago escaped.
Those who pursued a sociological search for the nature of human nature were not so sure.

Even so, two fundamental constants run through both conceptions:
first, an era of pure hunters (we now say hunter-gatherers, of course)
did exist separately from other eras; second, that era—although its
roots lay in the prehistoric past—is represented by "hunting" peoples
who live at any time, prehistoric, historic, or present. Thus, peoples
living today who may be classified as foragers bear witness not only to
their own lives but to those of prehistoric foragers as well. That is, not
only are living peoples conceived to be fit models for the remote past,
but that remote past itself is said to establish the parameters of life of
these living peoples.

Lee and DeVore are unequivocal on this point. Reporting the difficulties in defining "hunters" encountered at the 1966 Man the Hunter
conference, they state (1968:4): "An evolutionary definition would
have been ideal; this would confine hunters to those populations with
strictly Pleistocene economies—no metal, firearms, dogs, or contact
with non-hunting peoples. Unfortunately such a definition would effectively eliminate most, if not all, of the peoples reported at the symposium since, as Marshall Sahlins pointed out, nowhere today do we
find hunters living in a world of hunters." Nevertheless, in 1984 Lee
(1984:ix) could still think of his work among Zhu twenty years earlier
as being "like a race against time . . . [observing] . . . a foraging mode

of life during the last decades of its existence." It is this tautological reasoning that is most often invoked to justify modern ethnographic study of contemporary peoples who are consigned to a constructed past made present. Let us see how these themes were developed.

The Received Past

The Present without a Past

The history of the Kalahari, as written, reads like a kaleidoscope of unconnected slide shows thrown up on segregated screens. That southern African savanna called a desert still functions for many as an imaginary map—almost in the tradition of medieval geographers—on which names of various exotic peoples are entered or erased in accordance with some historiographic need of the moment to segregate those peoples conceptually—more urgent than spatially—from each other. In this the history of the region shares much with that particularist tradition in ethnography inflicted on it, which reports the presence of peoples extraneous to its purpose along with other exigencies of the environment—as it records annual rainfall—and then sets them aside.

Until recently, historians of the region were concerned primarily with tracing the emergence of first tribal, then modern, national states through the colonial nineteenth century and its aftermath. They did not find it necessary to elaborate the roles played by peoples considered marginal to this process. In Botswana, Tlou (1972:147)[3] began the move to broaden historical interest when he asserted that "the history of an area is more than just that of the ruling groups." He has taken his own admonition seriously and written extensively on all the Bantu-speaking peoples of Ngamiland, not just Batawana, but even he has relatively little to say about San-speakers (and Bakgalagadi) except that they were there first and live in the sandveld. Parsons (personal communication) has suggested that these peoples have been ignored because it has been too difficult to incorporate them into the narrative center of state political historiography, owing in large measure to a supposed lack of historical sources.

Recent interest in specific issues—the politics of traditional land tenure (Hitchcock 1978; Wilmsen 1982a, 1989) and a reevaluation of the nature of slavery and serfdom in the Kalahari (Tlou 1979; Miers 1983; Mautle 1986; Miers and Crowder 1988)—has stimulated research into the historical relations between San-speakers and the other peoples of the region. In Botswana, the establishment of the Bushman

Development Programme in 1975 (later the Remote Area Dwellers Programme) at a ministerial level of government led to the first significant investigations into relations among San and Bantu peoples since the League of Nations—inspired investigations of the 1930s (Wily 1979). And for Namibia, Lau (1979, 1981, 1984) has begun to correct the historiographic imbalance in that country. Nonetheless, in general San-speakers are still set at the threshold of history and then effectively lost from sight. Even in as encyclopedic a work as *A New History of Southern Africa* (Parsons 1983), Khoisan peoples are discussed— uncommonly fully but nonetheless mainly in terms of Stone Age and Iron Age development—in an opening chapter and then rarely mentioned again.

Anthropologists too have been caught in a contradiction. While illuminating in compelling ways the richness of San cultures and insisting rightly on the ancient heritage of San peoples, they have made a virtue of what they perceive to be the isolation necessary to preserve the integrity of those cultures, an integrity they have inextricably tied to their supposed antiquity. These ethnographers, although they acknowledge the presence of other peoples in the region, have felt that "circumstances and the aridity of the desert" (Marshall 1976:13) and "the vast distances of the Kalahari [have protected Zhu from] African or European contact until recent years" (Lee 1979:33).

Tanaka (1980:xii, 10–11), speaking of the Kalahari as a whole, finds that "the fact that a group of people with a population of several thousand is still living in the same fashion as human societies of almost 10,000 years ago is a miracle, although it can also illustrate the disadvantages of living in the Kalahari Desert, fit neither for cultivation of plants nor for domestication of animals." This contradicts his own observation that "many San . . . rely on the field and dairy products of the Kgalagadi . . . [these] Bantu tribes living in the Kalahari . . . show complete tolerance in the face of the San's parasitism and begging."

Such remoteness from the flow of history—a remoteness in the mind, as we shall see—was felt to be necessary in order to support the professed research goals of generating new insights into cultural evolution and reconstructing the properties of societies and economies of earlier human populations. Lee and DeVore tell us they chose to work in the northern Kalahari because "the research goals required a population as isolated and traditionally oriented as possible" (Lee 1965:2). For as they will say when we examine their motivation for joining Leslie White in a renewed search for lost authenticity in human relations, "The human condition was likely to be drawn more clearly here than among other kinds of soceities" (Lee and DeVore 1968:ix). I (Wilmsen 1983) have noted that most students, including myself, of Bushmen, as they were then still called, were swept into this intellectual stream and the evolutionary paradigm from which it flows. Brooks (1982:5) humorously recounts her gradual realization of the faults inherent in applying this paradigm directly to Zhu, and we shall shortly read excerpts from Howell's evaluation of the limitations it imposed on observations of these people and their neighbors. Needless to say, the associated ethnological program obviated the need to search for historical documentation of San peoples.

It is, as a consequence, still too easy to follow Van Der Post (1958) into *The Lost World of the Kalahari* and to suppose that *The Harmless People* of Thomas (1959) are not only enchanting but factual. These authors, to be sure, wrote partly fictionalized travelers' accounts for a popular audience, but they had a serious purpose: "A search for some pure remnant of the unique and almost vanished First People of my native land, the Bushmen" (Van Der Post 1958:3); and "studying the life and customs of the people of the Kalahari, who are called the Bushmen . . . the earliest human inhabitants still living in southern Africa" (Thomas 1959:6–8). This purpose was in tune with the anthropology of their time: "To find and study Bushmen who were living in their own way . . . we observed a way of life that had not changed radically in ages," as Marshall (1957:1; reprinted unchanged in 1976: 14) thought, echoing Murdock's (1959:61) influential text, which concluded that Bushmen were Paleolithic people who represented "actual remnants of that ancient population and their cultures [who] have survived into the historical period." To which Herskovitz (1962:60), in his equally praised *The Human Factor in Changing Africa,* added of the Khoisan that they had a "negligible degree of participation in influencing the course of events in the territories they inhabit." One wonders, then, if they were indeed part of the human factor.

Anthropology was itself in tune with the history of the region: "There are also the original people of the land, the Bushmen . . . moving about their traditional hunting grounds from water hole to water hole. . . . sometimes one may be lucky enough to come across a family group" (Sillery 1952:xii). Later historians, even those sensitive to the colonial destruction of indigenous societies, also spare little concern for San-speakers. Bley (1971:xxii) could write, "Like the Bushmen and Berg-Damara, the Saan were displaced by the arrival of later, more powerful tribes, and by 1830 none of the original inhabitants occupied a position of any importance in the territory." And this from Clarence-

Smith (1979 : 8): "In between [agricultural and pastoralist groups] live roving bands of Khoi or Twa hunter-gatherers, who have been of little or no historic importance."

But their pedigree is ancient. Viegas Guerreiro (1968 : 42) recites, with a few updates from more recent literature, for the Angolan Kqu the lineal descent from late Paleolithic "tribes" offered earlier by Schapera (1930 : 26)—who was himself cautiously updating Stow (1905)—for all Khoisan. Indeed, even the most thoroughly informed current ethnographies of San-speakers are founded on an identical premise: "The Kalahari San are among the few remaining representatives of a way of life that was, until 10,000 years ago, a human universal" (Lee 1979 : 1); "these communities in the central desert might provide . . . an impression of the life-style followed by all Kalahari Bushmen before their contact with Bantu and Europeans" (Silberbauer 1981 : 20). The theoretical basis for the ahistorical evolutionism with which these modern anthropologists entrench an ideology of isolation in their representations of contemporary San-speaking peoples is groundless. Vansina (1985) condenses the argument eloquently: "The time should be long past that hunter-gatherers . . . are seen as living witnesses to primordial conditions of life, as 'roots of heaven.' . . . unfortunately this image still lingers [and] has made it almost impossible it seems to shake off the old premises of study . . . [one of which is that] they live in the present and have little or no real history as their lives have been similar generation after generation."

Ethnography and historiography, thus segregated from each other, are linked with fiction in perpetuating a conceptual isolation of San-speakers, a conceptualization that tautologically justifies its own fictitious status. Paradoxically, these peoples, who are universally considered to be the longest-term living residents of the Kalahari, are permitted antiquity while denied history.

Like the rest of southern Africa, the political and economic structures of the Kalahari in the nineteenth century were differentiated in recognizable terms. A number of diverse social groups were articulated with what appears to have been a degree of relative autonomy for each in the early years of the century. There were Tswana agropastoral incipient states on the southern and eastern margins of the Kalahari by the mid-eighteenth century, but what the economies of the peoples they encountered may have been has not yet been made so clear. It is usually assumed that these latter were strictly foragers, or at most kept small stock, but this is poorly founded speculation. The situation was not so simple.

It is clear, however, that as the nineteenth century progressed the various Tswana groups were able to consolidate their positions and gain hegemony over the other Kalahari peoples and to appropriate an extractable surplus from them in the form of tribute. In the process, they incorporated these weakened indigenous peoples into their own social formations as a servile class. In the last quarter of the nineteenth century and the first half of the twentieth, Batswana were actively abetted in this process by a British colonial administration acting, above all, in its own interest. Gadibolae (1985; see also Wiley 1985), on the basis of previously unexamined archival records and recently acquired oral histories, reaffirms that even the minimum efforts made to control the conditions of San serfdom were initiated by the Colonial Office primarily to forestall adverse world opinion of their administration of the Protectorate.

The first question that begs to be asked, then, is to what extent these indigenous Kalahari social formations were altered, initially by African state expansion alone and later by colonial capital acting through those established states. It was, as it happened, at precisely the end of this period of hegemonic consolidation that the subjugated peoples of the Kalahari—especially those called Bushmen, San, or foragers—became the focus of anthropological attention. Consequently, a corollary question that must be asked is how this historic coincidence has led to a distortion of the ethnographic record of these peoples.

The uneven penetration of European merchant capital into the region is a second crucial factor. European traders were well established in eastern Botswana by the mid-1840s and only ten years later had saturated the farthest corners of Ngamiland in northwestern Botswana as well as adjacent Namibia (Parsons 1977:117; Tlou 1972; Tabler 1973). These traders, however, only consolidated to themselves what had been in effect long before they arrived. Marks (1972), Clarence-Smith and Moorsom (1975), Elphick (1975, 1977), Kienetz (1977), Lau (1982), Nangati (1980), and practically all the authors in Gray and Birmingham (1970), Palmer and Parsons (1977), Marks and Atmore (1980), and Birmingham and Martin (1983) provide overwhelming evidence that European-inspired market factors were felt in every part of central and southern Africa before the actual appearance of white men in those parts. As we shall see, European trade items were received into Namibia-Ngamiland more than two hundred years before the first white man set foot there.

To be sure, the preponderance of the new wealth thus generated in the nineteenth century went directly to European traders, while the small, but still significant, remainder available to indigenous economies flowed mainly to, or at least through, chiefs and local headmen who retained the lion's share for themselves. An example encapsulates the process:

Khama's income, now apparently freed from burdensome political reciproci-
ties, came from his measure of monopolistic control over the market between
internal and external trades at Shoshong. The income of the Ngwato king was
estimated at £3,000 in 1874 and at £2,000 to £3,000 in 1877, though it is not
clear whether this was in cash or cash value. The cash income was due in large
measure to predominant royal ownership of the means of production—the
king "owned" the land and the elephants and employed or hired out his serf
hunters. He extracted a 50 per cent levy on ivory production—the "ground
tusk" of every elephant shot in his domains, a common and venerable royal
prerogative in Southern-Central Africa. (Parsons 1977: 120)

There were exceptions, of course, but even where most rigidly true, the subjugated peoples—San-speakers and others—actually produced much of the surplus product channeled into commercial trade. This suggests that these peoples lived in societies already structured in such a way that they could organize themselves very quickly to produce an extractable surplus beyond what they had been providing as tribute to Batswana for decades and to earlier Iron Age chiefdoms for centuries.

Thus this case echoes others in southern Africa's colonial history. San traditionalism, so called, and the cultural conservatism uniformly attributed to these people by almost all anthropologists who have worked with them until recently, is a consequence—not a cause—of the way they have been integrated into the modern capitalist economies of Botswana and Namibia. The trajectory of this integration can be traced in the written and oral records resurrected in following chap-
ters. But before entering this path, we must turn to the reasons it has not led others into the Kalahari.

Setting the Savage Stage
In 1819, Christian Jurgensen Thomsen, secretary of the then recently established Danish National Museum of Antiquities, synthesized the work of his predecessors and arranged the museum's collections by "classifying them into three ages of Stone, Bronze, and Iron on the basis of the material used in making weapons and implements, dividing the specimens into three groups representing what he claimed were three chronologically successive ages" (Daniel 1950: 41).

Contemporary, living peoples entered as models into this scheme from the beginning; J. J. A. Worsaae, Thomsen's student, wrote in his *Primeval Antiquities of Denmark* (1849) that "having read how stone implements were at present used by Pacific islanders, and knowing that the Goths made no such use of stone implements, he concluded that there must have been a Stone Age" (Daniel 1950:44). Worsaae had been anticipated by Nilsson in 1834:

As witnesses throwing light upon ancient times I count not only antiquities, monuments, their different shapes, and the figures engraved on them, but also *popular tales,* which most frequently originate from traditions, and are therefore remnants of olden times. . . . [We ought to be able, by collecting] the remains of human races long since passed away, and of the works which they have left behind, to draw a parallel between them and similar ones which still exist on earth, and thus cut out a way to the knowledge of circumstances which may have been, by comparing them with those which still exist. (Nilsson, quoted in Daniel 1950:49)

Following his own recommended procedure, Nilsson distinguished four stages in man's development. The first—naturally—was the savage stage, when man was still a hunter.

Lubbock's *Prehistoric Times* ([1865] 1913) not only gave a name to this time before history[4] but set the savage Stone Age on bedrock by separating a Paleolithic hunting stage in prehistory from its Neolithic fishing and ceramic-making successor. Lubbock devoted fully a third of his long book to "the consideration of modern savages [because] if we wish clearly to understand the antiquities of Europe, we must compare them with the rude implements and weapons still, or until lately, used by the savage races in other parts of the world" (Lubbock [1865] 1913:430–31). Lubbock not only made it clear, as in this passage, that Europe was the center of interest in all these staged scenarios, he also anticipated another modern concern that troubled Lee and DeVore in 1968—that there were no longer any hunters living in a world peopled exclusively by hunters: "The present habits of savage races, while throwing, no doubt, much light on those of our earliest ancestors, are not to be regarded as representing them exactly, because they have been to some extent modified by external conditions, influenced by national character, which, however, is after all but the result of external conditions which have acted on previous generations" (Lubbock [1865] 1913:544).

In other words, if foragers were to be useful, it would be necessary to filter out from them what may have sifted down from the contamination of contact. Nevertheless, with suitable precautions in the employment of what we now call ethnographic analogy, "the archaeologist is free to follow the methods which have been so successfully employed in geology—the rude bone and stone implements of bygone ages being to the one what the remains of extinct animals [in relation to living species] are to the other" (Lubbock [1865] 1913:430).

The stage having been set, some action was called for. Morgan's *Ancient Society* ([1877] 1964:41–42) provided this:

Savagery was the formative period of the human race. Commencing at zero in knowledge and experience . . . our savage progenitors fought the great battle, first for existence, and then for progress, until they secured safety from ferocious animals, and permanent subsistence. . . . the inferiority of savage man . . . is, nevertheless, substantially demonstrated by the remains of ancient art in flint stone and bone implements, by his cave life in certain areas, and by his osteological remains. It is still further illustrated by the present condition of tribes of savages in a low state of development, left in isolated sections of the earth as monuments of the past.

Tylor ([1881] 1909:24) added a mobile element: "The lowest or *savage* state is that in which man subsists on wild plants and animals, neither tilling the soil nor domesticating creatures for his food. . . . [in some] regions they have to lead a wandering life in quest of the wild food which they soon exhaust in any place. In making their rude implements, the materials used by savages are what they find ready to hand, such as wood, stone, and bone, but they cannot extract metal from the ore, and therefore belong to the Stone Age."

There were confusions about just who fit where in these schemes. Worsaae's deduction from Polynesians using stone tools was one such, although this might be reconcilable with the fact that a distinction between a paleohunting and a neopotting Stone Age had not been made when he wrote. Lubbock ([1865] 1913:431) could say that "in some savage tribes we even find traces of improvement; the Bachapins, when visited by Burchell, had just introduced the art of working in iron."

As we shall see in chapter 3, these Tswana-speaking Batlhapa of southern Africa were possessors of vast herds of cattle and other domestic stock, long accustomed to ironsmithing. In the same breath, Lubbock asserts as proof of the eternal constancy of forager life that Bushmen, among others, "lived when first observed almost exactly as they do now," although it is unlikely that he was acquainted with more than the latest thirty or forty of the then three hundred years of European reporting on these peoples. These confusions are hardly to be wondered at, given the embryonic state of ethnographic reporting at the time.

Yet by 1880 the basic defining characteristics of a savage, foraging stage of human existence were in place. These will seem familiar to any survivor of a standard contemporary introductory course in anthropology: (1) the foraging way of life has its roots in a Paleolithic past that occurred long before recorded history; (2) this way of life depends exclusively on hunting and gathering wild foods regardless of when in time (Paleolithic or later) and where it is found; (3) its technology is simple and based entirely on naturally occurring raw materials; (4) social groups, limited by these constraints, are necessarily small and are virtual replicates of each other; (5) these groups are usually compelled to be highly mobile in their search for food. There was also already the caution that the effects of contact with higher cultures had to be accounted for before inferences about the evolutionary significance of any particular group of foragers could be justified. Engels ([1884] 1972:97) added some now quaint speculations on stage variations in sexuality and marriage, noting, however, that some things are just too bizarre to exist any longer, even among savages: "The primitive social stage of promiscuity, if it ever existed, belongs to such a remote epoch that we can hardly expect to prove its existence *directly* by discovering its social fossils among backward savages."

But it was Pitt-Rivers in 1875 who sounded a note whose echoes we will hear a full century later (p. 159). Borrowing from Lubbock the analogy of ethnological to paleontological materials, he asserts the by now unremarkable dogma that "amongst the arts of existing savages we find forms which, being adapted to a low condition of culture, have survived from the earliest times, and also the representatives of many successive stages through which development has taken place in times past"; he adds, however, that "two nations in very different stages of civilization may be brought side by side, as is the case in many of our colonies, but there can be no amalgamation between them. Nothing but the vices and imperfections of the superior culture can coalesce with the inferior culture without break of sequence" (Pitt-Rivers [1875] 1906:18–19).

It is in fact precisely this latter argument that is invoked by both anthropologists and administrators in decrying the present condition and future prospects of southern African San-speaking peoples. In the next chapter we shall hear it said that these San peoples are on the "threshold of the Neolithic, stripped of the accretions and complications" of later evolutionary stages, and furthermore that this condition retards their social incorporation into and economic participation in modern national states. It is taken as axiomatic that peoples in a "lower stage of evolution" will eagerly grasp at the vices of their betters while remaining ignorant of those benefits that could raise them materially and morally to new heights. Implicit in this is the notion that forager social formations are incapable of change on their own. Furthermore, change, in the event that it is stimulated by external agencies, will be gradual. Contrarily, those on a "higher plane" never wish to fall beneath themselves, although they may sometimes be compelled to do so by a capricious nature.

All of this raises a fundamental question: Before there were peoples on a higher plane, how did anyone ever become anything other than a foraging savage? The answers offered pointed to that same capricious nature, which either elevated population numbers above the sustaining capacity of resources or depressed resources below the requirements of populations. Either condition forced innovation. After "higher levels" were attained, the answer was obvious: those in a lower condition would naturally aspire to the higher once it was made known to them. But they could reach this apotheosis only through a "break in the sequence"—that is, by escaping their intrinsic primitiveness. Morgan ([1877] 1964:540) was among the few who thought that savages might sometimes rise, "for it was by this process [of imitation] constantly repeated that the most advanced tribes lifted up those below them, as fast as the latter were able to appreciate and to appropriate the means of progress."

Primitive Critique of Civilization

We must turn to the second intellectual trajectory of nineteenth-century Euroamerica to unravel the reasoning behind these rather odd propositions, which we shall presently meet again in modern guise. The architects of the developing Continental sociology of the latter half of the nineteenth century shared many of the precepts of their ethnological contemporaries, although they had different agendas and were generally not preoccupied with evolution in itself. Loomis and McKinney (1957:1) point out that Tönnies ([1887] 1957), in *Gemeinschaft und Gesellschaft* (translated by them as *Community and Society*), was concerned to address the questions "What are we? Where are we? Whence did we come? Where are we going?" These are, with perhaps the exception of the last, the classic antiquarian and evolutionary questions; posing them presupposes a recognition of, if not an intent to investigate, the proposition that there are problematic historical antecedents to where it is we are.

Tönnies was aware of this and wished to merge formal and historical sociology in order to better address his questions. He is quite clear on this point ([1887] 1957:34, 42, 252), although he does not dwell on historical, let alone prehistoric, referents: "Gemeinschaft is old. . . . the natural relationship is, by its very essence, of earlier origin than its subjects or members. . . . Gemeinschaft by blood, denoting unity of being, is developed and differentiated into Gemeinschaft of locality . . . a further differentiation leads to the Gemeinschaft of mind, which implies only co-operation and co-ordinated action for a common goal." That is to say, original kinship among individuals is natural and unanalyzable—either by those in it or by those observing it—but this kinship eventually becomes identified with territory and ultimately emerges as an ideology of sociality through which individuals recognize their community of interests. Or, "all three types of Gemeinschaft are closely interrelated in space as well as in time. . . . the earlier type involves the later one, or the later one has developed to relative independence" (Tönnies [1887] 1957:42).

Gemeinschaft is the earlier, simpler stage of sociality when all associations of persons were replicate segments, the polar opposite of modern Gesellschaft, characterized by atomization of social forms and alienation of individuals. The crucial theme here is that small-scale, earlier, "old" Gemeinschaft is the authentic, "natural" state of human sociality, whereas large-scale, current, derivative society is artificial. The key attribute making Gemeinschaft the center of focus is this authenticity—the true state of human existence, one that may be regained by study and effort. I argue that it is this quest for authenticity that fuels the fascination with foragers—with true, untrammeled "primitives"—that exists to this day in Euroamerican thought and its authenticating agent, ethnography.

Later, in a convoluted passage—resonant of German mystical painters and architects of the time—concerning centers of development radiating toward new nuclei spawning yet others in the evolving chain, Tönnies ([1887] 1957:252) says that this "refers only to different stages and types of collective life." But the Gemeinschaft stage, at least, cannot change without external stimuli, particularly trade; it continues to exist in varying forms today. There is a vague, unstated suggestion that it cannot change because it is pure.

I am unable to find that Tönnies specifically attributed Gemeinschaft to a savage—or any other kind of—Stone Age, but the passages quoted above, along with his occasional references to the primeval core of spouses, the tents of nomads, and other then-current ethnographic attributes of that primitive stage, plus the fact that we know Tönnies was conversant with the ethnology of his day, seems to suggest that he had in mind something of the kind. He says, for example ([1887] 1957:37), that Gemeinschaft is characterized by a "perfect unity of human wills as an original or natural condition," that is, by a collective conscience. Perhaps more tellingly, he quotes copiously from Maine's *Ancient Law* ([1887] 1957:182–183) wherein the condition of the modern family is traced through reverse evolution to its simple roots in prehistory.

Durkheim too eschewed evolutionary intentions, but he called upon historical transformation processes in aboriginal societies that in the words of mid-twentieth-century anthropologists sound very familiar today. He followed Tönnies in contrasting simple, original society to complex, derived society such as he saw his contemporary Europe to be. This original, simple society was based upon mechanical solidarity, an unproblematic cultural unity. Its attributes are (1) aggregation of replicate segments composed of relatively undifferentiated individuals; (2) common beliefs and sentiments; (3) communal, collective property; (4) uninhibited mobility within the group's domain; and (5) self-sufficiency of segments.

The segmentary building block of mechanical solidarity is the horde, "a social aggregate which does not include, and has never included, within itself any other more elementary aggregate, but is directly composed of individuals. The latter do not form, within the total group, special groups differing from the whole; they are in atomic juxtaposition . . . the horde is thus the protoplasm of the social realm and, consequently, the natural basis of classification" (Durkheim [1895] 1966:83). Social "species" are the different forms elemental hordes take on as they adapt to pressures from the environment and from other societies (cf. Hirst 1975:126–27).

Mechanically solidary societies continue to exist throughout time essentially unchanged from their initial state; indeed, they cannot change except through external stimuli. Such societies are incapable of generating any other social form from within themselves (Hirst 1975: 132), for "we know that the segmental arrangement is an insurmountable obstacle to the division of labor, and must have disappeared at least partially for the division of labor to appear . . . [and this is contingent upon] an exchange of movements between parts of the social mass which, until then, had no effect on one another" (Durkheim [1893] 1964:256). For such change to occur, "relationships must have formed where none previously existed, bringing erstwhile separate groups into contact . . . [thus breaking down] the isolated homogeneity of each group" (Giddens 1971:78).

Before such contact went too far, one could still turn to "the simplest and most primitive" peoples to study the origins of human institutions. For Durkheim these were the Australian aborigines to whom he turned—apparently after reading English ethnologists (Giddens 1971:105)—to "discover the causes leading to the rise of the religious sentiment in humanity." Such a turn seems to contradict Durkheim's avowal that "man is a product of history. If one separates men from history, if one tries to conceive of man ouside time, fixed and immobile, one takes away his nature" (quoted in Giddens 1971:106). It is a turn from which few have retraced their steps.

Marx is not so easy to pin down, as Althusser and Balibar discover just twenty-eight pages from one another. Althusser (1970:197), while acknowledging that "we must say that *Marx did not give us any theory of the transition from one mode of production to another*," devoted an entire appendix to "survivals" from modes of production subordinate to capitalism and to "*the theory of the transition from one mode of production to another* . . . since every mode of production is constituted solely out of the existing forms of an earlier mode of production." Balibar (1970:225) proposes a diametrically opposite reading. In considering the same "survivals," he says that the "definition of every mode of production as a *combination* of (always the same) elements . . . affords [the possibility] of periodizing the modes of production according to a principle of *variation* . . . [that conveys] the radically *anti-evolutionist* character of the Marxist theory of the history of production (and therefore of society). . . . Marx does tell us that all the modes of production are *historical moments,* but *he does not tell us that these moments descend one from the other.*"

I shall not attempt to resolve these divergent readings; I wish only to invoke an atmosphere in which to appreciate the extent to which Marx was in accord with those of his contemporary ethnologists and sociologists whose views regarding prehistoric and contemporary foragers have been condensed in preceding paragraphs. In volume 1 of *Capital,* Marx ([1867] 1906:199–200) declares: "No sooner does labour undergo the least development, than it requires specially prepared instruments. Thus in the oldest caves we find stone implements and weapons. . . . [Benjamin] Franklin therefore defines man as a toolmaking animal." Although he does not cite Lubbock,[5] Marx ([1867] 1906:200) continues with an analogy between paleontology and ethnology that echoes *Prehistoric Times:* "Relics of by-gone instruments of labour possess the same importance for the investigation of extinct economical forms of society, as do fossil bones for the determination of extinct species of animals." In a footnote to this passage, Marx notes approvingly that "prehistoric times have been classified in accordance with the results not of so called historical, but of materialistic investigations . . . viz., into the stone, the bronze, and the iron ages."

Earlier, with Engels in *The German Ideology* ([1846] 1977:68–69), Marx had specified the social conditions of the prior ages—conditions, moreover, that survived in the "antagonism between town and country [which] begins with the transition from barbarism to civilization, from tribe to State, from locality to nation, and runs through the whole of history to the present day." Those aboriginal conditions were (1) individuals united by bonds of family, tribe, and land; (2) human individuals as themselves instruments of production subservient

to nature; (3) landed property relations those of direct natural domination and communality; (4) the premise of locality; (5) exchange
chiefly that between men and nature.

In *Capital*, Marx ([1867] 1906:366–67) elaborates on this theme:
"Co-operation, such as we find it at the dawn of human development,
among races who live by the chase, . . . is based, on the one hand, on
ownership in common of the means of production, and on the other
hand, on the fact that in those cases, each individual has no more torn
himself off from the navel-string of his tribe or community, than each
bee has freed itself from connexion with the hive." Such individuals
and such "tribes living exclusively on hunting or fishing are beyond the
boundary line from which real development begins" (Marx and Engels
[1846] 1977:146).[6]

These tribes are highly mobile, remaining in an area only long
enough to exhaust its resources. Differentiation in the division of labor, hence progress, occurs with the transition to settled agriculture
contingent upon environmental conditions, population increase, inter-
tribal contact, and the "internal structure of each tribal character."
Giddens (1971:25) remarks that "the similarity to Durkheim may
be noted."

In all this, it seems rather clear that Marx shared the basic tenets of
his contemporaries with respect to a prehistoric era set in polar opposition to our own. Because Marx's picture of modern society and its
historical trajectory from its predecessors was itself in opposition to
that of his sociological protagonists, his view of the relation of modern
society to its historical antecedents was radically different from theirs;
but it is unclear from the very few references Marx makes to it whether
this applies to prehistory as well. It is clear, nevertheless, that Marx
did not assign to foraging peoples of his day the role of remnant relic
of an evolutionary past but situated them along with all other peoples
as products of history in his overall scheme of social development.
In this he was in radical opposition to Tylorian evolutionist and Durkheimian sociological conceptions of foragers. I shall elaborate on this
difference in the next chapter.

The analogy Marx drew between sociality and the mechanical connection of bees to a hive, however, along with the assertion that foragers live "beyond the boundary line from which real development
begins," sounds like a Gemeinschaft construction. When the analogy
to bees is read in conjunction with the proposition that differentiation
in the division of labor begins with the transition to agriculture, it appears that Marx also thought of forager society in terms of static, replicate units. Despite this, it is important to keep in mind here that

Marx recognized that foraging peoples had, "thousands of years ago," performed the first historical act; they had interposed instruments of labor between themselves and nature and had constructed social relations of production through which these instruments were engaged. Thus foraging is historically created, and contemporary foragers are products of historical contingencies, not of a natural essence or an evolutionary stasis.

There does seem to be a contradiction here, for if foragers are subject to social transformations in the employment of instruments of labor, then differentiation in the division of labor must occur, and peoples living exclusively by hunting and fishing cannot be beyond the boundary from which development begins. On this point Marx seems to retain an element of the Gemeinschaft / Gesellschaft dichotomy. Indeed, Krader (1976:166; emphasis added) interprets Marx in just such terms, saying that "while the primary separation or alienation of mankind from nature is indeed a human universal, the alienation of man in civilized society is not the same thing, while at the same time it is somewhat the same, the same in a *distorted* way. Civilized humanity is farther removed from nature. . . . alienation of humanity from nature and of human beings from each other go together." Diamond (1974:353) tells us Krader means that "Marx conceived primitive society as *the* critique of civilization."[7] This is, of course, pure Tönnies and seems at variance with Marx's criticism of the premise of a primordial "natural" condition of humanity. In any case, for Marx the attributes of a prehistoric foraging era appear to be noticeably different neither from Lubbock's and Tylor's evolutionary constructions nor from Tönnies's and Durkheim's sociological constructions. Current forager mode of production theorists draw on this sketchily outlined prehistory of Marx instead of his fully developed historical presentation when they reformulate nineteenth-century evolutionary sociological models.

Morgan ([1877] 1964:8, 506) clearly articulated the uniformitarian principle underlying both these nineteenth- and twentieth-century formulations: "The experience of mankind has run in nearly uniform channels; human necessities in similar conditions have been substantially the same and the operations of the mental principle have been uniform. . . . [Furthermore], the tribes of mankind may be arranged, according to their relative conditions, into successive strata. When thus arranged, they reveal with some degree of certainty the entire range of human progress from savagery to civilization."

Tylor too adopted the doctrine as his own; for him, "in good uniformitarian fashion, survivals united the causal processes of the pres-

ent with those of the past" (Stocking 1987:163). The parallels to
Tönnies, Durkheim, and Lubbock need not be repeated.

Search for Authenticity

From the end of the 1930s, Steward began to restate these formulations after they had lain dormant for nearly half a century. He combined
key elements from both the evolutionary and the sociological trajectories of the previous century (which in any case, as we have seen, are
not all that easy to disentangle) into what came to be called a theory
of multilinear sociocultural evolution. Steward (1938:1–3) felt that
greatest success in analysis of the determinants of any society "should
attend analyses of societies which evince a less complicated history [of
internal development, borrowing, and adaptation to a particular envi-
ronment], whose structure is simpler in content and form, and whose
institutions were most extensively patterned by subsistence activities."
    These societies were integrated by "the biological or bilateral family
[which is] the most stable sociopolitical group" (Gemeinschaft of
blood), by the distribution of "residences with reference to food resources, water, and other natural advantages; communal hunting and
fishing" (Gemeinschaft of locality), and by the ideological intervention
of integrative social features—among them "extended kinship," "fes-
tivals" and "ceremonies," "shamanistic activities," and "warfare"
(Gemeinschaft of mind). This is Durkheimian mechanical solidarity
writ with new ethnographic ink, taking as the point of departure
"human ecology or the modes of behavior by which human beings
adapt themselves to their environment." But in this early formulation Steward (1938:260–61) dealt gingerly with evolution (and with
Marx); the peoples he described were designated "primitive," but they
were so primarily because they had an uncomplicated history—and
that mainly archaeological—and lived closer to nature, where ecology
"clearly predetermines and delimits certain features of social and political groups."
    Twenty years later White (1959) appropriated the entire evolution-
ary program of Morgan, Tylor, and Lubbock while retaining the Tönniesian and Durkheimian social elements built into Steward's cultural
ecology. He, however (1959:278), reached back to the eighteenth century to embrace Rousseau as much as the German idealists who influenced Tönnies: "Crude and limited as primitive cultures may have
been technologically, and wretched and poor as life may have been for
many—but far from all—peoples living in tribal organization, their
social systems based upon kinship and characterized by liberty, equal-

ity, and fraternity were unquestionably more congenial to the human primate's nature, and more compatible with his psychic needs and aspirations, than any other that has ever been realized in any of the cultures subsequent to the Agricultural Revolution, including our own society today." One thinks of Hesiod here as much as of Morgan.

These sentiments strike a responsive chord in those who, in company with Diamond (1974:220), see anthropology as "the natural heir of the Enlightenment, the axial age of contemporary civilization." For Diamond, as for most of the ethnographers whose work in the Kalahari we shall delve into, one of anthropology's major tasks is "a puzzled search for what is diminished . . . [for] wherever civilization arises, the primitive in man is subordinated; it withers away, grows attenuated or is replaced" (Diamond 1974:120). It is hard to know what this means without first having absorbed an appreciation of how the "primitive in man" was constructed out of the European conception of the "naturalness" of small-scale societies as opposed to the artificiality of industrial society. The leitmotif of Diamond's (1974:208) search enshrines that construction in an unabashed leap over the nineteenth century to an eighteenth-century "search for the utopia of the past" upon which to forge the future.

For this search, with its haunting, mystical evocation of Tönnies insinuating itself into the Rousseauean wreckage, "*primitive* implies a certain level of history, and a certain mode of cultural being . . . [a mode of being inexorably] obliterated or attentuated by the processes of civilization . . . pre-civilized and, yes, a priori human possibility has practically disappeared from our cultural lexicon. . . . Without such a model (or, since we are dealing with men and not things, without such a vision), it becomes increasingly difficult to evaluate or understand our contemporary pathology and possibilities" (Diamond 1974:118–19).

In this search, ensconced as it is in an earlier evolutionary stage, "a certain level of history," those most primitive of primitives—those who came before and remain as our alter ego, those whose continued existence is a self-imposed rebuke to our self-defined failure as their successors—cannot be freed from their forager fate, even if they do not subscribe to such a role for themselves. This reductionist tendency in anthropological thought is bound up with "tendencies towards myth, ritual, and primitivism" in a new twentieth-century intellectualism to whose construction anthropologists contributed significantly in post–World War I America (Isernhagen 1982:157). It constitutes an idealist search for authenticity to be achieved by "a return to an ideal(ized) original state of being through a shedding of historical attributes . . .

[identifying] ontological man progressively more as ideal man, or even as man as he has never been but should have been . . . less prehistoric than ahistorical, less the potential than the imaginable man" (Isernhagen 1982:183–84).

The Invention of "Bushmen"

It fell to the nineteenth century to invent its nativity in ancient hunting savagery, which is quite a different thing from simply gaining awareness of its ancient hunting ancestors. Hobsbawm (1983:3, 8) has remarked that in the profound and rapid social transformation of the later nineteenth century, with its attendant need to accommodate the aspiring political ambitions of an expanding bourgeoisie, invented traditions served a reassuring function. In this atmosphere, constructions of evolutionary stages and sociological forms molded in imaginable configurations played important roles. To paraphrase Hobsbawm (1983:2), these stages and forms established their own past that, in contrast to the constant change and innovation of the current world, offered an unchanging, invariant structure for at least some parts of social life; they provided "sanction of precedent, social continuity and natural law as expressed in history."

"Bushmen" were invented in this intellectual environment. They, or something like them, had to be made available to certify the ontological quest. The historical dimensions of this invention are the subject of "the past recaptured," but first we must grasp the ideological components, in extension of the foregoing discussion, that dictated the modern shape given the "Bushman" image. Gilman (1985) points out that it was physiognomy that first aroused scientific and popular interest—the black body as opposed to the white. But the mere noting of difference was not enough for "the radical empiricists of late eighteenth- and early nineteenth-century Europe. To meet their scientific standards, a paradigm was needed . . . rooted in some type of unique and observable physical difference" (Gilman 1985:212). The antithetical position to the white body was found in the black, especially the Bushman-Hottentot female, with her "primitive" steatopygous physique, her "primitive" genitalia, and her "primitive" sexual appetite. Gilman (1985:229) notes that Hegel and Schopenhauer believed that all blacks remained at this most primitive stage and that their contemporary presence served to indicate how far Europeans had extricated themselves from this swamp. Bushmen were placed at the nadir of this scale of humanity. Bachofen drew on these ideas to construct this primitive promiscuous horde as the initial stage of human sociality.

But "Bushmen" as social beings rather than natural history specimens did not yet figure prominently in those formulations. Although various of these peoples were mentioned in many travelers' accounts, official reports, and dispatches from 1761 onward (even much earlier at the Cape), the first full-scale ethnographic field investigation of any "Bushmen," that by the German Siegfried Passarge among the Zhu, was conducted in the 1890s. The resulting publications did not appear until 1905 and after; though of considerable merit considering their time, they appeared too late to have much influence on theoretical constructions, which in any case were by then moving in new directions. "Bushman" did not yet carry the ethnographic authority accorded the often-cited American Indians, Australian Aborigines, and Eskimos, among others.

That did not, however, shield "Bushmen" from being categorized along with these other colonized peoples, or from being isolated conceptually as an undifferentiated enclave among more "advanced" Africans (those at a "higher" evolutionary stage). This conceptual isolation was a prerequisite to their administrative isolation and was a major contributing factor in their deepening social and economic isolation in the emerging colonial social formation that has left its legacy in Botswana and Namibia today. This was the path to the divided present; it led from an indigenous past that was very different: "The colonial reification of rural custom produced a situation very much at variance with the pre-colonial situation" (Ranger 1983 : 254) and had replaced prior relations among peoples with a created microcosmic society. Iliffe's (1979 : 324) observation that Tanganyikan natives created tribes in order to function within the colonial framework applies very much to the Kalahari, as we shall see. It was also in the interests of colonial administration to codify and reify custom as a means of consolidating its control. Ethnographers were recruited to provide this codification and to help ensure that this colonial world was manageable by certifying that it was divisible.

Their own words on the matter are revealing. Radcliffe-Brown (1923 : 142–43), newly appointed first head of the School of African Life and Languages at the University of Cape Town, worte in the *South African Journal of Science*, "[The study of African culture] can afford great help to the missionary or public servant who is engaged in dealing with the practical problems of the adjustment of the native civilization to the new conditions that have resulted from our occupation of the country."

Seven years later, in their "introductory Note" to *The Khoisan Peoples of South Africa*, the first volume in a series on native peoples published by that very same school, Driberg and Schapera (1930:v) reiterated Radcliffe-Brown's thesis:

To the administrator, the missionary, the economist, and the educationist, each in his own way now moulding the life of the Native into conformity with the standards of European civilization, a thorough knowledge and under-standing of the people with whom he is concerned is an indispensable prelimi-nary to the completion of his task. It is the hope of the editors that applied anthropology no less than the academic science will find in this series the groundwork upon which it may build for the future.[8]

This anthropological program was designed to serve the emerging seg-regationist solution to the harsher effects of domination; it was a "syn-thesis of liberalism and 'scientific racism,' which would hold out the prospect of evolution for individual blacks while avoiding genetic de-generation [of whites]" (Marks and Trapido 1987:8). "An intellectual organizing principle was required to validate this synthesis or compro-mise. The development of an anthropological notion of 'culture' came to serve this purpose admirably" (Dubrow 1987:80).

Wright (1986:105–6) draws the inescapable conclusion that this ideological context in which anthropologists operated "served to ori-ent their critical faculties in a way which made for the existence of an intellectual blindspot as far as questioning the notion of tribe was con-cerned." He goes on to observe that the thus reinforced continuance of a system of administration that emphasized "tribal" divisions was one of the major structural reasons why collective terms—such as "Bushmen" and later San (Wright, however, referred specifically to Nguni)—survived so long without being called into question. Marks (1969:126), also concerned with Nguni, argues that the retention of such all-inclusive terms with their connotations of timeless homogene-ity are the first obstacles in the way of our understanding the peoples so categorized. Ranger (1983:261–62) summarizes succinctly the point we have reached when he identifies the "ambiguous legacy that is 'traditional' African culture; the whole body of reified 'tradition' in-vented by administrators, missionaries, 'progressive traditionalists,' elders and anthropologists . . . [and declares that we have to free our-selves] from the illusion that the African custom recorded by officials or by many anthropologists is any sort of guide to the African past."

The Need to Name

In the invention of the requisite categories of tribal administration, considerable effort was devoted to investing names with meaning. The epistemological status of these names, as of all categorial names, is constituted in the ideological valuation of their predicates. For example, living in a "state of nature" was savagery to nineteenth-century evolutionists, so much so that savagery was considered to be the defining characteristic of the initial stage of human existence. In the later half of the twentieth century, however, living in this same state is again considered by some to be utopian (or at least quasi-utopian), so much so that it could be called the original affluent existence. In both cases the terms are applied attributively to anyone (or any group) who satisfies the predicate requirements of the concept "initial stage of human life"; these are the defining criteria mentioned several times in the preceding discussion of nineteenth-century evolutionary and sociological schemes. Everything else about such individuals or groups is contingent, both as empirical fact and as observational object; those things that in the next chapter we shall find Howell and Burchell avoiding are examples (cf. Schwartz 1977:13–41). In this investment process, language—not only the names that as labels encode the predicates of the categories of discourse but the specialized lexicon of the discourse itself—carries the burden of the work of reifying those categories and "helps to establish the authority which re-presentations require if they are to be seen as representative" (Alonso 1988:35).

By now it is well known that the term "Bushman" is anglicized from Dutch/Afrikaans "Bosjesmans/Bossiesmans" in its many spellings. The etymology of the Dutch term is in constant and sometimes contentious debate, revolving around the ideological investment of this term itself. It is important to emphasize that "Bushman" came into use during the 1680s in the Cape area only after thirty years of Dutch applications of other "terms obviously derived from native usage" (Parkington 1984:156). "Within a few years it had, along with 'Bosjesman Hottentot,' become the standard Dutch equivalent of the older [indigenous] Khoikhoi terms" (Elphick 1977:24). Those terms were Soaqua or Sonqua (Elphick (1977:24; Parkington 1984:151), which some authors derive from a root common to San of current usage; I shall take up this term in a moment.

Parkington (1984:156) sets "Bushman" in its original context of use. Within a few years of the founding of the Cape settlement in 1652, local pastoralist groups were called by their generic self-referents or by the names of their leaders; when explorations into the interior beyond the Cape boundaries became frequent, unknown peoples—many without domestic stock—were encountered. Europeans relied on their interpreters to supply names for these peoples, and "a new link in the chain of terminology was added. Before the end of the seventeenth century the term *Bushmen* or *Bushmen Hottentot* complemented and replaced *Sonqua Hottentot* to describe these pepoles" (Parkington 1984:156–57). These changes occurred at a time "when increased Dutch interference was causing massive, and irreversible, changes in indigenous group relations. *Bushmen* relates more clearly to these changes" (Parkington 1984:164). Parkington suggests that Soaqua should be understood to refer to the aboriginal hunter-gatherer social formation of southern Africa, whereas Bushman refers to pastoralists and foragers whose social and material fabric had been disrupted by Dutch intervention. As these dispossessed groups—along with escaped slaves and deserters from the Cape Colony, some of whom were white Europeans—sought to establish a mode of existence away from Dutch control, "Bushmen," as applied to them, "became a wastepaper basket term for all those who lived by hunting, gathering, and stealing" (Goodwin and van Riet Lowe 1929:147). Or as Gordon (1984:196), citing Nienaber (1952), glosses it, "'bandit.'" Elphick (1975:23–42), however, marks the much broader indigenous use of the term "San": "KhoiKhoi themselves made no such clear and systematic distinction between peoples, their term 'San' having wide reference to both hunter and small-scale pastoral groups" (Elphick 1975:41).

Gordon contributes to the many confusions to be found in the literature of the region that perpetuate distortions in the application of this term; we shall encounter others in following chapters. He says (1984:216, citing Moritz 1980:21) that the missionary Carl Hugo Hahn, in 1851 one of the first Europeans to enter the northern part of what is now Namibia, recorded in his diary that "his Herero servants referred to the Bushmen as 'Ozumbushmana' [*sic*], a term clearly derived, as he recognized, from Dutch." But Hahn recognized a great deal more; his original published account (*Petermanns* 1859:299) reads: "Our people call the Bushmen Ozombusumana (Sing—Ombusumana), a corruption of the Dutch name. The true name, by which they have otherwise been known to the Ovaherero, is Ovaguma [Lau tells me this is written ova-guruha in Hahn's diary]. The new name will surely displace the older, and its etymology will perhaps later give philologists a headache."[9]

Gordon is eager to show that penetration by outsiders (in this case, Ovaherero) is recent; he therefore overlooks the obvious—Hahn's Herero servants were employing pidgin language forms in conversing with a European. This is an instance of the expediency with which, in the early years of their association, "Africans as a rule adopted the restricted jargon of their immediate European masters" (Fabian 1986:139).

Hahn's Herero servants no doubt did say to him that certain "Bush-

men" were ozombusumana. But what were they telling him? The form
of the term used provides a clue: the Otjiherero noun prefix (class 10)
ozo- is applied to livestock as well as to most animals in general. The
use of ozo- in this case thus carried the meaning "those Bushmen are
our chattel," hardly an indication of unfamiliarity. Hahn was clearly
aware of this; in his own dictionary (1857 : 151) he gives omu-kuna
(pl. ova-kuna) as "Buschmann." The first full study of Otjiherero, that
by Brincker ([1886] 1964 : 145), who worked among Ovaherero from
1863 to 1889, has omukuru as "einer, der verlängst gewesen ist . . . die
Alten, Ahnen": "one who formerly existed . . . the ancients, ancestors." More recently, Katjavivi (1988 : 1) writes Ovakuruvehi, "the ancient (or original) ones." Irle (1917 : 16), in his German-Otjiherero
dictionary, translates Ahne (ancestor) as "omukuru." These glosses
are in keeping with Guthrie (1970, 3 : 310), who attaches the notions
of ancestor and grandparent to his proto-Bantu root *-kúúkù. Modern ethnographers note the same term applied by Herero-speakers
to specific peoples. Marshall (1976 : 17) says that Ovakuruha is the
Herero term for Zhu. Vedder (1938 : 136) restricted Ovakuruha to
those people he called Saan, the Heixum (Hai-‖'om) of current terminology, whom he distinguished from other Bushmen.

Otjiherero has another term, ovatua, derived from the proto-Bantu
root *-túá (Guthrie 1970, 4 : 122): "The most likely original meaning was probably either 'pygmy' or 'Bushman,' and presumably referred to the indigenous inhabitants originally encountered by the
speakers of proto-Bantu." This root also has the apparently secondarily acquired connotation "member of neighboring despised tribe."
Hahn (1857 : 150) has the form omukoatoa, which he glosses "Einge-
borener": "native." Brincker ([1886] 1964 : 157) has omutua, "Volker
vorzukommen": "people who came before" and notes that it appears
as such in many Bantu languages; these glosses reflect Guthrie's first
meanings. Brincker, however, captures the derogatory connotation as
well: "Die Grundbedeutung scheint 'Buschmann' im verächtlichen
Sinne zu sein": "The original meaning appears to be 'Bushman' with
its contemptuous connotations." Local usage conforms to these dictionary glosses. The Ovambandru people with whom I work in Botswana
insist that Zhu—who are the archetypal "Bushmen" of ethnography—
are not Ovatua (that is, not "Bushmen" or "member of despised tribe")
but Ovakuruha (that is, "ancestral," "those who came before"). Ovatua
do exist, they say, but in distant places.

Setswana elides the common Bantu root as rwa; with the plural
prefix (class 1) ba-, designating the noun class pertaining to humans, this becomes Barwa. Brown ([1875] 1979 : 16) renders this term

"Bushmen." However, the root with the locative prefix (class 7) bo-becomes "borwa": "the country of the Bushmen, hence the south to people living farther north" (Brown [1875] 1979:34); and "kwa ntlha ea Borwa" refers to the south. Digging deeper, we find "batho ba ntlha": "the first people" (Brown [1875] 1979:231); hence, except for the reference to the south, this term is cognate with other Bantu forms meaning aborigines. In practice, as we shall shortly see, it was applied to all sorts of people in particular circumstances, not only to those we today identify as San-speakers. The current form in use in Botswana is Basarwa, but this form does not occur in the nineteenth century and begins to appear only in the 1960s. A related form, Masarwa, was commonly used from the early nineteenth century or perhaps somewhat earlier to denote "Bushmen of the Bechuanaland Protectorate" (Brown [1875] 1979:183), that is, of the Kalahari;[10] this form employs the plural noun prefix (class 3) ma-, which is applied to non-Tswana and to persons of undesirable characteristics or social inferiority (Cole 1975:81). This term appears to derive from the secondary, acquired meaning of the root *-túá, "despised neighboring tribe."

Thus we find three sets of contrasting pairs: Dutch, Sonqua/-Bosjesmans; Otjiherero, Ovakuru/Ovatua; Setswana, Barwa/Masarwa. In each case the first term referred to known peoples of proximate location and carried neutral or positive connotations of aboriginality in some sense. The second term referred to newly encountered frontier peoples or rumored peoples of distant location and carried negative connotations of despised foreigner. In Dutch and English these transformations in usage occurred during the period—late eighteenth and early nineteenth centuries—when those groups were rapidly expanding geographically and consolidating their gains. These changes in nomenclatural referents were ideological impositions by newly hegemonic powers upon subordinated peoples who were thus interpellated as subjects in a new order of social relations. No longer a serious threat to European power, San-speakers acquired "characteristics that the powerful commonly find in those they have subjugated: meekness, innocence, passivity, indolence coupled with physical strength and stamina, cheerfulness, absence of greed or indeed desires of any kind, internal egalitarianism, a penchant for living in the present, inability to take initiatives on their own behalf" (Pratt 1986:46). This appears to be the first transition toward "bushmanness"; these same characteristics are attributed ethnographically to "Bushmen" today.

At the beginning of this transition the various Tswana groups were not yet dominant over other groups, but as their hegemony solidified during the course of the nineteenth century, the predicate attributes of San-speakers in Tswana ideology changed from original inhabitant to bloodthirsty marauder to childlike dependency. On the other hand, Ovaherero never established lasting hegemony in their sphere of influence; as a consequence, ovatua for them are situated somewhere over the horizon, and this term, when it is used at all, has only vague referents. Ovaherero usually refer to most local groups by their generic self-referents. The details of these processes are taken up in chapter 3.

This brings us back to San. As noted already, Parkington derives this term from the same Khoikhoi root as Soaqua, which he says (1984:164) "should be referred to not as a title but as a description of a set of strategies that varied from almost complete independence [from livestock keeping] to clientship [of livestock keepers]." He says further (1984:158) that it seems certain that Soaqua was not originally meant to be capitalized "in the sense of referring to named communities" but referred to a particular and widespread life-style, which depended heavily—but apparently not exclusively—on foraging. Indeed, Vedder (1938:124) derives San from the Nama verb "sa": "to gather wild foods." Sixty-five years earlier, however, Theophilus Hahn ([1881] 1971:3)—although confessing that he was uncertain of the derivation—traced this term to the root "SA, to inhabit, to be located, to dwell, to be settled, to be quiet. Sā(n) consequently would mean Aborigines or Settlers proper. These Sā-n . . . as they are styled in the Cape Records, are often called Bushmen . . . a name given to indicate their abode and mode of living. . . . Sā(b) has also acquired a low meaning, and is not considered to be very complimentary."

This Khoikhoi/Nama term, now written San, thus seems to be fully parallel in meaning and history to Bantu rwa/tua-kuruha, moving from protoneutral/positive to acquired negative value. As we shall see, however, Nama-speakers in northern Namibia seldom used San but usually addressed and referred to peoples by their generic self-referents, by leader names, or by borrowed terms such as Bosjesmans.

Thus, before the emergence of ethnicity as a central logic, which began toward the end of the seventeenth century at the Cape but not in the Kalahari until the nineteenth century was well begun (I will take this up in chap. 7), Khoikhoi "sa" and Bantu "tua/rwa" forms were primarily epithets of origins with economic connotations. Group identification followed the self-usage of individual social units. As a consequence of struggles to control, first, commodity production for the European mercantile market and, later, units of labor for industrializing South Africa, all of those native terms acquired negative connotations and became categorical denominations that replaced group denotations in general reference. Their origins aside, all these forms are impositions upon peoples to whom they are foreign; they retain their acquired derogatory signification and are intensely disliked by those to whom they are applied. This dislike is gaining recognition in Botswana's popular press (Leepile 1988 : 9), reflecting a growing awareness within the country of the pejorative connotations of Basarwa as well as of Bushman. These terms should all be relegated to archives, and the use of self-referents of self-defined social groups should be reinstated.[11]

Elphick (1977 : 25) identifies another acquired connotation of the native terms: "This Bushman-Hottentot (or San-Khoikhoi) dichotomy has become one of those time-honored pairing mechanisms by which scholars automatically organize, but also distort, the complexities of historical reality." To these have been added the forager/food producer and primitive/civilized dichotomies, anthropological analogues of those native terms. We have seen how these later dichotomies came into existence. All the terms have been reified in the agenda of anthropological practice, where they now serve as abstract signposts authenticating claims of knowledge about the society in which that practice takes place. In ethnographic discourse, they interpellate natives as the ontological categories required by that agenda. These categories are designed to segregate historically, economically, and politically the peoples they label and thus to isolate them socially—and often racially—from those who apply the terms. The explicit rationale for such categorization is that it creates a set of criteria according to which those placed in it are thought to be more or less homogeneous and readily distinguished from others whose assigned category predicates are different. In the indigenous classifications, these categories mark social distance; in the academic classifications, they mark supposed prehistoric persistence, a marking they have essentially lost in native vernaculars. In fact, the terms lump together more than a dozen living southern African peoples (plus several others who have disappeared under colonial pressures and introduced diseases) who have distinct languages and traditions and whose economies cover the entire spectrum of indigenous forms from extensive foraging to intensive agropastoralism.

Primitive, savage, hunter-gatherer, forager, Bushman, Basarwa, San; the names have changed, their predicates and the premises from which these are drawn retain their negation of historically constructed objects. An analytical discourse that unquestioningly accepted these homogenizing categories, appropriate only to the needs of its own moment, has left us nothing but a stereotype of its subject.

2

The Poverty of Misappropriated Theory

Once we are persuaded to doubt that it is possible arbitrarily to isolate certain phenomena and to group them together as diagnostic signs of an illness, or of an objective institution, the symptoms themselves vanish or appear refractory to any unifying interpretation. . . . [This] suggests a relation of another order between scientific theories and culture, one in which the mind of the scholar himself plays as large a part as the minds of the people studied; it is as though we were seeking, consciously or unconsciously, and under the guise of scientific objectivity, to make the latter—whether mental patients or so-called "primitives"—more *different* than they really are.

Claude Lévi-Strauss, *Totemism*, 1963

Return to Authenticity

Lee and DeVore (1968:ix) conclude their preface to *Man the Hunter:* "We cannot avoid the suspicion that many of us were led to live and work among the hunters because of a feeling that the human condition was likely to be drawn more clearly here than among other kinds of societies." Their suspicion was surely correct, supported as it is by many avowals in the then burgeoning literature of just that motivation. Service (1979:1), for instance, opens his vista on *The Hunters* in pure Tylorian fashion: "We cannot know all that we have gained in acquiring civilization until we know what we have lost." Lee and DeVore (1968:3) further express a basic aspect of that position; their words resonate with those of Nilsson, written in 1834, that we read a few pages ago: "It is appropriate that anthropologists take stock of the much older way of life of the hunters [because] the emergence of economic, social, and ideological forms" in this initial cultural stage predates organizational forms that came into being during what they call "an incredibly brief transitional phase of human history . . . [that] emerged within the last 10,000 years and [is] rapidly disappearing in the face of modernization."[1] Again Lee and DeVore read their audience accurately, for this view was once more in anthropological favor.

Lorna Marshall (1976:2) records that her family elicited little en-

couragement from anthropologists when, in the early 1950s, they
planned an expedition to the Kalahari and offered to investigate the
native peoples of the remote parts of that region. Steward's human
ecology and White's revival of cultural evolution would have to gain
adherents to give these peoples anthropological life. Their time was
drawing near. As Marshall was bringing her expeditions to an end, Lee
approached the corner of the Kalahari she was leaving, "intrigued by
reports of a large cluster of semi-independent !Kung groups" living
there (Lee 1979:10). Lee (1976a:10) records that his interest in the
San was sparked by Sherwood Washburn, who argued that studying
living foragers could illuminate the evolution of human behavior, and
by Desmond Clark, who suggested that studying contemporary forager campsites would throw light on prehistoric sites uncovered by archaeologists. Lee, along with DeVore, "chose to work in Africa rather
than Australia because we wanted to be close to the actual floral and
faunal environment occupied by early man" (Lee 1976a:10), as Paleolithic hunters had come to be called. To Lee (1984:1) these "semi-
independent" Zhu offered "our last hope for success" in realizing that
elusive evolutionary goal, the capture of primary authenticity.

Lee (1968:343–44, 1979:434) explicitly grounds his program in
"the uniformitarian approach to evolutionary reconstruction following the term widely used in nineteenth-century geology." This is the
program advanced by Lubbock, appropriated almost verbatim by Pitt-
Rivers, and given its clearest expression by Morgan and Tylor. Appropriately, Lee's (1969:47) goal is "to show that the Bushmen exhibit an
elementary form of economic life . . . and . . . to trace, from a primate
baseline, the origin and evolution of human energy relations." He can
do this because to him Bushmen are "in one sense on the threshold
of the Neolithic" (Lee 1972a:342), "stripped of the accretions and
complications brought about by agriculture, urbanization, advanced
technology, and national and class conflict" (Lee 1974:169). Thus
stripped, they do have "a Stone Age-type existence, [providing scope
for] this search for an ultimate reality" (Katz 1976:282). I shall return
to these echoes of Lubbock, of Morgan, and of Tylor cradled in Gemeinschaft and swaddled in Durkheimian mechanical solidarity often as I
consider the poverty of misappropriated theory.

"Bushmen" also have "a rapidly disappearing way of life" (Lee
1976a:3). The Harvard Kalahari Project ended in 1972, by a happy
coincidence with the end of the "Bushman" era—the end, that is, of
what was defined as a free foraging state, for now these people seem
quickly and with enthusiasm to have taken on the ways of the neighbors they previously shunned.[2] Now, Lee (1976a:8) assures us, "less

than 5 percent of the San simply hunt and gather for a living." From this point we begin to hear of "the !Kung's new culture" (Lee 1976b), a new culture brought about by that "break in the sequence" foretold by Pitt-Rivers—a crossing, that is, of the "threshold of the Neolithic." Bollig (1988) calls attention to the inconsistencies that arise from this new view.

Clearly, the discourse of Stone Age savagery has changed little during the 150 years it has been part of existential Euroamerican consciousness. And it continues to play the role initially reserved for it, that of metaphoric underpinning for the self-recognition of that consciousness. The metaphor continues to demand its tangible witness in order to secure its credibility. In the nineteenth century, living persons were taken from their homelands to be displayed in colonial capitals as representatives of their savage state. Among those from southern Africa was Saartjie Baartman, the first "Hottentot Venus," who was exhibited throughout Europe for five years between 1809 and 1815 and dissected by Cuvier after her death (Schrire 1984:4; Gilman 1985:213–29). Ethnography now fulfills this need; it can do so for modern tastes grown somewhat squeamish about using actual bodies in this way because, as Gilman (1985) tells us, displaying difference and writing about it serve the same ideological function. The question we have to ask then is, When does the ethnographic version force the evidence to "conform to the well-known myths of the culture of the scientist" (Perper and Schrire 1977:449)?

Howell (1986:3), a member of the Harvard Kalahari Project and author of one of its more distinguished books, offers one opinion, predicated on the awareness that "we must reconsider the meaning of what we saw there, and what we made of it." She describes (1986:6–7) how the historical context was missed in 1968: "Here are the hunter-gatherers of the dreams of someone who wants to go to the living source for illumination of the archaeological remains of Early Man."[3] She then catalogs machine-sewn cloth clothing, store-bought implements and utensils, familiarity with trucks and guns, wage labor, and multilingual people. Lee (1984:123–25) adds to this catalog: "Every !Kung in the Dobe area had a son, nephew, or relative working for the Blacks, and all the San paid regular visits to one cattle-post or another to drink milk. . . . In fact, they found life on a Herero cattle-post downright luxurious."

But these things we ignored, relatively speaking, because we didn't come all the way around the world to see them. We could have stayed near home and seen people behaving as rural proletariat, while nowhere but the Kalahari and a few other remote locations allow a glimpse of "the hunting and gathering way of life." So we focus upon bush camps, upon hunting, upon old fashioned customs, and although we remind each other once in a while not to be romantic, we consciously and unconsciously neglect and avoid the !Kung who don't conform to our expectations. (Howell 1986:7)

Exactly 150 years earlier, Burchell ([1824] 1953:54) avoided the same things among the Bushmen he spent some time with on the Orange River, whom he considered the most uncivilized, most destitute, and lowest of the human race, and whom he unquestioningly defined as pure foragers. Nevertheless, as Schrire (1980:22) remarks, "If ever there were an instance when the evolutionary implications of savage life were instantly negated, Burchell's example is it." For he describes kraals full of sheep (as many as two hundred), goats, and cattle ("some 50" in one alone) belonging to these people. But all these livestock are passed over without comment or are assumed to have been stolen, without pause to wonder why—or how—these animals were kept rather than killed by "hunters."

Howell continues: "Some of the causes of the misconceptions arise from the original task of seeking out the unspoiled, untouched remnant population of the original hunter-gatherers. When you go hunting for that goal, you may continue to search until the evidence is such that it isn't obvious that you haven't found it."

Howell (1986:7) correctly identifies that mysterious time, "the ethnographic present," existing somewhere in an undisturbed past made present, as serving "to transform anthropology from a natural science to a work of fiction in which the anthropologist is invited to use the society apparently being studied as a mirror for the simple reflection of the concerns of the anthropologist's society." But this is only one facet of a larger misconception, for ethnography is itself a rhetorical form, an invention created to bring back from the primitive world to nineteenth-century Europe the cosmic and worldly—that is, the ideological—reassurance that its place in the industralizing colonial world was indeed as it saw it to be and was secure (cf. Stocking 1987:232).[4] Thornton (1980:6–7) dissects this impetus of ethnography as a function of European concern with morality in situations of flux:

Since the evolution of the time was, in practice, a moral classification of nature and society, the other moral concerns of missionaries and colonialists easily took their places beside it. The still-smoldering debate between "Creationists" and "Evolutionists" concerns the linkage of mankind to nature through a prehistorical common ancestor. . . . What was at issue, both among believers in Darwin and the brotherhood of Christ, and what was common cause, was essentially moral classifications which gave Europeans an identity and justified their actions.

Tylor ([1881] 1909:401) made the motivation of this common cause abundantly clear: "Savage and barbarous tribes often more or less fairly represent stages of culture through which our ancestors passed long ago, and their customs and laws often explain to us, in ways we should otherwise have hardly guessed, the sense and reason of our own."

In this discourse, ethnography's role has not changed: "The !Kung were re-selected for further studies during the 1960s by investigators anxious to bring back to a troubled capitalist country fighting a painful war in Vietnam a message of liberation, peace and social justice" (Howell 1986:10). This has been no secret; Lee (1979:461) ends his book with this "Lesson of the !Kung": "A truly communal life is often dismissed as a utopian ideal, to be endorsed in theory but unattainable in practice. But the evidence for foraging peoples tells us otherwise. A sharing way of life is not only possible but has actually existed in many parts of the world and over long periods of time." This is that "crystalline structure which the best preserved of primitive societies teach us is not antagonistic to the human condition" (Lévi-Strauss [1960] 1967:49). Both Lee and Lévi-Strauss voice here a deep concern for that return to authenticity that reemerged in the 1960s, a concern that fostered a heightened awareness of ecology and embraced a variety of "back-to-the-land" movements as an aspect of a general search for a simpler utopia. It is no accident that at that time foragers became once more a center of public and academic attention after decades on the periphery of interest.

Diamond (1974:208) conjures the ghost of Tylor more unabashedly: "The search for the primitive is, then, as old as civilization. It is the search for the utopia of the past, projected into the future, with civilization being the middle term. It is birth, death, and transcendent rebirth, the passion called Christian, the trial of Job, the oedipal transition, the triadic metaphor of human growth, felt also in the vaster pulse of history. And this search for the primitive is inseparable from the vision of civilization." Indeed, for Diamond, a future utopia detached from the precivilized past "becomes a nightmare."

It is just in that "vision" of Diamond, in that "sense and reason of our own" felt by Tylor, that Howell depicts a rerun of the quixotic odyssey of the missionary explorer David Livingstone, whose nineteenth-century footsteps we shall shortly retrace through the Kalahari. But even Howell is unaware that she and her companions walked onto a stage first set to play to a colonial audience. The categorial script of their search was already written for them; the characters had long since learned their cues. It is that unawareness that underlies the incompatibility between the Harvard "researchers' sincere desire to be sensitive to the !Kung's situation in present historical cirumstances . . .

[and] . . . their project of viewing the !Kung as a complex adaptation to the ecology of the Kalahari desert, and an example of how our ancestors lived" (Pratt 1986:49). The reason behind that unawareness— a reluctance to allow historical impediments to deflect the quest for a purer past—is also responsible for the widespread willingness among anthropologists (and, needless to say, the public as well) to overlook the serious methodological flaws of the Harvard Kalahari Project.

Revival of the Primitive Critique

Better than anyone else, Lee and DeVore (1968:11–12) articulated the goals and strategies of the renewed search for authenticity. As a key part of their program, they offered a trial formulation of the characteristics of forager organization. These are:[5] D-1: "the basic hunting society consisted of a series of local 'bands' . . . [among which] it is probably necessary to continually redistribute the population . . . in order to maintain food-gathering units at an effective level"; D-2: "from the very beginning there was communication between groups, including reciprocal visiting and marriage alliances," "ritual," and "sorcery," which enable people to "change residence without relinquishing vital interests in land and goods"; D-3: because of the need to be mobile, "property has to be kept to a very low level . . . [resulting in] a generally egalitarian system . . . [in which] the lack of impediments in the form of personal and collective property allows a considerable degree of freedom"; D-4: "flexible organizations that allow people to move from one area to another"; D-5: "lack of concern that food resources will fail or be appropriated by others." This is vintage Durkheim (p. 18 above) buttressed by the evolutionist consensus of Lubbock, Morgan, and Tylor (p. 14). Lee (1979:117) later rebaptized this formulation the forager mode of production in a Marxian sense; however, Marx does not enter into the original 1968 version and does not appear in the reference list or the index of *Man the Hunter* or, for that matter, in *Kalahari Hunter-Gatherers* (Lee and DeVore 1976).

Lee and DeVore also repudiate Service's (1962) patrilineal band model of hunter social organization. This model has since been all but abandoned, an abandonment to which Lee's work has contributed in significant measure. But in the basic rationale for the study of "foragers" and in the premises upon which to base such studies, they are in complete accord with Service. A brief recounting of Service's statements will establish the correspondence in their positions. Service (1962:8) asks, If forager culture is not an environmental adaptation made long ago "and preserved into modern times because of its isolation, then what is it?" He answers his own question by asserting that the culture of "primitive" forager societies is constituted by Tylorian survivals into the present of "ancient cultural forms . . . paleolithic in type." The hallmarks of these survivals begin with (1) "the nomadism required by the foraging economy," leading to (2) a "simplicity and meagerness . . . of the material culture" and (3) "small size of the community . . . lacking the integrative devices of higher levels of sociopolitical evolution" so that (4) "the subdivisions of the society are thus all familistic," lacking (5) "specialized or formalized institutions or groups that can be differentiated as economic, political, religious, and so on" (Service 1979: 4–5). The study of these primitive societies provides a ground for "collecting useful facts with which to think more realistically about past stages of human evolution" (Service 1962: 9). Yellen (1984: 54) sums it up nicely when he says of anthropological perceptions of Zhu, "This San group has been used as a kind of narrow and opaque window to the Pleistocene."

In the major compilation to date of his work in the Kalahari, Lee (1979: 2) reaffirms this position: "Our ultimate goal is to use data on hunter-gatherers to illuminate human evolution . . . [however,] only after the most meticulous assessment of the impact of commercial, governmental, and other outside interests can we justify making statements about the hunter-gatherers' evolutionary significance." He restates (1979: 117) the characteristics of forager band organization that were his trial formulation in 1968. I set these out fully here to stress that, although now called "features of [the forager] mode of production" derived from Marxian inspiration, they are simply rephrasings of the earlier band formulation of Durkheimian dimensions. Indeed, since this characterization of foragers sets off from a notion of natural constraints, and since strong doubt has been expressed that such a notion should be deemed Marxian (Kahn and Llobera 1981: 320), it is doubtful that this formulation can be considered a mode of production in a Marxian sense.

Nevertheless, the features are: (1) hunters "must be mobile and cover a wide area in order to find sufficient food" (this is D-1 above); (2) "despite a variety of ideologies of land-ownership, all hunters have developed elaborate rules for reciprocal access to resources" (D-2); (3) "the need to move around sets limits to the amount of material wealth a family can possess" (D-3); (4) "because of the annual and regional variability in resources, hunter-gatherer group structures must be flexible enough to adjust to changing opportunities" (D-4); and (5) "the environment sets upper limits on group size" (D-5). Because

Lee—in company with nineteenth-century evolutionists and sociologists and with Steward, White, and Service—considers these features to be forager universals, he can call upon a uniformitarian doctrine, as they do, to justify the conflation of prehistoric with contemporary peoples. Lee (1979: 6, 115) is also as firmly attached to the Malthusian model as is Le Roy Ladurie, whom he invokes in support of his notion that natural mechanisms constantly keep Zhu population in "proper" relation to resources (cf. Hilton 1985: 4).

That Minimal Primordial Dimension

Meillassoux anticipated Lee; his construction is based on a literal reading of Marx's distinction between land as subject of labor and land as instrument of labor. He says (1967), "The use of land as *subject of labor* amounts solely to the extraction of the necessities of life from it, as it is the case with hunting or collecting." Such use fosters "instantaneous" production that, once shared, frees the hunters from "any further reciprocal obligation or allegiance." There is no ground for the emergence even of extended family organization at this forager level: "The basic social unit is an egalitarian but unstable band with little concern for biological or social reproduction." Only with the emergence of agriculture is the material base available for "the emergence of the '*family*' as a productive and cohesive unit and of '*kinship*' as an ideology" (Meillassoux 1972: 99). The Tönniesian-Durkheimian idea of replicate parts applies, for the forager "mode of production does not require continual membership of the same group [since cooperation is] impromptu and ad hoc." Obviously, there can be no basis for kinship, land tenure, or any other organizing social principle among foragers so conceived.

This conception was, of course, in error when it was born, as even a superficial examination of the results of decades of research condensed in *Man the Hunter* reveals. Long before, Tönnies, Durkheim, Morgan, Tylor—even the prehistorians Lubbock and Pitt-Rivers—had postulated kinship to be the basic organizing principle among primitive peoples; all but Tönnies identify hunters in that category. Sahlins (1965) more recently offered an empirically grounded theoretical formulation specifically of the role of kinship reciprocity in "forager" society. Before Sahlins, Marshall (1957, 1961) had presented an empirical description of such reciprocity for the Zhu people she called !Kung San or Juwasi. Both absolutely contradict Meillassoux's formulation. And of course there was the vast Australian and American literature.

Far more significantly, Benton (1984: 125) points out, "It is one thing to argue that in some social formations, reproduction of the economic relations requires an intervention into the economic on the part of non-economic social practices, and quite another to argue . . . that in these formations, the relations of production are in fact *constituted* through this non-economic intervention." If relations of production were constituted by kinship, then—again as Benton (1984:125) points out—relations of production could not be identified independent of the kinship system, and any attempt to analyze economic impositions on the operation of that system must retain a dubious status.

Terray (1972:142) wrestles with this problem and recognizes what I shall later refer to as strategy-selected memory in the construction of kinship relations, but he ends up admitting that, for him, "one essential problem remains, posed by the existence in kinship relations of a genealogical base," a base he declines to define. Meillassoux (1967) too is concerned with this genealogical base, finding it superseded by kinship "as an ideology" in agricultural societies but unmodified among foragers, where he finds it reduced to "a minimal dimension, that of the conjugal nucleus" (1973:193).

It seems obvious that this undefined minimal dimension of the genealogical base as conceived by Terray and Meillassoux must be interpreted as being primordial, that Gemeinschaft of blood that is the "natural" relationship, "by its very essence, of earlier origin than its subjects or members." For them, while this essence recedes in importance in the construction of kinship as social complexity grows ("biological families" become replaced by "functional forms associated by consanguinity" [Meillassoux 1964:168; quoted in Terray 1972:142]), it is the only dimension of kinship that exists for foragers. It must follow from this that forager kinship, so conceived, is primordial, hence ahistorical and radically unanalyzable. It seems to me that this is what Clammer (1978:3) has in mind when he criticizes "the common view that the structural determinants of all 'primitive' societies are always kinship in the last analysis," but that analysis never takes place. Certainly this view, in one form or another, is common not only to Terray and Meillassoux but also to Lévi-Strauss, Sahlins, Godelier (as Terray [1972:143] was perhaps the first to point out), Lee, and others, such as Hindess and Hirst (1975), who have appropriated the work of one or more of these authors (Keenan 1977:63). Terray (1972:147), by failing to analyze that "'element' [genealogical base] whose nature remains to be defined," falls into the pit that he clearly saw and tried to avoid.

Meillassoux (1973:190) goes on to assert that "the *social organization of work* involves age groups rather than kinship groups, since the latter do not coincide with any co-operative productive units." There is a logical error here: kinship groups, which according to a major premise of Meillassoux's schema do not exist in the foraging mode of production, can neither coincide nor not coincide with productive units in that mode. Meillassoux here falls prey to the same evolutionary sophistry we will find in Sahlins.

There is also a factual error in Meillassoux's presentation at this point. He misrepresents Marshall and asserts (1973:90n.) that she is incorrect in describing Zhu social relations as being founded on kinship: "In fact," he says, "kinship is not the principle of social organization involved. As she [Marshall] says elsewhere, (p. 345) membership of a band derives more from choice than from family imperatives." But let us turn to what Marshall (1960:345) actually wrote: "Birth accounts for most membership in bands . . . marriage is the second important factor. . . . Choice and circumstance are also factors. Where there is choice, such as married couples have after bride-service is fulfilled, or a widowed mother might have between offspring, or a sibling between siblings living in different bands, the relative adequacy of the resources would influence the choice." It stands without comment that choice is not an independent organizational option; kinship, as depicted by Marshall, in this passage and in chapter 5, is primary in directing choice.

The attenuation of the concept of kinship to a primordial condition of existence leaves no alternative but to equate the kinship system (if it is even proper to speak of such a thing in this vein) with relations of production. The labor process and surplus extraction, accordingly, must be conceived as undifferentiated in kinship relations. As a result, relations of production are reduced to secondary consequences of technical necessity.

Lee does not fall victim to this error; he recognizes forager social integrity, especially in his earliest work (1965:98–99, 139). Later, when he applies a mode of production lexicon with key elements of Meillassoux's construction, he subordinates this integrity by offering a forager mode of production whose five components are a hierarchical construct based on environmental constants. In this he follows faithfully the lead offered a decade earlier by Meillassoux as well as by Terray. Taylor (1979:151) carefully dissects this approach and finds it can be reduced to the identification of elements and their combination in a process of production—in simpler terms, a typology. Like all typologies, this one obscures the basis for analyzing social relations, which is presumably its intended purpose. Similarly, Godelier (1973) reduces human social relations to the product of the evolution of chronologically antecedent forms that develop in response to functional constraints imposed by a combination of environmental and technological forces; foragers are way down on the scale. Clearly, these constructions are all legacies of Morgan, descended through Engels in the Marxian genealogy and through Steward in ecology to their multilineal standpoints of today.

Attempts to insert social dimensions more firmly into these Marxian-evolutionary schemes have been hampered both by inadequate ethnography and by underdeveloped theory. This is not to assert that social dimensions are categorically excluded by students of San-speaking peoples. Silberbauer (1982:26–27) speaks of factions, cliques, the exercise of political power, and strategies for decision making among Gcwi. Lee (1982:52) mentions multiple options exercised by Zhu individuals in a number of social situations and (in apparent contradiction to his earlier denial that foragers may have fundamental conflicts of interest) strategies of competition among Zhu groups for recruiting members. But Silberbauer (1982:24) sees these things as Gcwi manipulating their society to fit their environmental requirements, whereas Lee (1982) finds that the characteristics of foraging life lead to shallow spans of social continuity. This brings them both back suspiciously close to Meillassoux's position, key elements of which—specifically the immediate relation between production and consumption—Lee (1979:118) appropriates.

That Characteristic Paleolithic Rhythm

At issue is not merely a consideration of the acquisition and distribution of the immediate product of land but, more fundamentally, of prior questions concerning distribution of property—both landed and instrumental—among specific social groups and of the forms of extraction relationships existing among these groups. These problems are dealt with, in the modern ethnographies of San peoples we are considering, in the first instance by denying their existence, describing a "primitive" economy in terms of consensual relations aimed solely at provisioning more or less egalitarian holders of resources—land, labor, and such—while simultaneously assimilating these problems to the authors' basic ecological models, insisting that the distribution of property and the successful application of consensual relations among foragers will be subject to essentially the same input/output pressures as the appropriation of the product itself. Discussions of production as such tend to be avoided or to be reduced to a species of resource exploitation, that is, to a mechanical application of techniques of production.

It is thus no distortion to claim along with Taylor (1979:162) that in all these studies "phenomena such as kinship, religion, etc. are analyzed as *'functional necessities' in relation to the level of productive forces.*" An economic/ecological productive "base" is objectified, with the result that all variations in social relations are reduced to secondary consequences. From this perspective it is easy to view continuity in social relations as reflecting stability in ecological conditions, with perturbations tending to oscillate around some equilibrium state, and for change to be seen as adjustments to external impositions—either drastic alterations in the productive base or injection of disruptive social forms through contact with peoples at a higher stage of sociocultural evolution.

Sahlins has articulated this position most clearly; beginning with what he calls Bushman subsistence (1972:23), he "detects again that characteristic paleolithic rhythm," whose "first and decisive contingency" still requires that sine qua non of nineteenth-century savagery, "movement to maintain production on advantageous terms" (Sahlins 1972:33). Speaking of what he calls this "primitive reality," Sahlins continues (1965:139), "for the present purpose 'economy' is viewed as the process of provisioning society (or the 'socio-cultural system'). No social relation, institution, or set of institutions [in this primitive reality] is of itself 'economic.' . . . This way of looking at economics or politics . . . is dictated by the nature of primitive culture. Here we find no socially distinct 'economy' or 'government,' merely social groups and relations with multiple functions, which we distinguish as economic, political, and so forth" (Sahlins 1965:225). Such mundane distinctions are hardly necessary among the fortunate few in this primitive reality, for here "a pristine affluence colors their economic arrangements, a trust in the abundance of nature's resources rather than despair at the inadequacy of human means" (Sahlins 1972:29).

Sahlins, of course, did not come to this position without precedent; he himself cites Evans-Pritchard (1940:91), who said that Nuer "economic relations, if such they may be called, must conform to this general pattern" of direct social relations. The meaning of direct social relations is found in Sahlins's (1965:141) grand division of economic transactions into two types: reciprocity, the direct relation, which is "a *between* relation, the action and reaction of two parties [individuals]," and redistribution, which is "socially a *within* relation, the collective action of a group." Gemeinschaft in its mechanical solidarity has not forsaken us.

In application, of course, the boundary between these divisions is more often blurred than not, as typological boundaries tend to be, especially when so few types are distinguished. Sahlins recognizes the resulting need to qualify specific instances (that is, to say that there are few pure cases); however, in discussing hunter-gatherers he is consistent in finding economic transactions to be "vice-versa movements between two parties" (1965: 141). Specifically, and of most immediate interest to our purpose, he finds this to be true of "Bushmen"; Lee (1979: 118, 437) agrees. Much earlier, Schapera (1930: 143, 149) had said of peoples placed in this category that "all their industries are essentially domestic" and "there is no well-developed system of organized government" among them, although he acknowledged that there was still much to be learned about the social life of those peoples.

Now, all of this is very curious: peoples whose social relations have "*merely* multiple functions," none "socially distinct"? What might this mean? Let us examine Sahlins's text further. We must begin with the recognition that for Sahlins (1965: 140) primitive relations of production are ecologically based. They are determined by "familial requirements" with "direct access by domestic groups to strategic resources" and are dominated by a division of labor according to sex and age. This is essentially a mechanical contract between man and nature. Social dimensions at this primitive level are inscribed by exchange transactions.

It seems, however, that even in practical terms exchange in the total primitive economy also holds a different place than it has in other economies, "more detached from production," "less firmly hinged to production in an organic way," "less involved in the acquisition of means of production," "biased toward the commanding imperative of food." This is an evolutionary stage concept, which draws a line between a "primitive" conceptualized in a priori terms and other social forms. Kinship, in its analytic incarnation, is its measure. This demarcation is made clear in the text (Sahlins 1965: 140–41), where the litany of attributes characterizing primitive exchange just recited is bracketed by a pair of phrases that on inattentive reading appear irreducibly irreconcilable. We read that, in primitive communities, although "the social compact has yet to be drawn," these same communities are "societies ordered in the main by kinship."

One may ask, How, if the *social compact* has yet to be drawn, might *societies* exist and, furthermore, how might they be ordered by kinship? Sahlins is in a quandary here; he clearly intends to suggest not that there are no social relations among foraging peoples or that they have no society, just that theirs are relations of a different order. His difficulty is evident in his continually contradictory and inconsistent— and unanalyzed—resort to the vocabulary of kinship structure.

Far from being irreconcilable, however, it is just here that the evolutionary stage division is in fact most clearly drawn. In Sahlins's schema, kinship, at least for "primitives," is primordial, uncomplicated by problematic social constraints. The hidden proposition here, despite the substitution of "spectrum" for "typology," is that this primitive is but a finer tuning of the lower scale of Steward's levels of sociocultural organization, with foragers assigned to the family level. Family, on this evolutionary scale, arises sui generis, intrinsic to living human individuals; those who do not fit the mold are "displaced and decultured persons" (Sahlins 1965:158). True, as people move upstage complications intrude, and the nineteenth-century echoes that reverberate throughout this narrative are this time voiced by Sahlins himself. "The reasoning is nearly syllogistic. . . . Take as the minor premise Tylor's dictum that kindred goes with kindness, 'two words whose common derivation expresses in the happiest way one of the main principles of social life.' It follows that close kin tend to share, to enter into generalized exchanges, and distant and non-kin to deal in equivalents or in guile. . . . There is something real to this view; it is not logical sophistry" (Sahlins 1965:149–50).

It did not seem to be logical sophistry a quarter-century ago when foraging peoples were commonly consigned in evolutionary thought to uncomplicated simplicity in social relations, and we believed we could explain ourselves to ourselves through evolution alone. But it not only is sophistry, it is false. Sahlins's formulation reduces kinship to an intuition, forgetting that kin and affinal relations are the social products of strategies pursued in reference to determinate economic and political conditions (Bourdieu 1977:36). As Meillassoux (1960:38) remarks, "At the economic level 'primitive man' was not quite a man since he was not a 'homo oeconomicus'" (it seems that Meillassoux here means simply man engaged in economic activity, not economic man as profit maximizer). That cogent observation notwithstanding, Meillassoux (1960, 1967, 1972, 1973)—after dismissing Sahlins as a liberal economist (Meillassoux 1972:104)—finds no contradiction in adopting all the essential evolutionary stage elements of his primitive program. As we have seen, Meillassoux's basic division is derived from Marx and Engels and is founded on a "radical difference" between a foraging mode of production, in which land is a "subject of labor," and all other modes of production, in which land is an "instrument of labor." But the rest of this formulation is a mixture drawn from Tönnies, Durkheim, and the proponents of primitive savagery, who drew a similar distinction.

Despite programmatic differences of emphasis on exchange and production, the salient features of Sahlins's ecological model and Meillassoux's materialist model have much in common. A brief comparison will bring these commonalities to the surface. For Meillassoux, foragers are united in a kind of family or tribal community in which transactions are chiefly between man and nature; for Sahlins, domestic family groups have direct access to resources. Meillassoux asserts that the organization of work involves age-mates only, since kinship has formed no groups that could coincide with cooperative productive units; Sahlins proposes that functionally distinct social groups do not yet exist among foragers.[6]

For Meillassoux too, as regards foragers, the emergence of the family as a productive and cohesive unit and of kinship as an ideology has not taken place (his chiding of Marx as being "too simplistic" on the matter notwithstanding; Meillassoux 1972:97); for Sahlins the social contract has not been drawn. Meillassoux says forager societies have no internal structural contradictions; Sahlins tells us that among foragers close kin share, nonkin deal. Finally, as a result of these unevolved social forms, "actually hunting may be unable to develop into any other mode of production" (Meillassoux 1973:201). Here we hear the ghost of Durkheim insisting again that mechanical solidarity was an "insurmountable obstacle to the division of labor, and must have disappeared at least partially for the division of labor to appear." The implication that social relations beyond the primordial family arise only with food domestication is inherent in Sahlins's bipartite schema. In all this, the affinity to Lee's mode of production is apparent.

As They Begin to Produce, So We Begin to Know Them

But Marx's ontology is quite different. Central to Marxian thought is the proposition that human social relations are not primordial but are constructed by human agents through their labor: "The first historical act is thus the production of the means to satisfy these needs, the production of material life itself. And indeed this is an historical act, a fundamental condition of all history, which today, as thousands of years ago, must daily and hourly be fulfilled" (Marx and Engels ([1846] 1977:48). It was this realization, first enunciated by Marx and Engels in *The German Ideology,* that set them apart from their contemporaries. It is clear that they understood this to apply to all peoples everywhere, at all times—as necessarily part of the human condition "thousands of years ago" as today. "It is quite obvious from the start that there exists a materialistic connection of men with one another, which is determined by their needs and their mode of production, and which is as old as men themselves. . . . [Men] themselves begin to distinguish themselves from animals as soon as they begin to *produce* their means of subsistence" (Marx and Engels [1846] 1977:50, 42). This is "the first historical act"; all men are in history.[7] Forager mode of production theorists, along with Lévi-Strauss and others, have seriously misread Marx on this point, drawing as noted already from the weakest part of his writings, the prehistory, rather than from his mature thought.

It is this misreading that appears to have dictated the technicist determinate form of forager mode of production constructions (cf. Keenan 1977; Richards 1983). There is a further confusion, this one centered on the subject/instrument of labor dichotomy. As is often the case, Marx's metaphoric presentation contributes to this confusion, but a close reading of the little he has to say in *Capital* about the beginnings of human labor may bring a bit more clarity to the discussion. I have already noted that for Marx "tribes living exclusively on hunting or fishing are beyond the boundary line from which real development begins"; such peoples thus seem implicitly to be conceptually relegated to a stage of savagery. But it is important to emphasize that individuals are already connected by "tribe or community" (Marx [1867] 1906:367; p. 20 above). Equally important, they already possess "specially prepared instruments" of production, as evidenced by "the oldest caves [in which] we find stone implements" (Marx [1867] 1906:200). As Krader (1976:163) has said, the context here indicates that Marx was alluding not to the beginning of agriculture but to the beginning of humanity, when the first separation from nature was accomplished. I think Marx is best understood to mean that "Stone Age" peoples—at least those we would today call Upper Paleolithic *Homo sapiens*—were associated in social relations beyond the family and engaged in labor by interposing instruments of production between themselves and subjects of labor.

But what are those subjects of labor? And what is the status of land in this conception? Again, a careful reading of *Capital* may help. The initial statement is fairly clear: "All those things which labor *merely separates from immediate connection with their environment,* are subjects of labour spontaneously provided by Nature" (Marx [1867] 1906:199, emphasis added). Among these subjects of labor are listed soil, water, fish, timber, and ores; this is, of course, an indicative list, not an exhaustive one. Marx continues in the next paragraph: "Leaving out of consideration such ready-made means of subsistence as fruits, in gathering which man's own limbs serve as the instruments of labour, the first thing of which the labourer possesses himself is not the subject of labour but its instrument. . . . As the earth is his original larder, so too it is his original tool house. It supplies him, for instance, with stones for throwing, grinding, pressing, cutting, &c. The earth itself is an instrument of labour."

It seems to me that here Marx conceives "earth" in the dual sense it carries in European thought, that of being at once preexisting global substance and abstract cradle of existence, the ancient Greek Gaia from which most of the other elements of the cosmos were born but from which nothing was taken being but one manifestation of that notion preserved from the past (in Hesiod, for example). Thus soil is a subject supplied by instrumental earth.

Further along, Marx ([1867] 1906:201) reiterates this notion: "Once more we find the earth to be a universal instrument of this sort, for it furnished a locus standi to the labourer and a field of employment for his activity. . . . Labour has incorporated itself with its subject: the former is materialised, the latter transformed. That which in the labourer appeared as movement, now appears in the product as a fixed quality." Once more the dual character of earth is invoked, this time both as general physical object of labor and as specific subject defining the extent of the field of individual labor. It would perhaps stretch the metaphor too far to read a concept of landed property into this, but it seems to me that the germ of such a concept—"labour has incorporated itself with its subject [including soil]"—is here.

Finally, it seems clear to me that—if the reading of Marx's placement of Paleolithic peoples I offer above is accepted—Marx included forager relations to instruments of production and to land among those of other humans. One last quotation appears to establish this point. This notion of earth as instrument of labor and of the labor process that is associated with it "is the necessary condition for effecting the exchange of matter between man and nature; it is the everlasting nature-imposed condition of human existence, and therefore is independent of every social phase of that existence, or rather, is common to every such phase" (Marx [1867] 1906:205).

From this formulation it seems to me inescapable that to segregate a foraging mode of production on the basis of land as a subject of labor is to deny full humanity to modern "foragers," a nineteenth-century notion subscribed to neither by Marx nor by any of the modern proponents of such a mode of production. On these ontological grounds, it appears that current constructions of a forager mode of production are irretrievably flawed and must be abandoned.

There are also solid epistemological grounds for such abandonment. These have been examined thoroughly before and need be reviewed only briefly here.[8] P.-P. Rey's (1973) warning against the danger of antiquarianism in the proffered Marxian models of precapitalist societies is pertinent in our present context, an antiquarianism, as I have tried to show, that fosters constricted readings of Marx's skeletal prehistory. Kahn and Llobera (1981:323) are correct to point out that Rey's warning needs to be elaborated if it is to be drawn into significant participation in current debates; the arguments presented in this and the previous chaper—which indeed exist as a subtext to the entire book—are intended as a step toward meeting that need. It is essential to remind ourselves at this point that Marx was concerned exclusively with capitalism. His remarks on precapitalist conditions, particularly those called primitive, do no more than set his principal discussion in the frame of his overall outlook on human history; they develop neither a theory nor a methodology for apprehending precapitalist formations. While it might still be argued that Marx did not look upon "primitive" humanity as a prehistorical subject (although the discussion thus far suggests to me that he did), most of his followers have been drawn to this form of thinking. This, along with the direct application of Marx's theory of capitalism to noncapitalist formations, has left Marxian studies of foragers in no different a position than their evolutionary and structuralist predecessors.

In this context it is not difficult to see that the forager mode of production, as constructed by Meillassoux and Lee at least, is an empiricist model, an ideal type abstraction, implying that its explanation lies in the concrete reality it is drawn from. Meillassoux (1978:133) speaks in these terms of "models embedded in one another at the most complex stage of the demonstration [that] are presented in a logical progression that can possibly be regarded as an 'ideal' historical production." These constructions are built on an acceptance by their authors of concepts and methods of traditional anthropology as used by nineteenth-century evolutionists. This, as Kahn and Llobera (1981: 294) point out, "allows them to treat existing 'primitive' societies as *pre*-capitalist [and to] adopt the implicit evolutionism of traditional anthropology." Bradby (1975:127) points out that *precapitalist* used in this way has a double meaning: historically prior to capitalism and technologically inferior to capitalism. On either count, forager mode of production theorists situate their subjects on a dubious existential plane. Unlike his French colleagues who deny this charge, Lee enthusiastically embraces it, finding moral superiority in subordinate contrast to capitalism. To all of these writers the base/superstructure metaphor is not a hypothesis but an empirical fact amenable to direct scientific verification. Thus, for example, foragers are restricted to their condition of existence by foraging, and if we can find foragers who forage we have verified this proposition.

Kahn and Llobera (1981:287) suggest that Meillassoux means simply mode of subsistence when he uses the term mode of production (this despite Meillassoux's [1972:98] own warning against confusing mode of production with way of life). He is in this regard closely aligned with Lee, who approaches his forager mode of production even more narrowly by identifying a series of elements and their combination in a process of production. This is the "weak usage" of the concept (Clammer 1978:12) and "is the first 'pitfall' to be avoided in analysing pre-capitalist models" (Taylor 1979:151). Taylor (1979: 162) sums up the consequences of falling into this pit: "The constraints imposed by the conditions of production, themselves determined by the development of the productive forces, express the conditions for the reproduction of the social formation. Phenomena such as kinship, religion, etc., are analysed as *'functional necessities' in relation to the level of development of the productive forces.*"

If all of this seems familiar, one might refer back to Durkheim or, if one would rather, follow Taylor (1979:6–9) into more recent decades where one will find Parsons's voluntaristic theory of action derived from that nineteenth-century source. The premises and propositions of this formulation need not be recast; it need only be pointed out that their operant subjective consequences are that, for individuals, actions and choices are limited only by imposed constraints of the physical environment and the cultural system, which set limits on available goals and means. This is precisely the forager mode of production as described for us, hemmed in by environmental strictures upon a simple stage attainment in technology and social relations. Indeed, Lee (1979:335) goes so far as to suggest that San-speaking "foragers" consciously strive to restrain their wants and needs in order to preserve their equilibrium state.

But needs cannot be defined in terms of an unproblematic human nature. Marx ([1859] 1971:197–98) argues that there is a systematic relation between production and consumption that must be sought in the structure of the mode of production itself. Production differentials are accompanied by consumption differentials that are independent of abstract "needs." This is the domain of Sahlins's concern, but in adopting a Chayanovian equilibrium model—Sahlins (1972:87) calls it Chayanov's rule—of need satisfaction he detoured more deeply into the evolutionist cul-de-sac he had previously built for foragers. For these peoples "the norm of domestic livelihood tends to be inert. It cannot move above a certain level without testing the capacity of the domestic labor force, either directly or through the technological change required for a higher output. . . . it has an ultimate ceiling" (Sahlins 1972:87). Sahlins thus aligns himself with the nineteenth century and with Lee.

These positions may be maintained because all forager mode of production theorists accept, to one degree or another, the atomistic metaphor of instances—that is, of an economic base surmounted by a juridico-political superstructure and topped off by an ideological peak (Terray 1972:97). These instances are more or less coextensive with the evolutionary levels of technology, sociology, and ideology—those levels, that is, set by Lee and DeVore at the beginning of human time. Particular structures of these instances or levels are associated with each mode of production, and changes in structure are seen to result from "an inexorable deterministic evolution of one fundamental antagonism, between the 'relations and forces of production'" (Taylor 1979:159), that is to say, between the instances of the mode of production and its environment. It is a tenet of these theorists that prior systems must disappear before more evolved forms can appear. This tenet seems to be, in turn, the foundation for the insistence by modern ethnographers of "foraging" peoples that these peoples have been historically isolated—otherwise, the implication is, they would have disappeared in Tönniesian fashion.

According to the assumptions of the socioeconomic typologies presented as one or another forager mode of production, it matters little whether we examine contemporary or Paleolithic "foragers" so long as the basic structures of their technosocial relations are assumed to be the same. The authors of these constructions would no doubt claim to have avoided neoevolutionism, but they nevertheless do not treat forager societies as segments of larger social formations but hold them up as typical of an evolutionary stage.[9] Among other things, this allows one to read bushmanness into the lives of some, but not other, Kalahari peoples and thus to believe that one has seen "Bushmen." The epistemological naïveté of this practice renders current constructions of forager modes of production untenable.

Foragers Come to Class

There is a way out of this impasse;[10] it grows from a discourse regarding the articulation (or disarticulation, according to Amin 1974, 1976) of formerly colonized peoples in modern nation-states and more broadly in a world system. We may begin by briefly examining the debate revolving around the notion of a world system. This system has been defined by Wallerstein as a multiple cultural system that incorporates "minisystems" such as tribes: "Most entities usually described as social systems—"tribes," communities, nation-states—are not in fact total systems" (Wallerstein 1974:347–48). Wallerstein credits Braudel with the initial formulation, but in its currently employed form this world system is ineluctably bound up with propositions set forth by Frank (1967, 1969) to account for the "development of underdevelopment" in the colonial era and afterward. That underdevelopment took place through an "active process of appendagization [of the satellite colonies to the European metropolis] and distortion [of native social formations in the colonies]. . . . for Frank, as more recently for Wallerstein, there is but a single 'world system,' and it is capitalist through and through" (Foster-Carter 1978a:49). Laclau (1971) also envisions a unitary world system, but one that intensified or invented "precapitalist" modes of production to articulate with.

I subscribe to important elements in this world system formulation; specifically, that most entities usually described as social systems, tribes, and so forth are not complete social systems, and that there is—and has been for the centuries I shall be mainly concerned with—a unitary world system. Indeed, the data to be presented in the following chapters make it very difficult to think otherwise as far as the Kalahari is concerned.

However, necessary as these propositions are for a viable analysis of the material to follow, the world system as a whole has come under devastating criticism for both its theoretical weaknesses and its empirical lacunae. I will sketch in these criticisms here as they are pertinent to my own agenda. The weaknesses of Frank's underdevelopment theory and from it Wallerstein's modern world system have been summarized by Skocpol (1975), Brenner (1977), Cooper (1981), and Nash (1981) as well as others. First, they substitute teleological direction for an analysis of process; second, they treat market factors as deterministic and treat production as a mechanical derivative of those factors; third, they see native engagement with capital as futile in the face of inevitable domination by the world system; fourth, and most crucial, they fail to consider class structures of native social formations and the various ways these were restructured to meet the challenge of European encroachment.

The first three of these defects bear family resemblances to those already identified in forager mode of production proposals; we need not concern ourselves with them again. Besides, the failure to confront class structures is fatal in a far more material way. Brenner argues this most forcefully. He demonstrates (1977:27) in considerable detail that world systems of the Frank-Wallerstein variety are unable to analyze the outcomes of their own premises because "they fail to take into account either the way in which class structures, once established, will in fact determine the course of economic development or underdevelopment over an entire epoch, or the way in which these class structures themselves emerge as the outcome of class struggles whose results are incomprehensible in terms merely of market forces." Let us see how this criticism applies to our immediate central interest.

Dupré and Rey (1973:132) begin their critique of Polyani's substantivist economics with the declaration that they wish "to put all economic and social systems on a genuinely equal footing and to think their articulation." I read this to mean that they wish to remove all vestiges of an evolutionary typology of forms of exchange ("'market,' 'prestation-redistribution,' 'reciprocity'") from the analysis of precapitalist economic systems, at least as these are, or were, found in Africa. Applying their critique to a reanalysis of the work of Meillassoux (1960) on the Ivory Coast Gouro, they reach a conclusion somewhat different from that of Terray (1972) and of Meillassoux himself regarding the existence of class relations among the Gouro. In contrast to the latter two theorists, Dupré and Rey (1973:153) find that elders in that society carry out "a class function which has no constituted group for its support." This is hardly an unequivocal conclusion, but it does open the debate more widely to the consideration of class relations in precapitalist social formations. Benton (1984:118–26) gives an excellent summary of the terms under which that debate has proceeded, and I shall call upon his work frequently in what follows.

I think Bloch (1983) must be correct in asserting that insisting on classlessness and freedom from exploitation as features of precapitalist societies precludes a theoretical—or even an adequate descriptive—characterization of such societies, although Mattick (1985:249) is equally correct in pointing out that this is a problem in Marxian anthropology, not of the possibilities inherent in Marxian theory itself. Or as Benton (1984:123–24) puts it, "By failing to pose the question of the relations of production of lineage society as anything but *technical* necessities, [the protagonists in the debate] all manage to preserve intact their *assumption* that these relations are communal in the face of considerable evidence of important differences between categories of economic agents in their access to conditions of production and reproduction." Dupré and Rey (1973:143) do indeed see—and Rey (1975) reiterates—that recourse to such technicist imperatives is tantamount to saying that "societies based on redistribution and reciprocity could not tolerate antagonisms and tensions in their midst," a corollary they reject. Yet they stop short of recognizing that class relations may structure such societies.

Terray (1975:89, 133) has in the interim become "far less categorical" in his denial of the existence of relations of exploitation among the Gouro. He then extends this analytical reversal (1975:87) and significantly advances the discussion with his realization that "it is not possible to give class a universal definition, valid for all modes of production." Building on this realization, Clammer (1978:6) points to the fallacy of unanalyzed "claims that, firstly, class relations are a characteristic only of capitalism—where capitalism does not exist neither do class relations (even of a different kind), largely because of the subsidiary claim that in primitive societies differential access to wealth is *not* related to questions of rank, status and power; and, secondly, that relations of exploitation do not occur within the productive situations discovered in such societies." Clammer (1978:14) argues further that, even if class relations are subsequently shown to be characteristic only of developed capitalism, it is nevertheless not legitimate "to define out of existence on semantic grounds, socio-economic relationships and structural positions which are related both to differential access to wealth and to status and power, such that the former is the principal mechanism in determining the latter."

Class, in other words, is no more a monolithic given than is kinship; its presence or absence in any particular instance must be demonstrated by an analysis of the circumstances to be found in each instance itself. As Benton (1984:124) says of the debate surrounding the Gouro, "In the absence of any attempt to specify, in terms of available ethnographic material, precisely what is and what is not 'communal' appropriation, there are no theoretical decision procedures to settle such questions as the class characteristics of lineage-based societies." Lee (1979:119), although arguing vigorously against any form of status differentiation in "foraging societies," appears to concur with Benton on this point: "How widespread these practices [extraction of surplus product and labor] are and whether they constitute [among Zhu] 'exploitation' in the sense of appropriating a disproportionate share of the labor of others are questions for continuing investigation." The real issue, of course, is not an acrimonious debate over whether exploitation and accumulation can occur in "forager" social formations, but analyses of this question in real, concrete noncapitalist societies (cf. Harbsmeier 1978). It is not clear at this point in our theoretical development whether class must be a feature of noncapitalist formations, as Marx states it must of capitalist formations, but the foregoing discussion provides ample incentive for investigating the question. At the end of chapter 6, I conclude that class relations do appear to be inherent in San social formations.

For all its inconclusiveness, this debate has opened the way to a less restrictive conception of class relations. Terray, in the passage quoted, has already provided the manifest for such a turn from cultural solipsism. In this, he is joined by Marks (1982:16), who sees it as "a curiously mechanical, Eurocentric view which would deny these migrants [black mine workers in nineteenth-century South Africa] the appellation 'working class' because their consciousness was still partly formed and informed by their very recent experience in contracting rural options." Cliffe (1977:195) decries the restrictions on our ability to understand it imposed by "the widespread popular misconception . . . that African rural society is classless." Echoing a recurring theme of this book, he attributes this misconception to those who, "trying to authenticate some utopian alternative, cultivate the myth of traditions of equality in Africa." Benton (1984:122) calls very clearly for an empirically grounded examination of this issue. Expanding upon his critique of the Gouro debate, he notes that Hindess and Hirst (1975) claim (correctly, according to Benton) that all modes of production must necessarily extract a surplus in order to reproduce social relations from generation to generation. He then asks rhetorically, "So what distinguishes those modes in which appropriation of the surplus is exploitative and constituative of class oppositions from those in which it is not?"

We may pose that question in an even more challenging way: What distinguishes varying forms of class relations in different social formations? In Taylor's (1979:73) terms, "There must be a basis for distinguishing between the different forms of surplus-extraction characteristic of different modes of production." To examine these questions, I shall follow a suggestion made by Terray (1972:145) that an analysis of class relations should deal with its subject in the same way as an analysis of kinship relations. That is to say, at least as I read it, an analysis of structural relationships must proceed hand in hand with an analysis of the specific historical realization of any instance of that structure. As with kinship, so with class: "The unity of the entity . . . can no longer be taken for granted but has to be proved" (Terray 1972:141). Class manifestations and functions, accordingly, may be expected to vary among social formations.

To extend that argument, consider that the very essence of class arises in the historical construction of contradictory strivings of persons who, consciously or not, constitute their efforts in a common ground opposed to similarly constituted efforts by other persons. Given such a dynamic generation of class relations, variation in their realization is only to be expected.

Indeed, as Mattick (1985:249, 1986) is at pains to remind us, Marx explicitly dissociated himself from "the Enlightenment-Romantic tradition of 'universal history'"; a universality in which classes arise unproblematically on cue when specified conditions present themselves. Again, as with kinship, setting class relations in an encompassing historical dynamic removes from them the fallacy of primordial essence, a fallacy expressed in this fashion: as kinship—with its "element whose nature remains to be defined"—emerges upon the human escape from animal nature (or, as for Meillassoux, after a transitional forager stage), so class, in the grip of that essence, emerges upon the attainment of capitalism. Classes, however, like kinship, are made by people and acted upon by them. If the materials for their construction are present, one would expect them to be constructed. As Wallerstein (1979:196) has said, "Class analysis is only meaningful to the extent that it is placed within a given historical context." Watt (1983:81) crystallizes the issue succinctly by noting that, although it is not necessary to accept deterministic models of class differentiation in Africa, "the prismatic processes of local inequality and commoditization cannot be ignored." It appears then to be at least plausible, and potentially productive, to ask whether class relations are components, variably realized under specific conditions of production, of all human social formations—indeed, whether any human social formation can exist without them.

There will follow, in chapter 6, an exploration in pursuit of that question, based on the material pertinent to Zhu that I will present. I should stress once more, however, that this pursuit has very little to do with a quite different question, that of relations of production among foragers. In the Kalahari, we are some two thousand years too late for that.

I enter this exploration with Cohen's (1978:73) assertion that "a person's class is established by nothing but his objective place in the network of ownership relations, however difficult it may be to identify such places neatly." It is true that Cohen is speaking here of relations between proletarians and capitalists, relations that may just now be on the verge of dominance in the Kalahari (Parson 1979), but the phrase "objective place in the network of ownership relations" has a wider referent. In other words, wherever ownership can be extracted as a meaningful term of relations there must be its reciprocal, nonownership. The mere fact of ownership does not, of course, require the existence of classes. But if relations of ownership are associated with other asymmetrical relations (leadership, for example), and if some groups within a social formation can control these relations to their advantage and reproduce their control at the expense of other groups, then the essential elements of a class structure appear to be present.

Given such a structure, the processes of production and distribution, and their transformation, are, as Berry (1985:6) states, "never determined by the strategies of a single group but [arise] from the struggles among many." Thus "the fact that kinsmen or patrons and clients depend on one another for services and support may mask but does not alleviate the tensions arising from differential access to wealth and power" (Berry 1985:13). Carstens (1970:8) sees the dynamics of these struggles in this way: "It is only by the manipulation of their [southern African peasants'] internal status systems that they are able to gain access to other status systems which are located in the higher class. The strategy of status manipulation is best seen then as a means for crossing class boundaries."

To complete the preliminary argument, it remains only to stress with Taylor (1979:148) that accumulation—barter or monetary or even capital—is not confined to capitalist formations. We shall see that the circulation of commodities is as old as the Early Iron Age in the Kalahari; the differential accumulation of wealth has been a constant feature of the region from that period onward into the present. The differential consumption of livestock and exotic commodities at hierarchically organized Iron Age sites, the asymmetrical access to means of livestock production and commodity exchange to be documented for the nineteenth century, and the continuing asymmetry of that access in the present all attest to exploitative relations of surplus extraction. Benton (1984:123) reiterates the obvious when he says that if a surplus is extracted, "then this extraction implies a *power* to extract it. That power, like any other power, must derive from material and social resources."

This brings us to a final objection voiced by Schneider (1977:20), who maintains that, since Wallerstein views trade in luxuries as nonsystemic, he cannot explain the expansion of polities interested only minimally in basic commodities (she cites fifteenth- and sixteenth-century Portugal, but as we shall see, the eleventh- to eighteenth-century polities of southern Africa centered on Mapongubwe, Great Zimbabwe, Khami, and Monomotapa are also in this category). Schneider touches on a deficiency common to social theorists who are unacquainted with current advances in thinking among prehistorians (in southern Africa, Denbow 1986; Denbow and Wilmsen 1986; Parkington and Hall 1987). Brenner (1977:32–33, 53), for example, whose analysis is otherwise incisive, can say that in precapitalist societies production for exchange without reinvestment for improved production is the norm. He continues: "Pre-capitalist economies, even those in which trade is widespread, can develop only within definite limits, because the class structure of the economy as a whole determines that their component units—specifically those producing the means of subsistence and the means of production, i.e., means of survival and reproduction, rather than luxuries—neither can nor must systematically increase the forces of production, the productivity of labour, in order to reproduce themselves."

Now this is rather disconcerting.[11] In the first place, it should be unremarkable by now that luxury goods may enter into the material reproduction of class differentials. Furthermore, it seems essential that precapitalist social formations are not under an imperative to change the productivity of their labor; if we were to think they were under such an imperative, we would not have escaped the teleologist trap we have sought to avoid. However, if they cannot change that productivity, we seem to stand again at that barrier to "primitive" development thrown up by nineteenth-century ethnologists and sociologists and now manned enthusiastically by their forager mode of production replacements.

Brenner's concern is, of course, with the development of capitalist economies in relation to precapitalist formations, and he devotes relatively little attention to the latter. Nonetheless, his assertion (1977 : 53) that the historical processes involved are "understandable only in terms of the conflictual processes, processes of class transformation and class struggle, which tend to emerge from the contradictory character of the pre-capitalist social relations themselves" is retrogressive in the same way as Godelier's (1970) derivation of the Asiatic mode of production from the evolution of contradictions inherent in forager and pastoralist kinship. Taylor (1979 : 161) rightly terms this a reduction to an autodevelopment of the structure of a mode of production (but note that Godelier does posit a transition from foraging, something his colleagues are reluctant to do).

But what about noncapitalist formations? Cooper (1981 : 302) cautions that we have to be more subtle than searching for "the elusive kulak" and instead need to understand precapitalist class structures and their reshaping by capitalism. To do this, we must begin by examining the articulation of production with circulation and consumption in noncapitalist modes of production, "its other moments," and in relation to the sociological and ideological "other levels" of these modes. "Only then can we pose the problem of the existence of the

particular relations of production that determine this system of production . . . on which its class structure is based" (Taylor 1979:152).
Then, in the articulation of two or more modes of production, transi-
tions may be analyzed as shifts in relations of dominance, thus allowing a "variety of actual historic cases and possible outcomes" to be
theoretically comprehended (Benton 1984:130).

In his seminal examination of the concept of articulation, Foster-
Carter (1978a, 1978b) tells us that Althusser introduced the concept
without defining it but used it as "an anatomical metaphor to indicate relations of linkage and effectivity between different levels of
all kinds of things"—except, it seems, modes of production (Foster-
Carter 1978a:54). P.-P. Rey apparently was the first to "'think' the
articulation of modes of production," which he formulated as a process in time without acknowledging this shift of usage (Foster-Carter
1978a:55–56). This makes for a rather vague concept, and I confess
I am unable to offer much clarification. Moreover, Berry (1985:6)
points out that in using it many writers "have treated modes of production as structural entities rather than as historical conjunctions of
material conditions and social relations, and they have, accordingly,
found it difficult to explain social transformations." This is emphatically true of forager mode of production theorists.

Nevertheless, along with Foster-Carter (1978a:74) I find that "what
is important about the term 'articulation' is the questions that it has
made it possible to raise." Two resulting issues are particularly important to my purposes in this book. First is a rejection of "the sterile assertion of the analytical priority of relations of production over those
of exchange and indeed all else" (Foster-Carter 1978a:76); in the
analysis of the Kalahari we shall soon embark on, it will become apparent that things are not so simple as to assign priority uniformly to
any single "moment" or "level" of the social system. Again, Foster-
Carter (1978a:77) declares that "too little attention has been paid to
other 'instances' and 'practices' than the economic," notably politics,
kinship, and ideology. This is, as he says, "a clarion call for *class*," a
call that needs to be heeded in the Kalahari of "foragers."

I think we thus arrive at a position from which to question whether
the base/superstructure metaphor is at all helpful and to realize, along
with Kahn and Llobera (1981:311–12), that it is unfortunate that
"the 'economy' was identified with matter and consequently given primacy over the other aspects of society. . . . [They add that] to adopt a
materialist, as opposed to an idealist standpoint, is not to assign primacy to the economic but to renounce the use of metaphysical principles like Hegel's absolute spirit [such as Lee sees guiding Zhu, who

he thinks are, or were until recently, striving to retain their pristine state, or as Lévi-Strauss sees urging 'primitives to annul any possible effect of history on their lives']. . . . there are no autonomous spheres termed economic, political, and ideological."

The Uses of Ecology

This brings us to the second important issue raised in the concept of articulation, which is perhaps a corollary of the first: an avoidance of narrow economism, or ecologism, which in the forager paradigm has come to amount to the same thing. This, in concert with a world system perspective that does not preclude active, dynamic roles for "mini-systems," has a potential to overcome the universalizing ahistoricism that restricts much social theory—I am here thinking, of course, primarily of that ahistoricism purporting to engage "foraging" or, more generally, "primitive" peoples—and to overcome that Marxism that has too often fallen into a "mechanistic theory of stages of development of nation states" (Wallerstein 1977:6). As we have seen, in forager models based on those species of theorizing, production either does not take place or is an automatic function of physical existence. Perhaps this is why ecological models, either with or without animal analogies, are deemed especially amenable for appropriation to them.

Only Silberbauer (1981:xiii) among ethnographers of San peoples seems to recognize that an ecological paradigm "is not a substitute for a theory to explain . . . the consequences of interaction" among the analytical categories of society, demography, subsistence, and environment. This is where the difficulties in appropriating that paradigm begin. Analysis, in that appropriation, is restricted to a qualitative assessment of forces impinging on forager society from within; forces considered external either are omitted from consideration or are treated in terms of the researcher's environment, not that of the people under study. Ordinarily, no testable data are given upon which to judge these forces; when data are submitted, they are almost invariably inadequate to meet sampling standards. This is a fatal flaw. For without rigorously acquired and applied data, be they quantitative or qualitative, ecological anthropology—not to speak of systematic ecology—is simply anybody's game of "my nature is more real than yours." No one gains in such a game.

Indeed, what we are given in these forager models (and they do conform more closely to what are thought of as models rather than modes of production) is economic determinism in ecological guise set at the beginning of human time. Brenner (1976:30) points out that models

of economic process constructed in terms of "objective" forces—ecological imperative is such a force—will yield results in which the response of the economy is seen, in model terms, to be more or less
automatically in the direction of supply and demand. And from what
we have been told in these models, that is indeed it; the land produces
what it can without prompting, and society constrains its demands
upon land and upon itself in balanced proportion. It is a stage of primitive communist bliss (Lee 1979:460–61), even though near the end of
the saga we are told that, after all, modern "hunters are poor" (Lee
1979:454).

Lee, as noted previously, returns to Morgan and Tylor to invoke
uniformitarianism as epistemological support for this static view of
forager history, a formula shared implicitly by the other authors whose
work we have examined. But he—and they—misconstrues the principle: "The uniformity required is not in nature's activities but in our
account of them" (Goodman 1967:94). It is not that the world is unchanging; the world of foragers, along with the worlds of tribes and of
chiefdoms and of nations, changes continuously. They are, in fact, all
the same world. Making that world intelligible to ourselves requires
consistency in observation and presentation. It is that consistency that
we seek in systematic ecology and that we do not find in any of the
proffered "forager" models. In them, data and analysis are ad hoc and
directed toward demonstrating normative constructs. Departure from
an assumed norm is seen as atypicality rather than variation. Adaptation, a key concept in the paradigm, useful for gauging the articulation
of social and material forces, becomes in such a schema merely a retrospective assessment of survival, or perhaps of Tylorian survivals. We
are left with anecdotal ecology.

Needless to say, this is a problem not of evolution or of ecology but
of a particular ethnographic appropriation of these fundamental processes of life to its own use. Ecological study of social formations is
valuable in itself, but the integrity of this value is subverted when the
results are extrapolated uncritically onto some projected past made
present. Whatever primitiveness there may be in our human heritage,
it surely was left behind in the presapient Pleistocene. Today very few
archaeologists of the Paleolithic would agree that any *Homo sapiens*
society of that period was primitive. How much less so any living
peoples—unless we insist on thinking of them as retarded or devolved,
conditions for which Lubbock ([1865] 1913:431) long ago found
scant evidence. Ecological knowledge is crucial if we are to understand
our presapient and sapient past or cope with our present, but that
knowledge cannot be obtained by ethnographic analogy, any more

than ecological analogy can give us anything but clues to the historical course to the present.

Ecological studies are essential for specifying the nature and limits of natural forces of production that members of social formations must contend with. But neither an applied science of ecology nor even an advanced theory of ecology—in itself—can provide the theoretical framework needed to analyze the articulation and transformation of social systems. Godelier (1977: 124) states the matter succinctly when he says that Marx was right "to declare that man's problem was not in his original unity with his conditions of production, but his separation from them." Among their other defects, the models we have encountered are united in equating economic constraints on modes of production with the purely technical constraints of resource exploitation (cf. Asad 1978: 58). Furthermore, the anecdotal ecology presented in these models does not permit an analysis of the role of contemporary social divisions in access to ecological productive capacity on the one hand or to the fruits of production on the other; therefore an analysis of class differentiation in these regards—such as is carried out in chapters 6 and 7—is not possible. Far from being superfluous for such an analysis, systematic ecological data are essential and are presented along with the argument in those chapters. But before examining the present, we must find out what we can of how this present came to be.

3

The Past Recaptured

We were made to believe that we had no past to speak of, no history to boast of. The past, so far as we were concerned, was just a blank and nothing more. . . . It should now be our intention to try and retrieve what we can of our past . . . to prove that we did have a past, that it was a past that was just as worth writing and learning about as any other. We must do this for the simple reason that a nation without a past is a lost nation, and a people without a past is a people without a soul.

Sir Seretse Khama, *Botswana Daily News*, 1970

The Recovered Past
Initial Pastroforaging
In decrying this manipulation of the African past, Sir Seretse, Botswana's first president, was addressing all citizens of his newly independent country, but to some his words carry double force. For none of Africa's peoples have been so effectively isolated in this manner as those of Botswana, Namibia, and Angola, variously merged into one or more of the categories Bushman, San, Basarwa, hunter-gatherer, or forager. These stereotypic categories must be deconstructed in order to expose the reality of human history lying behind them.

Written and oral records fail, however, at the very moment when precolonial social formations were already experiencing the thrusts of European capital. Consequently, especially for the subjugated peoples (who were, in any case, marginal to the interests of the recorders), these records enshrine already penetrated formations. Foster-Carter (1978a, 1978b) and Godelier (1978) have emphasized that it is just those precapitalist forms—those that existed before colonial penetration—that are transformed in the colonial encounter. We therefore have firm reason for looking behind documents and memory in order to learn with archaeological aid as much as we can about these earlier formations.

Evidence is beginning to accumulate that suggests ceramic-making pastoralists were present in a very large portion, if not all, of southern

Africa by about 2,000 years ago (table 3.1; fig. 3.1). This evidence is still too sparsely represented to support more than tentative and speculative syntheses, yet a somewhat coherent picture is emerging of pre–Iron Age pastoralists occupying the fringes of the Kalahari—from about 200 B.C. to A.D. 400—as part of their far wider range in the region. Ceramics assigned either to the earliest Iron Age (Evers 1981; Huffman 1982) or to the latest Stone Age (Denbow and Campbell 1986; Yellen and Brooks, n.d.) are spread thinly across the northern half of southern Africa. The presence of such ceramics at Magopa in the western sandveld of Botswana at the end of the first century B.C. (Yellen and Brooks, n.d.) is of particular interest because it provides direct evidence that Dobe-NyaeNyae, where Zhu have lived for a very long time, was engaged with this pre–Iron Age pastoral system from its inception. Sheep are known to have been kept during this period in Namibia at Mirabib (Sandelowsky, van Rooyen, and Vogel 1979) and in Zimbabwe at Bambata Cave (Walker 1983); cattle were present in Botswana at Lotshitshi on the edge of the Okavango Delta slightly before A.D. 300 (Denbow and Wilmsen 1986). These sites, plus a handful of others in Botswana (Denbow and Campbell 1986) and Namibia (Kinahan 1984a, 1984b),[1] begin to fill the geographical vacuum that had previously existed between the Cape coast and central Africa, where for several years domestic stock dating before A.D. 500 have been known to be present (Robertshaw 1978; Smith 1983).

It is generally assumed that the peoples associated with these early pastoralist economies must have been Khoisan—or, perhaps better, ancestors of modern Khoisan. Such an assumption fits well with accumulating linguistic evidence that much of the basic pastoral vocabulary used by speakers of southern Bantu languages is derived through a Khoisan intermediary (Ehret 1967, 1982; Ehret and Kinsman 1981). In addition, Köhler (1987) finds, in the Angolan-Namibian border area, Kxoe vocabularies for cattle and pastoralist activities, as does Vossen (1984) for the central Khoe of Botswana. Barnard (1986:6) notes that Khoe terms for cattle have undergone one of the regular sound shifts from Khoikhoi that are characteristic of Central San languages, thus indicating that the word has not been reborrowed in recent times. This is further evidence that stockkeeping predates Bantu entry in the region.

Developed Pastoralism

In contrast to the scarcity of earlier sites, there is now firm evidence for aligning the eastern part of the Kalahari with the known Early Iron Age

Table 3.1. Chronology of Food Production in the Kalahari

Location and Site	^{14}C Years	Date
Western sandveld		
Xgi	110±50	A.D. 1840
Otjiserandu	140±50	A.D. 1810
Kgwebe Hills	<185	A.D. 1765
Kgwebe Hills	195±75	A.D. 1755
Depression	305±75	A.D. 1645
VunguVungu	320±45	A.D. 1630
Magopa	360±50	A.D. 1590
Depression	370±75	A.D. 1580
Qomqoisi	420±50	A.D. 1530
Depression	470±80	A.D. 1480
Xgi	495±45	A.D. 1455
Nqoma	860±60	A.D. 1090
Kapako	840±50	A.D. 1110
Xgi	810±60	A.D. 1140
Nqoma	970±50	A.D. 980
Nqoma	970±50	A.D. 980
Nqoma	970±70	A.D. 980
Nqoma	980±60	A.D. 970
Nqoma	1,000±60	A.D. 950
Nqoma	1,100±80	A.D. 850
CaeCae	1,150±60	A.D. 800
Divuyu	1,190±70	A.D. 760
CaeCae	1,230±50	A.D. 720
Nqoma	1,220±70	A.D. 730
Divuyu	1,220±70	A.D. 730
Nqoma	1,290±60	A.D. 660
Divuyu	1,330±60	A.D. 620
Divuyu	1,330±60	A.D. 620
Divuyu	1,370±60	A.D. 580
Divuyu	1,400±70	A.D. 550
Magopa	1,960±50	10 B.C.
River system		
Toteng	<185	A.D. 1765
Toteng	<185	A.D. 1765
Gwi	235±370	A.D. 1715
Xaro	360±80	A.D. 1590
Toteng	400±100	A.D. 1550
Serandela	800±80	A.D. 1150
Matlapaneng	970±50	A.D. 980
Matlapaneng	1,040±50	A.D. 910
Matlapaneng	1,120±110	A.D. 830
Hippo Tooth	1,120±190	A.D. 830
Qogana	1,190±80	A.D. 760
Chobe	1,190±80	A.D. 760
Serandela	1,220±80	A.D. 730
Matlapaneng	1,260±60	A.D. 690
Matlapaneng	1,270±80	A.D. 680
Lotshitshi	1,660±100	A.D. 290

Table 3.1. (*continued*)

Location and Site	^{14}C Years	Date
Eastern hardveld		
Toutswe	450±95	A.D. 1500
Domboshaba	450±80	A.D. 1500
Broadhurst	590±50	A.D. 1360
Domboshaba	490±50	A.D. 1460
Toutswe	645±95	A.D. 1305
Moeng	720±125	A.D. 1230
Toutswe	750±95	A.D. 1200
Moeng	795±75	A.D. 1155
Toutswe	755±75	A.D. 1195
Commando Kop	835±55	A.D. 1115
Thatswane	840±75	A.D. 1110
Moritsane	855±75	A.D. 1095
Kgaswe	860±80	A.D. 1090
Toutswe	860±105	A.D. 1090
Moeng	880±80	A.D. 1070
Kgaswe	940±80	A.D. 1010
Kgaswe	960±80	A.D. 990
Maiphetwane	960±50	A.D. 990
Commando Kop	970±40	A.D. 980
Toutswe	990±75	A.D. 960
Taukome	995±75	A.D. 955
Moeng	1,007±120	A.D. 943
Thatswane	1,025±80	A.D. 925
Rraserura	1,130±80	A.D. 820
Moeng	1,185±120	A.D. 765
Thamaga	1,190±90	A.D. 760
Taukome	1,240±80	A.D. 710
Bisoli	1,240±80	A.D. 710
Taukome	1,265±80	A.D. 685
Bisoli	1,340±50	A.D. 610
Maunatlala	1,570±140	A.D. 380
Bambata Cave	2,145±60	195 B.C.

economies of the rest of southern Africa (Denbow 1984, 1986; Maggs 1977; Hall and Vogel 1980; Parkington and Hall 1987). A large number of sites in the eastern hardveld Kalahari of Botswana were established by pastoralists during the seventh to the eleventh century A.D. (table 3.1, fig. 3.2); the earlier of these contain ceramics similar to others that are distributed widely in Zimbabwe and northern Transvaal by A.D. 600.[2] Iron and copper tools and ornaments are abundant, and most if not all of them were manufactured locally. Rondavel houses of the kind still commonly made of a cow dung and clay plaster applied to wattle frames in the region are preserved at some places.

The agropastoral economic form of these settlements is evident in

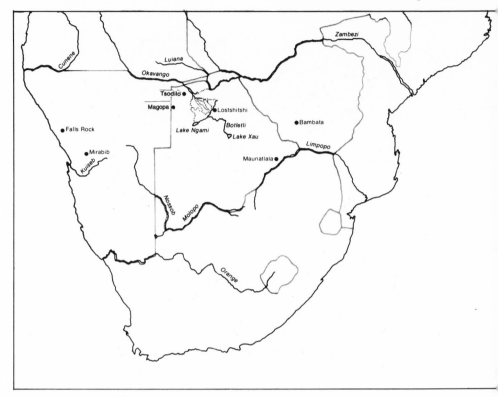

Figure 3.1. Archaeological sites containing pottery predating the introduction of metallurgy into southern Africa.

the remains of cattle, sheep, and goats, which at some of the larger sites make up 80% of the faunal assemblage, the remaining 20% being of hunted wild animals. Dung silicified by burning marks the presence of kraals[3] on most of the 320 sites known from this period; at the larger sites these reach diameters of 100 meters and depths of 150 centimeters, evidence that large herds were kept. Sorghum and cowpeas appear to have been the principal crops.

Finally, cane-glass beads manufactured in Indic or Arabic Asia and cowrie and conus shells, some of species that live only in estuaries of the Indian Ocean, were found at four of the largest sites. This is certain evidence that before 1,000 years ago agropastoral peoples in eastern Botswana participated in exchange networks that reached the east coast of the continent.

A tripartite hierarchy of settlements may be discerned in terms of

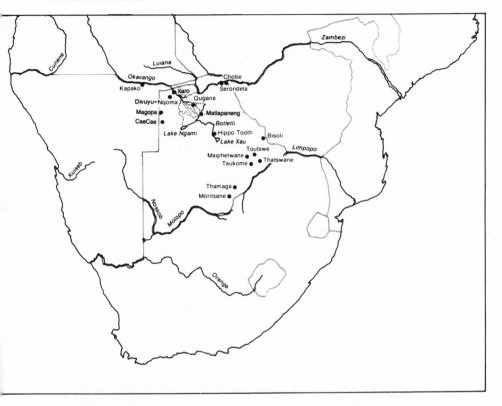

Figure 3.2. Agropastoral and metallurgical sites with radiocarbon dates between A.D. 500 and A.D. 1000.

site size, location, length of occupation, proportion of exotic trade items, and relative numbers of domestic stock; social stratification of the inhabitants seems clear (Denbow 1984, 1986). Toutswemogala, one of the largest of these sites, covers about 100,000 square meters; it was occupied (perhaps with interruptions) for about five hundred years and contains a very large kraal deposit as well as many trade items. Second-level sites, such as Taukome and Thatswane, cover about 10,000 square meters and appear to have been occupied for only two hundred to three hundred years. Kraal deposits, though large, and trade goods, though numerous, do not match those of Toutswemogala. At the tertiary sites, kraals are very small or absent, stone artifacts typical of the Late Stone Age of southern Africa predominate, and re-mains of hunted animals usually outnumber those of domesticates. This is in contrast to the larger sites, where stone artifacts are virtually nonexistent and hunted animals few; foraging appears to have been more important at these smaller settlements than at larger centers.

Social stratification is further indicated by the age at slaughter of cattle at these sites. At Toutswemogala, as also at the later chiefdoms established at K2 and Mapungubwe, prime young to middle-adult animals were killed in far higher proportion than were juvenile and aged animals. These prime animals are most desirable as food, but they are also the reproducing cohorts of a herd. In contrast, juveniles (probably yearling bull culls and runts) and old, postreproductive animals were most often slaughtered at Taukome; this is the slaughter strategy practiced in rural Botswana today by subsistence farmers, who emphasize herd maintenance at the expense of meat production. It appears that at this early date members of an elite social stratum were already able to extract prime food resources—along with a surplus product distilled in value as exotic trade goods—from subordinate classes for their own use. Many, if not most, of the prime animals slaughtered at Toutswemogala must have been obtained from lower-ranked locations, for a sustained offtake of breeding stock would quickly reduce the resident herd to unsustainable numbers. It may be appropriate to think of tertiary site herders as cattle managers for centralized elites rather than as cattle owners in their own right.

The history of pastoralism in the western sandveld Kalahari has a similar chronology, although it differs in a number of significant social and economic details. Divuyu, the name given to an agropastoral occupation of the Tsodilo Hills (fig. 3.2) that took place during the sixth and seventh centuries, is a fully developed Early Iron Age site very rich in ceramics, iron and copper tools and ornaments, and ivory. Iron was smelted at the site, as indicated by the presence of slag. Sheep and goats were mainstays of the economy, but cattle appear to have been rare and to have been kept elsewhere.

Divuyu ceramics have clear design affinities to roughly contemporary sites in central Angola (Clark 1968; Sousa Martins 1976; Ervedosa 1980).[4] Divuyu also appears to be related in ceramic design to the site of Madinga-Cayes near the mouth of the Congo River in Congo Brazzaville (Denbow, Nanima-Moubouha and Sanviti 1988). The date of Madinga-Cayes in the beginning of the first millennium B.C. fits well with a hypothesis of Bantu expansion proposed by Heine (1973). According to this hypothesis, a Kongo nucleus of Bantu languages formed in the lower Congo Valley about 3,000 years ago, and from this the Herero language cluster moved into the Cunene-Okavango region "das von Khoisan-sprachigen Wildbeutern und Rindernomaden bewohnt war": "where Khoisan-speaking wild food collectors and cattle nomads were living" (Heine, Hoff, and Vossen 1977:65). This cluster (Herero, Nyaneka, Kwanyama, and Ndonga) includes many of the Bantu languages spoken in that same region of Namibia-Ngamiland today. Pfouts (1983) estimates that these languages became differentiated in the region beginning between 1,500 and 2,000 years ago, an estimate that fits well with the initial date (A.D. 500) for occupation at Divuyu. Thus several independent lines of evidence agree that proto-Herero-speaking Bantu peoples entered the western part of southern Africa roughly 2,000 years ago, where they found Khoisan-speaking herders. As already noted, Ehret proposed twenty years ago that these Bantu-speakers obtained cattle, or at least a cattle-keeping vocabulary, from Khoisan herders in this region.

Two marine shells of Atlantic coast origin (Cerithiidae) and two iron pendants were found at Divuyu; the pendants are virtually identical to specimens of the same age found in Shaba Province, Zaire (van Noten 1982, fig. 31). These items indicate that Divuyu peoples maintained exchange systems with the coastal and interior areas from which they had recently moved. Thus, during the first centuries A.D. this northern margin of the Kalahari was already actively part of a wider sphere of production and exchange extending throughout a large portion of the Angolan and Kongo river systems. Fish bones and river mussel shells found at Divuyu are further evidence for such exchange, these probably from the Okavango Delta some 70 kilometers away where a site, Xaro, with Divuyu-like pottery has been found or from farther upstream where sites such as Kapako have long been known. Relatively small communities of Bantu- and Khoisan-speakers appear to have intermingled throughout this entire region on relatively equal terms. Economic and linguistic—and therefore social—transfers appear to have flowed freely among these communities, with the result that pastoral economies became well established in the Kalahari. The dimensions of these transfers and their effects on local populations are not yet known; however, it is reasonably clear that the roots of Namibian–western Kalahari pastoral economies lie in this early Khoisan-Bantu interrelationship (Wilmsen 1978; Denbow 1986; Denbow and Wilmsen 1986). Elphick (1975:33–35) summarizes European descriptions from as early as the seventeenth century that may reflect similar relations between "San foragers" and "Khoi herders."

From between A.D. 700 and 1,000, a number of agropastoral sites are now known in the region. The largest of these is Nqoma,[5] situated on a low plateau of the female Tsodilo Hill (fig. 3.2), the main components of which are dated to the ninth and tenth centuries. Cattle, some of a humpbacked variety, were paramount in the economy of this site, but sheep and goats were also common. Sorghum, millet, and possibly melons were grown, but mongongo nuts and *Grewia* berries—along with wild faunal remains—indicate that foraging continued to be important. Rondavel houses were constructed, and an elaborate variety of ivory, iron, and copper ornaments, along with many iron tools, was made on the site. Cane-glass beads and marine mollusk shells, including money or ring cowrie, *Cypraea* sp.,[6] provide firm evidence that Nqoma was an important local center in intracontinental trade networks that extended from the Indian Ocean coast by the ninth century. Freshwater mussels and fish continued to be imported from Okavango communities.

Another site, Matlapaneng, northeast of Maun on the eastern side of the Okavango Delta, is contemporary with Nqoma. Cattle, sheep, and goats were kept there, and sorghum, millet, and cowpeas were grown. Matlapaneng was as large as Nqoma and had all its material characteristics, but there are two significant differences between the sites. Matlapaneng is not nearly as rich in metal ornaments or East Coast trade goods; in this respect it resembles the secondary sites of the eastern hardveld, such as Taukome, rather than Nqoma. In addition, Matlapaneng ceramics are overwhelmingly allied with those of the hierarchical east,[7] and this must mean that its social, economic, and political ties were in that direction rather than northward as those of the Tsodilo sites had been until this time. It appears that the dominant centers of the hardveld, Toutswemogala and others, were extending their economic interests into the western sandveld at this time; indeed, some Nqoma ceramic motifs display eastern influence, evidence that these interests were penetrating deeply into the west. It seems that this was the beginning of hegemony from the east that was consolidated by about A.D. 1000.

A series of smaller sites can be assigned to the general time span of the eighth through eleventh centuries, although only one has been dated (fig. 3.2). At CaeCae, ceramics, iron, and cattle are contemporary with those at Nqoma and Matlapaneng. At the nearby sites, Qubi, Magopa, and Qangwa (Yellen 1970, 1973, Yellen and Brooks n.d.; Wilmsen, n.d.a), similar ceramics as well as iron occur in small quantities. All of these sherds are thin and appear to have come from small bowls or dishes. Just across the border in the NyaeNyae area of Namibia, Kinahan and Kinahan (1984:21–22) recovered ceramics from thirteen of twenty sites they investigated; they state that some of these ceramics may be related to charcoal-tempered Iron Age wares in Botswana. In the Delta area, small undated components containing ceramics similar to those of Matlapaneng are present at Lotshitshi and near Tsau.

A hierarchical site structure may be discerned in the foregoing description, not unlike that described for the eastern hardveld during this same set of centuries but not so elaborate. Nqoma appears to be at the apex of this western settlement hierarchy; it covered about 20,000 square meters and was occupied (perhaps intermittently) for about four hundred years. Nqoma yielded a predominantly pastoral fauna with an even higher proportion of cattle to sheep and goats than found at the larger centers in the east; it contained moderate numbers of exotic trade items. In addition, Nqoma has the richest (in both quantity and variety) and most elaborate metal ornament inventory now known for any site of its time in the entire southern African region.

At CaeCae, on the other hand, although occupation debris is found throughout an area of more than a square kilometer, settlement seems to have occurred in small clusters similar to present-day homesteads in the area, which also are spread over more than a square kilometer. There is no way to determine how many of these clusters may have been occupied simultaneously, but it is unlikely that aggregate occupation area at any given time would have exceeded 2,000 square meters. Information provided for Qubi (Yellen 1973) indicates that the same may be said for this location. The other sandveld locations, though known only by isolated, small test excavations, appear to be similar in most respects. Contemporary levels at Lotshitshi are also in this range. As already noted, ceramics and metal occur in very small amounts at these sites, cattle (also in very small numbers) are known only from CaeCae and Lotshitshi, and exotic trade items are absent from all current inventories.

It appears that an elite was established at Nqoma that was able to exercise sufficient hegemony over the inhabitants of secondary settlements to appropriate the overwhelming preponderance of imported goods (glass beads and marine shells) that entered the western sandveld as well as the bulk of locally manufactured surplus product (metal and ivory ornaments) that was not exported. Some local products must have been exported, for we may assume that imports were desired and thus were expensive and had to be obtained for value; otherwise they would be more widely distributed among many sites. It seems likely that Nqoma elites were also able to extract the required exchange value from their subordinates, probably from as far afield as CaeCae, Qubi, and the other sandveld communities, to judge from the presence of contemporary ceramics at these sandveld places.

We must consider the significance of these few sherds scattered about those places in the western sandveld. While it appears to be true that Early Iron Age and later ceramics are associated with pastoralists in southern Africa, it does not necessarily follow that these ceram-

ics were part of the means of pastoral production; indeed, some of
the most common forms are patently unsuitable for such functions.
Hendrickson (1986:20–25, 37–40) has reconstructed vessel shape
and size profiles from 473 sherds recovered from Divuyu, Nqoma, and
Matlapaneng. According to her analysis, 72%, 80%, and 43%, respectively, of the sherds from these sites came from small bowls, many
of which were shallow, dishlike forms that I calculate had capacities of
a half-liter or less. These dishes had relatively thin walls, were often
elaborately decorated, and often had a red slip applied to exterior sur-
faces. Of the larger pots, the most common appear to have had a
maximum capacity of about 1.5 to 2.0 liters, although a few were
larger. Some of these pots were large enough to have been useful for
storing milk or water; they could also have been used for milking,
although this is unlikely because they break too easily. Most of these
ceramic vessels thus appear to have been designed for food preparation and serving, while more durable wood and leather containers
were used for high-risk purposes (such as milking), as they are in the
Kalahari today.

If it is true that Early Iron Age ceramic vessels were designed to
function as nonproductive utilitarian items, primarily for personal or
household use as cooking/serving/eating dishes, they would have had
equally important functions as material manifestations of the relations
of production in the pastoral/pastroforaging social formation of the
time. In such functions they would be invested with associational
value as attributes of dominant centers, so that pottery dishes would
confer prestige on their possessors. Accordingly, ceramics (especially
personal serving dishes) would be desirable prestations in social relations beween those dominant elite centers and their rural sources of
supply, where local people would prize them as symbols of higher
status. So as not to debase that value, the centers could be expected to
parcel out these prestations carefully, limiting them perhaps to senior
members of local descent groups (or some such persons) who would
have been responsible for channeling a locally produced surplus—a
form of precapitalist commodity—back to the centers. Local products
that could have been commoditized in this way include ivory, rhino
horn, ostrich feathers and eggshells, gum arabic, aromatic woods (Cape
sandalwood, *Spirostachys africana*) and corms (*Mariscus* spp.), red
dye woods (*Pterocarpus angolensis*), and limonitic red pigments. The
pigments (known from several sources in the CaeCae-Qubi-Qangwa
area but absent from the Delta and Tsodilo) could have been the
source of media for red slips on Nqoma, and Matlapaneng, bowls and
dishes as well as for paintings on rock walls at Tsodilo. Ivory, rhino

horn, and gum arabic were important in the interior trade with the Indian Ocean coast during this time (Freeman-Grenville 1962) and may have been exported from Nqoma. Dye woods are known to have been highly prized trade items at least as early as the sixteenth century (Martin 1972), when they were used in dressing leather goods, as they still are today in southern Africa. In addition, both pigments and woods are used to make cosmetics and are today in great demand for this purpose; it is not difficult to suppose that they were equally desired in the past. The recurrence of a similar pattern of site inventory at five known locations in the western sandveld suggests that these locations participated on the same level in a social formation dominated economically by Nqoma (about 100 kilometers away on average) and possibly similar centers that are as yet undiscovered.

Thus, in the earliest well-documented period (A.D. 600–1000) of agropastoral penetration into the Kalahari, a regional differentiation of settlement organization and an associated difference in social formations can already be discerned in the archaeological record. In the east there was clearly an appropriation of indigenous Khoisan forager, and probably pastroforager, systems by Bantu-speaking peoples who colonized the area in numbers and quickly established a hierarchy of settlements around their central towns. The smaller, tertiary sites in this organization accurately reflect in their size and content the domains of pastroforagers whose position in the imposed social hierarchy into which they were incorporated was economically subordinate to that of pastoralists. Jim Denbow and I suspect that a fourth, solely foraging, level exists, but we have not yet identified examples. It appears that by the end of the first millennium A.D. eastern Kalahari communities were differentiated socially and economically in a manner similar to that of historically known and contemporary social formations found in that same region. This picture conforms to what is known for the rest of the eastern half of southern Africa (Huffman 1982).

In the western half of the subcontinent, full agropastoralist economies with ironworking and transcontinental exchange networks were introduced at the same time as in the east. Bantu peoples were surely involved in the process in the northern peripheral zones where transmission must have taken place, and there is some historical evidence (which we will review in a moment) that they penetrated much farther south. But Bantu hegemony as it now exists was not established in the western Kalahari until the mid-nineteenth century, and at first only to a limited extent. It appears, rather, that early agropastoral economies were transferred among indigenous cattle-keeping pastroforagers, who could only have been Khoisan-speakers, and to entering Bantu-speaking small stock-herding and horticulturalist ironworkers. The mechanisms for these transferrals are not yet entirely clear but probably followed long-established lines of interaction and then became internally differentiated according to local conditions. Forager and herder polities were less hegemonically structured in this area than in the east, as they are known not to have been in historic times until disrupted in the nineteenth century, first by the Tswana and then by European capitalism.

As trade with the Indian Ocean grew in scale, however, and gold became a major export from the interior while fine India cloth was imported to places like Ingombe Ilede on the Zambezi River (Phillipson 1977:193; Phillipson and Fagen 1969), the nearer peoples on the eastern highlands of present-day Zimbabwe organized trading networks to their own benefit (table 3.1, fig. 3.3). The routes to the ocean from the west were truncated beginning in the eleventh century by Mapongubwe, then followed by the developing Zimbabwian states—Great Zimbabwe and Khami (Birmingham 1983:25; Garlake 1973; Huffman 1982). From then on the western Kalahari was reduced to the status of producer rather than receiver in the Asian trade. Matlapaneng seems to have been one of the first outposts of this subordination. Salt, ivory, and cattle from Namibia-Ngamiland probably continued to enter the Angola-Congo trade to the north as these products are known to have done in the nineteenth century (Miller 1976, 1983:121, 127). Shells, metal, and dried fish were probably among the items distributed in return, but we cannot document their entry into Namibia-Ngamiland until the Portuguese initiated an Atlantic-oriented trade in the sixteenth century. Beads from this trade are found at the beginning of the seventeenth century at VunguVungu (Sandelowsky 1979) and Xaro on the Okavango (Denbow and Wilmsen 1986), at Homasi in the NyaeNyae pans (Kinahan 1986), and in upper levels on the Nqoma plateau at Tsodilo.

A series of sites dating from the twelfth to the nineteenth century documents the continuity of ceramic—and metal—using agropastoralists along with foragers in the sandveld into the time of recorded history. Sherds of a type called Bushman ware by Kinahan and Kinahan (1984:22) are most numerous in the NyaeNyae sites; these have been radiocarbon dated to the late sixteenth century (Kinahan 1986:115). Similar ceramics with radiocarbon dates in the same century are found at Qomqoisi and Depression Shelter at Tsodilo, as well as at Magopa (Yellen and Brooks, n.d.), CaeCae (Wilmsen, n.d.a), and Toteng (Robbins 1984). A colonial trader boom in the nineteenth century, based on

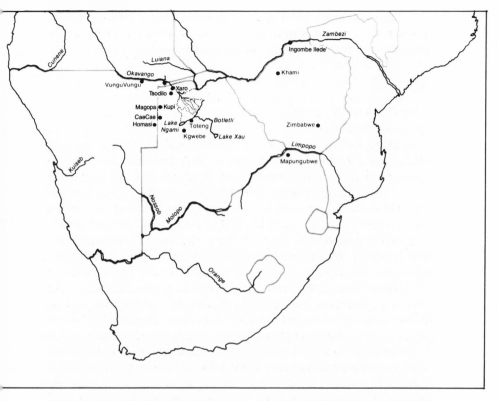

Figure 3.3. Archaeological sites containing pottery dating between the twelfth and nineteenth centuries A.D.

ivory, ostrich feathers, and cattle, brought into the region a wide variety of Europeans, with their quest for wealth, their goods of many kinds, and their force of arms, and transformed its economy and society once again. A sherd from an English white-body cup with an embossed rose and a fragment of an iron spoon found at the Kupi site near Qubi are residues of this trader activity in the Dobe-NyaeNyae area that we are about to examine.[8] A thin Mbukushu component at Tsodilo and similar Herero levels at CaeCae, which date to the turn of the twentieth century, record the pauperization of the region that followed this brief nineteenth-century flash of relative wealth.

Some of the newcomer Europeans also began to write about what they saw. In Ngamiland, the resultant link between archaeological prehistory and recorded history is made at the Kgwebe Hills, where

the artifactual assemblage and a radiocarbon age conform to traditions that this was the site where the Tawana branch of the emerging
Ngwato state first established itself in 1795.

The Recorded Past
The "Great North Road"

When the Batawana arrived in the Lake Ngami region, Bantu-speaking
Bangologa, Bayei, Ovambanderu, Hambukushu, and the San-speaking
Zhu, Cexai, and Nharo were already settled there, many with substantial herds that the Batawana were at first not strong enough to confiscate (Tlou 1972:140). The newcomers gave the name Kgwebe to the
place where they first settled. This name derives from that of the San
leader then living there (Nettleton 1934:344; Peters 1972:220–21),
and by using his name—or more likely adopting existing use of it—
for that place, Batawana acknowledged his prior right of possession
(Wilmsen 1985b).

In both Tswana and San ideology, right of possession of some section of land stems from membership in a legitimately constituted social
group recognized to have hereditary association with that land; in the
Tswana view, at least some of that land must be used for pasturage or
planting (Schapera 1943; see chap. 5). To be in that state of possession
is to have at least partial economic independence, and as Tlou (1972:
138) notes oral tradition holds that the Kgwebe peoples were independent at the time of Tawana incursions. That the headman's name,
Kgwebe, was retained by Batawana is good presumptive evidence that
his group owned livestock. Furthermore, the aggregate herds of the
different peoples of Ngamiland appear to have been extensive; it was
to these that Batawana followed earlier Hurutse and Kwena traders in
1795. The formation of the Tawana state in Ngamiland was in part
motivated by a desire to control those cattle as well as the ivory of
the area, whose value was inflating rapidly in the European-inspired
mercantile system then spreading through southern Africa (Parsons
1977:114).

Just fifty years later, Cotton Oswell, Mungo Murray, J. H. Wilson,
and David Livingstone spearheaded the British thrust to the same
riches (fig. 3.4). On the first of August 1849, they reached Batawana
on Lake Ngami from the southeast by following the Zouga (Botletli)
River after traveling northward from Shoshong, the main town of
Bangwato (Livingstone [1857] 1912:51; Oswell 1900, 1:189). They
were the first Europeans to travel that route and to see the lake. In a
letter dated 3 September of that year to Arthur Tidman, foreign secre-

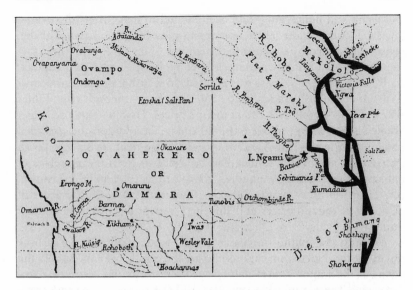

Figure 3.4. Livingston's route from Sechele's town (just off the bottom of the map) through Sekgoma's town (Shoshong) to Lake Ngami and later on to Sebuatwane's town (Linyanti); this became known as the Great North Road. The star marks the location of Letsholathebe's town (called Batuana on the map); Sorila is the Tsodilo Hills but is placed too far north and west. CaeCae does not appear on the original, but for orientation a triangle has been added to mark its location. (This is a photographic enlargement of a section of a map showing Livingstone's travels in Africa published in Livingstone ([1857] 1912); fig. 3.7 is a larger portion of the same map.

tary of the London Missionary Society, which was read to the Royal Geographical Society, Livingstone announced to the world—that is, to Europe—that Lake Ngami had been discovered (Schapera, ed., 1961, 1:131–38).

Of course, these Europeans were led to the lake by natives who knew the way because they had been there many times before; Oswell wrote (1900, 1:121), "One of them who had in former years been at the 'Great Water' was appointed guide." As an instance of this ongoing trade, Bakwena ivory dealers—taking with them bullets, beads, sugar, horses, and tobacco, among other things—took advantage of the caravan coalescing around Livingstone's party (financed by Oswell, an English gentleman on leave from his bank who was not concerned with profit but not averse to paying his expenses by hunting and buying ivory) to pursue their long-standing trade with Ngamiland (Tlou 1972:172; Schapera, ed., 1959, 1:15). Indeed, Livingstone (a Scots missionary)—and especially the British traders then active among

Bakwena and Bangwato—had been invited to make this "discovery" by the Tawana Kgosi (chief, sometimes glossed king), Letsholathebe, who wished thereby to increase the volume of his trade with these foreigners who had finally gotten close enough for unmediated contact.

If Letsholathebe's desire was granted, so was that of the Europeans; Wilson, an English trader, made £500 on the two-month trip (Tabler 1973:122)—about $12,500 at today's prices. Oswell's expense ledger totaled £642/4s/6p, about $16,000 today; in addition, he provided the Livingstones—David and Mary—£290 for their own needs "with the remark that as the money had been drawn from the preserves of our estate (elephants) we had as good a right to it as he" (Listowel 1974:56); in other words, Oswell's total outlay was on the order of $25,000 at today's prices and still there was profit, obtained entirely from ivory.

More to the point, an eastern wagon route (figs. 3.4, 3.5)—"the Road to the North for capital and to the South for labour . . . the focus of the wagon routes that splayed out north and south to Zambezia and the Cape" (Parsons 1977:113)—to the ivory and cattle riches of Ngamiland had been opened to direct commerce with established mercantile capital at Grahamstown and the Cape. It would no longer be necessary for the emerging British Empire to gain access to the interior indirectly through Tswana middlemen such as the Bakwena who guided Oswell, Livingstone, and Wilson or through the Griqua (people of combined Khoi and European parentage), who were already active on the Chobe River. Part of the strategy of the British at the Cape—to circumvent the thrust of the Boers up through the Transvaal in their own efforts to capture land and markets—was thus taken a step forward.

There was keen competition for this European trade among the Tswana groups. A brief digression into the circumstances surrounding Livingstone's expedition will reveal not only the scope of this competition but also the degree to which the Kalahari was already interlaced with trade routes. The direct route from Kolobeng, then the Kwena capital, through the desert to Lake Ngami was both shorter and advantageous to Bakwena because it avoided Bangwato, who wanted to act as middlemen (Tlou 1972:176). It was along this route that Batawana invited Livingstone to travel. He wrote, "Seven men came from the Bataoana [Batawana], a tribe living on the banks of the Lake, with an earnest request from their chief for a visit. But the path by which they came to Kolobeng was impracticable for wagons, so, declining their guidance, I selected the more circuitous route by which

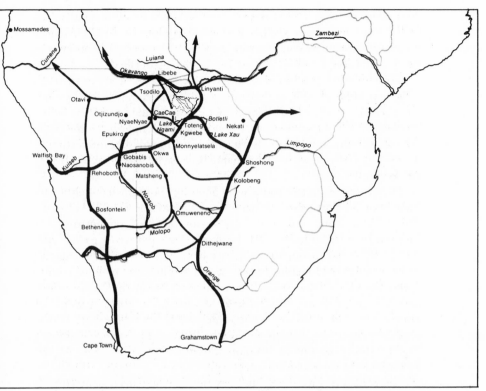

Figure 3.5. Major trade routes in the western half of southern Africa in the middle of the nineteenth century; the heavier lines mark the routes most frequently used by Europeans.

the Bamangwato [Bangwato] usually pass" (Schapera, ed., 1961, 1:131).

About this latter route, Livingstone ([1857] 1912:35) noted that "Sekomi [Sekgoma], the chief of the Bamangwato, was acquainted with a route which he kept carefully concealed, because the Lake country abounded in ivory, which he obtained in large quantities at small coast to himself. Sechele . . . always alive to his own interest, was anxious to get a share of the trade." This came to be known as the Great North Road.

In pursuit of this interest, Sechele, the Kwena Kgosi, sent two oxen along with a request to Sekgoma to allow Livingstone to use the route. The request was refused, but with Sechele's active assistance Livingstone went anyway. The Mokwena "appointed" to guide his party was called Ramotobi, now spelled Ramothobe (Tlou 1972:171), which means "a person who frequently goes away." Ramothobe knew the route well; Livingstone ([1857] 1912:47) was astonished: "The knowledge retained by Ramotobi of the trackless waste of scrub through which we were passing was surprising . . . one clump of bushes and trees seemed exactly like another. Yet, as we walked together, he remarked, 'When we come to that hollow we shall light upon the highway of Sekomi; and beyond that again. . . .'" It would be interesting to know if this man was given that name because he was an active trader on the route.

The central Kalahari route was, however, not ignored—either by natives or by Europeans. A Scots trader, MaCabe (1855:413–34), followed that route during the dry season of 1852. Livingstone met him returning from his second trip to the lake and wrote to his wife, Mary: "He went through the desert having 24 oxen to each waggon. They lived on wild melons for twenty days. They [the melons, tsama] seemed to sustain the strength of all animals better than water; dogs & everything eat them" (Schapera, ed., 1961, 2:200). Batswana, of course, also continued to use the route, and later first the Boer Dorstland Trekkers in 1875, then the Ghanzi Trekkers in 1895 went along it (fig. 3.5 shows the network of more important routes in use during the second half of the nineteenth century).

The British too were playing both sides of the fence; while consolidating their gains with Batswana, they continued to supply essential arms to the Boers, whose Great Trek to the Transvaal and later attempts to annex Bechuanaland were as disruptive of native political structures as were the difaqane wars of the 1820s (see p. 90 below). Sechele's brother Kgosidintsi attacked British policy in a letter to the missionary Moffat: "Is it because we have not white skins that we are destroyed like *libatana* [beasts of prey]? Why do the English assist the Boers? Why do they give them power over lands that are not theirs to give? . . . They have driven their white Bushmen [Boers] into our country to kill us. . . . and if we ask to buy powder we get none. No, no, no! Black men must have no ammunition: they must serve the white man" (Nangati 1980:129). It is within this volatile environment that we must examine the evolving status of the San-speaking peoples of the region.

By no means were all the references to "Bushmen" that these first travelers made confined to the bushlore sort, such as Oswell's account of running down a Bushman woman with his horse to induce her to lead him to water (Oswell 1900, 1:189–91). Livingstone ([1857]

1912:39), for example, observed: "A few Bechuanas may go into a village of Bakalahari, and domineer over the whole with impunity; but when these same adventures meet the Bushmen, they are fain to change their manners to fawning sycophancy. . . . these free sons of the desert may settle the point by a poisoned arrow."

We have already seen how Burchell ([1824] 1953:197; see p. 36 above) found "Bushmen" "possessed of *large herds of cattle.*" No more concise depiction of the variety of economic circumstances in which San-speaking peoples were found in the early nineteenth century and the changes then being imposed by combined difaqane and colonial pressures can be given than this by Livingstone (Schapera, ed., 1961, 4:161):

> The Bushmen of the Desert are perhaps the most degraded of the human family. Those near the river Zouga [Botletli] look much better. The river supplies them with fish and "tsitla" [bullrush roots], and they seem expert in the use of bow & arrow, for they have killed nearly all the lions. The Botletli are real Bushmen in appearance and language, yet about twelve years ago were in possession of large herds of cattle. (We saw specimens of their cattle, the horns of which measured from six to eight feet from point to point.) The Bushmen are very numerous on all sides of both Lake and River.

Livingstone ([1857] 1912:119), on his second trip to the north, again mentions San stockholding, this time in the dry plains north of Ntwetwe Pan: "Came among our old friends the Bushmen. . . . They refrain from eating the goat, which is significant of their feelings to the only animal they could have domesticated in their desert home."

Those people Livingstone called Botletli are today called Bateti (or Deti by linguists) and are said by Schapera (1953:83, Schapera, ed., 1961, 4:161) to have referred to themselves as BaUra (a variant spelling of Barwa), but this term, if indeed some Bateti applied it to themselves, was surely an admission by those particular people of impoverished economic status rather than a designation of group identity. There can be little doubt that these peoples owned substantial herds, for Sebetwane told Livingstone ([1857] 1912:65) that "twice he had lost all his cattle by the attacks of the Matabele [Amandebele]. . . . he stocked himself again among the Botletli, on Lake Kumandau [Lake Xau], whose herds were of the long-horned species of cattle."

Further assurance that many San-speaking peoples were accustomed to managing cattle at this time is provided by another remark by Livingstone, this time in a letter to William Thompson dated 17 September 1853: "All in the party knocked down by fever. . . . But for two Bushmen who managed the loose oxen and other wise assisted, we could not have moved" (Schapera, ed., 1961, 4:241). He was at this point 100 kilometers north of the Botletli River, and—since he made a point of distinguishing between Bateti and other San-speakers—it is likely that he refers here to men of a different group.

Livingstone ([1857] 1912:113, 116) also records San participation as primary producers in the ostrich-feather and ivory trade: "It requires the utmost address of the Bushmen . . . yet the quantity of feathers collected annually shows that the slaughter must be considerable." Later he states ([1857] 1912:119) that the "Bushmen profit" by the sale of these feathers. Another group of San-speakers, some of whom are described as being "at least six feet high," killed many elephants with their long-bladed spears. These statements, plus those of other Europeans who came immediately after Livingstone, offer convincing evidence that San peoples were producing for the Cape and Moçambique markets before any whites came into the area.

I shall return to the significance of these records in the closing section of this chapter, but it is revealing to insert at this point some observations made twenty-three years earlier in the Kwena region—those of Andrew Geddes Bain in 1826 (Lister 1949:55). Bain describes cattle "remarkable for the amazing size of their horns"; these cattle were the progeny of animals raided from Bakgalagadi ba Ngologa in the 1770s. These latter people had been Bakgwatlha who came to be designated Bakgalagadi (this means simply people of the Kalahari Desert) after having been driven into the desert by Bangwaketse (Schapera 1942:2–3, 1953:83; Ncgoncgo 1977). In the process, by capturing Ngologa stock, Bangwaketse first came into possession of the western sandveld type of long-horned cattle, and to this day they apply the term *dingologa* (things of the Bangologa) to cattle of this type. Campbell (1982:18) places a branch of Bangologa with herds of such cattle in Ngamiland by the beginning of the eighteenth century, at least one hundred years before Batawana arrived. Okihiro (1976:128–29) finds that these people began their northward move from the Molopo River between 1550 and 1600.

Other cases of changes in nomenclature applied to peoples who had been marginalized during this period can be noted to give perspective to the tangled mixture of "bushmanizing" terminology institutionalized at this time. Schapera (1942:3) records that a group of northern Cape Batlhapa (those Setswana-speaking "Bachapins" mentioned by Lubbock as having just learned pastoral ways; see p. 14 above), who had been rich cattle owners at the beginning of the nineteenth century, suffered devastating losses in a series of battles and raids. They subsequently allied themselves with a Korana group (a Nama-speaking people) and were then—until they recouped their losses through raids of their own—called Barwa by Bangwaketse who drove off their attack at Lobatse: "It was at Pisane that a war broke out between Molete and the tribes of the South, some people called Barwa—bushmen" (Botswana National Archives [hereafter BNA] 1926b).

The location of that battle is still called Phata ea Barwa (Bushman Pass). But pristine fellowship notwithstanding, it appears that alliances, then as now, were ephemeral; Kinsman (1981:185) recites an account by the son of a wealthy Motlhapa who told John Campbell in 1815 that he lost his whole vast herd in a raid by Korana and thus "became a poor man, which obliged him for some time to live among the wild Bushmen, to sustain sustenance." One gathers from this that who you know was as basic then as now.

Beinart (1982:124) notes that in a similar instance Mpondo who had become impoverished of cattle by difaqane struggles sometimes took up a foraging existence, "earning for themselves the name *abatwa* [the Xhosa form of Barwa] as they adopted 'Bushman' hunting techniques." And, "Similarly, Knudsen noted about Tibot's group [of Nama allied with Jonker Afrikaner] (later part of Berseba): 'If they have cattle, this is their only mainstay; if their herds get depleted, their life goes, or they become Bushmen again'" (Lau 1982:131). Elphick (1977) has synthesized many analogous cases for the Cape from early European records.

Even more revealing, Hahn ([1881] 1971:3) wrote, "The Khoi-khoi often speak of !Uri-San (white Bushmen) and mean the low white vagabonds and runaway sailors who visit their country." Recall that Kgosidintsi referred to Boers as the "white Bushmen" of the British. Hahn ([1881] 1971:101) notes further: "The poor Namaquas are also called by the others, Bushmen, especially when they are servants, or if they lead a Bushmen's life, and have no cattle and sheep." It was often the case that no distinction whatever was made; the Reverend Mr. Wookey tended to fuse those peoples he called Bushmen and Bakgalagadi, while J. Moffat (BNA 1887) said of Bushmen that "their appearance, their walk and their language at once mark them out as Bakhalahardi." In other words, it was not necessary to be something vaguely "San" to be rwa/twa, "Bushman." I shall return to this point and its implications for San historiography.

Neither was it necessary to be "Bushman" to lose a battle. In 1855 MaCabe, the trader we met watering his oxen and dogs on melons, rode on a Boer commando raid against a small San settlement near the Molopo River. Three Boers were killed, and MaCabe narrowly escaped the arrows and guns of the victorious San defenders (Tabler 1973:74).

Atlantic Roads

A western flanking movement was also undertaken by the British. Thirteen years earlier than Livingstone's entry into Ngamiland, Captain (later Sir) James Alexander ([1838] 1967, 1:iv−xi) had been commissioned to explore what is now northern Namibia in order "to promote trade and . . . to become acquainted with the Damaras [Ovaherero]" and to extend British geographical knowledge of and commerce with that region (fig. 3.6). In other words, one purpose of Alexander's undertaking was to investigate Herero cattle as a source of food to supply the Atlantic shipping trade, principally the refreshing station at Saint Helena, and for the guano mines of Ichaboe Island (BNA, n.d.).

Alexander was not just wandering off into the wild blue yonder; like Livingstone, he had reasonably good information about the peoples he would meet and the products of the land all the way up to the Cunene and Okavango rivers, although he went only as far as the vicinity of modern Windhoek. His information was based on knowledge general to the native peoples of the Cape, who acquired it through social exchange networks and passed it on to their European masters. He could draw as well on four journals kept by eighteenth-century Dutch explorers of Great Namaqualand (roughly the southern two-thirds of present-day Namibia). Three of these journals are of interest to our purpose: that of Carel Brink, who went with Captain Hendrik Hop as far as Keetmanshoop in 1761; that of Hendrik Wikar, who lived north of the Orange River in the 1770s; and that of Willem van Reenan, who reached the copper mines at present-day Rehoboth in January 1792.

Brink (Mossop 1947:51), in 1761, describes the copper and cattle country of the people "called Damrocquas, though at times also Tamaquas . . . [and says that] . . . beads (of blue glass, some of which were oblong squares, some round) were obtained by them from another nation who lived still farther away and who were of a yellow or tawny hue and were named Sandamrocquas, but by others named Briquas or Birinas." Damrocquas and Tamaquas are probably alternate spellings of the same name. Dama/Tama (meaning black, dark) is a Nama term for Ovaherero and Ovambanderu; San combined with a form of Dama is Nama for Bushmen who are like Ovaherero in that they keep cattle; Biri/Bri (from biri = goat) is combined with qua (people) or nas (those of), thus Goat People, and applied by Nama to Batswana. Brink records two important pieces of information here: first, there are "Bushmen" who are herders; second, he lists a number of peoples who were links in the trade networks stretching into Angola. The multiplicity of

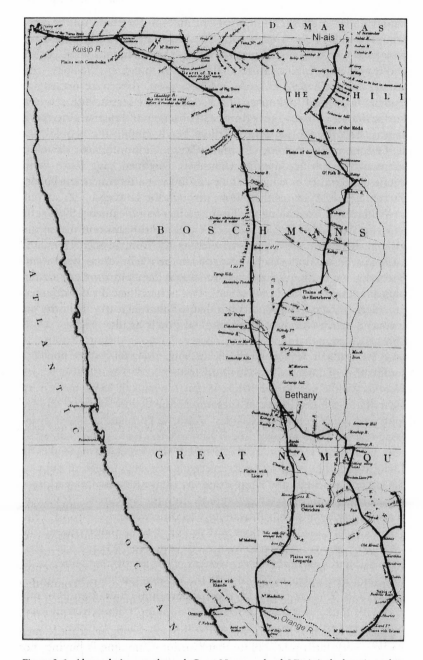

Figure 3.6. Alexander's route through Great Namaqualand. Ni-ais is the location where the dialogue with Aramap (Jonker Afrikaner) took place. (From a photocopy of part of Alexander's ([1838] 1967) original map.)

names underscores the multiplicity of links in the trade routes. Portuguese beads of the kind he describes circulated in these networks; they had been introduced into the Kongo two hundred years earlier and traded into Angola shortly thereafter (Birmingham 1981:26–39, 83; Miller 1983:132–34). As we have seen, they were present at VunguVungu, Xaro, Homasi, and Tsodilo in the seventeenth century. Furthermore, virtually every European observer of the early nineteenth century records the presence of these beads among the peoples described, no matter who or where they were. Okihiro (1976:187–89) summarizes such accounts by Campbell, Methuen, and Smith, who detailed the routes by which Bakaa and Bakwena received these beads. Tlou (1972:173) traces these links through the sandveld.

Wikar, who lived along the Orange River in exile during the 1770s (Mossop 1935:29–79), describes the eighteenth-century trade on the Orange River for these beads as well as for iron, copper, ivory, tobacco, cattle, and hides that was carried on between Nama, the Tswana Barolong and Batlhapa, and Samgomamkoa (San, plus gomas = cattle, plus qua; that is, cattle-keeping San). The archaeologically documented precolonial trade routes had continued to function, carrying newly introduced articles along with traditional goods as they became available. As Birmingham (1981:38) observed, "Long distance footpaths used by the salt traders probably became the avenues for the dissemination of European goods and influences." The English trader George Westbeech (Tabler 1963:49), at Linyanti in 1886, made very clear the continental span of these precolonial trade routes: "Had a long talk with Felisberto Guedes Sousa, a Portuguese trader from Benguela on the west coast, about Major Serpa Pinto [who claimed to have been the first person to have crossed Africa, a claim made also by Livingstone]. He laughs as does everyone else about here, about . . . his great explorings, and simply says, as I have long maintained, that he just came with the trading footpath from the west coast." It was on those earlier records that Alexander was proceeding.

Alexander's second purpose was to find a route that bypassed the "Kallihari desert" and communicated with the "Maquainas" [Bakwena]; that is, to tap the trade sources of the interior stretching from the Namibian central highlands into the Kalahari and beyond. Alexander ([1838] 1967, 2:157–59) records part of his conversation to this end with Jonker Afrikaner, the Nama captain: "I am extremely anxious to pass either through the Damaras of the plains [Ovaherero], or to travel towards the Eastern Ocean. . . . and I was in hopes that we had got beyond the Kallihari desert also, and that a belt of well watered country stretched across Africa from where we now are, to the country of the Maquainas. . . . 'This is not the case,' replied Aramap [Jonker Afrikaner]."

Alexander succeeded in his first assignment; the Cape Town traders Dixon and Morris were established at Walvis Bay just five years later in 1841 and began systematically to supply to the Atlantic routes cattle bartered from the interior (Naude 1931; Esterhuyse 1968 : 11; Kienetz 1977 : 556). Cattle had previously been obtained at several points along the Namib coast; American whalers are known to have bartered at various bays there before 1793 (Kienetz 1977 : 556). In 1836 Alexander ([1838] 1967, 2 : 90–96) met some of these Americans at the mouth of the Kuiseb, who traded muskets and powder for Nama oxen and small stock; he also found there skeletons of white sailors who had been killed in former years by Nama for interfering with their women (Alexander [1838] 1967, 2 : 80–81).

By the 1830s this trade had taken on substantial proportions; one American captain "expected to purchase cheaply two or three thousand cattle from the Nama in the interior and to return to the United States with a shipload of hides" (Kienetz 1977 : 556). Alexander ([1838] 1967, 1 : 102–3) records that this coastal trade depended on supplies from far into the interior. Indeed, "great numbers of livestock must have been sent out from the interior during the 1840s; [the Rhenish missionary Henrich] Scheppmann reported that during his stay at Walfish Bay between January and March 1845, 'exceptionally many ships have come here, six to nine at once; they come from Ichaboe and purchase oxen here.'" On his way to Walfish Bay, Scheppmann saw 350 ships with some 6,000 crewmen and workmen digging guano at Ichaboe (Kienetz 1977 : 557–58); these are obviously not actual counts, but they do indicate large numbers. It was these men—and those at Saint Helena—who were being fed with beef from the interior. The implications for interior peoples of this intense trade at a distance are substantial and will be examined shortly.

Alexander did not reach Bakwena or other Batswana, however, because he was dissuaded from any attempt by Jonker Afrikaner, who had gotten thirty pairs of tusks a short time previously on the Nossob, which he called the river of the Bechuanas, and wanted to preserve the route for his own use (Alexander [1838] 1967, 2 : 159–60). Nevertheless, British attempts to open a direct route from the Atlantic to the interior were not abandoned, and ultimately they succeeded.

The Time of Troubles

Before examining the next move of the British, it is necessary to consider some aspects of indigenous history that had occurred before

these incursions by Europeans, yet recently enough to have been recorded from the lips of witnesses. This will enable us to gauge the
degree to which indigenous peoples in the western half of the subcontinent no less than their eastern counterparts were being pushed, and
were pushing each other, into realignments of their previous political
geography, under pressures partly induced by the very people who
were doing the recording.

The difaqane (Setswana, mfecane in Nguni languages: the time of
troubles) wars of the 1820s, although originating in Natal on the far
eastern side of the continent, were overwhelming in scope, and their
consequences were felt even in Namibia and Ngamiland, where some
of the final battles were fought. These upheavals not only disrupted the
established order among peoples, they also left them less able to resist
subsequent Boer incursions (Ncgoncgo 1982a: 171) and thus made
them more receptive to English promises of protection.

Of immediate interest is a series of events that followed the battle
at Dithejwane, which took place in June 1823 (Thompson 1969:
391–446). The defeated Sotho group, who later, on the Linyanti tributary of the Zambezi, became known as Bakololo under Sebetwane,
went north and defeated the newly established Batawana at Toteng on
the tip of Lake Ngami. They were in turn defeated by Ovambanderu
west of the lake, who then occupied Toteng; this was about 1826 (Nettleton 1934, BNA 1926c: 5, Tlou 1972: 14). The Otjimbanderu name
for Toteng, Engarambuyu—to make poor with the spear—commemo-
rates this victory (Peters 1972: 221–22). Campbell (1982: 9) concludes that Otjiherero-speakers must have been in Ngamiland "well
before 1800 for by 1820 they were fighting the Tawana for grazing
rights just west of Lake Ngami . . . to this day there are Mbanderu (a
branch of the Herero) living at Omaweneno near Tshabong who speak
Nama, a Khoi language they must have adopted a considerable time
ago." Andersson's unpublished diary (State Archive Service, n.d.: 384)
records further confirmation of pre-nineteenth-century Ovambanderu
presence in the Kalahari: "Jonker confirmed all what we had formerly
heard of the Ovationa [Batawana], viz, that in former years they often
fought with the Damaras, whom they always conquered, and who then,
it appears, lived very far east." Recently collected oral histories sub-
stantiate these historical sources, with the caveat that Herero peoples
did not settle everywhere in western Ngamiland but seem to have been
most active in the Qangwa Valley and southward. I shall return to this
in the next chapter.

In about that same year, 1826, Bangwaketse were dislodged by

Mzilikazi's Amandebele, and some of them went westward, where they fought Ovambanderu at Matsheng near present-day Lehututu. In 1834, at Monnyelatsela near Ghanzi, the Ngwaketse Kgosi Sebego forced local Ovaherero to pay tribute to him (Schapera 1942:8–9; Campbell 1982:19). Amandebele, in turn, were forced by the Boers in 1837 to quit the Transvaal; they moved north to the Nata River at a place called Nekati and subsequently east into what is now Zimbabwe, whence they periodically for the next fifty years raided the cattle of the Kalahari and Okavango all the way into Namibia (Chirenje 1973: 13–17, 1977:30–31).

While the last of these events was taking place, Alexander was on the Fish River at about 25° south latitude, returning from his explorations to the north. One of his Nama guides, Hendrik Buys (Boois), told him they were near the old trade route followed by Bechuanas, who came to trade their small axes with the Namaqua for cattle, and that a few years earlier he had himself gone east from Bethenie across the Nossob River to hunt for ivory in the Kalahari (this would have been about 1830). This route was part of the network over which Barolong and Bakwena (the Birina of the Nama) had traded and raided since the seventeenth century (Parsons 1983:45); it was a link in the chain that had brought Portuguese beads to the attention of Wikar on the Orange a half-century earlier. In the southern sandveld somewhere east of the Nossob, Buys and his companions had come upon a town that had had many occupants but was then recently abandoned; a local Boschman (Bushman) told them it had been built by people called Manchatee,[9] who had been attacked there by Kamaka Damara (kamaka is a corruption of gomas = cattle; i.e., these were Ovambanderu) not long before. These battles are well remembered and can be dated with reasonable assurance. Kuruman, an Omumbanderu in his seventies in 1926, heard this account from his father: "Both Herero and Bandero were fighting with the Barolong and they were strong on both sides. The war lasted for some months because the Damara used to get fresh regiments from SW Africa & the Barolong were getting the mephato [age regiments] from South. However, later the Barolong pushed the Herero and Bandero out" (BNA 1926b).

Two items of testimony help fix the time of these events. First, Kuruman said that Katjamuwaha (Tjamuaha) was a leader in the fighting. And Moses Malata, an elderly Morolong in 1926, describes the capture of Herero black and white hornless pack oxen during the final battles. Vedder (1938:152) gives Tjamuaha's birth year as about 1790; he lists the oviuondo (year name) of 1832 as Ojongombondo, the year of the black and white oxen. Gibson (1977; see also Almagor 1980b) affirms the accuracy of Vedder's Herero oviuondo, so that we may place the events referred to in the first half of the 1830s.

There is further evidence for Herero peoples in places far beyond their present location. Alexander records that he had seen cattle with Herero dewlap cuts and Herero captives at Nama encampments in the vicinity as well as much farther south. He bought one of these captives, a boy about nine years old, for two cloth handkerchiefs and two strings of glass beads; he named this boy Saul Sheppard and later educated him in England at Woolwich (Alexander [1838] 1967, 1:219–25). Sheppard later, as secretary to Tjamuaha's son Maharero, played a key role in negotiations with Palgrave when England briefly considered annexing South-West Africa.

We shall shortly return to these Ovaherero and the significance of their unexpected presence in these places, but first we must cast a preliminary glance at another group of people, these making their way rapidly northward. The Orlams (from Afrikaans, oor landers = people from other lands; they are called Ovakwena in Otjiherero)[10] were Nama peoples from the Cape who escaped enslavement in the colony by adopting guns, horses, ox wagons, and the accompanying accoutrements of a frontier existence (Kienetz 1977; Lau 1981). In 1823 Jonker Afrikaner led a commando of these mounted men from the Orange River to fight the Ovaherero south of Rehoboth. He remained in that central Namibian area, raiding northward and eastward for the cattle that he traded at Walvis Bay via the road he subsequently had had cut to that harbor before Alexander arrived in 1836.

By the first years of the 1840s, another group of Orlams under Amraal Lambert had settled at Naosanabis and Gobabis—where they defeated the resident Ovambanderu—and began to extract the ivory, feathers, skins, and cattle of Ngamiland for their trade to the west and south. A year later, in 1843, the Reverend Joseph Tindall established among them the second and third of the Wesleyan missions in Namibia (Tindall 1959). There was opposition to the Orlam advance, of course—as at Bosfontein in 1822, when local San-speaking people put up such fierce resistance that the Reverend Mr. Archbell was forced to flee the battle—but generally guns and horses prevailed.

The Orlams, because of their early monopoly of guns and horses, had great power and freedom of movement—so long as their ties to the trade of the Cape and Atlantic were not broken. But they were the creations of that trade and could not operate without it. To meet their need, the Orlams had to control large hinterlands whose indigenous populations—Nama, Herero, and Bushmen—were forcibly stimulated to supply from their own means the surplus product the Orlams required for their external trade. As has been amply recorded by many missionary observers and synthesized by Lau (1979, 1981, 1982), by 1850 the Orlams had substantially dispossessed almost all of the indigenous Nama (Ovaserandu in Otjiherero, the Red Nation, Rooi Nasi), as well as San-speakers, of Namibia and had subdued a large number of Ovaherero.

Nevertheless, in 1851, Carl Hugo Hahn (1984:509) could still write, "Unattached Namas, Bushmen, and Damaras are to be found in Hereroland."[11] That statement would become less true as the century progressed; Tindall (1959:142, emphasis added) had already remarked that in 1842 "the wild beasts of the field and the fowls of the air [had] *during the last few years* become accustomed to feed on human flesh"; this was in 1846. In 1851 Jonker himself extended his elephant-hunting grounds to Otjozundju; in 1846 he had raided the Ovambanderu in the east.

In the 1860s and 1870s, Ngamiland was considered the prime elephant-hunting ground of Africa, and this was the domain of Amraal, situated at Gobabis, where he was "visited annually by trading caravans of the Bechuana tribes. . . . [Tindall described the country in the 1840s.] . . . Cattle Damaras are very numerous; said to be very rich in cattle. Their number and extent of their country is unknown" (Tindall 1959:32).

Tindall speaks of thousands of people settled around Amraal at the beginning of the 1840s—Nama, Herero, Bergdamara, San; he also says (1959:119) that from 1846 to 1851 Amraal mounted at least one raid per year on Mbanderu cattle to the northeast. One example will suffice: "Set off north of Station with chief Ameral . . . on the third day halted at Epukuico [Epukiro]. . . . twenty miles riding brought us to another strong extensive irrigation [probably Otjunda, of which we will hear more]. . . . not meeting with the Damaras I wished to see, and hearing from others that they had fled farther north, convinced that the report I had heard was true, I returned." This was 14 March 1846; in the previous month, Tindall (1959:118) recorded that a Nama commando "attacked several Bushmen villages, robbed them of their sheep and goats . . . south east of the place, Elephant's Fountain."

A Bushman had told him (Tindall 1959:34) in 1843 that the Rooi Volk (Red People; i.e., northern Nama) were their main enemies who took their property. Since livestock was the principal property normally taken, we may assume that it was this the man was referring to, although of course it might also have been ivory or feathers. In any case, it would have been property of commercial value. There are no

records of raids for strictly domestic goods; most accounts of the time
agree that such property was usually destroyed. A similar oral account
was given to Köhler (1986:206) in which Kxoe assert that their cattle
had been taken from them by Hambukushu.[12]

Tindall's accounts of San stockholding in the west are roughly contemporary with those of Livingstone in the east. The German missionary Irle (1906a:158), writing of central Namibia in the 1860s (twenty
years after Tindall), substantiates the statement that some "Bushmen"
continued to own livestock at that time: "The Bushmen exist off wild
animals. . . . there, where they live together in small encampments
under a headman, they also have smallstock, goats and sheep.[13] Irle
(1906a:154–57) not only speaks of Bergdamara cattle—which, like
"Bushmen" cattle, were not supposed to exist—but reproduces a pho-
tograph of a kraal full of fat cattle belonging to these people.

San stockkeeping had been noted much earlier. Wikar (Mossop
1935:31) wrote in his journal of 1779: "Bushman Hottentots came
from the Zandveldskraal or Samgomamkoa. They have cattle but only
a few, and yet they do not steal, but, because they support themselves
by shooting game and what they find in the veld, they are called
Chaboup or Bushmen. . . . [further on (Mossop 1935:37) Wikar de-
scribes] Bushmen known as Nanningai . . . who have cattle." Elphick
(1977:27–28) lists numbers of such references and notes that the
term San could apply to all sorts of small-scale pastoralists as well as
to foragers, but not to wealthy stockowners or to genealogical members of the Khoikhoi clans.

Part of the process by which economic differentiation was intensified is well illustrated by van Reenan, writing in 1791 (Mossop
1935:315):

Asked why they kept no cattle as did the Namaquas, the Damraas [the Berg-
damara of the time] replied that they did have livestock in plenty, sheep, goats,
as well as horned cattle, but that the Namaquas had made themselves masters
of the flocks. . . . they also said that aforetimes they had defended themselves
against the Namaquas, but that since the use of iron had increased amongst
the latter they have many arrows and assigais which they trade from the
Bastard Hottentots [Orlams], and they no longer could carry on operations
against them.

The Namaqua van Reenan referred to were northern Nama, the Red
People, who, remember, had shortly thereafter increased their plunder
of Bushmen stock in the presence of Tindall.

Both ivory hunting and raiding were means of accumulating the
commodities with which to obtain the European goods that were be-

coming ever more vital to the maintenance of Orlam life. Coffee and sugar, cloth and china had become essential ingredients of that life, while guns and powder were required to maintain hegemony over others and thus ensure the steady flow of these exotic goods. Nangati (1982:142) makes a similar point for Bakwena in the 1840s: "In no time, foreign articles, such as utensils, brought by traders started to compete with indigenous manufactures. . . . the consumption of imported edibles, such as tea and coffee, luxuries, such as snuff, and ornaments, like beads and trinkets, became habitual. It should be noted that consumption of these goods did not go far down the social hierarchy." Traders, some in the guise of missionaries, were already there to supply these needs and to keep each tier of production in debt to its creditor. Tindall (1959:33, 36) provides a glimpse of a nineteenth-century huckster evangelist working the hot African frontier:

Assembled the people in the temporary chapel to hold a missionary meeting. . . . Chief Ameral spoke as follows. . . . "you whose ears must open must say that all we hear is true, and we must give." . . . seventeen head of cattle were subscribed, 98 sheep and goats and a few sjamboks [whips] . . . [and two weeks later] . . . was presented with 80 sheep by Jonker from his people . . . on Tuesday morning he gave a cow, and brought a cow and 5 additional sheep also a goat. I afterwards received another goat, a koodoo skin, an elephant's tusk, and 8 sjamboks. Had preaching this morning.

But there were not yet, in 1850, enough traders. They would soon arrive.

At this point we should turn our attention to more evidence for eighteenth-century trade to the north. Alexander ([1838] 1967, 1:172), southeast of what is now called Windhoek in 1837, spoke with Ovaherero who told him they were accustomed to trade with white men they called "Oban"[14] at a place north of the Cunene on an inlet of the sea: "We exchanged our cattle for iron to make javelins, for copper to make beads, and we also got knives and calabashes from them." Vedder ([1928] 1966:188) records that he was told in the 1920s by Ovaherero in the Kaokoveld that the cowrie shells they prized came from "the beaches of Angola." Gibson (1962:621) identifies the probable location of this trade as Baia dos Tigres, south of Moçamedes on the Angolan coast, and says that later Ovaherero traded ostrich feathers and ivory for guns.

The Portuguese had established trade outposts around Luanda in the early seventeenth century but did not become active in southern Angola until the latter part of the eighteenth century (Birmingham 1981:83, 116; Miller 1983:135), when coastal expeditions were undertaken and ivory began to be extracted from the interior. In 1790 Gregorio Mendes began exploration and direct trade on the rivers south of Moçamedes (Sousa Dias 1948:199–209); as we have seen, native trade here had already been carrying European goods for a long time. Ovaherero had tapped into this new European trade very quickly.

Fourteen years after Alexander, in 1851, Galton ([1853] 1971:199) estimated that Ovaherero still obtained half the iron they needed from the Portuguese, through the Ovambo from the north, the other half by then being supplied by the Orlam trade from the south. Carl Hugo Hahn (1984:510), who was with Galton at the time, wrote: "One finds there on the other side [of the Cunene River] Portuguese, who it seems are travelling merchants, who trade glass beads, etc. for ivory, and I think also cattle. Iron is to them [Ovambo and Ovaherero] more valuable than copper."[15]

Already in 1851, when Oswell and Livingstone met Sebetwane at Linyanti, they found: "On this Zambezi, as perhaps you know, the Portuguese have considerable trading stations. Sebitoane has only seen one of them, who came seeking slaves, but with the under-slave dealers he has had traffic for the last three or four years. . . . many of Sebitoane's followers were dressed in green baize, red drugget, calico, and cheap, gaudy cloth, some in garments of European manufacture" (Oswell 1900, 2:230, 245). Two years earlier on Lake Ngami, Oswell had observed that Letsholathebe already had limited access to European goods through native intermediaries of other tribes. Not long afterward, in 1855, the Canadian trader Green (1857, 1:535–39; Tabler 1953) reported that Mambari traders (of mixed native and European ancestry) had an established regular trade at Libebe in which they gave guns, powder, beads, and other goods for ivory, cattle, and slaves; he said that Portuguese gunpowder was in such abundant supply that it was traded to Batawana by Hambukushu. By then Lazlo Magyar, a Hungarian trader, with Mambari (*Petermanns* 1860:227–31; Fodor 1983) and others had been trading for two decades in the homeland of Angolan Kqu, who, we may be certain, relayed trade items southward to Zhu and others in the Kalahari below the Okavango-Cunene river systems.

First Steps to Underclass Submergence

The circumstances in which these peoples lived may be reasonably reconstructed. The last to receive guns, horses, and other newly introduced instruments of power were Ovaherero, Bakgalagadi, and "Bushmen." All these peoples were at first, in the early nineteenth century, farthest from the three major entrepôts of European trade routes in southern Africa and could receive only those things that nearer peoples had no use for or were willing to part with in exchange for products they could not appropriate through tribute or intimidation. This is part of the reason San-speakers, especially, but to a degree Ovaherero and Bakgalagadi as well, were disadvantaged relative to Tswana and Orlam groups. There is also no doubt that many San-speakers were already to varying degrees in the incipient stages of underclass submergence and were thus deprived of opportunities to acquire the introduced instruments of power.

During the first half of the nineteenth century, many San-speakers appear to have retained significant autonomy. Tlou (1972:140) says that at first a voluntary clientship in a form long existing among southern African groups was extended by Batawana to San and other Ngamiland peoples. A sketch of the first contacts between Batswana and San-speakers given by Tshekedi Khama, Kgosi of Bangwato, to the Reverend Mr. Haile (London Missionary Society 1935) as part of the LMS's investigation of slavery in Bechuanaland is highly illuminating:

I will now proceed to describe the contact of the Bamangwato people with the Masarwa. I have said that the Bamangwato are hunters and also a pastoral people. Therefore their first contacts came about in the hunting field, the Masarwa being themselves hunters. . . . There was in those times no question of overlordship of one people over another. It was simply a mutual understanding; at that time we had no strength by which we could force them to become our servants. If we had had such power the history of our contact with them would have been similar to the history of the white people with them.

Tshekedi was speaking of the mid-eighteenth century; at this time Tswana polities do not appear to have been radically different from those of contemporary Khoisan. At that time Bakwena, Bangwato, and the other eponymous Tswana groups were small and mobile (Okihiro 1976:13), probably not exceeding one hundred families who lived primarily from the milk of their herds, hunted meat, and gathered wild foods; short-season crops—mainly melons, cowpeas, and millet—along with some sorghum were secondary supplements (Okihiro 1976:65). There was no overarching Tswana unity, and leaders had only limited local authority.

Indeed, it may be that at this time some Tswana groups were primarily goat keepers, not great cattle herders, as the Nama designation Biriqua suggests (Parsons 1974a:647). Lichtenstein (Spohr 1973:81) says that at the beginning of the nineteenth century some Tswana groups got almost all their pack and riding oxen in trade from Khoisan, but such observations must be balanced against known fluctuations in the fortunes of conflict summarized earlier in this chapter. Biriqua seems to have been simply a Khoikhoi equivalent of the Setswana Barwa categorization of peoples considered economically inferior. It is also the case, however, that Europeans of this time seldom cite cattle as a major reason for dealing with Tswana groups on the Kalahari margins, as they do from before the beginning of contact with Nama and Ovaherero. Indeed, the efforts of Alexander, Livingstone, and others were geared toward reaching the greater riches they perceived to lie farther north and west.

In this fluid social mosaic, not only Tswana-speaking but other refugees from difaqane and Boer disruptions were recruited into those Tswana polities on the southern verge of the Kalahari—Kwena, Ngwato, Rolong, Tlhapa—who shared a double advantage: they were at once far enough away from the most severe of those disruptions to gain strength by incorporating many peoples dislodged in the struggles and near enough to the objects of mercantile desire that in part fueled those disruptions to reap the benefits of the harvest (fig. 3.7). The growth rate of these Tswana polities is astonishing. Some estimates are available. In the 1830s, Willoughby (n.d.) thought that no more than 300 people were associated with Sechele at Shokwane (Tshonwane), and Okihiro (1976:23–24) summarizes eyewitness estimates of Kwena population growth over the fifteen years following 1840: in 1843 Livingstone also reported 300 Bakwena under Sechele; these were joined in that year by about 350 booRatshosa and in 1849 by 3,600 other peoples, including Bakaa. In 1857 Livingstone estimated 20,000 "Bakwena" living in Sechele's town, Dithubaruba. Starting from similarly small numbers, Bangwato had grown to 600 households in 1842; in 1866 Shoshong, Sekgoma's capital and the center of eastern Kalahari trade, with nominally 30,000 inhabitants was the second largest settlement—after Cape Town—in southern Africa (Parsons 1977:115).

Recruiting all sorts of peoples irrespective of nominal designations was clearly the way these Tswana polities achieved the critical mass for political domination. Numbers alone were not enough, however; arguably, Orlam centers in Namibia controlled populations as large through the 1840s, yet they did not attain anything approaching the formative state status achieved by Batswana. Again, it was a fortuitous combination of factors that favored some Tswana groups—in reality, mainly Bangwato—in this regard. In the first place, their land straddled the most profitable trade route to the interior that, in Parsons's apt phrase, splayed out to all, not just one or two, of the major supply regions beyond what was then the frontier. European merchants along with native refugee recruits were sucked into this funnel.

A second factor was political. Kgari, Kgosi of Bangwato about 1826–28, is credited with rationalizing the incipient socioeconomic stratification in Tswana political structure to control both the spectacular increase in numbers of people subject to the kgosi and, more to the point, their equally spectacular increase in productive potential. The system Kgari instituted, called the kgamelo (milk jug) system, greatly enhanced the class ranking inherent in Tswana social structure and strengthened local elites by giving them direct economic and administrative control over the lower classes in their sphere of assigned responsibility. The system consolidated Ngwato dominance over other peoples in Gangwato, the country of Bangwato (Sebolai 1978:18). Sechele adopted this system for Bakwena soon after he became kgosi in 1831 (Okihiro 1976:135–36).

Cattle were critical in this system because they were lent out in patronage by elites to poorer clients under obligatory conditions, called mafisa, in which a client's assets were mortgaged against the safety of his patron's property and his support of the patron's interests. It was clearly to the advantage of second-level administrators, batlhanka, to arrogate all cattle in their districts to themselves, for they thus held not only the intrinsic value of the animals but also—by parceling them out in mafisa—their far higher mortgage value, by means of which the allegiance of subordinates was ensured (Parsons 1974a:648, 1977:114). Those San, Bakgalagadi, and other minorities who owned cattle were quickly dispossessed of their herds in this process, and many were reduced to landless servants (Schapera 1970:89; Parsons 1974a:648; Okihiro 1976:135–37). This latter group was thus transformed into an underclass called malata, serfs, in Sengwato and Sekwena (the Ngwato and Kwena dialects of Setswana). Even so, not all persons in the category "Bushman" were disfranchised in this manner; a substantial number were incorporated into the middle ranks of Ngwato and Kwena polities (Ncgoncgo 1982b:29).

Thus the status of those peoples undergoing subjugation was by no means uniform throughout the Kalahari and its fringes at the middle of the nineteenth century. Motzafi-Haller (1987) catalogs the process by which Bapedi of the Tswapong Hills in Gangwato were gradually brought under the hegemony of Ngwato rulers and subjected to tribute levies, labor extraction, land appropriation, and resettlement in the later eighteenth and early nineteenth centuries without being reduced to serfdom. Bakgalagadi lived at this time under varying conditions of dependency, partly as a function of modes of subsistence and

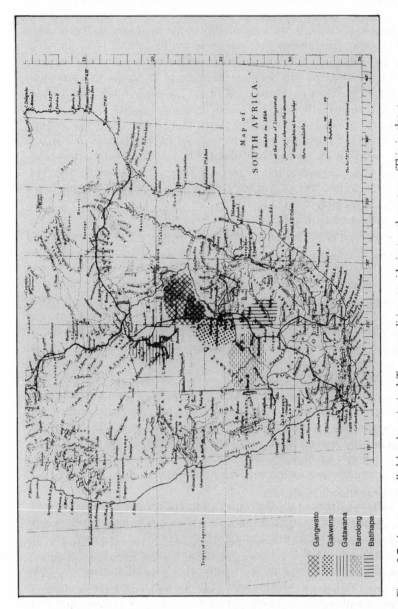

Figure 3.7. Areas controlled by the principal Tswana polities at mid-nineteenth century. (This is also a photocopy of part of the map of Livingstone's travels, a smaller portion of which is reproduced as fig. 3.4.)

partly based on location (Okihiro 1976:137). The same was true of San-speakers. In Ngamiland it was not until 1847, when Mogalakwe became regent, that Batawana were able to begin dispossessing San peoples there, initially only those living near the Okavango Delta (Tlou 1972:149). Mogalakwe accomplished this by introducing a form of the kgamelo system into Tawana social politics for the same reasons that had earlier motivated Kgari and Sechele, and with the same effect (Tlou 1976). A dispossessed serf class (bathlanka in Setawana) was created under the commoner class (basimane in Setawana); both were under the complete authority of ruling elites (dikgosana, those of the kgosi). As in Gangwato and Gakwena, some Bushmen in Gatawana— principally those who owned livestock—were absorbed into the Tawana polity; others withdrew into the sandveld (Tlou 1972:140–41, 149). It was that San majority relegated to the status of batlhanka and malata who later, in the playing out of the colonial process, became pauperized Masarwa, "Bushmen."

At the end of the 1830s the peoples of the Kalahari were distributed more or less as the Europeans found them. There continued to be sporadic fighting, but this was primarily for control of exchange commodities in the inflating market. Corresponding adjustments in the control of specific areas of land took place in this competition, to be sure. In general, however, except in Namibia, where first German and then South African administrations successively annexed ever larger sections of land and reduced native peoples to reservations, the political geography of the African peoples of the Kalahari that emerged about 1840 has been little changed until today. This is due in large part to colonial—and now postcolonial—administrative efforts to maintain the received status quo. That status quo came to be reified first by those administrators themselves and then by twentieth-century students of the region, most especially anthropologists, who thought it reflected ancient traditional land divisions. Figure 3.7 shows the approximate areas controlled by the different Tswana polities that feature prominently in this text.

As we have seen, however, the historical reality that brought about this distribution was quite different. Most dramatically, the different Tswana groups passed from a peripheral position in the region to almost uncontested dominance. In the west, the Orlams were equally expansive in terms of both space encompassed and numbers of people affected. Ovaherero-Ovambanderu, on the other hand, found the area they controlled greatly contracted, and at mid-nineteenth century they were sandwiched between Ovambo, Orlams, and Batawana in northern Namibia-Ngamiland. The various San groups, although they too were displaced and redistributed, are more difficult to trace because they are with rare exceptions referred to by generic terms such as Bushman or Masarwa. The few instances where it is possible to suggest the outlines of movements of these peoples are vague and poorly documented. Sheller (1977:5), for example, records oral traditions of Gxanna movements in the central Kalahari that were initiated "some decades ago" but does not investigate them further (see also Cashdan 1986). English et al. (1980:7) trace some of these movements to the Ndebele displacements of the difaqane period and note their far-reaching effects. The systematic collection and analysis of San oral histories has, however, barely begun; consequently, few firm delineations of movements can be made.

Linguistic evidence points to considerable displacement, but since fine-scale sociolinguistic research is also in its infancy in the region, little can as yet be drawn from it. Traill (1974) finds the Kqoo group of languages in southern Botswana-Namibia to be homogeneous in structure, with local dialectical variants; this suggests relatively recent geographic insulation of speakers of Kqoo dialects. Vossen (1984) posits a separation of Khoe (Central San) languages from Khoikhoi (Nama) at a time coincident with the introduction of Early Iron Age pastoralism into the region, that is, about 2,000 years ago, with more recent dialectical diversification characterizing some of these languages. The results of these studies parallel what is known for the Tswana languages; Setawana, for example, is subdialectically variant from Sengwato, from which it separated two centuries ago, and both of these are further divergent from closely related languages spoken in Transvaal and Lesotho. This suggests similar histories for the two language groups.

In general, however, it is not possible to reconstruct details of San movements from the few nonspecific references given in nineteenth-century accounts. Schinz (1891:394), for example, tells us: "A comparison of words from this dialect with others I gathered at a later opportunity from Bushmen who visited us indicates that the !Kung San tribe is spread not only through all the Omarambo Omatako, but it also stretches in an eastward direction to the vicinity of Lake Ngami."[16] Schinz is here speaking of Namibia-Ngamiland Zhu, not Angola Kqu. He does recognize dialectical differences—Zhu and Kqu are mutually intelligible dialects of each other, while within Zhu, Namibian and Ngamilandian have subdialectic variations—and his account provides valuable information for the presence of Zhu over a large area (he provides word lists that confirm this). Nonetheless, because Schinz then applies the same term (!Kung San) to all the "Bushmen" he meets in the region, we cannot trace the movements of these peoples with the same degree of historical confirmation available for the array of Tswana-speakers—whose speech is as diversified as that of the Zhu group—featured in this narrative. In fact, oral and archival accounts unanimously agree that Zhu did not live in the vicinity of Lake Ngami until late in the nineteenth century when they were taken there as servants of Batawana; the Lake vicinity was the domain of Cexai. This lack of specificity, of course, not only distorts the record but contributes significantly to the apparent invisibility of San-speakers in the history of the Kalahari.

At midcentury, 1850, in the sandveld, many Zhu were not yet subjects of any other group, and in the southwest the Kqoo probably were variably so, although local units of both language groups were certainly paying tribute and contributing labor to others. Theophilus Hahn (1895:23–24) says that as late as 1877—when he spent considerable time in the Gobabis area—the people he calls !a (Nhard or Cexai) north of Ghanzi recognized no overriding hegemony by others, nor did the !Gabi (Kqoo) of the Aminuis area. Nama military commandos ranged pretty much at will, but these were raiding forays, not conquests; after they quickly extracted the current crop of ivory and animals from an area, they withdrew to their home bases. It was only at those bases that Nama exercised anything like full political dominance. Herero-San relations were also varied and flexible. The respect accorded Zhu prowess by Ovaherero, recorded often by Europeans (e.g., Baines 1864:325) and usually attributed by them to a pervasive fear of San poisoned arrows (recall Livingstone's similar thought about Bangwato fears), was actually just one element in the factional disputes then raging over control of resources such as the cattle being pulled out of the interior into the Atlantic trade.

Something more fundamental was at work. To extend Okihiro's (1976:189) observation: European incursions, from an early moment, destroyed local polities and substituted raiding for trading as the dominant form of economic activity among them. Ncgoncgo (1982a:166) makes much the same point: the immediate legacy of difaqane and Boer incursions was that raiding became necessary for survival. In this environment it appears that San peoples at first could hold their own. Vedder (1938:138–39) records that in the mid-eighteenth century, after a failed attack against them by Ovaherero, "the greater part of their [Herero] cattle fell into the hands of the Saan [Heixum]" victors. And Bangwaketse, when fleeing Amandebele in 1826, "at Lehututu came across the Barolong of Molebe, who were running away from the Bushmen" (BNA 1926c). With the interposition of Tswana and European states and the Orlam commando, that ability was mortally impaired. Nangati (1982:142, 144) identifies half of their predicament: "Firearms became an instrument for the expropriation of means of production and subsistence. . . . the nobility achieved considerable power and increased the exploitation of the BaKgalagadi [and one must add, of the 'Bushmen'] through its ruthlessness." The other half was, of course, the corollary of this. San access to economic necessities—both outlets for their products (their means for accumulating exchange value) and sources of competitive supplies—was channeled through these same dominant exploitive powers. In this predicament, poisoned arrows were irrelevant; San peoples were subdued more by political factors than by force of arms.

In the east, as we have seen, the different San groups were in different degrees of subjugation—some Bateti, for example, possessed significant herds, while other San-speakers, nearer the consolidating Kwena and Ngwato powers, were already completely in the service of those powers. As usual, Livingstone ([1857] 1912:114) provides a cogent illustration:

At Lotlakani we met an old Bushman who sat by our fire relating his early adventures. Among these was the killing of five other Bushmen. "Two," said he, counting on his fingers, "were females, one a male, and the other two calves." "What a villain," I exclaimed, "you are, to boast of killing women and children of your own nation! what will God say when you appear before him?"—"He will say," replied he, "that I was a very clever fellow." I at last discovered that, though the word he used was the same which the Bakwains employ when speaking of the Deity, he had only the idea of a chief. He was referring to Sekomi, and his victims were a party of rebels against whom he had been sent.

It seems never to have occurred to Livingstone, despite the distinctions he often made, that not all "Bushmen" were members of the same "nation," any more than were those in the complex web that constitutes "Tswanadom" (Murray 1986:12), in which "the concept of Botswana as a political, social, cultural, or geographic entity did not [yet] exist" (Denbow, Kiyaga-Mulindwa, and Parsons 1985:2). What was obvious to his narrator escaped Livingstone; the various San groups competed as much for the scraps they could get as their masters did for the big money. This man clearly perceived his immediate interest to lie with his "lord"—who probably rewarded him now and then with a cow or a goat, and more regularly with milk and a shirt and tobacco—rather than with some "Bushmen" whose language he may not have understood. In the atmosphere of the time he was, to the detriment of his children's interests, probably correct.

In the remaining decades of the century, San peoples continued to experience rapidly fluctuating conditions. Some momentarily attained a measure of economic gain, but ultimately, with few exceptions, all who had not been absorbed as Tswana—rendering them no longer Bushmen—were reduced to the status of a propertyless class.

Heyday of the Hunters

The major occupation of the second half of the nineteenth century was the consolidation of gains by the emerging Tswana states, including an extension of hegemony over groups who were becoming more thoroughly subject to them. Along with this, and indispensable to it in the context of that time, was competition for trade and for European presence. In this competition, relative geographical location was an important factor in formulating strategy. Thus Letsholathebe in the far northwest invited traders and missionaries to come to him through the territory of other Tswana groups, but—to protect his control of trade—he refused to allow them to proceed to Sebetwane farther north. At the same time Sekgoma (Kgosi of Bangwato)—to maintain his position as monopoly middleman between the British and all of the interior peoples—tried to block the way along which Oswell and Livingstone would have to travel to Letsholathebe, while Sechele (Kgosi of Bakwena), whose daughter Wilson briefly married (this marriage, no doubt, perceived on both sides in strategic terms), urged them on in hopes of recapturing the trade advantage being lost to Bangwato.

Nangati (1980:128) writes, "Earlier, by inviting Livingstone to his settlement at Tshonwane in 1845, Sechele endeavored to solve, at a stroke, his problems of trade and defense"; Livingstone had no illusions about why the Tswana dikgosi were eager to bring missionaries into their orbits: "I need scarcely add that his wish, although sincere, does not indicate any love for the doctrines we teach. It is merely a desire for the protection of temporal benefit which missionaries everywhere are supposed to bring" (Schapera, ed., 1961, 1:127). Livingstone wrote to Tidman on 3 September 1849, "When Sekhomi, the Bamangwato chief, became aware of our intentions to pass into the regions beyond him, with true native humanity he sent men in front of us to drive away all the Bushmen and Bakalihari from our route, in order that, being deprived of their assistance in the search for water, we might, like the Griquas above mentioned, be compelled to retire" (Schapera, ed., 1961, 1:132).

We have already seen how the Orlam Jonker Afrikaner dissuaded Alexander from trying to connect the eastern and western trade routes and thus circumvent Afrikaner's own plans to consolidate the Walvis

Bay–Lake Ngami route under Orlam control. He accomplished this consolidation by the early 1840s, and for the next thirty years even European traders were subject to paying the Orlams what amounted to a toll for use of the route. Palgrave (1877, Annexures: vii–xxxiii) records in his special commission report in 1876 twenty-seven pages of testimony by traders that stresses especially the large levies in goods made upon them by the Nama on the Lake Road.

A trader, Kleinghardt, told his tale of woe in a weak voice:

> Before sun down a messenger came from Barend Beukes to tell me that I was not to go on, that they were going to hold a raad on the question as to whether I was to be allowed to go on. . . . [after several days during which Kleinghardt was forced to unload his waggon and had exhausted his supply of coffee, sugar, and tobacco as gifts]. . . . They said: no we must first speak about the payment. I said what payment. . . . They then left the waggon, I having paid in all £6 and they went away: and some returned with ostrich feathers and offered to trade for coffee and tea, and for nothing else. (Palgrave 1877, Annexure 2: ix–xvii)

He was echoed at this time even by Eriksson, who lost £800 in goods confiscated from one of his traders by Gobabis Orlams. Tindall (1959: 142–43) records an early (1843) instance in which the Walvis Bay trader Dixon had goods taken by the Rooi Volk (Red People) before being allowed to continue: "The Chief's oxen were yoked to Mr. Dixon's waggon and drew it up to the chief's residence. . . . the waggon was returned the following day. A chest had been broken open and goods abstracted. They paid their own price in poor cattle for these things and affirmed they owed no more."

Nonetheless, all three of the main colonial routes—of the British from the south and east, of British and, soon, Germans from the west, and of Portuguese from the north—were to coalesce in northern Namibia-Ngamiland in the 1850s (fig. 3.8), where the last untapped riches—before diamonds and gold—of southern Africa (ivory, feathers, and—of greatest importance—cattle) were to be found. There were many men waiting to tap them.

In mid-1853 Charles John Andersson followed the route from Walvis Bay to Otjimbinde over which he and Francis Galton had traveled in 1851 in their abortive attempt to reach Lake Ngami. Andersson now completed the journey and published a detailed description of the route, along with distances and time of ox-wagon travel between inhabited places and other locations where water could be found (fig. 3.9). The route, of course, was that used by natives long before, subsequently cut for wagons by Orlams, and traveled over in part—as

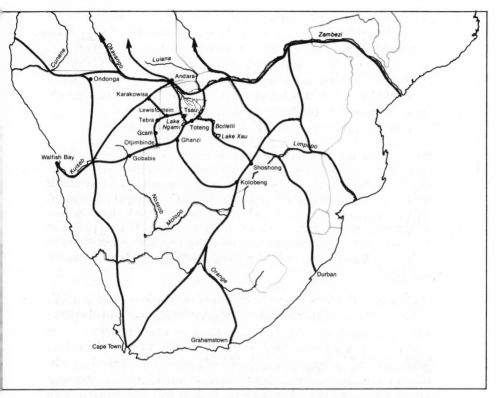

Figure 3.8. Major trade routes in the western half of southern Africa during the late nineteenth century.

we have seen—by European missionaries and traders a decade earlier (Andersson 1854; Tabler 1957: 123–29).

Andersson (1854: 5, 31) describes better than any secondary summary the immediate explosion in trade that occurred in the Lake Ngami region after Livingstone's announcement: "A year had hardly passed away, after its existence was made known, before its shores swarmed with civilized men. . . . [already in 1853] . . . beads were not sought after with the avidity they used to be, such quantities having been imported of late into the lake country, that (to use a vulgar, but very emphatic expression of Letcholatebe) 'the women grunt under their burdens like pigs.'" At that time, the value of the ivory obtained in the Lake region was already estimated to be £4,000 to £5,000 annually (Andersson 1854: 37).

The published journals of both Andersson and Galton are replete

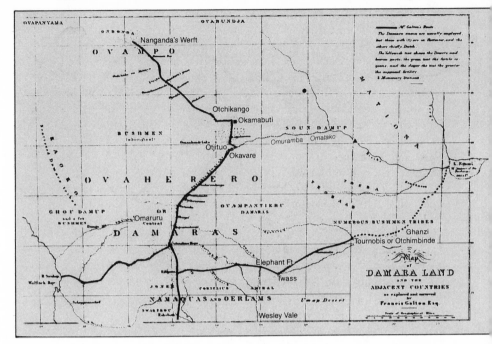

Figure 3.9. Map of Galton's travels (with Andersson) in South-West Africa in 1850–51; the dotted part of the route was followed by Andersson alone in 1853. Mationa is Batawana; Ovampantieru is Ovambanderu; Elephant Fountain is Gobabis; Soun Damup refers to those people called Damara today, not Ovaherero; notice that the route of the Omuramba Omatako from Otjituo (over which Galton did not travel) is incorrect and should run farther northward to Karakobis (marked by a solid circle). For reference, the position of CaeCae is marked by a triangle. (From a photocopy of Galton's ([1853] 1971) original map.)

with details about the interdigitation of peoples in the region; a few examples will bring this point forcefully home. Since we have already reviewed the extent of missionary-trader activity, it comes as no surprise to find references to Europeans living among the indigenous peoples in 1850, as Galton ([1853] 1971:254, 263) records: "I found a man settled here [at Jonker Afrikaner's town] who was of great use to me, and whom I engaged; he was white . . . I found him installed as Jonker's prime minister. . . . Eybrett, for that was his name, undertook to guide me to Elephant Fountain. . . . [Later, at 'Twas] . . . I engaged a Dutchman, by name Saul, whom I found there. . . . He was a well-known shot, spoke Hottentot perfectly, and was just the man I wanted." It is worth emphasizing that he also records as a matter of course the presence of San-speakers, Ovaherero-Ovambanderu, Batswana, and Nama in varying combinations at almost every location he visited.

Galton ([1853] 1971:266−67) confirms what Tindall had recorded seven years earlier, the presence of Ovaherero in numbers in the Namibia-Ngamiland border region: "we were now fairly *en route* [from 'Twas] and had entered the Bushman country. . . . the news of our shooting expedition had spread far and wide, and Damaras [Ovaherero] flocked like crows from all quarters to share in the food."

Galton ([1853] 1971:272) also notes a number of the rewards of European trade that were already a part of local domesticity, such as the large iron pot in which a Bushman at 'Tournobis (this the Nama name for present-day Rietfontein; the Zhu call it Dinqa and the Ovaherero, Otjimbinde) was cooking: "One of my men came to say that he had just found a Bushman cooking with a large iron pot; this was a sure sign of the neighborhood of civilized man. The Bushman said that it was given to them by people from a waggon some distance to the east, and who had gone to the lake the previous rainy season." These wagon people must have been among those "civilized men" who "swarmed" to the lake after Livingstone; it could not have been Livingstone, who was at the lake a full year earlier, in the dry season. Thus, within a half-year or so of its beginning, direct European trade at Lake Ngami had penetrated 200 kilometers westward, and its products were available to a wide range of persons.

The descriptions of the local people and their behavior toward each other found in these journals are also of considerable interest because they often undermine stereotypical views, not only those of the time but also many that remain current today. In 1858 Andersson (1861:200) was following the Omuramba Omatako in his search for a river route from the Lake region to the Atlantic; he noted that "the Bushmen of these regions are as stout, well fed, and good-looking fellows as one would wish to see. . . . they did not appear to be in the least afraid or suspicious." Far from running when they heard shooting, they were attracted to the sound, which seems to indicate that they were already familiar with gunshots and their implications: "We now had meat in abundance—indeed, more than we well knew what to do with, and I was anxiously looking out for Bushmen to eat it up, for I hate waste, when a werft of these people, attracted to the spot by the report of the rifle, made their appearance just as the carcass of the last killed animal was about to be served up" (Andersson 1861:186). To which Galton ([1853] 1971:177) adds: "Towards evening I saw Andersson walking like a chief, with a long string of Bushmen at his heels."

Andersson had with him at least a dozen Herero men, plus a number of women, but—in contrast to the generally held opinion that these peoples had nothing but unremitting hostility toward each other—

nowhere does he mention friction between them. In fact, his unpublished diary (State Archive Service, Windhoek, n.d., A83[1]:335) contains an entry for 24 May 1859 that reads in part: "It seems there is no truth in the story of their [Herero] having some time ago killed a lot of red people & Berg Damaras. They live, on the contrary, on very good terms."

Eleven years later one "fine-looking Bushman chief," who must have been Zhu, was known to Andersson (1861:205) by his Herero name Kanganda (ka = diminutive prefix, plus onganda = settlement; Little Village Man):

At about this time, just as I had returned one day from a hard ride in search of water, and, having been successful, was refreshing the inner man, a fine-looking Bushman chief stood suddenly before us. He had accidently come across my horse's spoor, and thinking the rider might belong to some white man's party (he had seen Messrs. Green and Hahn when on their way to the Ovambo), he unhesitatingly followed it up till he reached the wagon. I felt much gratified at this encounter, first, because the man could speak well of us to his countrymen, and, secondly, because he would be of the utmost service to us in guiding us to the springs, wells, and vleys, now very difficult to find. He (Kanganda was his name) agreed at once to accompany us for some distance, and I on my part, promised to kill an elephant for him and his people at the earliest opportunity.

The last clause of this quotation is particularly informative: it specifies that an *elephant* was to be killed. It thus appears that ivory constituted the value exchanged for guide service, not meat, or not meat only. In the mercantile rhetoric of the day, elephant meant ivory; if meat had been the value medium, any animal—perhaps several of them— should have served. It appears that these "Bushmen" Zhu were engaged in the trade.

San-speakers were also important in the news network that kept people informed about events over very large distances. Two rather dramatic incidents will convey the extent of these networks. Chapman (1971, 1:235) was trading at Lake Ngami in 1859 when, he says: "Other Hottentots from Amraal Lamert's have made a successful hunt northwards, where they struck the missionaries' and Green and Andersson's spoor. From them we learned that Mr. Andersson had reached a tribe called Ooakangarra [Ovakangara] or Ooabingwe [probably Ovambundju] on a fine river [the Okavango] in about latitude 17° S. and longitude 18° E., but was detained there by fever. These reports were verified a few days ago by the arrival of Andersson and Green themselves." Tabler (1953:41) quotes from Green's journal that when, in 1868, Livingstone was lost to public view in central Africa, Green was able to report at Walvis Bay "rumours current among the interior natives, that a white man, presumably Livingstone, was travelling north-west from the east coast above the Zambezi."[17]

It is well known that in his later writings Andersson, along with other Europeans, spoke disparagingly of San peoples, and several mention various atrocities committed both by and on these peoples; this is often invoked by modern capitalist writers as evidence for a constant state of hostility in "native" political relations. This is a distortion; as we have seen, in earlier times—before they had helped create an atmosphere of conflict—Andersson, as well as other traders, explorers, and missionaries, generally described San peoples and their relations to others in neutral or complimentary terms, and an individual could even be fine and good-looking (recall Galton's opinion) or "a fine, intelligent young fellow" (Andersson 1861:218). Part of the change must have been brought about by actions such as those of Andersson (1861:216–17) himself:

We succeeded in capturing all the inmates of a small Bushman werft. The whole party captured consisted of but a few women and children and two or three grown-up men. The poor people were of course desperately frightened. . . . Thinking it inadvisable at the time to make any mention of my need of guides, I merely gave them to understand that I was *en route* for the river. . . . My mode of proceeding answered well, for at an early hour the next day, on going to their werft, we found them enjoying themselves, in all security, by a roaring fire. Without a moment's delay I ordered two of them to arise and to accompany us. They were extremely loath to comply, but I soon gave them to understand that obey they must. . . . dreading the consequences of allowing the man his liberty, I hit upon the following expedient to prevent his absconding. I fastened his right hand to the wrist of one of my attendants. . . . The Bushman was then ordered to proceed, and, in order to prevent all chance of escape, I followed close at his heels. The man was in a desperate fright, and stopped repeatedly, begging hard to be let loose, but I turned, of course, a deaf ear to all his entreaties.

Perhaps more invidious was Galton's ([1853] 1971:177–78) tactic. After persuading some of the long string of Bushmen who had trustingly followed Andersson to be their guides, "one Bushman was to remain all night as a hostage; the others were to tell his wife. . . . Our new friend became quite uneasy at nightfall when his companions had left him alone, so we watched him alternately throughout the night to see that he did not run away. I do not think the poor fellow slept a wink . . . for I constantly caught his bright eye gleaming distrustfully round, whilst he pretended to sleep." Similar actions by other traders, by which San were "captured," "seized and secured," and otherwise forced to comply with orders that required them to abandon their own needs to serve the interests of the traders could not have contributed to continued trustful relations.

These early records contain clear evidence of San cattle. At about the point on the Omuramba Omatako where Schinz later crossed this ephemeral watercourse, Andersson (1961:187) was told by his Bushmen guides that "both Bushmen and black people lived on its banks; that both nations possessed cattle." He was lost in the Omaheke sandveld where Zhu live—indeed, he was very near NyaeNyae (figs. 3.10, 3.11)—when, on Thursday, 10 February 1859, he noted in his diary (but did not later publish): "Found a Bushman werft after catching a woman & presenting her with some tobacco, she had soon become pacified . . . saw at the werft oxen, calabashes, a [illegible] fish, etc." (State Archive Service, Windhoek, n.d., A83[1]:124).

Both Andersson and Galton found and used wells cut into the limestone floor of the Omatako at several locations, as did Chapman in the Ghanzi area, positive evidence that numbers of cattle were kept there: "The day was hazy, but Andersson made out something like green grass, five or six miles to the north-west, and the guide found a bushman who directed him in that very course; so we went there, and found not only dry rushes but also a troop of baboons. This was a sure sign of there being water somewhere near, and after looking about a little we came upon wells" (Galton [1853] 1971:175).

In a synthesis of the country that was soon to become German Südwestafrika (*Petermanns* 1878:306–11), there is an extensive description of the area spoken of by Andersson: "The Herero have at places where the calcrete is not too hard nor too thick dug holes into the ground from which day after day they water their large herds. . . . Most of the names marked on the map of the Omaheke, or sandveld [this includes the NyaeNyae-Dobe area], are such places and pans at which are often found considerable [numbers of] Herero camps."[18] Chapman (1971, 1:166), writing of the Ghanzi area in the mid-1850s, recorded: "At intervals there are large wells dug by the Damaras [Ovaherero] to water their cattle, with wooden troughs into which they diligently scoop the water as it percolates through the sand. Large herds of Namaqua cattle were grazing in every direction, herded by strapping Damaras."

In 1862 a Herero man gave Baines (1864:324–28), at a place "the Bushmen call it Karran" (Karang), an accurate description complete with travel time of the route from where they then were to the "traders' road" in the Omurambo Omatako. This is convincing evidence that this Herero man—no doubt along with others of his people—was as

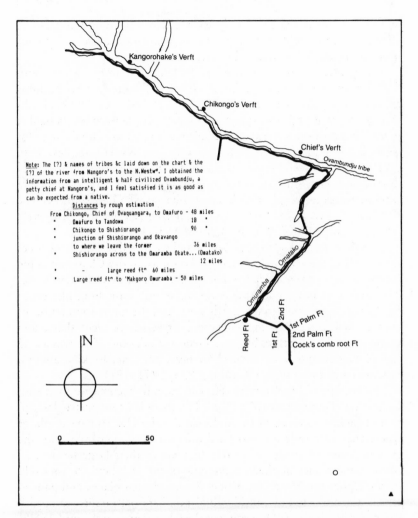

Kangorohake's Verft

Chikongo's Verft

Chief's Verft

Ovambundju tribe

Note: The [?] & names of tribes &c laid down on the chart & the
[?] of the river from Nangoro's to the N.Westw'. I obtained the
information from an intelligent & half civilized Ovambundju, a
petty chief at Nangoro's, and I feel satisfied it is as good as
can be expected from a native.
    Distances by rough estimation
 From Chikongo, Chief of Ovaquangara, to Omafuro - 48 miles
    "   Omafuro to Tandowa   18   "
    "   Chikongo to Shishiorango   90   "
    "   junction of Shishiorango and Okavango
          to where we leave the former   36 miles
    "   Shishiorango across to the Omaramba Okate...(Omatako)
                                             12 miles
    "   -   large reed ft" 60 miles
    "   Large reed ft" to 'Makgoro Omuramba - 50 miles

Omatako

Omuramba

Reed Ft

1st Ft

2nd Ft

1st Palm Ft

2nd Palm Ft
Cock's comb root Ft

N

0   50

O

▲

Figure 3.10. Tracing of a sketch map in Andersson's unpublished diary (State Archive
Service, Windhoek, n.d.). 'Makgoro Omuramba, the last place mentioned in the marginal notes, is not marked on the map but must be at the end of the drawn route, which
measures fifty miles from Reed Fountain. Reed Fountain is Karakobis; Nangoro's in the
notes refers to Chief's Verft on the map—this is an earlier location of Andara, which
subsequently was moved some miles downstream. The location of Gautcha is indicated
by an open circle and that of CaeCae by a triangle in the lower right corner. Scale in
miles.

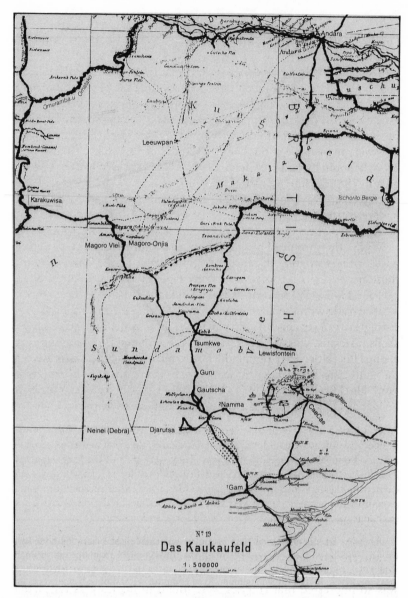

Figure 3.11. Composite map made from photocopies of Langhan's *Deutscher kolonial Atlas in Vier Blatter* (1894) and Passarge's (1907) map. Magoro Vlei is in the correct direction and distance from Karakuwisa (Karakobis) to be the same place that Andersson called 'Makgoro Omuramba (fig. 3.10). Magoro/'Makgoro is of Setswana form and seems to be Mokoro, meaning a narrow road; Vlei (Afrikaans) and Omuramba (Otjiherero) both mean valley, so we seem to have Narrow Road Valley or Narrow Valley Road. Lee (1979:41, fig. 3.2) and Harpending (n.d.) show the place-name Mokoro in about the location given on this map. Onjia, in Magoro-Onjia, is of Otjiherero form and may be Onjira, a road, which agrees with the Tswana form. Tschorilo Berge is the Tsodilo Hills; Tsumkwe is Tchumque; 'Gam is Gcam; 'Namma will be met as tgoma, Ngoma, or Gnoma in the text, its modern Setswana spelling is Ncama; 'Kai'Kai is CaeCae as shown.

familiar with Ngamiland trade routes as was Ramothobe with the eastern routes.

When he finally reached the Okavango at Libebe, Andersson (1861: 239) collected from the inhabitants the names of the peoples known to be living in the different directions from that place: after listing the already well-reported river peoples, he writes, "To the southward only Bushmen and impoverished Herero exist." This impoverishment was, however, an instance of fluctuating fortunes of pastoralists, in this case brought about by raiding. Chapman (1971, 1:166) wrote of the Ghanzi area in 1856: "Here we met a party of Damaras, poor, emaciated and scabby creatures, equalling in poverty the most wretched Bushmen I had yet seen. They were once the possessors of immense flocks and herds, and owners of the soil where they now grubbed for roots."

Within this mosaic of peoples a lattice of trade networks transferred goods over very long distances. A glimmering of the dimensions of those networks is recorded frequently in European accounts. Galton ([1853] 1971:172) records that at Okamabuti "the Ovambo carry on a cattle trade with the Damaras. . . . two Ovambo caravans, each consisting of from twenty to thirty men on foot, come here with beads, shells, assegais, wood-choppers, and such like things, which they exchange for cattle. They obtain the beads and some of the assegais from the half-caste Portuguese traders who frequent their northern frontier." He describes in detail ([1853] 1971:178–79) one such caravan he met at Otjikango and says there were four such yearly:

After a little time three Blacks were seen running from the direction of Otjikongo. As soon as we could make them out clearer, the Bushmen and Damaras all called out "Ovampo," and so it was. They were part of the long-expected caravan. . . . their necks were laden with necklaces for sale, and every man carried a long smoothed pole over his shoulder, from either end of which hung a quantity of packages. These were chiefly little baskets holding iron articles of exchange, packets of corn for their own eating, and water bags.

An idea of the value of this trade is given in oral histories that say Ovaherero gave a young ox for a single cowrie shell (Alexander [1838] 1967; Vedder 1938:138, [1928] 1966:188). Later Passarge (1907:40) was so impressed that cowries were found in quantity as far inland as Ghanzi (these worn by a "Buschmannweib") that he exclaimed, "Welche Geschichte mögen die Kouriemuscheln hinter sich haben!": "What stories these cowries must have behind them!"

Galton ([1853] 1971:198–99) tells us that his own caravan consisted of a motley crew traveling together to trade with Ovambo: "I counted in our caravan 86 Damara women, nearly half of whom had yelling babies on their backs, and 10 Damara men. Our party consisted of 14, and the Ovampo of 24; making about 170 souls in all; 206 head of horned cattle were driven along, independently of our own, and were the result of Ovampo barter. . . . The 86 women went on various speculations,—some to get work in Ovampoland, some to try and get husbands, others merely to sell their ostrich-shell corsets." Keep in mind that Galton's was the first European party seen in the region, yet there seems to have been no inhibition on the part of native peoples of all kinds to join it or to run toward it. Note also that Galton's enumeration of people totals 134, while he says there were about 170 in the caravan. We know there were Bushmen in the group— for Galton has them calling out at the approach of Ovambo traders— and we may assume that they made up the 36 or so unaccounted for. Another instance of the ephemeral Bushmen.

Theophilus Hahn (1895:614–15) describes some details of San trade: "The Gabe Bushmen of ‖Nuis shewed me beautiful embroideries of their own make from white, pink, blue, black and green beads, which they said they had bartered from the Ghanse or !Ai Bushmen, and these had again bartered the beads from the Batoanas of the Lake for ostrich feathers, leopard and jackal skins." CaeCae people have described the same route to me and told me that it extended, as far as their grandfathers' dealings were concerned, through Qangwa and Tsodilo to the Mbukushu at Namiseri and Muhembo on the Okavango.

Passarge (1907:40) found beads in abundance in the western sandveld: "As jewelry there are necklaces of white, red, and blue glass beads worn around the neck or stuck in the hair so that they hang in loops across the forehead." [19]

There was conflict, of course, and Green (*Petermanns* 1867a:8–12) gives a glimpse of it in a letter to Hahn: "More of their [Herero] trade caravans came along to us and as soon as they noticed us, they took up a warlike position. . . . This is not to be wondered at, as they have lost cattle to Nama robber bands." [20] That was by no means the first, or the fiercest, instance of conflict in trade; both the historiography and the anthropography of the region are full of bloody tales. But as Lau (1981:38) insists, it was not "one damn crime after another," and—to call upon Hailey (1953) in anticipation—relations among groups were "at all events liable to readjustment." Among these readjustment processes was incorporation, as Ncgoncgo has noted. Presently we shall meet Tautona, an Omukwena (Nama) whose grandmother when a child was captured in a battle with the Mbanderu Tuvare family that took place near Windhoek in the 1860s. Tautona's grandfather was a Tuvare, and his children now are identified as Zhu and live with the senior Tuvare family at CaeCae.

Carl Hugo Hahn (*Petermanns* 1867b:285–86) documents both

the scope of indigenous trade and the interdependence of different peoples in it:

Our Herero eagerly buy [from Bergdamara] ostrich eggshells which are a much sought after trade item by the Ovambo. . . . At the lowest estimate that I can make, 50 to 60 tons of copper ore must go yearly to Ondonga. The Bushmen [Heixum] are so jealous of this trade, that to this day they have not allowed strangers, not even people of Ondonga, to see the places where they dig. . . . Also, other Bushmen prepare salt from saltpans in the form of sugar-loaves and bring them to Ondonga to sell, from where they go on to other tribes, so that the salt trade is fully as important or even more important than that of copper.[21]

Passarge (1907:85) said that ostrich eggshell beads had "very high value and, as we shall see, played a large role in earlier trade."[22] Vedder ([1928] 1966:183) records that salt still had a premium value in the early twentieth century, worth as much as tobacco. Tommy Kays, who came to Ngamiland as a trader's son in 1913, recalled that salt and gunpowder were equally valued at that time (Wilmsen 1985b).

Chapman (1971, 1:143) offers some insights into eastern Kalahari indigenous trade in the 1850s:

[My Bushmen] begged me to shoot an ostrich, as they were collecting black feathers to adorn the heads of Matabele warriors. . . . We moved onwards, the Bushmen showering maledictions on the vultures, for I had refused them permission to burthen themselves with the ostrich flesh, as they were bending under the weight of my packages and large junks of eland flesh. It is beyond their comprehension how we can be so prodigal as not to remain till we have devoured the flesh we kill.

Chapman, of course, wanted the white feathers, which were then expensively fashionable in Europe.

In the Ghanzi-Gobabis section of Ngamiland he noted, in 1855 (1971, 1:167), Portuguese beads and cowrie shells obtained from the northern trade routes:

The Damara women wear several strings of heavy and cumbersome iron beads round their legs, also a few common Portuguese beads, which they informed us came from Nangoro's, chief of a large nation far to the northwest and near a river Cunene. . . . Their headdress is a curtained hood or bonnet of skin like a helmet, ornamented with a string of cowries, and having leathern horns erect at the back, besides a heavy appendage of probably 10 to 20 lbs. weight of rude iron beads, the most prized, hanging down their backs.

It was this long-standing trade over which the Tswana dikgosi sought to retain control while attempting to gain control over the rapidly developing new European trade. In the process, their suzerainty

over the reduced classes of Batswana and—with even more effect—
over non-Tswana peoples was solidified as they tightened their grip on
indigenous trade. Their efforts to control the Europeans, while multi-
faceted and partly successful in the short run, were ultimately frus-
trated: "There has been a game of diplomacy between Chapman and
the Bechuanas all the morning, the object of the latter being to persuade the Bushmen to bring the tusks of Chapman's elephants to them,
or at least within their power" (Baines 1864:409).

Observe, first, that San "Bushmen" were not automatic pawns in
these negotiations; instead, their services seem to have gone to the
highest bidder. In this case it turned out to be the European. Next,
notice that there were simply too many traders to keep under surveillance, especially as they covered so much ground. Tabler (1973) summarizes the biographies of 333 adult male Europeans and Americans
who traveled, traded, preached, or settled in Namibia and Ngamiland
between 1738 and 1880; in the rest of the region there were many
more. Of indispensable importance, the traders had the ultimate ter-
minals of consumption of exported products at their command; chief
or servant, all had to sell through them. The traders also held the im-
port commodity needs of local peoples in their hands:

The Hottentots [in 1861] at Elephants Fountain, owing partly to the profit of a
successful elephant hunt last year, are much better dressed than formerly. The
women, who wore native dress, are now mostly clad in European clothes, and
none of the men are so ragged and dirty as they were. This will continue while
Amraal lives, but at his death, or after the decline of the ivory trade or the
coming of lungsickness, I expect a great falling off in their temporal and spiritual state. (Chapman 1971, 1:231)

Profit was the lure that brought these men here; ostrich feathers
sold in England for £45 sterling per pound (about $1,000 at today's
prices) and ivory for 7 shillings ($7, or about $280 for an average tusk)
in 1860 (Esterhuyse 1968:13). Gordon-Cumming ([1850] 1904:254),
who in 1844 was perhaps the first white hunter in the Kalahari, wrote:
"Although I voted these matters an immense bore, it was nevertheless
well worth a little time and inconvenience, on account of the enor-
mous profit I should realize; I had paid £16 for a case containing
twenty muskets, while the value of the ivory I demanded for each fire-
lock was upward of £30 [that is, a pair of tusks], being about 3,000
per cent., which I am informed is reckoned among mercantile men
to be a very fair profit." Note that Gordon-Cumming is buying, not
shooting, this ivory.[23]

Andersson's spoor to Lake Ngami was traced in reverse, about nine months after it was laid down, by Frederick Green, who had come up on the eastern—Great North—road of the Bangwato. On this trip Green was guided in the vicinity of Lake Ngami by Ovaherero, but from that point he says (1857:664), "I am positive that we should never have reached Walvis Bay" were it not for a "Bushman" guide.

San participation in the rapidly expanding mercantile economy was by no means limited to the role of guide, any more than it had been in previous trade. Green also records that "Bushmen" brought ivory from the desert to barter; this was in 1855 and was not the beginning of San involvement in that trade. During the following three decades they became probably the principal producers of both ivory and feathers as well as of pelts (Okihiro 1976:161). In addition to their being much sought after as laborers, San participation in the trade took several forms. Mackenzie (1871:179) remarks on the extent of business between the servants and guides of traders and chiefs' subjects, especially San and Bakgalagadi, and Passarge (1907:10) says that the trader Franz Müller told him that in the beginning of the 1880s "Bushmen" by the hundreds gathered at his wagons to trade. Much of this was relatively insignificant domestic barter and in fact acquired the name trade on the side.

Of far greater consequence to both the San-speakers and the traders was production for the ivory and feather trade. Parsons (1977:118) summarizes early records:

It is evident that Cumming penetrated an already existing trade network relaying ivory toward the Cape. The ivory that he obtained from Sekgoma in the Shoshong Hills had been transported from the Boteti by the porterage of Kgalagadi serfs. The Tswana were exporting ivory, karosses, and ostrich feathers southwards in exchange for "beads of all sizes and colours, brass and copper wire, knives and hatchets, clothing for both sexes, ammunition and guns, young cows and she-goats" (i.e., for breeding) obtained in the relay trade of white, coloured, and other black groups. The Ngwato themselves did not hunt the elephants of which they sold the ivory prior to 1844; Sekgoma bought the ivory with beads from skilled Khoisan hunters (Ura or Denassana) on the Boteti. It was horses and guns, introduced and maintained by Cumming and his fellow Scotsmen like David Livingstone, which enabled the Ngwato and other Tswana themselves to maximize the production of ivory and feathers. Serf hunters armed with firearms were sent out by the king, or hired out to alien hunter-traders on payment of one musket to each hunter per trip.

Chapman (1971, 1:185) provides a vivid description not only of the hunt but of the social context in which it took place in the 1860s:

The natives of Lake Ngami hunt elephants about with their Bushmen and dogs, and if possible drive them into a bog, where the Bushmen kill the whole.

They sometimes have a hard struggle, and many a fellow loses his life in the contest. Every year several of the most daring men are missing, killed by the elephants and buffaloes. Some Bushmen are expert with their spears, and I knew one little man, his arms as delicate as a lady's, to kill 3 elephants out of a troop in a short time; but this is sheer dexterity and not often met with. The Bushmen usually drive them a long distance, yelling and with their dogs also worrying them. . . . They drive them to where their masters, the Bechuanas, are waiting to steal the honour by firing one or two long shots at random. Then they leave the Bushmen to perform the rest, they taking the merit and the tusks and the meat as well.

This scene that Chapman lays before us must not, however, be extrapolated to the whole show. Herero and Tswana hunters, along with the Nama already mentioned, were—and are—as skillful as their San counterparts; they produced a proportion of the ivory traded to Europeans. Gibson (1962 : 624) cites several nineteenth-century sources that specify Herero trade in ivory and ostrich feathers; Passarge (1905 : 82) is of the opinion that Herero and Nama rifles reduced animal numbers to the point that subsistence hunting was no longer a viable pursuit.

McKiernan (Serton 1954 : 133, 177) records specifically that traders regularly visited such supposedly remote places as Gcam and Tebra (Debaragqu in NyaeNyae); on Sunday, 5 August 1877, he was at Ghanzi, where he noted in his journal: "Thomas is going to send Lou with Gamble, with a cartload of goods, to trade in the Gaam Veldt. . . . they left on Tuesday afternoon. . . . [on 25 November 1878] . . . Lou came back in the evening; he left Clay to the southeast of this place, on his way to Teabraa Fountain. He will go out to Omoruru by Ochaharawa [Otjiarua]."

In 1877 McKiernan's party was already fifteen years behind. Robert Lewis, Karobbie to his Herero partners, had begun hunting and trading in the Kaukauveld in 1863, where he left his name as Levisfontein (Afrikaans form of Lewis Springs, spelled Lewisfontein on early maps) by which Qangwa in Ngamiland was known on maps of Botswana until 1968. He and Eriksson (remembered at CaeCae as Karuapa Katiti, Little White Man), shot elephants throughout western Ngamiland at that time. Already in 1885 Schinz (1891 : 358) found the spoor from the west to Lewisfontein well marked: "On 6th May we reached Karakobis . . .; this was an important stage for us, since we now had to leave the aforementioned highway in the bed of the river [Omuramba Omatako] and follow the wagon spoor that swung to the right, and head toward the southeast."[24] It took him just thirty-six hours to reach Lewisfontein.

San persons were trusted caretakers of Herero and Nama cattle and apparently stuck to their jobs even when under attack: in a letter to Andersson dated 19 May 1864, Green (State Archive Service, Windhoek, n.d., A83[2]: 97–99) wrote that all the Herero fled from an attack by Jonker's Nama but that a Bushmen herdsman sent a message saying he "intends sticking to the cattle until they are again attacked." Twenty-eight years later, on 22 April 1892, Hendrik Witbooi (Gugelberger 1984: 68) wrote to the trader Duncan that they had lost only two men in heavy fighting with Herero, one of whom was "a Bushman who guarded the cattle."

Other primary sources document the widespread extent of San production for the commodity market. Chapman estimated that fifteen to twenty thousand pounds of ivory was exported annually from Ngami-Namibia during the 1860s. That rate of production was maintained into the 1880s. In the east, the average annual export through Shoshong was estimated to be about eighty thousand pounds in 1879 (Esterhuyse 1968: 13; Parsons 1977: 121). At best, half of this production could have been shot by Europeans; almost surely, they shot much less. The remainder must have been produced by hunters native to the different localities of production, many—if not most—of whom were San-speakers. Consequently, for more than two decades these local hunters would have had to have killed approximately three hundred elephants in Ngami-Namibia each year and four times that many in the east to have produced their share of the ivory that was exported from the region.[25] Chapman (1971, 1: 186) estimated that during the 1860s "on a rough calculation, 2000 to 3000 elephants are killed annually south of the latitude of Lake Ngami."

But it is not only exports that are significant, although their production on the scale we have just witnessed in cameo profoundly redirected indigenous economies. An idea of the scope of manufactured goods imported into the region during the second half of the nineteenth century can be gleaned from the company ledgers of Axel Eriksson. Eriksson was apprenticed to Andersson and inherited the trading enterprise upon the latter's death. His company maintained the largest trading network in the region; beginning in 1869, he kept as many as sixty ox wagons at a time on the routes to most of the places between Walvis Bay and Lake Ngami and northward into Ovamboland. An appreciation for the size of this trade is given by Esterhuyse (1968: 12), who has compiled the sources on Eriksson: "In 1876 he already had approximately twenty Europeans in his service, and by 1878 the number had doubled. In that year his stock was estimated at R12,000. Amongst other things 1,000 rifle-barrels, 20,000 lb. of gunpowder,

600 gallons of brandy, 39,600 lb. of coffee and 51,000 lb. of sugar had been imported the previous year."

Until about 1870, Europeans were remarkably immune from the competitive conflicts they helped inflame among indigenous peoples. Except from the Orlams, with whom they maintained a mutual piracy designed on both sides to monopolize markets, they could expect almost complete cooperation. San, especially, had a good reputation. McKiernan (Serton 1954:170–71) wrote in his diary on 11 October 1878: "In my 4 years' experience with Bushmen, I have found them to be the most civil natives in the country. They are lazy and unreliable, it is true, but if decently treated are always friendly."

This situation was changing rapidly in the 1870s owing, at least in part, to the actions of some of the traders who made Andersson's and Galton's earlier seizures seem tame. We have already noted how these two men contributed to the underlying basis for the transformation of San attitudes, but other examples are readily called up. On 11 October 1878, about twenty miles south of Karakobis [Karakowisa], McKiernan entered in his journal:

Rode down to Merton's place yesterday; saw Merton, Tretow and the Erikson brothers. Albert Erikson had just returned from the eastward, and reports the killing of Wm. Wilkinson by Bushmen. Wilkinson came into this country with us. . . . he was supplied with guns, ammunition etc., necessary for hunting, and went into the bush, accompanied by 2 young Boers and a lot of Bushmen. After Thomas was killed, word was sent him to come in and render an act of property in his possession, to which he answered that he would not come in, neither would he return the property. The two Boers came in, saying they could no longer remain with him; that from the way he was treating the Bushmen, they feared they would all be murdered by them. Everyone knowing the Bushman nature concurred in the opinion that Wilkinson would be killed by them, if he persisted in his manner of dealing with them; and so it has turned out. Bates and Dixon, white men on that side, expect to recover the property and send it to us. Nothing has been done to the Bushmen, nor do I think there will be. No one thinks enough of the man to revenge him. (Serton 1954:170)

This occurred in the region of pans lying between NquaNqua, Nyae-Nyae, and CaeCae where Zhu lived. Notice that personal property and other traders were assumed to be safe.

A new element was introduced when the Boer Dorstland (Thirstland) trekkers moved slowly though Ngami-Namibia from 1875 to 1881 on the way to their promised land in Angola. Although these people were ardent hunters of elephants, they traveled with full families and herds looking for a place to settle. They also brought with them their disdain for African peoples and injected their own attitudes and actions into an atmosphere that was already charged with violent change. They did, however, rely on "Bushmen" to supply some of their basic needs, even if they had to pay well: "The men were compelled in this out-of-the-way country to barter with the Bushmen for water. . . . The Bushmen had to draw the water from the ground with reeds, and for a calabash containing five bottles of water, one had to pay five pounds of gunpowder" (Postma 1897:31).[26] Ovambanderu at CaeCae remember a song composed when a party of these men, having left their thirst-weakened animals to look for water, walked into Otjimbinde: "Who are these people who come out of the bush walking without horses? Where do they come from?"

The Boers must have appeared to the Zhu, among whom they established their kraals during 1876–79, as on the one hand a serious threat to their land, from which they could expect hardly any benefit in the form of cooperative participation in the hunt and its spoils. On the other hand, they must have appeared—indeed, must have been— far more intractable than the traders. This situation, of course, erupted into hostilities. The first of the Boer trekkers wintered at Tebra in 1878; they too record trouble with the local Zhu (Prinsloo and Gauche 1933:29–30):

On investigation, we found a Bushman arrow stuck in the horse's body, and we were immediately very uneasy. We knew it was the work of Bushmen. Oom Willem had gone into the bush at midday to find game meat which was all on which we lived. The evening came on us and we could see nothing in the dark, but early the following morning at five we took after the horse's way from Oom Willem. We had to follow the horse's spoor, and after we followed it for a considerable time I heard Faan call out, "Here lies poor Oom Willem." The others of us ran there but found that Oom Willem must have been dead a long time with a poisoned Bushman arrow in his side. . . . "Come, Faan," I yelled, "let's go follow the vermin and kill them." Faan was then right by me, and so one and another except for two who stayed by Oom Willem. After an hour's ride, we saw quite a number of Bushmen and killed as many as possible. We could not, however, find too many. These Bushmen had as a chief or captain a "Bergdamara" more cunning and deadlier than a snake.[27]

Collapse of Merchant Capital

Coincident with this new form of intrusion, the ivory/feather trade vanished in the 1880s when the elephants were hunted out and feathers went out of fashion in Europe, the small demand remaining now supplied by newly established ostrich farms at the Cape. Parsons (1977:

120) notes that in Gangwato, "Khama had inherited a situation in the 1870s where actual hunting in his country was becoming severely limited. The elephant herds of the plateau in Khama's Country had been largely exterminated by the new firepower, and commercial farming in the Cape Colony was beginning to challenge the northern trade in ostrich feathers." George Westbeech lamented in 1886:

Some Bushmen also arrived from Africa [Klaus Africa, a Griqua], H. Wall and August, they it appears came across a troop of elephants and killed six. . . . According to native talk, since the veldt has been hunted by the Bushmen for two years and by a number of people from Lake N'gami to whom Luwanika gave permission to hunt, the elephants have been driven through the river. . . . I am much disappointed, as we always considered the Linyanti the best of hunting veldt, but now it is not worth the trouble of hunting it. (Tabler 1963:63)

Briefly, at the end of the 1880s and in the first half of the 1890s, a minor economic boom, brought about principally by construction of Cecil Rhodes's railway from the Cape to Bulawayo, developed on the "missionary road" (no longer the north road from Shoshong that Livingstone, Oswell, and Wilson had followed to Lake Ngami but now deflected eastward before turning north again along a route that subsequently became the boundary between the Protectorate [now Botswana] and Rhodesia [now Zimbabwe]); this in turn stimulated an export of cattle from Ngami-Namibia (Clarence-Smith and Moorsom 1975:374).

Consequently, cattle and their accompanying cowhand jobs passed through many communities along the routes through CaeCae, Levisfontein/Qangwa, Ghanzi, and the other tsetse-free areas of the region and on across the Kalahari to the line of rail.

The result of all this activity was that many European traders were constantly in contact with native producers of sought-after items—ivory, ostrich feathers, cattle, and hides. These producers, as we have seen, were understandably not loath to circumvent the tributary demands of their chiefs and suzerains. There can be no doubt that the resultant terms of trade, although nowhere recorded, were, even by the then-current lopsided standards, extremely advantageous to the Europeans, who wasted no time learning to bypass the chiefs. This direct involvement with the primary producers reached substantial proportions in some places and had a significant reorienting effect on the economic focus of the native peoples there. This was a transient moment, but it had lasting consequences.

Insofar as its strength could sustain interregional economies, the miniboom in the east collapsed in 1896, coincident with the onset of

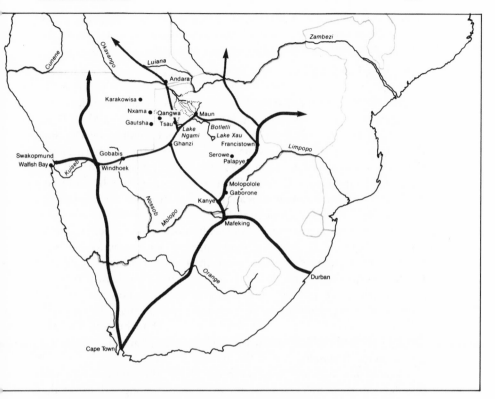

Figure 3.12. Principal trade routes of the twentieth century.

rinderpest, which wiped out most of the cattle and wild ungulates of southern Africa. Both the indigenous and the European economies of Ngami-Namibia, which had fused—as had their counterparts throughout the Namib-Kalahari—during the previous half-century into an interdependent if not a unitary formation, became correspondingly moribund. Trade routes were correspondingly drastically reduced (fig. 3.12).

Passarge (1907:10, 118) records that in 1897, at the very places where Müller had a dozen years earlier attracted hundreds of people to his trading wagons,

The merchant, Franz Müller, a fine observer and unquestioned expert on the Kalahari, assured me that the number of Bushmen has declined since his trip at the beginning of the eighties. Before, they gathered in hundreds around his wagon and brought very many pelts to trade; now one sees in these same places ever fewer, often not a single person. . . . The extermination of the wild animals and the failure of melons have brought about, in my opinion, this unfavorable prospect. . . . Trade routes appear not to have stability in the country of the Bushmen, rather they underwrite barter among tribes.[28]

In the Ghanzi kalkpan (in 1895, two years before the rinderpest epidemic), where thousands of cattle and many "Bechuana, Damara, and Nama" had been noted by the earlier traders, Captain Fuller, who was sent to reconnoiter the suitability of the area for settling Boer farmers, found that "Massarwa are the only inhabitants, except that there are two or three BaTawana cattle-posts on the northern edge" (Public Records Office, London 1895 : 141). Three years later the Boers were settling in on their farms in Ghanzi, which they now held in free-hold. In the Namibian high plateau, first the British in 1876 had made a feeble, halfhearted attempt to induce European settler-farmers, and then the Germans beginning in 1884 set in motion their colonial settler policy. Robert Lewis, who was sometimes referred to as Maharero's prime minister, played an active role in trying to secure the British position and, when that failed, in trying to subvert German efforts.

Land itself, not just its easily skimmed product, now became the object of colonial acquisition. To the hunters and traders, the only significant question about the ownership of land had been whose authority over it they had to deal with. The settlers, backed by imposed government, demanded that authority for themselves.

As suddenly as it had been set in the 1850s, the commercial scene dissolved in the 1890s. If Galton's caravan of yelling babies on the backs of mothers following hundreds of cattle in search of markets and mates was perhaps a rare Fellini-like exaggeration of the more mundane daily routines of the trade routes, many people of all kinds were nonetheless constantly engaged in those trails of trade. If, too, Tindall, in his zeal to find souls to save and tithe, may have exaggerated in thinking there were thousands of people in the vicinity of Amraal's kraals, there were certainly many hundreds of several different groups, along with thousands of their cattle. And if Müller's hundreds of Bushmen clamoring around his wagons are probably better reduced to scores, still there were those scores, and Müller was by no means the only competitor for their attention. Even if every community was not itself visited regularly by traders, a glance back to the map of trade routes through Ngami-Namibia in the 1860s to 1880s (fig. 3.8) will reveal that few people of the region could have been farther than two good days' walk from one of these routes—and, as we have seen, the routes were busy.

All that changed in the 1890s. During the previous decades the entire region had pulsed with activity; everybody had had a piece of the everyday action, no matter how that eventually worked against long-term interests. Now the region seemed as empty and remote as it was later conceived to be. In Gatawana, Passarge attributed this to an actual reduction in the number of Zhu people (he did not consider that there may have been others, even though he describes long-established relations with Batawana), due, as he thought, to his correctly perceived reduction in game supply. But it was not that; there are no grounds for supposing a decline in numbers of Zhu or of any other peoples. The Kalahari, it is true, had been sucked dry of commoditizable wild animals, but it was only selectively destroyed, and those San—and Herero, and Tswana—people who found it necessary could manage reasonably well on the diet of nuts and berries left to them, with odd additions of flesh from the remaining animals, as they are recorded by ethnographers to have done.

What could not be overcome was that they now had relatively little to offer in trade and less with which to buy from traders. And except for a few cattlepost jobs, their labor, just recently valued highly if rewarded poorly,[29] had become virtually worthless in a now nonexistent market. There did remain a few incentives for others to come to them, and a few for them to go to others; trade, as we shall see, continued, but at a fraction of its former scale.

The remoteness imagined by outside observers beginning with Passarge was not indigenous but was created by the collapse of mercantile capital, which had in its genesis and growth dismembered well-worn native links of communication. There remained only localized channels of trade along the old—precolonial—intraregional routes over which skins and hides were now the major exports, bartered primarily for inadequate supplies of tobacco, salt, iron pots, and marijuana.

Inevitably, all this activity benefited empire but few others. Those European traders and hunters who arrived wealthy left wealthy; a few others made, then usually lost, fortunes; the majority could neither shoot straight nor keep ledger books and were simply carried by the tides; many died painfully and destitute in the bush. Andersson's death seems a metaphor for their fate:

At length, on the sixth day, we arrived at Typandeka's abode, Mr. Andersson being then quite exhausted, when I immediately made his bed in the cart, and from this bed he was never able to rise without my assistance. . . . The third day after our arrival at Typandeka's werft, he said to me, "Axel, my last day is near;" and on the following one, June 27, he called me, and afterwards wrote his last letter to his wife. He then named to me the prices of some articles for sale, and cautioned me not to leave Damaraland until the hunters went west. The day after Typandeka's visit we set out; but first I tried to make Andersson's bed in the cart as comfortable as possible, notwithstanding which he, at the least jolting of the vehicle, would cry out with the agony it caused him. Early on the third day, as I was assisting him in his bed, something seemed to break in his stomach, and he suddenly grew worse, and a kind of green slime came running from his mouth. He said, "Now, Axel, it is all over for me." He then requested me to read some Psalms suitable for a dying person, which I did; and having read them over twice, he remarked, "How beautiful is the Swedish Psalm-book!" and continued, "Greet Een, and tell him how sorry I am not to see him again"; and added, "I am now satisfied to die, I suffer so fearfully." The next day he appeared a little better, and on the following one, the 4th of July, we left the last of the Ovaquamyama werfts, early in the morning, but were necessitated to make two trecks to enable us to reach the water. In the afternoon, Mr. Andersson became very sick, and the whole of that night and the following day the slime aforementioned was constantly running from his mouth; his weakness had now reached its extreme point. In the afternoon he, however, asked for a piece of fried liver, which I immediately prepared, and some of which he ate, but scarcely a quarter of an hour elapsed ere he died [he was forty years old]. As I could not bury Mr. Andersson's remains in a place where I might not afterwards be enabled to find them, I inspanned, and made a moonlight treck; and next day, about noon, arrived at the first werft of the Ovaquambi. Here I decided to make my master's grave; but the chief Nauma would not consent to his remains being interred so near to him, and I was therefore compelled to retrace my way back about a quarter of an hour; and there, between two trees on the right of the road, I found for him a resting-place. I had only an axe and a tin dish with which to make the grave, and this was in hard, clayey soil. (From Axel Eriksson's letter to Andersson's widow, Andersson [1875] 1967:327–31)

The peoples of the Kalahari, except for a few families who became elites, were left with a travesty of what they had previously possessed in their land and with little else other than, possibly for some, their versions of romantic dreams of glory days in their heads. A Zhu man, Gcaunqa, said it simply to Alec Campbell at Tsodilo, "God made whites with everything; he made blacks with cattle; but he made Zhu with fuck-all." Gcaunqa recognized in this order of things not its cosmological rightness, but the existential despair it engendered. And an unnamed Zhu said, in 1920, at Tsintsabis in Namibia: "Elephants, lions, and game of all kinds abounded and have only disappeared since the white man came and shot them in large numbers" (Gordon 1984: 203). Not only had the ivory-bearing elephant and the horned rhino been virtually exterminated, but the staple larger antelope had been shot to a mere numerical shadow of their former selves for their hides, while much of their flesh fed vultures in the prodigality of the time.

The surplus native product of the region had been exhausted, and nothing had yet been introduced to replace it. Indigenous peoples responded by retrenchment, European traders by retreat. Those who were able clustered around the growing new nodes of government, colonial now as well as tribal, and their satellites along the reduced main routes of communication between them, leaving once-active centers such as Gobabis and Shoshong almost deserted and their hinterlands drained. The region had been restructured for the third time in a hundred years. Neither the economy nor the social relations, nor yet the requirements of the people, were as they had been a half-century before. The reins of external control passed in the process from the ad hoc hands of merchants to the policy-conscious care of colonial office administrators, British in the newly declared Bechuanaland Protectorate, German in what was now Südwestafrika. Where merchants and missionaries had dismembered networks, administration proceeded to enclave the segments.

4

The Past Entrenched

It is one of the inescapable problems created by the extension of Colonial rule that it tends to stereotype inter-tribal relations which were previously fluid, or were at all events liable to readjustment by the methods employed in more primitive communities.

Lord Hailey, *Native Administration in the British African Territories*, 1953

Consolidation of the Underclass

The stereotypes Lord Hailey (1953) identified at mid-twentieth century had long before been institutionalized by colonial administrators. Anthropologists and historians, in their turn, validated these rigid views of "intertribal" relations and overlooked the earlier fluidity also noted by Lord Hailey. By the time official records came to be written in the interior of southern Africa, San-speakers there had been reduced to peripheral political and economic positions. British colonial administrators, preoccupied with applying policy to native populations, were generally indifferent to aspects of local life that did not enter directly into the concerns of commerce and control. Still, Ranger's (1978:109) observation that dominated classes did not produce archives and were not much reflected in them is only partly correct; the archives contain a great deal more about San-speakers than has been suspected.

Indeed, just as it became clear in the preceding chapter that it is possible to understand the role of "Bushmen" in the developing merchant capital economy of the Kalahari and in the various forms of Tswana state participation in that economy as it emerged during the nineteenth century, so for the twentieth century it will be possible to extend to San-speaking peoples the insight of Palmer and Parsons (1977:5) "that the nature of inherited colonial economies of Central and Southern Africa cannot be understood, and therefore be changed wittingly, without historical analysis of how and why contemporary social and economic distortions originated."

In Südwestafrika, the German policy of military conquest and domination, which came into being under von François during the early

130

1890s, resulted within fifteen years in the virtual decimation of all indigenous peoples, who were reduced thereby to labor pools without autonomous leaders and with no independent means of production beyond their barest needs. The British policy of indirect rule applied in the Bechuanaland Protectorate assigned subordinated peoples such as San-speakers to the administrative domain of Tswana dikgosi. Despite some efforts to bring subjugated peoples into the system, advantage remained with these chiefs and their own people—those people, that is, who could claim allegiance within the Kwena, Ngwato, Tawana, or another of the recognized Tswana polities. In this atmosphere peoples who could not claim such allegiance, among whom, of course, were unassimilated San-speakers, rose to official attention only when they became irritants to the colonial system. Although this happened often enough, these were considered marginal events in the course of empire. Not surprisingly, then, San-speakers appear, on superficial examination, to have only an ephemeral existence in historical records of the time. Consequently, standard ethnographies and historiographies relegate San-speaking peoples to silence in all of this. But as we shall see, many of these peoples played active roles on both sides and in significant phases of that process.

With the collapse of hunting, a hunter's life was no longer worth as much as it had been—not to himself, now left with only a reduced subsistence supplement, nor to centers of accumulation, where emphasis shifted from quick tributary extraction to longer-term sustained production. In practical terms this meant that cattle were now unchallenged by ivory as the central source of wealth in the Kalahari (cf. Schapera 1970:103).

The kgamelo system is well suited to tributary extraction of capital value when, as in hunting, the means of production remain largely with subordinated ranks. Until the 1890s, the largest proportion of income of the dikgosana (heads of royal families) was derived from ivory, feathers, and skins collected by San and Bakgalagadi (Public Records Office, London 1899). In herding, however, the means of production—cattle in this case—remain in the hands of herd owners. Khama saw this and moved to bring the new relations of production under chiefly control (Parsons 1974a:653). To do this, he restructured the kgamelo system to bring about in effect the capitalization of labor and land. Part of his reform reassigned cattle of the tribal herd to commoner and vassel ward heads, thus enormously increasing the power of these lower-level functionaries.

Khama also nominally freed serfs, ostensibly giving them the right to dispose of their labor in their own interests, and brought some—

though hardly all—of his own serfs into positions of free stockholding. This was illusory; his decree was almost universally ignored. Those
elites who could control the largest number of cattle and serfs stood to
gain the most in this new system.

In fact, the conditions in which serfs found themselves had deteriorated. In the economic reality of the time, there were very limited opportunities for freed serf labor. As primary producers during the years
of mercantile hunting, they had had some bargaining power in the disposal of their product. This power had declined as state capital consolidated its strength and hunting became less remunerative; now, as
obligatory herders, they were completely at the mercy of their masters.

Hunting labor could be, and was, successfully converted to herding
labor; indeed, as we have seen, these forms had never been fully segregated during the previous two millennia. There is an inescapable condition, however: it takes fewer herders to adequately manage one
hundred cattle than it does hunters to kill one elephant. By the 1890s
the tusks of an average elephant had declined in worth to a bit more
than £10 (from £30); an ox at the time was worth about half that.
In addition, elephant numbers had been drastically reduced. Consequently, a very successful hunter might yield his patron £5–10 in ivory
value per year. A herdsman, on the other hand, would have in charge
five or six times that value in oxen as the salable fraction of a much
more valuable herd. There was little incentive for a herd owner to accommodate more herders than necessary.

Furthermore, wives and children of herders fill significant market-
productive roles in cattle management, whereas those of commercial
hunters are confined to producing principally for domestic household
consumption. In other words, a cattle owner needs to engage fewer
families than a merchant hunter, thereby reducing the lateral spread of
economic opportunities. The inequalities inherent in this conversion
for the underclass whose labor secured the herds is readily apparent.
There were substantially fewer places for herders than for hunters,
even in the expanding cattle economy.

It is also readily apparent why members of that underclass, who were
mainly San-speakers, should compete for positions. The system had
quite suddenly alienated San labor from the land more thoroughly than
had been possible before and had thereby created a captive surplus labor pool with essentially only a single outlet. Those San-speakers who
could capture a cattlepost position obtained a measure of security in
the system—at the bottom of the heap, but in it. There were, to be
sure, a few San families in Gangwato who managed to retain or accumulate small stockholdings; we shall shortly examine their fate in the
second and third decades of the twentieth century.

In the years just before 1900, a number of San-speakers were also able to obtain jobs on the Kimberley diamond mines; most of these men tried to pass as "Bechuana" (Tswana), some successfully (Parsons 1983:119). The remainder—those whose labor was not immediately needed, and these were not only San peoples—were now without direct means to participate in regional economies. They were relegated to the more inaccessible and difficult ecological zones of the Kalahari, falling deeper and deeper into foraging, which had become a condition of poverty in the overall structure of society. They thus became a secondary labor pool, maintained at no expense to the controlling classes, who could draw upon this underclass at will to free their own members for cash-earning opportunities, education, and the "lifestyle of the 'new elite' that spanned Southern Africa" (Parsons 1977:136).

The earlier chiefdom-states had been tied together by lopsided but nonetheless mutual mafisa and kinship relations and had been regulated by tributary mechanisms passing domestic products and exchange commodities up and down the line (Nangati 1982). With the penetration of mercantile capitalism, this preexisting structure of reciprocity, which had articulated the state hierarchy with various forms of communal property relations, was at first strengthened to facilitate the flow of commodities from producers to merchants. As the nineteenth century entered its third quarter (the time of Livingstone, Andersson, and their collaborators), those in the higher echelons of the political hierarchy (dikgosi and dikgosana, the chiefs and royals) found it increasingly easier to siphon off for themselves an ever-larger fraction of the reverse flow of exchange value. Thus, former "relations of reciprocity were transformed into exploitative relations . . . for purposes of profit in the modern cash nexus" (Parsons 1974a; see also Wilmsen 1982a; Denbow, Kiyaga-Mulindwa, and Parsons 1985). In the process, the dues and privileges of earlier elites (in theory, simply their share of community property) were "increasingly translated into private family fortunes of a colonially favored aristocracy" (Denbow and Wilmsen 1986:1514). Previously flexible relations of production were transformed into ethnic categories defined by criteria of race, language, and economic status.

These doubly dispossessed people foraging increasingly invisibly in the now "remote" bush were entirely dependent on their kin at cattleposts to pass on to them what snippets they might of their acquired needs: tobacco, coffee, tea, sugar, cloth, pots, and buckets; the list is long. In the end this process made San peoples appear to be traditionally landless and created the squatter communities filled with an unemployed underclass—Tanaka's parasites—that are mentioned, only to be discounted as aberrant, in every ethnography of these peoples. The current consequences of these historical processes will be examined in detail in subsequent chapters.

Resistance

Yet it is too easy to dismiss San-speakers as being uniformly without power or influence at the beginning of the twentieth century. True enough, many were in that predicament, but others retained significant means for influencing their relations with dominant groups, as well as among those groups themselves. Archival records reveal the extent of those means along with the degree to which relations among peoples continued to be transformed in the colonial arena. As it was for the preceding decades dominated by merchant capital, it is necessary to examine events in the region as a whole in order to assess adequately the continuing economic and political submergence of San-speakers in the early part of this century.

A case in point. On 2 September 1903 Merwyn Williams, the first full-time resident magistrate to be appointed to Ngamiland, wrote to the resident commissioner at Mafeking:

Sir, I have the honor to report that the bushmen at Gnoma [Ncama] have killed three of Sekgoma's people lately. . . . Gnoma is a post belonging to Tome a Batawana & is situated this side of Karakubis & has always been considered as Sekgomas country the line is not defined so I dont know whether it mightnt be in German Territory or not However I can easily go there and capture the lot if I have your permission, the place is not marked on any map. . . . Last year I reported the Bushmen at Karakubis for killing 7 of our people now they are at it again Gnoma is not far from Karakubis. . . . I should say that *Gnoma* is outside this reserve & in German Territory although it has always been a Batawana cattle post. (BNA 1903a)

This dispatch set off a chain of correspondence that reached the Colonial Office in London more than once and continued for exactly four years. The event that inspired this reaction led to administrative decisions that had a bearing on Zhu economics, on the fate of Herero refugees fleeing the Germans a year later, and on Sekgoma's difficulties in retaining his chieftainship.

The case is worth following in detail for two reasons. First, it took place in one of the areas (the combined Dobe-NyaeNyae area of Lee and Marshall) upon which the contention of San isolation from external events has been most strongly argued (fig. 4.1). Second, to a greater extent than most, the records for this case contain the views of all the principals to the events in question: of the British—and, reported in this, transcribed descriptions by Zhu (who were agents in the events)— and Sekgoma's own account, along with the final dismissal of his claims

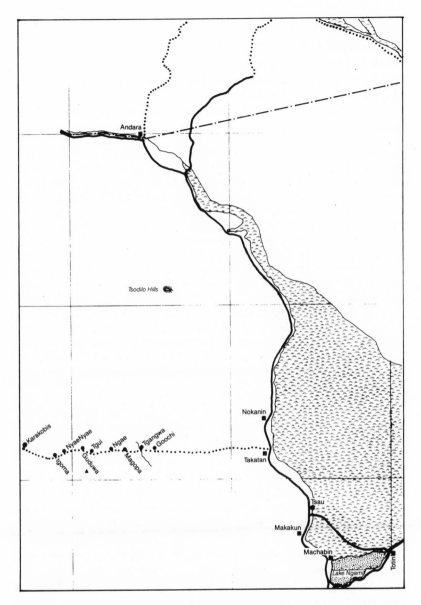

Figure 4.1. Composite map compiled from four sketch maps made by British colonial agents in 1903–6. The places named on the road out to Karakobis are those where Sekgoma's cattle were rustled or where Herero refugees were located after the 1904 battle at Hamakari. The modern Setswana spellings of these place-names as used in the text are as follows: Goochi is Gqoshe; Tgangwa is Qangwa; Ngae (not identified); Tgui (called Baobab Pan on one map) is Cgi, a pan noted for its large baobab trees; Guduwa is Gcuwa; tgoma is Ncama. CaeCae does not appear on the original maps but is indicated by a triangle for reference. Sources are BNA 1903c, 1904b, 1905d, 1906.

after he had been deposed. There are also detailed eyewitness accounts
of subsequent German pursuit of Ovaherero to this place—during the
final stages of their subjugation of these people—the ramifications of
which we shall examine shortly.

On 5 November 1903 Williams again reported to the resident
commissioner:

I have just returned from a place called Ngunda a little to the east of Karakobis
and near the place where the Bushmen have murdered some of Sekgomas
people I saw some Bushmen who gave me full particulars of the affair. In the
parts not far from Karakobis there are numbers of Batawana cattle posts &
until quite recently they were also posts at Karakobis itself but the Bushmen
killed the people & all the cattle there last year they killed 7 men & lots of
cattle & were not punished. The country about there is swarming with Bushmen who go up to Bamangandas and Nynganas [Andara] continually & not
long ago at the time that Pasch & family were killed there were a lot of Bushmen present & saw & probably helped in the afair afterwards when the
Bushmen wanted some of the meat of the oxen taken they were told to go and
get some themselves from the Batawana who live near Karakobis so they returned there & killed the Batawana servants who were herding the cattle &
took some cattle to Bamanganda's to buy loot & anything they could get that
had been taken from the dead white man's waggons some cattle they killed at
Tgoma [Gnoma in Williams's previous dispatch] others they slaughtered at
Karakobis & ali. (BNA 1903c)

The British were interested only in consolidating their own rule.
Sekgoma was far too independent for their purposes, and they recognized that cattle, because they could be lent in patronage, were the key
to his maintaining a loyal following. Thus the British administrators
were not entirely displeased with Zhu cattle thieves, as Resident Commissioner Panzera made clear to his superiors regarding the case (BNA
1903d): "Sekgoma's position is strengthened by the acquisition of
cattle." The British were, moreover, concerned not to intrude on German possessions (BNA 1903b): "The dispatch of an expedition to
punish the offenders would probably result in difficulties with the German Authorities, but in view of the disquieting effect which these continued outrages on his border might have upon a Chief of Sekgoma's
disposition, I think that it will very likely be necessary to send a reinforcement of police to N'gami." Williams (BNA 1903c) had, however, already made that move unnecessary when he "decided to bring
the cattle away from that place & nearer to the river & to avoid a recurrence of this sort of thing." The administration, consequently, not
only did nothing to help retrieve the cattle, but also prohibited Sekgoma
from taking independent action.

Sekgoma was deposed in 1906 and exiled to Gaborone, where a year later he made his final attempt to have his cattle returned to him (BNA 1907a):

Sekgoma Letcholethebe states: In 1903 some Masarwa of Ngoma and Karekubisa took some cattle belonging to me. . . . Mr. M. Williams told me that he had received a reply to the effect that I, Sekgoma, was not to go and recapture those cattle, that the government would return them to me. Mr. M. Williams asked me the number of the cattle taken by the Masarwa, I gave it to him in writing; there were one hundred cattle at Ngoma [Gnoma], and there were 60 at Karekubisa, not including calves just born. . . . To this day these cattle have not been returned to me. . . . I had bought 60 of these cattle after rinderpest and the other hundred were their progeny. I had bought them with money realized by elephant's tusks, skins, hides, horns, etc. . . . I had earned that money and the cattle were my own property. This is all I have to say.

The administration, having achieved its goal, replied, again through Panzera (BNA 1907b):

Please tell Sekgoma that the Government authorized no one to promise him that the cattle which were killed and raided at Gnoma by bushmen would be restored to him. It is very much to be regretted that it was not possible to bring the offenders to justice, but the Secretary of State was not prepared to authorize the Protectorate Admin". to take steps against the robbers, and it was impossible to allow Sekgoma himself to employ force against them.

The "full particulars of the affair" given to Merwyn Williams by Zhu participants reveal the immediately antecedent events that led to the raids. It would be superficial, however, to interpret either the particulars as given, or Williams's miscomprehension of them, on their surface appearance, as representing what was at issue. The statement "go and get some [meat yourselves] from the Batawana who live near Karakobis" cannot have been intended to mean that Nyanganda's people were merely refusing to share their spoils with Zhu (which in any case they were unlikely to have done when it came to those parts of the slain oxen that were immediately eaten). The raids that followed were not simple rustling for a few meals; far too many cattle were captured for that, and substantial numbers were driven to Andara, where they were turned over to Nyanganda. To understand these events in full, we must fill in some details in the history of Tawana-Zhu relations and then consider two key aspects of Sekgoma's policy toward Andara.

In 1891, when Sekgoma became kgosi, he followed Ngwato precedent and began to centralize control of the emerging Tawana state to himself by eliminating many aspects of the kgamelo system (Tlou 1972:228–31; Dikole 1978). His aim was to broaden his support

base by spreading positions and property more widely among junior
elites (dikgosanyana), commoners (basimane), and aliens (including
San and other batlhanka) in order to gain their allegiance (Dikole
1978 : 6, 11). To widen this base even further, Sekgoma, as Khama had
done before him, also attempted—with as little success—to abolish
the servile status of subject peoples such as San. As part of his policy,
cattle taken in raids were declared to be morafe (community) herds;
some of these were sent to remote sandveld locations where "needy
families [could] enjoy milk and meat as well as herd them. . . . such
cattle were distributed at outlying cattleposts" (Dikole 1978 : 7).

We know from eyewitness accounts that such cattle were present in
the Dobe-NyaeNyae area at the turn of the century:

The Bushmen have care of the cattle, and at the beginning of the dry season
must bring them back properly. They have for their part right to the milk, as
much as is not necessary for the calves. Thus, for example, there was in January 1897 a goat kraal of Killitibwes solely under the supervision of Bushmen in
the Makabana Hills, in February it was farther south in the sandveld. The
chief of the Aukwe at Garu had, at Djarutsa, a cattle kraal of the Batawana
chief Sekgoma during the rainy season 1897–98 and went with the cattle at
the beginning of the dry season to the Debravelt [in which lies NyaeNyae].
(Passarge 1907 : 121, writing of the years 1896–98)[1]

More specifically, Lee (1979 : 79) records a seventy-year-old Zhu
man's (whose name was Qam) version of what appears to have been
mafisalike contractual loan arrangements whereby Tawana cattle were
kept at CaeCae during the 1890s:

Before I was born white hunters would visit /Xai/Xai [CaeCae] and shoot the
elephants with guns. My #tum ("father-in-law"), #Toma!gai, worked for the
whites. When they left, the zhu/twasi were all alone. My #tum said, "Let's go
to the Tswana, bring their cattle here and drink their milk." So my #tum organized the younger men and went east to collect the cattle. . . . the Tswana
came up to visit and hunt, then they went back, leaving the San to drink the
milk. Then my #tum got shoro [tobacco] from the Tswana and smoked it. . . .
Later they drove the cattle out to Hxore pan, where they built a kraal and ate
the tsin beans of Hxore while the cattle drank the water. So they lived, eating
tsin, hunting steenbuck and duiker, and drinking milk. . . . At the end of the
season the cattle boys loaded the pack oxen with bales and bales of eland
biltong and went east with it to collect the balls of shoro and sometimes corn.
These they would deliver to my #tum, #Toma!gai.

Partly to supply these cattle, Sekgoma pursued a policy of extensive
raiding into the region north of the Okavango River as far as the
Luiana River. Beginning about 1900, he claimed that region as part

of Gatawana on grounds that decades of Tawana ivory hunting, tribute and tax collecting, and cattle raiding there had gone effectively unchallenged.

Sekgoma's policy, thus combined with the aftereffects of merchant-hunter intervention, created a highly fluid, unpredictable, and essentially unstable economic and political environment in this northwestern part of the Kalahari. Not the least factor in this instability was British alarm at Sekgoma's raids across German Caprivi (in order to reach the Luiana), incursions for which they feared retaliation. Nyanganda was exploiting this environment in his own interest by enlisting Zhu as accomplices in his attempts to retaliate against Sekgoma's raids and to recapture some of his cattle. True, Sekgoma stated that the particular cattle taken had been purchased by him; even if so, this would have been a technicality of no importance to the other actors in the scene.

What is important to note, however, is the presence of other cattle-posts in the western sandveld area—at CaeCae and the Tebraveld as well as at other places—reported by Passarge and Lee. Some were "solely under the supervision" of Zhu. We may assume that those cattleposts where Zhu were in control were relatively immune from predation because these Zhu herders would be kin of the raiders, who would have benefited in more concrete ways from the labor investment of their herder relations.

We also know that, like some Kwa and other San-speakers in Gang-wato, some Zhu in Gatawana acquired small herds. Lee (1979:409) found in his Dobe area that "many men had owned cattle and goats in the past." It was this turn-of-the-century period to which the older of these men referred. Some of their cattle may have survived from earlier decades, some were certainly the product of Sekgoma's policy, and some were probably retained from raids.

The "loot" Zhu obtained from Nyanganda when they delivered the raided cattle was more likely compensation for services rendered than goods purchased, contrary to Williams's assumption. However that may be, it is clear that Zhu continued to be primary producers—the majority, as in the rest of the Kalahari, in the interest of others, a few acquiring small interests of their own. We shall examine their fate in a moment.

Onset of a Labor Vacuum

First we must turn briefly to the German war against Ovaherero and Nama and its immediate antecedents as they affected the basic economy of the region and deepened the pauperization begun by the traders. The initial act of Leutwein, the second military governor of Südwestafrika, upon his arrival in 1894 was to negotiate with Andreas Lambert at Gobabis by executing him "in the interests of the state" and then confiscating the property of those of Andreas's followers who still lived there. Since only thirty rifles and thirty horses were captured, "it seems that the number of men bearing arms cannot have been much greater" (Drechsler 1980:75). This is in marked contrast to the large number of strongly armed men mentioned at this place by Tindall and the many travelers and traders who came immediately after him.

Leutwein followed this action by denying the Ovambanderu their grazing land in the eastern part of the colony and finally by executing their leader, Kahimemua, along with the Omuherero Nikodemus (Kambahahiza Kavikunua, Maharero's older brother's son) in 1896. In their resistance to his harassment, Leutwein recognized that the Ovambanderu "were defending their means of subsistence, especially their cattle herds" (Leutwein 1906:111). It was just those herds he was after.

The confiscation of Herero cattle served multiple purposes. First, the needs of the army for draft animals and food were thereby supplied, and large numbers were sold to German settlers at nominal prices to stock the farms being allotted in the area. Of greater importance, however, the basis of Herero economy and with it the ability to mount effective defense of their land would be broken. Consequently, these pastoralists would be deprived of any independent means of social reproduction and would be reduced to a dispossessed labor pool available to satisfy German needs. This was a major aim of Leutwein's policy. To these ends, the capture of cattle was declared a major priority of the fighting; three thousand head were taken at Otjunda, in the Omaheke, in May 1896, and Leutwein claimed that twelve thousand head were captured from the Ovambanderu during 1896–97 (Leutwein 1906:111; Drechsler 1980:94; Sundermeier, n.d.:42–44). Tohoperi Tuvare recalls that his father was one of the few survivors who fled to the Bechuanaland Protectorate from the fight at Otjunda.

Rinderpest struck at this time, and after it passed itinerant traders are said to have begun collecting their debts by confiscating cattle directly from Herero kraals, reportedly without resistance (Eich 1899: 579; Bley 1971:127). At the turn of the century, Ovaherero were left with a fraction of their former cattle and were being transformed into a wage labor force. There were those in Germany who thought that rinderpest had been very beneficial to the development of the colony (Drechsler 1980:98).

A sporadic but significant flow of Ovambanderu back into previously known parts of Bechuanaland began at least a decade before the official beginning of the German-Herero war (BNA 1897; Schapera 1945:11; Alnaes 1979a, 1979b; recall also Tohoperi's account just mentioned); von Lindquist reported to Berlin in 1897 that "some small bands of Herero have of late emigrated. . . . leading the way was a 40- to 50-strong group from the Grootfontein area who set out in a northeasterly direction. It remains to be seen whether they have gone to British or Portuguese territory" (von Lindequist to Hohenlohe-Schillingsfürst, 14 October 1897, quoted in Dreschler 1980:98). They went, of course, to Ngamiland, where they had long-standing claims such as that recorded by Alnaes (1979a:3, 11) that the Mbanderu chief, Munyuku (circumcised in 1834; Schapera 1945:36),[2] father of Kahimemua, lived part of his life in Ngamiland (see also Nettleton in BNA 1926c). Sundermeier (n.d.:6) was told that in the time of Kahimemua's father's father, Tjozohongo (born ca. 1750; see genealogy fig. 6.9), "From Rietfontein east the whole Ghanzie plain was all Mbanderu country." A site near Qubi is said by current residents of the area to have been a place where Katittewe (the father's father of the CaeCae Tuvare family heads and mother's father's father of Tautona's Zhu family at CaeCae) and his Mbanderu group lived with Zhu at about this time or slightly later. This move reported by von Lindquist was to have repercussions later for all the peoples of the region, especially for Ovaherero fleeing the Germans in 1904 (Alnaes 1979a, 1979b). There were others farther north in the Tebravelt who took no part in the conflict to follow; these were Ovambanderu under Nikodemus Kavarure (the nephew of Kahimemua and actual father, as seed raiser in levirate to Kahimemua's son Kangariri, of Kaheranju), who felt their home was there where they were, not westward at Hamakari (the Waterberg). Alnaes (1979a) recorded oral histories confirming the presence in the NyaeNyae area of Ovambanderu of Nikodemus's group months before the battle of Hamakari.

At this point, a turn to the recitations of six Mbanderu elders recorded by Sundermeier (n.d.:43, 54) in 1966 will shed some light on the situation. Just before the fire fight at Otjunda, Kahimemua untied the knots of each family head on the thong of the clan (omuvia omurangere) as a sign that each would die in the coming battle. He did not untie the knot of his brother's son Nikodemus but told him that he would trek to a country where he would find a calf from their clan's sacred cow. In 1904, before hostilities erupted into war, Nikodemus did just that "and received sacred cattle" in the Onyainya-Qangwa area; this appears to confirm Mbanderu presence in that area. Alnaes (1979b:4) was told that in 1904–5, after the war, the head of a family was able to "borrow" seed stock in this manner from relatives already established in Ngamiland; she says that most refugees had such relatives to call upon.

It is cogent to pause here for a moment and recall Chapman's (1971, 1:231) thoughts of thirty years earlier: "But at [Amraal's] death, or after the decline of the ivory trade or the coming of lungsickness, I expect a great falling off of their temporal and spiritual state." Chapman could not have foreseen the German imperial imperative that brought about Amraal's death, but he did foresee the decline of the ivory trade and the falling off of the temporal and spiritual state that would accompany these events.

There were native counterparts to Chapman who had also foreseen the collapse of the whole show; Witbooi is eloquent in a letter to Maharero dated 30 May 1890 (Gugelberger 1984:43−44):

My dear Captein Maharero Tjamuaha! To you, Paramount Chief of Damaraland, I address this letter today. I have received a letter from Dr. Göring from which I take it that major changes are taking place which force me to add my own commentary. I understand from that letter that you have placed yourself under German protection. Dr. Göring therefore has become rather influential, and it is in his power to give orders in what concerns our ways of life. . . . My dear Captein! Do you really know what you have done? Do you know for whom you have done what you have done, and against whom you have done what you have done? . . . Dear Captein! I am positive that you will regret your decision! You shall regret forever the fact that you have given not only your land but also your chieftaincy into the hands of the white man. The war between us two is the lesser evil. . . . Despite all this I am hopeful that our war can lead to a just peace! But that you had to succumb to German protection, assuming on top of this to have acted wisely, that shall become a burden to you as if you were to carry the sun on your back!

It should come as no surprise that such awareness had hardly any effect on efforts to stay in the show for as long as possible. Three letters written by Witbooi on 28 June 1891 reveal just how strong was this urge. The first two are to the trader Robert Duncan (Gugelberger 1984:57−58):

Beloved and noble Mr. R. Duncan! I am reporting to you that I have heard about German activities to which I cannot agree and which perhaps will hinder us with our work. These events provoke thoughts. The Germans entered our lands and are enforcing their laws. I have been informed by some of my officials that signs proclaim German laws [about firearms] in the stores at Rehoboth. . . . All their activities take place on my roads and my territory. But I had better not look too closely so that I avoid becoming a cause for their actions. I am only involved with the Hereros, and you know that this involvement has been going on for quite some time. The Hereros refuse a peaceful settlement. Therefore, dear friend, get going and try to provide me with arms and ammunition as you have done in the past. I greet you and remain your friend and Captein.

From the second letter to Duncan on that same day:

My beloved and most noble Mr. Duncan! I beg you to please help me out with some money so that I can try to obtain arms and ammunition here in Rehoboth. Fortunately, arms are still available there, but only if one can pay cash. Please do help me, my dear friend, as you have always helped me in the past. I fully rely on you! Please respond to this note instantly. The Hereros are getting closer and closer. I greet you all and remain Your friend and Chief.

And then this:

Dear Gibeon Community! I address these lines to you. Through Gert Pinaar I have asked you a favor. So far I have not received an answer. I repeat my plea. Be careful and work, dear Community. Do not get attached to material goods. Have a meeting and try to buy ammunition. We have to do our best to obtain all the firearms and ammunition which is still in the possession of traders here in the country. Those Germans are rather powerful, and they move with gigantic steps. But the work of the Lord is faster. Please hurry, dear Community! You are helping yourselves by helping us. Please do not reject this plea. Please do obey, I urge you. Herewith I inform you, Sub-Chief Abel Christian Isaak and Petrus Cloete, that I am going to sell your oxen which are with me for firearms. I greet you all and remain Your Captein.

But on 15 September 1894, Witbooi himself did what three years before he had warned Maharero against; he signed a treaty with Major Leutwein in which "Chief Witbooi promises, for himself and his successors, to support his Majesty the German Emperor and his government against any and all internal and external enemies by providing men capable to serve in the military, immediately and without conditions, when and as needed" (Gugelberger 1984:57–58, 128).

The German-Herero war took place from January to August 1904; it was extended against the Nama immediately thereafter. It was an avowed war of extermination; sixty thousand people are said to have been killed. In it "it was irrelevant whether those attacked had been involved in the war or not and whether they were Herero, Bergdamara or San ('Bushmen')—the German soldiers were anyway incapable of distinguishing between them" (Drechsler 1980:159). Irle (1906b), who had worked his entire adult life in the country, was moved to ask, "Was soll aus den Herero werden?": "What shall become of the Herero?" and extended that question to the other peoples decimated in the slaughter.

The varying roles Zhu played in the conflict are brought to light in

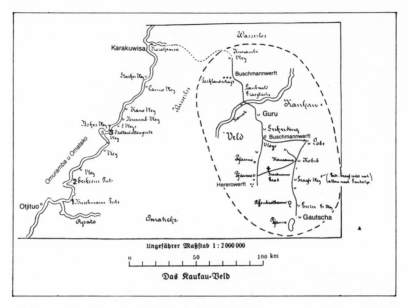

Figure 4.2. Photoreproduction of a map of the KauKau Veld (the NyaeNyae area) published in von Deimling (1906). Places important to the text discussion have been set in type. The numbers mark well-known hand-dug water holes: 1, Buschmann Putz (Bushman Pit); 2, Erikson's Putz—dug by Axel Eriksson; 3, Hottentotenputz—presumably associated with Nama-speakers. CaeCae does not appear on the original, but its location is marked with a triangle for reference.

documents of the times; these roles were complex and hardly uniform among individuals, any more than were those of Ovaherero (or for that matter of Europeans) themselves. Detailed accounts of Zhu in various associations with hostilities are given by von Deimling (1906), von Herrenkirchen (1907), and other memoirs of German Schutztruppe; some of these occurred in the heart of the NyaeNyae area (fig. 4.2):

> The captain of the !Kung Bushmen went to see Graeff. . . . of the entry of certain Herero bands, which he regarded as unauthorized intruders, he appeared little in favor; hence he promised his willing assistance. . . . the march to Gautscha, in the heart of the oasis, set out. Another, larger band of Hereros had settled there; indeed it happened that the enemy, because of Graeff's previous attack ran away in fright. Thus was even that distant part of the colony cleansed of the enemy.[3] (Bayer 1909:244)

It seems, however, that some of those memories exaggerate events, for Graeff later told Lt. Col. Trench, British attaché to the German forces, that "in the vicinity of Gautscha he met numbers too strong for him to tackle and fell back on Grootfontein" (BNA 1905b).

The assistant magistrate at Tsau, Merry, went out to investigate the German attacks and obtained a Herero description (BNA 1905a):

It appears that about the 5th of April [1905] just after daylight, the Damaras observed a party of about twenty mounted men, accompanied by Bushmen approach their village. As they appeared to be coming from the direction of the Protectorate, the people imagined they were British, and were encouraged in this idea by the information they had received of the recent visit of Sub-Inspector Surmon to the district, they therefore made no attempt to escape. The mounted men, about half of whom were white, the others being Damaras, dismounted and at once opened fire, killing three men and women, the remainder fled into the bush and escaped. Later on in the day two of the refugees returned to the village to endeavor to recover some of their belongings, and on their return journey saw the Germans, with a Scotch Cart at Guduwa, some 18 to 20 miles this side of NyaiNyai. . . . Four Bushmen who accompanied the patrol were recognized by the Damaras, they had been living with them at NyaiNyai.[4]

Factional conflict was a factor, as it had been forty years earlier when Baines recorded hostilities between Zhu and Ovaherero, but relations between these peoples were not all hostile. The "!Kung captain who sought out Graeff" objected to the unauthorized presence of *particular* Herero groups, and Mbanderu oviruzo of Nikodemus had been in the area for six months or longer without recorded conflict (Alnaes 1979a:3; Dreschler 1980:144–55; Sundermeier, n.d.:53). This should be expected; Kahae Tuvare told me, "Onyainya kakurusu Nikodemus": "Onyainya is the old place [that is, the legitimate place, omahi] of Nikodemus." Other Otjiherero place-names in the area— Otjikarema, Guru, possibly Djarutsa[5]—point to long-standing Mbanderu residence; and Schinz (1891:400) records that people he called Herero were living at Rietfontein in 1881.

Zhu at CaeCae accommodated refugees from the fighting. Tautona, the Nama man we know who was eighty-six in 1980, remembered the route through the Omaheke along which he and others fled to CaeCae; they took that route because it was the one they were accustomed to using to reach that place. Kahae Tuvare, an Omumbanderu, seventy-three in 1980, said that his grandfather and father lived at Qangwa and had often watered their cattle at CaeCae; consequently it was to these places that his relatives escaped: "My father's father, Katittewe, as well as other ancestors, went to Letsholethebe to ask to live at Qangwa. . . . this is a Zhu place and does not have a Herero name. . . . after the war they stayed there for two years then went to Nokaneng and Tsau. . . . we returned here [CaeCae] when the British were asking for men for Hitler's war [1939]."

Herero-Mbanderu factionalism was if anything more intense as a result of the strains of the German pressure; after their defeat at Water-berg, Samuel's Ovaherero set out to take revenge on Nikodemus's Ovambanderu, who had refused to fight with them. The British magistrate and Sekgoma at Tsau were kept informed of events, in part by Samuel Sheppard—the son of Alexander's ward, Saul Sheppard, and one of the 1896 immigrants to Gatawana—who "had been sent to the border by Sekgoma to make enquires on the spot" (BNA 1904a):

Messengers dispatched to the Chief from the vicinity of the border arrived at this station yesterday reporting that a considerable body of armed Damaras [Ovaherero] was then approaching the border of the Reserve with the object of attacking the group of Herero [Ovambanderu] refugees whose rumored presence in the neighborhood of Karakobis on their way hither I reported in my communication of the 3rd Sept. . . . The accompanying rough sketch may I trust give some idea of the position [fig. 4.1]. . . . Some of the Herero fugitives concerned informed me that the party recently reported as approaching the border which had threatened to attack the Hereros then encamped at the well called Tgangwa [Qangwa] was being led by Frederick Maharero son of the Paramount Chief Samuel and that accompanied by only a small number of men he had made a demonstration against the refugees occupying the position named who immediately fled abandoning their cattle which he seized. (BNA 1904a)

In the middle of 1905 a number of these Mbanderu refugee groups were still in the border area. The visit by Surmon that Merry referred to was undertaken in March of that year in order to ascertain the degree of Herero settlement in the northern part of the Protectorate (BNA 1905c):

I have the honour to report for your information that after leaving here on the 12th Ultimo I did patrol to the west visiting a Damara post near the border about five days journey from here on horseback. The Damaras I saw were about twentyfive in number, consisting of several families, and had about twelve head of cattle. These people told me of about 30 families of Damaras living all together a little further west [these were those attacked by Graeff]. . . . Those on this side of the border are said not to have had any communication with people in Damaraland for several months.

Manuel Marenga relates that those Mbanderu families remained at Qangwa for more than a year because it was a place to which they had rights and thereby afforded them a location at which to conduct the series of ceremonies necessary to install Nikodemus as their new omuhona, chief. Marenga says this is what Kahimemua meant when he told Nikodemus he would find a sacred calf there. As they said, "Well, we must not be children, without a chief, so the Batawana will say 'Oh, so you have no chief, so you will become Tswana and work for us.'" For, as the saying is, leaderless men are women. On the other hand, immigrants with a recognized leader were formed into their own ward under the headmanship of that leader; such wards retained a political voice within Tswana merafe (Schapera 1938 : 19–24; Tlou 1974 : 60). The Ovambanderu of Nikodemus did not wish to be incorporated as batlhanka under Tawana hegemony; this led to continuing struggle between these groups.[6]

Maps based on Sheppard's reports and Surmon's trip show Ngae (unknown), Tgangwa (Qangwa), Muhupa (Magopa), and several of the NyaeNyae pans as the places where Ovaherero were living at the end of December 1905, nearly a year and a half after the battle of Hamakari (fig. 4.1). Sekgoma wanted to keep them there and restock his cattle-posts with them as herders.

But the Germans at first were worried about retaliatory raids and formally requested that the British high commissioner in Johannesburg instruct his resident magistrates to move all Herero refugees farther into the Protectorate, away from the border. This was done, the British being themselves nervous about conflicts with the Germans. In fact, Williams (BNA 1904a) reminded his superiors that after the Zhu raids a year earlier he had already cleared Tawana cattle from the area. He goes on to list a number of potential clashes and says that in consequence of these "it is a subject for congratulations that I some time ago secured the removal of all Sekgomas cattle posts in that neighborhood."

It was the British policy of protecting their own interests in Gatawana that had denuded the western sandveld of cattle, not adverse ecology or raiding. We may be sure that no unduly fine distinctions about ownership were made in these removals; any Zhu cattle would have gone east with the rest, as did Zhu herders of Tawana cattle. Indeed, (as will be detailed in chapter 6) those Zhu now living at Tawana cattleposts in the Nokaneng-Tsau area near the Okavango Delta trace their coming to those places to the events of this time. In 1906 Mathiba rescinded the reforms made by Sekgoma and thus in essence reenserfed those Zhu and other San-speakers of Gatawana living where Tawana cattleposts were concentrated. This completed their disfranchisement and tied their labor to Tawana needs. In the western sandveld, Zhu—though just as thoroughly enmeshed in the Tswana-dominated economic formation—retained considerable political autonomy and freedom of action.

In Südwestafrika, the Germans simply confiscated cattle for themselves. They also killed or drove out as many native peoples as they could. Just three years later, when they realized that Leutwein had been correct in seeing natives as a needed labor pool and that they had erred in driving that labor away, the Germans attempted to persuade Ovaherero to come back to Südwestafrika. They had some success (BNA 1907c): "Capt. Streatwolff at Tsau has persuaded 20 Herero to return to South West." They also turned to other sources. While eliminating San from their land to make room for incoming German colonist ranchers, police were instructed that "firearms are to be used in the smallest case of insubordination . . . [except] . . . if some of the male Bushmen who have been arrested are strong enough to work, they should be handed over to the district authorities at Lüderitzbucht to work in the diamond fields" (quoted in Gordon 1984).

Clarence-Smith (1979:70) has noted that the opening of copper mines and diamond fields at the end of the first decade of this century created an acute shortfall of labor in Namibia. This was in keeping with the rest of the subcontinent. A dominant economic factor in the Kalahari region became, in the first half of this century, the supply of migrant labor to meet those mining needs. San-speakers, as before, were engulfed in this regional process.

Ngamiland Shots for Universal Emancipation

World War I brought another brief flurry of fighting to the borders of Ngamiland. Just two weeks after the war began in Europe, German forces attacked Quagganahai (in Ngamiland) near Rietfontein, and on 17 August 1914 they "took a very strong Herero fort in the Kaukauveld on the south of Guru 160 miles east of Grootfontein" (BNA 1914b). This was Onyainya, hardly a fort but a cattlepost.[7] For keeping track of German movements, the British considered "Masarwa and Makwengo Bushmen" to be the best intelligence agents and arranged for Mathiba to support ten San spies in the field, although it was thought doubtful they could be sent to the Grootfontein area, where "Bushmen" had assassinated two German officers earlier in the year and were subject to being shot on sight. These "Bushmen" and Tawana dispatch riders were to "scout their old hunting grounds on the sandvelt to the west," where they were stationed at Nqoma and Xaudum (BNA 1914a).

Nine months after these southern African skirmishes of World War I, Herero refugees were still entering the Protectorate. Among those who came to Ngamiland in the aftermath of the war was a Boer, Piet Venter, whose Herero name was Kurundu. Venter's wife, Retia (Lydia), was known as an Omumbanderu after her father and her mother's father (who was Katittewe), but her mother was a Nama whose mother was, by a Nama husband, the mother's mother of Tautona. Venter and

Retia were at CaeCae about 1918, a date that can be reasonably fixed because their son Kakuna, who was seventy-two in 1984, remembered that he was about six years old at the time. They subsequently went to Qubi; Marshall (1960, fig. 1), on her first map of the area, has the place-name Venter, which still locates their homestead there. Four years later, at Makakung in 1922, the Venter household served as a channel both for passing confidential information among native peoples and for implanting divisive rumors in the British administration.

During 1922–23 three sets of events took place in Ngamiland and the then recently mandated Trust Territory of South-West Africa, under Union of South Africa administration. These events cannot really be seen as part of a unified conspiracy, as both the British and Union administrations feared, but they did have common origins in widespread dissatisfaction with the nature of those administrations. They also were influenced by international attempts to unify action against colonial oppression. Again, the events are worth examining in detail because they reveal how the peoples of the region were interlinked, how the shape of events was contingent on the history of the region, and how the region continued to be meshed with the rest of the world.

The first series of events came to a head in 1922 when the magistrate at Gobabis, Captain van Ryneveld,

was shot by Bushmen on the 26th [July] and died by the same day. . . . these Bushmen have been raiding cattle for several months past on a scale which hasn't been experienced before and threatening anyone who went in pursuit of them. . . . At the present time there is also some form of agitation going on amongst the Hereros, and some of the Bechuanas. On one or two occasions recently these agitators have come over from Bechuanaland. . . . They wear rosettes of red, blue [actually black, although I'm told that some of the dyes were false and ran blue] and green at their native meetings, and have been explaining how war should be made against the Europeans. . . . should you have reason to suspect that any of your natives are constantly crossing the border and are members of any socialistic or other political society I should be glad if you would advise me. (BNA 1922a)

Police operations were initiated in the northern part of Gobabis District, and many Zhu were rounded up. Most of them were released; however,

rather more than 100 were dispatched to Gobabis but . . . a number escaped and 7 have not been recaptured. Amongst these were Zamekou [Samkao, a common Zhu man's name] and his principal adherents. Zamekou himself appears to have obtained an influence over the whole of the Bushmen in his area which has been most unfortunate. They have been implicated in stock thefts

upon an unprecedented scale and have fired not only at the Police but also at
private individuals. . . . We are informed that there is a water hole a good bit
to the north of Rietfontein and probably within your district which is an old
haunt of the wilder Bushmen. Do you know anything about it? . . . All the
tame Bushmen are agreed that Zamekou has a base somewhere near the border
to the N.E. of this [Rietfontein] and as he disappears in that direction from
time to time for considerable periods this is probably true. (BNA 1922b)

Cuzen, resident magistrate at Ghanzi, had to make inquiries before
he could report that NyaeNyae existed just "three days Journey on
foot North of Rietfontein." It is a measure of changed conditions
brought about in a decade or so that the Union magistrate in Gobabis
did not know of NyaeNyae and that Samkao could "disappear" into
an area where previously British officials had gone easily when investigating cattle raids. Neither Samkao nor any of his adherents was ap-
prehended, although a camel corps detachment was sent to search for
them (Almagor 1980b:70 records that, in consequence, 1922 in some
oviuondo year lists in Ngamiland is called "ojozongamero": "camels").

In these changed conditions, Zhu—along with other San-speakers—
continued to use the means at their disposal to protect their own interests. Cuzen (BNA 1922c) had previously been told the reason for these
raids by Zhu who had come into the Protectorate from South-West
Africa: "They informed me that they could not live under the existing
laws in S.W.A., as they are punished for killing game and must carry
passes. . . . If they are not allowed to kill game they would kill cattle."

At almost exactly the same time, Nettleton, the resident magistrate
at Maun, transmitted to the government secretary a sworn statement
made by a Mosarwa man named Samson, who said: "While at Makakon a few miles south of Tsau I was spoken to by a Mocuba, named
Tau, who is living with a Mosarwa woman at Makakon. He told me
that he had been to Maun lately and Chief Mathiba told him and
others who have posts away from Maun to sell their oxen and buy
guns. Tau told me that when the people had sufficient guns, the Batawana would make a war against Europeans. . . . I reported the matter
to my master, Mr. C. Lewis" (BNA 1922d). Samson heard that story
while visiting his sister, Tau's wife, who lived in the Venter homestead
at Makakung. Two Herero visitors told it to him with the intention
that it should reach the administration and embarrass Mathiba, perhaps weakening his authority. Given his relationship to the principals—
actually, even without such relationship—it is hard to imagine that
Samson was unaware of his role in this scene. Nettleton says the Herero
hoped to gain a better hearing from the British for what they viewed to
be demeaning treatment by the Batawana. He calls the story "RUB-

BISH" and offers this analysis: "We may take it as a certainty that Bolshevic (or German) activity must be at work on the Damara in S.W.A. and from that source of contagion Damara emissaries must undoubtedly be coming over to our side to infect our Damara in Ghanzi and Ngamiland. . . . The Damara have no country of their own and therefore Bolshevic propaganda appeals to them" (BNA 1922e). It appears to have been Lloyd George himself, then prime minister of Great Britain, who raised the specter of bolshevism in a dispatch to Jan Smuts, prime minister of the Union of South Africa, in which he urged that this threat not be allowed to spread (Willan 1982:245).

That "Bolshevism" appeared in Ngamiland in the person of Samuel Sheppard, whom we have met before: "Samuel Sheppard is the native who travelled from Maun to Ghanzi, held meetings at Kalkfontein, then proceeded to Lehututu and towards the Upington District [in the Union of South Africa] eventually reaching Windhuk after months of travel. . . spreading sedition among the natives through whose villages and kraals he may have passed" (BNA 1923b). Toppe, the acting magistrate at Gobabis, sent Sheppard back to Ghanzi on 4 April 1923 with the remark: "From what I am able to gather it would appear that this man has travelled practically all over the country . . . and I fear he has been spreading the doctrine of 'Africa for the Africans' en route" (BNA 1923a).

The doctrine was that of the American visionary Marcus Garvey and his Universal Negro Improvement Association (UNIA), which reached South Africa through the agency of black sailors who passed it on to dockworkers at Cape Town, Port Elizabeth, and Durban, where parts of the doctrine were incorporated into the philosophy of the recently formed Industrial and Commercial Workers Union (ICU). In South-West Africa it began in a group of Liberian and Cameroonian deportees who had been settled at Lüderitz (Emmett 1986:20). Sheppard, who knew English tolerably well (BNA 1905a) and also spoke Setswana, could have become acquainted with the movement both through direct contact with its advocates and through newspapers such as *Black Man* and *Abantu Batho* that radiated UNIA ideas throughout southern Africa (Marks and Trapido 1987:40).

In February 1921 a UNIA branch was established at Lüderitz, in association with a branch of the ICU: "Within eighteen months the 'Black, Red, and Green Rosette' was to be seen throughout much of the Protectorate [South-West Africa] . . . [where it spread] first to other urban centers and ultimately to the bush" (Pirio 1982:23–28). Hill and Pirio (1987) set this spread into South-West Africa in its subcontinental context. Sheppard is also reported to have traveled to the Up-

ington District, where he may have come in contact with members of
Sol Plaatje's Liberty Hall group, centered in Kimberley, who were
at that time actively studying the UNIA message (Hill 1983; Willan
1982:267). Sheppard carried this message to Ngamiland.

As far as the mandate administration was concerned, the situation
was becoming tense, although the native commissioner kept matters
low key. A police informer, David Ngxiki, reported:

> On the 13th Sept. [1922] Fritz (Herero) . . . said that three days beyond
> Gobabis [that is, in the Onyaiyna-CaeCae area] there were alot of natives in-
> cluding Hereros, Bushmen, and American negroes waiting for the white people
> to come there to start a fight. There are altogether about three hundred natives
> there with rifles, and some without rifles. They still want more arms. A herero
> came from there to get recruits. I could not find this boy. . . . Fritz asked me if
> I had heard what the Bushmen at Gobabis did to the Police and the Magis-
> trate. (State Archive Service, Windhoek 1922a)

There were, of course, no three hundred rifles,[8] and the "American
Negroes" were Liberians; only one of them is known to have gone to
the more remote parts of northern South-West Africa, and I have not
been able to find that he reached the Onyaiyna-CaeCae area. However, Sheppard clearly was not alone. Nor was South-West Africa
the sole direction from which emancipatory efforts impinged on the
area. Kahae Tuvare remembers seeing the black-red-green rosettes as a
boy; he says they were brought to Sehitwa by people of Nikodemus's
(Kavarure) group who came from Rakops to the east. Four years earlier Nikodemus, because he vigorously protested the terms of Tawana
rule over his people, had been allowed by Mathiba to resettle first at
Chobe, then at Rakops on the Botletli. Almagor (1980b:70) records
the oviuondo year name of 1918 as "Ojoruntjindo": "Nikodemus's
movement" (to Chobe).

Nikodemus had lost his bid to lead the Ngamiland Ovambanderu
to the superior claim of Kaheranju, but he was strongly affiliated
with Venter through the latter's wife, Retia, and through her to both
Ovambanderu and Zhu in the western sandveld (see genealogy, fig. 6.9).
Networks such as these were—and are—important channels of information; this seems to have been the route through which the message
of Garvey reached CaeCae, NyaeNyae, and other "remote" locations.
A letter is known to have been circulated in early 1922 calling for the
unity of Ovambo, Nama, Damara, Herero, and San peoples in an effort
to overthrow mandate authority (State Archive Service, Windhoek
1922b). It appears that Samkao and his group heard this message and
perhaps acted on it. Ngxiki continued, "The trouble if it arises will

begin on the eastern border of the District when the rain starts." In the event, not much trouble arose—other than the death of a magistrate, some cattle rustling, and bureaucratic anxiety—but it does seem certain that remote Onyaiyna-CaeCae had wider international feelers than we have been led to believe.

Herero discontent was deepened when Union promises to restore their possessions in land and cattle after the war were not fulfilled. In Vedder's ([1928] 1966:163) supercilious—and unconsciously cogent—phrase, the seed of American apostles of freedom did fall on well-tilled Herero soil. Vedder took this metaphor from the *Diamond Fields Advertiser* (6 September 20), which announced that Garvey's message would be "seed on fertile soil" of black discontent; but to extend the metaphor, that seed could not germinate and take root in southern Africa because "of the mismatch between the millenarian expectations of its supporters and its organizational and political capacity" (Marks and Trapido 1987:42). It took only momentary root in Ngamiland. When asked if he knew anything about it, Marenga, who was not yet born at the time but had heard about it from elders, replied: "Oh, that. Yes, they came all around here and had those ribbon badges." His curt dismissal reflected, in part, his own disdain for the people who claimed to represent the Garvey movement but who absconded with the contributions made to the cause (Kandovazu 1968 says that R8,000 was taken in this scam). Marenga's response also reflected the frustration of those who told him of the movement and its end in Ngamiland.

The Underclass Solidified

Frustration was the order of the day. Raiding in the nineteenth century was a response to unequal trade relations and was a way to transfer exchange value in a distorted market system. Successful raiders could expect a viable—if unfair—return for their efforts. Now in the first decades of the twentieth century there was no longer raiding of large herds for value but small-scale stock theft for immediate meals, the transition brought about by utter exclusion of the reduced classes from legitimate economic channels.

Other avenues were explored as well. At least from the teens of this century, Ovambanderu have made persistent attempts to reestablish their old cattleposts in South-West Africa, especially at Onyainya, Ncama, and Gcam. These efforts were persistently challenged by Tawana rulers, who wished to retain control over both people and cattle, and by SWA authorities, who were fearful of strengthened Herero resistance to their policy of establishing white farms in the area. By 1918 or thereabouts, Boer farmers established themselves at Gcam (testimony of Dam Y/741; see chap. 6). Gordon (1984:217) cites a case that occurred in 1935: at that time, 138 Ovambanderu/Ovaherero with over eight hundred cattle and four hundred goats said to belong to a Tswana owner at Magopa were forced to leave the Gcaucha area by South-West African police acting at the request of the Tawana kgosi, Mathiba. This episode is well remembered at CaeCae because, according to a resident of that place, Halengisi, who was among those forced to move, Zhu and Mbanderu as well as Tawana cattle were involved. Other cases will be discussed in subsequent chapters.

Some San-speakers—surprisingly, given the overwhelming odds— managed to hold on to small herds: "In the Bangwaketse Reserve, for instance, the Masarwa, who used to pay tribute in skins to the Bakgalagadi, having become educated to the use of money, now take their skins to Hawkers and Traders, and to the dismay of the latter, often demand market prices in cash. Many of them acquire cattle of their own as a result of their trading" (BNA 1927). Joyce (1937; BNA 1938), in a thorough survey, found that in Gangwato there was, on average, one beast (cow, bull, ox, or calf) for every two to five San families (his figures were partly actual counts and partly estimates; significantly, Joyce did not include San-speaking, cattle-keeping Bateti in his survey). The distribution was, moreover, highly skewed; one man— with forty head—owned 9% of all the cattle belonging to Gangwato San-speakers (other than Bateti) at the time, and less than 10% of all San families owned any stock at all. Thus at this time, in the 1930s, while a handful were better off economically than were most Tswana rural poor, the fact remains that the vast majority of San peoples were below even that low standard of poverty.

Even these small holdings were confiscated—as often as not through the legal mechanisms of the courts. The Molele and Mobusetse families are often mentioned as having been particularly favored by Khama and having built up independent herds (BNA 1944a; Sebolai 1978:26). In 1944 the Moleles with their herd of thirty-six cattle and fifteen goats were "banished from Crown Lands" by magistrate court and removed to Ngwato District to come under Bangwato control; all firearms belonging to them were confiscated (BNA 1944a). By the mid-1940s, the principal veterinary officer of the Protectorate reported only ninety-eight head of cattle owned by San peoples in the entire northern two-thirds of the Ngwato Reserve (BNA 1946); in some sort of compensation, some of these were said to be in better condition than those belonging to Bangwato (BNA 1940a).

Without the benefit of magistrate, but equally effectively in kgotla, a Zhu man, Tcashe (K/921), at CaeCae during the early 1950s, was fined all of his four cattle to compensate an Omumbanderu for the loss of one ox stolen and eaten by Tcashe's cousins, who owned no live-stock—one beast for each of the four offenders, a penalty in keeping with Tswana law, which extracts full payment from each offender.

Simon Ratshosa (BNA 1926a, 1927; Parsons 1974b) threatened to bring these injustices to the attention of the world in 1926 (even though the immediate cause of his announcement was a dispute with Tshekedi over the ownership of a certain group of "Bushmen"). The British be-came concerned about world opinion, and a series of investigations en-sued. At the conclusion of one of these investigations, the London Missionary Society (Livingstone's sponsor) assured the administration that all was really according to "native" custom; perhaps a few adjust-ments were needed to conform to contemporary notions of personal liberty, but it would take time to make "Bushmen" understand about civilized cattle keeping (LMS 1935).

Tshekedi (BNA 1933, 1934, 1935; LMS 1935) taunted the admin-istration, challenging them to take charge of the situation themselves if they were genuinely concerned, as he noted they did in other matters—the control of trade, for instance. Then he added a pointed, sarcastic slap (BNA 1934): "I add to this namely, that the Magistrates were a party to this procedure also, before and after this Declaration [of abol-ishment of serfdom]. We obtain passes from the Magistrates for the express purpose of bringing back Masarwa deserters. If this be a sin, then it is a sin committed not only by Tshekedi and the Bamangwato but also by the Government though they now hold themselves aloof." This brief flurry of not too painful soul-searching seemed to satisfy everyone. As for San-speakers, they had gained the status of pawns in administrative power plays, to be fought over as line items in bureau-cratic budgets.

Tagart (1933:7), in the first of a dreary series of investigations, had seen the core of the matter clearly. Although his recommendations were as pasty as any, he saw that the San present was articulated with the economic, political past and future of the region as a whole:

The fact is that there is little opportunity for any natives to obtain paid em-ployment either in the Bamangwato Reserve, or indeed in other parts of the protectorate. It is probably not going too far to say that this has been the most potent factor in perpetuating the servile condition of the Masarwa, and re-mains the greatest obstacle in the way of their emancipation. Had there been a steady local demand for free native labour it is inconceivable that the Baman-gwato could have maintained the present system, and until greater opportunity for independent employment presents itself, it is difficult to see how the Masarwa can be helped to emerge from the condition of apathy and dependence into which they have lapsed.

The escape valve for Tswana labor was migration to South Africa, principally to the mines. Schapera (1947:38–39) estimated that in 1938–40, 28% of all adult male Batswana were away on migrant labor; that proportion rose to 46% during World War II, when about ten thousand men from the Protectorate served in the British army. In contrast, only forty-two San men—all with Tswana names—from Gangwato were registered as being on the mines in 1936 (BNA 1938); this list, of course, does not include those who successfully "passed" as Tswana. Tswana men would have been unable to avail themselves of migrant employment without a supplementary labor pool from which to replace the absent work force on cattleposts and fields. San men, prevented from going to the mines in proportionate numbers, supplied the bulk of that necessary labor supplement (this is taken up in detail in chap. 7).

Tagart was alone in that vision of all peoples of the region integrated in a single political economy. To most others San "Bushmen" had disappeared, not from the land but from notice. It had taken almost two thousand years to accomplish, but in 1940 Tshekedi—who nearly a decade earlier had testified that when San-speakers first received Batswana into the Kalahari they were equals—now could say they were rootless, without an ideology of property and place (BNA 1944b). Rey (1932:288), then resident commissioner for the Protectorate, wrote in the *Geographical Journal* that, away from the Botletli—in the sandveld Kalahari where Livingstone, Oswell, Campbell, and others had painted vivid word pictures of many people shooting ostriches, elephants, and each other—no inhabitants were known. Lord Hailey (1953:290–93) devoted only eight paragraphs in five thick volumes to "the servile people" of the Kalahari, almost all of those paragraphs lifted from Tshekedi's testimony to the London Missionary Society.

Nevertheless, a place where glass beads from Asia, mollusk shells from the eastern sea more than 1,500 kilometers away, and—it is no longer unreasonable to suppose—colorful cloth were important trade goods more than a millennium ago is not isolated. A place where early in the nineteenth century a boy is bought for cloth and glass beads, educated in England, and returns as a man to prepare his son in turn to be an emissary of a twentieth-century American-inspired ideology is not without contacts to the world. People who repeatedly assassinate their oppressors, reappropriate portions of their confiscated property, and contribute to causes for the realignment of policy are not passively dispossessed by choice or circumstance.

The conclusion is inescapable: it is not possible to speak of the Kalahari's isolation, protected by its own vast distances. To those inside, the outside—whatever "outside" there may have been at any moment—was always present. The appearance of isolation and its reality of dispossessed poverty are recent products of a process that unfolded over two centuries and culminated in the last moments of the colonial era.

5

The Ideology of Person and Place

I am not afraid of raising this point, which does not mean to say that the Masarwa are no people at all, but merely shows what the position is today. Also with regard to the assertion that they have nothing to do in the work of governing themselves . . . *we* were in the position of the Masarwa before the Government came into the country. We used to rule ourselves and even after the Government entered we were told we should rule ourselves, but now at the present day we see the Government taking away our own self-government, and the rules which they make for us they do not ask us about before they make them.

Tshekedi Khama, testimony to the London Missionary Society regarding the Masarwa (Bushmen), 1935

Concepts of Possession

By applying a particularist, synchronic ethnology in their approach, ethnographers of San peoples brought the appearance of social and economic separation in the Kalahari up to date. Passarge set the tone for ethnographic reporting of San-speakers when he divided "Das Leben der Buschmänner in früheren Zeiten" (Bushman life in earlier times) from that "in der Jetztzeit" (in the present). This observational present of his was 1896–98 and featured Zhu—in addition to their "traditional" role as foragers of wild resources—as husbandmen of cattle and goats. Passarge also says that Zhu were associates of Batawana and Ovaherero and in the immediately preceding decades had been—but were no longer then—participants in mercantile trade. His earlier time, by which he meant later precolonial centuries as representative of prehistoric millennia, was the same except that husbandry, external contact, and trade were subtracted while foraging was extrapolated to fill the void, thus eradicating the rich history of associations we have just witnessed.

Modern ethnographers of San peoples have not looked far beyond Passarge in considering social relations among Kalahari peoples; none have ventured past the closing years of the nineteenth century to seek the roots of these relations. Lee (1979:401, emphasis added) voices

the opinion—first enunciated by Pitt-Rivers in 1875 (p. 15 above)—
explicitly shared by all of them regarding that period: "The nature of
the contact [between Zhu and Batswana], in socioevolutionary terms,
occurred between *more or less adjacent stages* within the sequence of
precapitalist social formations."

With respect to associations between these peoples during the
middle of this century, however, Lee (1979:53) provides the only
manageable data. These are revealing. Of the rather stable population
of about nine hundred persons who lived in the Dobe area during the
1950s and 1960s, 43% to 49% were Bantu-speakers, primarily Ovambanderu and Batawana. Put another way, barely half the inhabitants of
the area were Zhu when ethnographic observation of these "isolated
Bushmen" was at its peak. These proportions have not changed in the
1970s and 1980s and probably are also representative of at least parts
of the nineteenth century and earlier times, although data do not exist
on which to base actual calculations. Lee (1979:401–12) concedes
that this large Bantu presence has had significant influence upon Zhu
since 1960, but only since then, and even this he attributes mainly to
the establishment in that year of a European presence in the Bushman
Affairs Office at Tshumqwe in Namibia. He discounts earlier associations as of little importance in social, political, and material terms.

Lee's (1979:404, table 14.1) "chronology of events in the Dobe-
NyaeNyae areas" has the following listing: "1870s first visits of
Tswana hunters to area" (followed in the 1890s by cattle); four entries
later, the "arrival of the first year-round black settlers" occurred about
1925. No one seems to have asked how, in about 1925, Bantu aliens
could systematically settle at every major water source in the area and
gain—with no recorded protest from Zhu, despite the supposed im-
placable hostility between these peoples that had previously kept them
separated—immediate control of the disposition of those waters, di-
verting the bulk to sustaining their own herds. Since no form of conquest took place, the answer must lie in the way people perceive their
relations to land, how rights to use of particular portions of land are
distributed, and the history of prior distributions of those rights. The
general outline of prior distributions is discernible in the history of the
region just examined; specific details of family land relations are central to the next chapter concerning production relations. I shall take
up here the structure of perceptions and rights to land of the peoples
we are concerned with.

It is not surprising that the structure of San land tenure has been
overlooked, despite the promising beginning made by Lee (1965:198):
"[Zhu] do not lead a nomadic way of life. Each summer they move up-

country to the seasonal waters and each winter they fall back on their permanent waterholes." A tenent of evolutionary models in anthropology is that San relations to land have been autochthonous and are based entirely on unproblematic egalitarian principles of social relations. This tenet is entailed in Lee's separation of "adjacent stages" of social development cited a moment ago. The underlying motive forces forming these relations have been attributed to principally ecological imperatives centered on resource procurement necessities (Meillassoux 1967, 1972; Lee 1979; Silberbauer 1981; Tanaka 1980; Cashdan 1980a, 1983).

Now one may reasonably argue that the ecological principle that allocation of land and rights to its use is fundamental to the distribution of members of any species in space is congruent with the sociological principle that residence rules are essential to the continuance of associations of persons in place as viable polities. But one must remember that these principles are at best congruent, not identical; they have different referents and impose different orderings on their subjects, a point too often overlooked by ecologically oriented anthropologists.

Silberbauer (1981:192–93), for example, in unable to decide about Gcwi relations to land. When discussing utilization of their habitat, he attributes to them stabilized bands whose members have exclusive rights of exploitation in their territory. When discussing ownership and kinship he is not so sure, for he finds "no clear structural factor which determines band membership" (1981:140). Similarly, prospective recruits to a band unit ask permission of the owners of territories "to drink their water" (1981:141). These recruits appear to wander in from somewhere, stay for a shorter or longer time, and perhaps eventually wander off; those who stay the longest become the new "owners" of the territory. Silberbauer can find no basis for stability of residence or group membership, because none of the owners he interviewed (there are only six in his sample) were "demonstrably descended from the founders" of the territories in which he found them, although he acknowledges that inevitably real and classificatory kinship links are established and there is a high (but unspecified) probability of a kinship bond among members.

There is a contradiction of logic here. If there is stability of member rights in territory, there must also be stability of membership. Silberbauer fails to find the connection because, first, he conflates ecological territory with sociological tenure, and second, he looks for lineal descent groups with namable ancestors and finds only shallow lineages in this sense. Furthermore, of seventy-three men whose marriages he analyzes (he appears not to have interviewed women), Silberbauer finds that only 11% were married to MBD or FZD (see chap. 6, n. 2) at the time they were interviewed. On this basis he concludes that Gcwi marriage arrangements spatially disperse rather than consolidate kin, despite the fact that bilateral cross-cousin marriage is said to be preferred. Actually, demographic processes being what they are, 11% realized PsC unions is about what one could expect on average. Silberbauer (1981:148–50) then records that all first marriages are indeed between terminological cross-cousins and lists in this category, in addition to MBD and FZD, the more distant collaterals MMBSD, FFZDD, MMMBSSD, and FFFZDDD, plus others; a total of thirty-four kinship positions are said to be covered by this term. We are told nothing of marriages between persons in these positions.

This can be neither a shallow system nor a divisive one. At any given time, many of the thirty-four positions will be unfilled for any current person, who in addition almost surely will be unacquainted with numbers of potential mates in those positions that are filled. For that person to know that a descendant of certain ancestors, along with terminological equivalents, is a potential mate, the system must be comprehended in considerable depth and detail. Silberbauer makes it clear that it is so comprehended. This requires membership in a group that is stable—though not necessarily static—in person and place. Silberbauer confines his analysis, however, to first-cousin marriages intact at the time of his fieldwork, despite the fact that all first marriages are between terminological cross-cousins (Silberbauer 1981:149–50); he of course finds relatively few current first-cousin unions among adult males, but he tells us nothing about the status of other-cousin unions.

Tanaka (1980:127–34) presents data to support an argument for stability of social groups in place. He demonstrates that Gcwi residence groups are linked in a regular manner of kinship relations; eleven of his "residential clusters" (sample size is eighteen) contain twenty parent-child links between constituent households, nine contain fourteen sibling links, and only three have no kin ties with other families in the group (two of these comprise a single married pair each). Furthermore, he shows that primary kin ties link adjacent groups and that the relationship among residence units is structured in space as a direct function of kinship distance. Tanaka is at pains to dissociate his findings from Steward's patrilineal band and Service's derivative patrilocal band models; nevertheless, his evolutionary model compels him to maintain that Gcwi social integration is low. This also leads him to deny corporate status to Gcwi kin-resident groups despite his own evidence that they are stable in space, have generational continuity, and employ these factors in assessing tenure rights.

Lee too is concerned to undermine the earlier unilineal, patrifocal characterization of forager society; and he is equally concerned to place Zhu ownership of land on a resource-producing basis. His clearest statement of this is in his discussion of nqore (pl. nqoresi) ownership (n!óre = place in land/country),[1] in which he argues for a boundless universe of nqoresi that is both functional and adaptive in a world where group sizes and resources vary seasonally and yearly. Although nqoresi are collectively "owned" by sets of female and male kin who inherit land from generation to generation, association is said rarely to extend as far back as the grandparental generation (Lee 1979:60). Part of the problem lies in Lee's failure to take into account Bantu- and European-induced displacement of Zhu in the past two centuries; part lies in his persistent imprecision in the use of terms and presentation of values. An example: he says (1972b:129, 1979:61) that "the half-life of a core group's tenure of a n!ore can be estimated at 30 to 50 years." It is unclear what he means here. If half-life of a core group means that half of any particular set of adult persons will be absent at the end of a specified number of years, then, given a life expectancy of about forty-five more years at age twenty (Howell 1976:76–77), it is inevitable that that group's tenure will be on the order of less than fifty years. If infants and children of the same set of adults are included in a core group, then a half-life of thirty years results in a probability of 0.25 that current core group members will still be in place sixty years hence; that is, into the second ascending generation, based on a generation span of thirty years (Howell 1976:214, 335). If the oldest "owners" are at about their expected life span (sixty-five years), as they are likely to be, then the modal residential continuity for any given cohort will be in the range of 120 years. Matters are further complicated by the fact that children are born in almost every year, thereby changing the composition of core groups; the half-lives of these groups must consequently be recalculated annually. It is difficult to find any meaning in such arbitrary calculations; indeed, we shall find that the notion of core group itself has outlived whatever usefulness it may once have had. With Terray (1972:96), I regard the notion of "core" as of purely descriptive value.

Now consider that Lee (1979:338–39) says that Zhu inheritance of land is ambilateral. That is, a person may inherit rights to land from either parent or both, but whatever the individual case, inheritance is through parent(s) from parent's or parents' parent(s) in a continuing line. However, in the examples Lee gives—there are only two—core membership is said to have altered owing to the incorporation of affines and the loss (for unstated reasons) of other persons, many of whom were also affines. Nowhere does Lee attempt an effective analysis of kinship and affinity among the members of his delineated groups. Furthermore, he considers marriage primarily in functional terms of resource procurement and distribution. This is relevant, of course; Godelier (1966, 1975) argues that in forager societies kinship functions as production relations. Lee never draws the two clearly together, however, and he takes into account neither the generational-continuity nor the kin-incorporating nature of Zhu marriage; he cannot therefore recognize the corporate nature of Zhu landholding. He does, however (1979 : 340–41), noting the presence of residual named groups, postulate a higher degree of corporateness in the past than he now finds, but he does not discuss what may have brought about the change.

Another approach to the issue is patently needed. Paradoxically, it has been concern for the articulation of putatively remnant forager societies within modern capitalist states that has pointed to the most rewarding direction in which to pursue analyses. San land tenure, far from being an ecological given, is part of that social universe negotiated by San persons in their day-to-day relations with others, not only those acknowledged to be comembers of a particular group but those of other peoples who share the same geographical space. Land, and rights to its access and use, is a continually recurring factor in these negotiations. It goes without saying that San-speakers have developed inherent political structures for organizing these negotiations both in their internal dimensions and in relation to other peoples whose distribution overlaps or interlayers with their geographical space. I take up a detailed consideration of the actual realizations of these structures in chapter 6.

Consequently, it is necessary to examine the comparative systematic similarities of San social relations to land with those of other southern African peoples. In stressing these similarities, I am aware of the danger of imposing structural uniformity where none exists and have tried to avoid tendencies in that direction. I do not envision anything like *a* San system of land tenure, much less that such a thing might be simply a subspecies of southern Bantu—or Tswana or Herero or whatever—systems. Nor by drawing on some principles adduced for other societies do I intend to suggest that the structure of San land tenure can be comprehended entirely through models derived for those societies. Indeed, I specifically reject the applicability to San systems of significant parts of those models. I wish only to demonstrate that San systems, although exhibiting important distinctive features, share with other systems a number of equally important common principles for relating persons to place. These common elements have their ontogeny in the long history of association among these groups, a history we have seen distorted by colonial interventions that have obscured longer-term regularities.

Also obscured is the fact that San social relations to land and the structures for confirming these relations are as fully developed as are those of their neighbors, with which there is significant overlap. Establishing this point undermines arguments of San inequality in this regard. It is this rather than a postulated unproblematic relationship or a shared *corpus juris* among the examined systems that this chapter addresses.

In contrast to the ecological concept of territory that focuses on productivity and the means of production, the constitution of land tenure locates people within the social matrix of relations to land, where productive activity must take place. In light of the discussion to this point, it is not surprising that the structure of San land tenure set in its social matrix has been overlooked. Marshall (1960, 1976), Lee (1965, 1979), Yellen (1976), and Yellen and Harpending (1972) include sections on spatial distributions of the people they call Kqung, as do Silberbauer (1965, 1981) and Tanaka (1969, 1980) for the Gcwi, Heinz (1972) for the Kqoo, and Cashdan (1984) for the Gxanna. All these authors look upon their subject groups in isolation and offer no more than generalizations drawn from limited descriptions of a few particular cases. Barnard (1979) makes a similar point. Moreover, in keeping with their commitment to the separate-enclave notion, these authors could not notice that San-speaking peoples share structural elements of property relations and tenure common to a number of societies in southern Africa; accordingly, they misconstrue San land tenure practice as well as its interdigitation with other systems.[2]

On the other hand, Wiessner (1977, 1982) successfully places some aspects of Zhu settlement dynamics in a broader Zhu social framework. Hitchcock (1978, 1980) and Cashdan (1986) discuss contemporary Kwa and Gxanna relations to land in eastern Botswana as they are enmeshed in dominant Ngwato and Kwena systems. Both allude to interlocking Kwa-Gxanna and Ngwato-Kwena customary claims to landownership at the local level, and Hitchcock shows how this differs from higher-level administrative as well as anthropological views on the matter. Neither he nor Cashdan, however, develops these descriptions to formulate a basis for Kwa-Gxanna customary claims, other than physical presence of persons on specific parcels of land, an argument that can be—and has been—negated by assertions that such presence is the result of squatting, not tenure.

We must search elsewhere. By definition, nonliterate societies do

not keep written codifications of their constitutive principles of ownership. The only avenue for comprehending these principles in such societies is to examine the logic of social relations that governs their
concept of material possession and its extensions without forcing these
into a Western model. But we must proceed with caution. It is now
thirty years since Bohannan (1957, 1965) argued that it is inappropriate to transfer conceptual and institutional categories of Western
law to African societies. At the same time, Turner (1957), following
on Colson's (1953) earlier study, demonstrated that in some African
societies cooperation in and competition for such assets as land are
constrained by a prevailing structure of social relations that can be
understood only in the context of extended social processes.

Nevertheless, despite sixty years of intensive development of this
processual paradigm that began with Malinowski (1926) and owes
little or nothing to Western legal theory (see Comaroff and Roberts
1981 for a summary history of this development), derivative Western
formal models have been implicitly applied to San polities. Even con-
certed efforts to dissociate San property relations from those of Europe
take the form of normative contrasts to an Anglo-American model
(Silberbauer 1982; Lee 1972a, 1979, 1982) rather than analyses of the
indigenous African matrix within which San systems are historically
set. Thus Leacock and Lee (1982:10) are able to assert the anomaly
that means for resolving interpersonal conflicts are necessary in San
societies, whose members are "free from fundamental conflicts of interest." They are able to do so because they apply a Western jural
model of conflict and decision making to these societies, although
both the nature of interests and the concept of what constitutes resolu-
tions are fundamentally different from Western modes.

There is also the problem of translatability. MacCormick (1983), a
jurist, stresses that it is particularly necessary to determine native conditions of use of terms; for example, whether some apply only to land
or have a wider domain. As Carstens (1983:60) reminds us, Maine
had already made this caution abundantly clear in 1861. Another jurist with considerable anthropological experience, Roberts (1979),
cautions that presenting indigenous concepts in the form of legal rules
organized in Western categories encourages the use of such distorted
rules in artificial ways that will damage native intents and interests. As
Bennett (1985) observes, "The courts go to great lengths to preserve
the integrity of their own system, even although the law they are supposed to apply is African customary law." As we shall have occasion to
see, this indeed happens not only in authoritarian Namibia but also in
democratic Botswana with respect to contemporary San rights.

For untangling the issue of San tenure relations to land, Gluckman

(1971:45–46) offers guidance.[3] The argument may be distilled as follows: "Property law in tribal societies defines not so much rights of persons over things, as obligations owed between persons with respect of things. . . . The crucial rights of such persons are demands on other persons in virtue of control over land and chattels, not . . . any set of persons, but persons related in specific, longstanding ways. . . . To understand the holding of property, we must investigate the system of status relationships; we must deal constantly with relations to property." Ownership constrained in this manner cannot be absolute because property acquires its critical role in a specific nexus of relationships. In these circumstances, there can be no definition of ownership in the sense of incontestable control such as inheres in modern capitalist conceptions of property relations. Rather, being in a property relationship involves being bound within a set of reciprocal obligations among persons and things: everything, and especially land and rights to its use, must be subject to a complex of claims arising from this social matrix. In essence, real-property relations so conceived are flexibly defined rights over someone or something in terms of social relations: "Rights to property . . . are attributes of social position" (Gluckman 1965:163). Entitlement seems a better gloss than ownership for such a notion of relations to land, and I shall use this term.[4]

Gluckman did not employ a dialectic vocabulary, yet the essential dialectic dynamic of property is apparent in his formulation: the reciprocal discourse among members of a social universe conducted in historical, not mechanical, nature. It is this dialectic element that I take from Gluckman. For foragers, as for anybody else, persons create property. They create it in reference to each other, not in reference to objects or to space or to the use of objects in space. Use, production, takes place within a conception of real property—within a conception of persons in relation to each other with respect to place. Within that conception, the social rules and processes defining relations of production and disposition of the means of production are as fully articulated for foragers as for anybody else. This crucial and self-evident point is subverted in current ecological and Marxian models of forager cultural order.

I should make it clear that I depart from Gluckman's construction in two important ways. First, no codified *corpus juris* such as he seems to have found among the Barotse can be attributed to San-speakers, nor for that matter, to Ovaherero or Batswana (cf. Comaroff and Roberts 1981), who are also considered in this analysis; I neither make that attribution nor follow an analytical procedure that requires it. Second, Gluckman assigned major importance for property relations to the status hierarchy inherent in Barotse social organization and considered rights to land to be held in a graded arrangement of administrative estates. This assessment has been criticized (White 1963; Biebuyck 1963; see Comaroff and Roberts 1981:5–11 for an extensive evaluation of the controversy), and the status relations that can be attributed to San peoples have few of the attributes perceived by Gluckman (I examine these in the next chapter). Ovaherero differentiate between two statuses; Loth (1963) and Werner (1980) recognize at least incipient, if not fully developed, class relations in these statuses. One of these is that of ovandu ovahona, which is usually glossed "chiefs" (ovandu plus ovahona; sing., omuhona = "Haüptling"/ "chief"); Brincker ([1886] 1964:141) gives, in addition, "einer der viele Güter hat," which may be glossed "wealthy person." Thus ovandu ovahona are wealthy, chiefly people. The other status is ovandu oviriri = "commoners"; Brincker ([1886] 1964:51) glosses the verb iriria as "sich gewohnen," "to accustom oneself [in this context, to poverty]." Thus Otjiherero recognizes two status distinctions based on wealth, primarily the possession of cattle. Schapera (1945) provides firm genealogical evidence that hereditary chiefly lines were able to reproduce their status over many generations. Among commoners, a person's standing is determined more by immediate contingencies within class limitations. Vedder (1938:146–47) says that "it was only the man who possessed a hundred head of cattle and round about a hundred followers . . . [who could] . . . call himself *Omuhona,* or chief." The outlines of Tswana class structure were reviewed in chapter 3; again the negotiability of status within classes is clear (cf. Comaroff and Roberts 1981). I do not adopt the hierarchical aspect of Gluckman's model.

Instead, I take the "attributes of social position" by which rights to property are obtained to be entailed simply by virtue of native membership in a group, that is, by ascription at birth or adoptive incorporation into a specific set of related persons. Acquisition of new status by a person is constrained in scope and direction by that person's initial membership in such a group and hence is an extension of ascription (cf. Comaroff 1978). Abandoning hierarchical ladders does not impair the theoretical foundation for the argument to follow. On the contrary, it opens the possibility of a more fundamental analysis of the way property is woven into the social fabric of San society. As will become clear, flexibility of spatial organization for San peoples—and for Ovaherero and Batswana—rests on a fluid and negotiable social field in which a repertoire of rules is constantly activated and continually reassessed by individuals in the course of everyday interaction.

In this social field, "norm and reality exist in a *necessary* dialectical relationship" (Comaroff and Roberts 1981:247) that gives form to the San universe.

That social field must be brought into prominence in order to set equally variable functions of production in their proper context. For San-speakers, it must also be made comprehensible within the broader social sphere of southern Africa in which it has always existed. This is especially urgent today, when a centuries-old legacy of precapitalist and capitalist disfranchisement is being legitimated in legislation for lack of well-grounded and persuasive arguments that this dispossession should be corrected rather than concretized.[5] Guenther's (1981:117) concern that "plans drafted or implemented by governments on behalf of their hunter-gatherer minorities may adversely affect these minorities if they use the faulty notion of hunter-gatherer territoriality as a guiding principle" has all too real a basis in already-implemented policy. Gluckman's insight, modified as mentioned, provides an indispensable first guide to endeavors to alter this situation.

As I see it, the principal heuristic value of Gluckman's effort is that it stresses the flexible quality of property rules and the leeway allowed in their application during negotiation of individual cases. Theoretically, by identifying the dialectic between person and property mediated in a social field, it restores kinship to that central logic of San social relations from which it has been analytically divorced by ecological and related Marxian endeavors overly influenced by evolutionary stage notions.

Beyond that, and more important in the overall scheme of things, read in this way property is removed from the arena of pursuit of means to overcome necessity and is situated where it is in fact created: in the political definition of how these means are to be pursued. San relations to property (land, chattels, and the rest) can then be seen as inhering not in a different natural order but in a social order that organizes persons and relations of production differently. This too opens the way to their social formation in terms of its own structure set in the concrete locus of its African history.

Kinship and Tenure

The initial discussion will center on Zhu relations to land; then the systems of other San groups will be summarized and their congruence with that of Zhu will be made clear. Subsequently, the underlying principles of kinship and group membership as the basis for San tenure entitlements will be shown to be compatible in essentials with those of Herero and Tswana land tenure.[6]

There is agreement among researchers on the ecological-geographical correlates of Zhu land division: space is partitioned so that each demarcated section of land contains enough food and water resources to sustain the user group in all but the most unproductive years. The basic unit is called nqore (pl. nqoresi).[7]

There is, however, disagreement among anthropologists about the mechanisms of place affiliation. Marshall (1976:184) notes that a person, no matter where residing, identifies primarily with nqore of origin (birthplace); Lee (1979:338) agrees and gives the example of people who told him (1976c:94), "No, we are not of /Xai/Xai; /Dwia is our earth." While it is true that a person identifies primarily with birthplace, this must not be construed (and is not construed by Lee) to imply that rights in other nqoresi may not subsequently be acquired. Such identification with birthplace is made to locate a person in an appropriate social geography; anyone familiar with that person's network will automatically fill in many kinship details without further prompting. Marshall (1976:184) says that nqore affiliation is inherited unilaterally through either parent. Lee (1979:338) says that inheritance may be unilateral or bilateral with a strong unilateral bias, tending to patrilateral (however, refer back to note 4). Wiessner (1977:50–51) says that inheritance is strictly bilateral but that additional affiliations are acquired through marriage. This lack of agreement arises because these authors consider nqore inheritance to be primarily a means for associating individuals with geographic territory. I shall return to this point.

Marshall (1969:344–45) brings a thoroughly commodity-oriented view to her depiction of Zhu relations to land. Although she does recognize that kinship plays a role in forming these relations, she holds that relative adequacy of resources causes people to "flock" around an "owner" of productive land. She has altered her view to the extent that she no longer thinks of an "owner" as a headman (1976:191–95; however, see my discussion in chap. 6), but the resource function of Zhu spatial organization has been retained in her most recent presentation.

Lee (1979:58, 334) too defines nqore in resource terms—he again uses the word territory here as he did in his original discussion (Lee 1965:137–48) of what he than called Zhu territories. He has now reversed his (1972b) interim view that Zhu have no concept of land-ownership by asserting that "the !Kung do own the land they occupy"

(Lee 1979 : 337), but he does so in an anecdotal manner that puts him in a position indistinguishable from that of Marshall. Lee (1979:58–63) envisions a core group of owners who compete with other core groups to recruit members in order to increase productive output (1979:457, 1982:53) and thus create a radiating chain of affines who may stay together for two generations or so (Lee 1979:60–61). The main adhesive holding some people together while keeping them well spaced from others is personality (1982:52) and observance of rules of conduct (1979:338).

The adhesive, however, dissolves in the face of the unpredictability of rainfall, with its consequent variable resource production, this being a "powerful argument against territoriality" (Lee 1979:352) that induces Zhu to "*consciously* strive to maintain a boundaryless universe" (Lee 1979:335). In this contradictory ecology, Lee (1979:339, emphasis added) says that "ownership of *land* passes from parent to child." Even so, since he investigates only one generation of such passages, he finds shallow and diffuse inheritance and guesses (his term) that a significant rate of moving about in the nqoresi occurred in pre-contact as well as in contact times (Lee 1979:333–39). It is true that Lee's respondents—all male—were of different ages and generations, but he reports inheritance from their immediate parents only, not for antecedent or subsequent generations; thus his investigation is of parent-to-child transmission only and has no deeper generational implications.

More to the point, it is not land itself that is inherited. What actually is inherited is a set of status positions binding an individual to a network of obligations owed between persons, among which are those with respect to land. It is through this network that persons become associated with geographic space. Among Zhu, a person's primary nqore of identification is always that person's birthplace. As I shall demonstrate, there is a very high probability that this birthplace will be in at least one parent's nqore. Thus an individual Zhu's tenure entitlements in land are a dynamic function of a regional kinship net initially defined by ascription through birth into a descent group and later reinforced by marriage. As will become clear, in a proper (preferred) marriage a person does not acquire a wholly new entitlement(s) but does reinforce entitlement(s) already held. In adoption, which occurs rarely (I know of only two cases), ensuing entitlements are also already at least partially held, since adoptees are children of siblings or cousins of adopters. Thus, as argued above, acquisition is merely an extension of ascription. Ascription is bilateral, with entitlements at birth vested equally in the nqoresi of both parents. To make this clear, the kinship matrix in which San land tenures are set must be elucidated. I shall begin with the Zhu case, concentrating on the active dialectic among Zhu kinship, marriage, and inheritance of land.

Zhu Kinship

Since Marshall (1957), no one has reported fundamental work on Zhu kinship and marriage.[8] Fabian (1965) and Barnard (1978) identify contradictions in her work, and Marshall (1957:14) herself noted that some critical points remained to be clarified. The contradictions, however, do not lie in Zhu kinship relations as has been supposed but spring from two apparently minor oversights in Marshall's otherwise meticulous analysis. Marshall (1957) gives male-centered consanguineal terms correctly, excluding, however, the suffix mà, which she considered strictly a diminutive marker. This led her astray, especially in association with her second decision to adopt an exclusively male egocentric paradigm, although she does list terms used by women. She was consequently unable to discern the systemic relation between terms, especially those applied to affines. Nor did she recognize the reciprocity in male- and female-centered terms that lies at the terminological heart of transformation from kin to affine.

To facilitate comparison with Marshall's work, I shall enter Zhu terminology through male-centered terms for consanguines and then move on to the female-centered paradigm. Marshall's diagram 1 (1957:6) gives these male-centered terms correctly; my figure 5.1 is an expanded kinship diagram that incorporates those terms in the orthography of Snyman (1975). Figure 5.2 is a nearly identical diagram to which have been applied female-centered terms. Since this was written, Lee (1986:83) has provided a lucid description of the contrasting-gender kin universe terminology.

As is readily apparent, adjacent-generation terms are the same for egos of both sexes, and there are only two such terms, aside from áiyá (own mother) and m̀bá (own father). One of these is gxa (g‖à̰ = "tante," Snyman 1975:27), "aunt," designating adjacent-generation female collateral and encompassing parents' female siblings and generational equivalents plus own siblings' and cousins' female children and equivalents. The other adjacent-generation term is tsu (tsù = "oom," Snyman 1975:80), "uncle," designating adjacent-generation male collateral, parents' male siblings and generational equivalents, plus own siblings' and cousins' male children and equivalents.

In ego's and alternating generations, however, there is a fundamental difference; terms here are linked to gender of ego. For males, male offspring of tsusi-gxasi are in the qu (!ú = "naam," Snyman 1975:

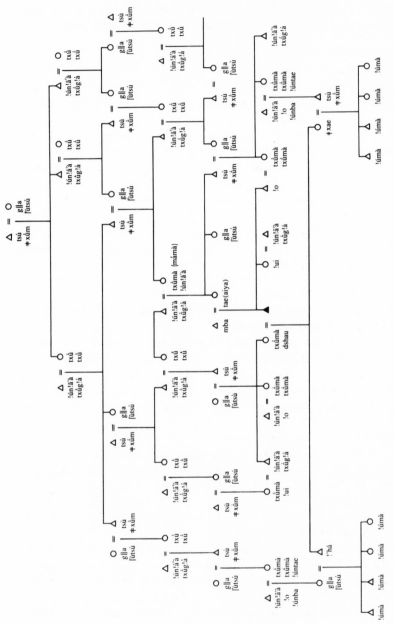

Figure 5.1. Kinship terminology, male ego. Upper terms are consanguineal; lower terms are affinal. In Snyman's orthography (1975:27) g‖a is written g‖à.

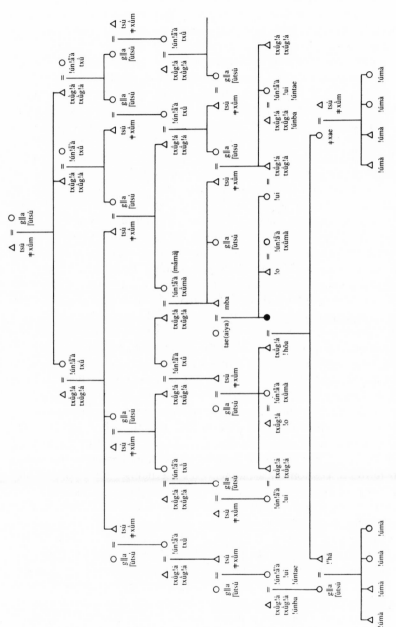

Figure 5.2. Kinship terminology, female ego. Terms arranged as in figure 5.1.

121), "name," relationship, as are female offspring of these parents for female ego. Notice that in her diagram 1 Marshall makes female ego's parents' fathers as well as all male cousins qunqa (!ú!ā̄'à, literally older name: "name giver") to her; since Zhu names are gender linked, this cannot be true in the consanguineal terminology, although it is applied —reciprocally to name giver's spouse and especially affinally—as a term of respectful affection. Complementary to this qu relationship is a tru (txů) relationship that is also gender linked: for female ego, male collaterals in own and alternating generations are trugqa (txů̄g!à); for male ego, female collaterals in these generations are truma (txůmà). Again, Marshall assigns affinal terms in the female consanguineal paradigm, as she must do, having placed male cousins in the qu category.

It is important to summarize at this point. In ego's first ascending generation, father's brothers (FB) and mother's brothers (MB) are termed tsu by both male and female ego; father's sisters (FZ) and mother's sisters (MZ) are termed gxa by egos of both genders. These terms are also applied to male and female kin, respectively, in generations alternate to this one. In ego's generation, however, male ego applies the name term qu with appropriate suffix to male offspring of both parents' siblings (FBS, FZS, MBS, MZS) as well as to all male relatives in parents' parents' (FF, MF) and children's children's (SS, DS) generations; female ego applies the same term to the female counterparts of these persons (MZD, MBD, FZD, FBD, MM, FM, DD, SD). Male ego applies truma to females in these generations (FBD, FZD, MBD, MZD, FM, MM, SD, DD); female ego applies trugqa to their male counterparts (MZS, MBS, FZS, FBS, MF, FF, DS, SS).

As figures 5.1 and 5.2 make clear, these terms are indefinitely extendable both laterally and vertically; but though extensions are worked out in practice through recitation of detailed terminological chains, this does not make kinship, as such, all-pervasive. To anticipate the discussion for a moment, the mechanism for distinguishing kin from nonkin is what Marshall (1957) recognized as the name relation. This is expressed by the term qunqaakwe (!ún!ā̄àkwe: !ú, plus n!ā̄, plus à = reflexive connective particle, plus kwe = together), which may be glossed "name sharers to each other," or as Marshall (1976:214) records, "jusi [sic] e!ka "kaiakwe": "people who own each other," or as I would put it—in keeping with my earlier considerations about the transliteration of concepts of ownership—"those who have each other." By applying this relational term to each other, the members of this group specify their inclusive bilaterality by intergenerational reciprocal naming through both mother's and father's lines. Lee (1986:88, 93) notes that all persons who share a name claim descent from the same original name bearer but that, when discussing their own kin, categorial distinctions are explicitly and sharply drawn —which reciprocal name sharers (we might say set of namesakes, as distinct from those who simply have a name in common) one has is crucial in practice. As we shall see, this is a group that most anthropologists would recognize as a local descent group, but one that carries many of the functions of a kindred for individuals.

It is also important to note that trugqa and truma are not primitive terms but are compounds of a stem, tru, and a suffix, gqa or ma. The stem component will be considered when affinal terms are introduced. The suffixes are possessive particles. That they are not diminutives as Marshall thought, or more broadly relative age markers, is clear from the fact that trugqa is always used no matter what the relative ages of persons, as is truma with certain revealing exceptions to be noted in a moment. Although it has the same form as mà (diminutive), mà is a possessive (cf. Snyman 1975:42; Köhler 1971:502); for example, dshàù mìmà = my wife. The morpheme gqa is never diminutive and is associated with the possessive gá (Synman 1975:10; Köhler 1971:502; Heikkinen 1987:13), as in žù a gá = your/his/her realtive and in sisi o mì gasi = my things. With regard to truma, Ssao Xau told me, "This word is one [example] only, with this ending, so that all of them end with mà. So that when they end with mà then it is to point to the fact that it is something of mine or a person [relative] of mine. Or a person I call mine. Yes." [9]

The possessive character of these elements is found in the term mama (màmà), which Marshall (1957:15) consigns solely to a role as a term of affection, which it indeed has, as (as already noted) does qunqa. But mama is a kin term denoting parent's mother (Snyman 1975:43 gives "ouma": "grandmother"). The stem mà is associated with a whole set of lexical items expressing incorporation in a group: mì = self, m̀ = us, mà = own child, mạ̀'á = to give birth to/to carry a child, mhìsì = own children, and the possessives mà and m̀ as in m̀bá = my father (cf. Snyman 1975:42–44, who gives comparable Afrikaans glosses). Mama thus is a reflexive possessive that may be glossed "she who bore us" or "she who carries us"; its extension as a term of affection serves to express mutual incorporation in a kinship group. Strong evidence for this is that ascending-generation trusi in ego's own descent line but not in collateral lines (and never in descending generations except in a show of affection), along with spouse's equivalent trusi, are always addressed, and usually referred to, as mama. This is done to show respect by stressing the closeness of their relationship.

Affinal terms are given beneath their consanguineal counterparts in figures 5.1 and 5.2. Notice first that the trugqa-truma reciprocal pair has affinal as well as consanguineal denotations: upon marriage into a group, a man's consanguineal trumasi in that group remain trumasi, but his consanguineal qunqasi-qumasi become affinal trugqasi. In like manner, a woman's trugqasi remain such, while her qu relations become trumasi. For both sexes, consanguineal tsu becomes father of spouse and is termed tcum (≠xũm). I have already noted that trugqa and truma are compounds; it should now be apparent that their stem along with tcum may be glossed "in-law": "Let us suppose that that person is my in-law, he is my uncle, now I marry his daughter. I must call him ≠xũm because I have married from his family. . . . It shows respect. Yes! It is inherent in that word that it shows great respect. Yes."[10] Thus trugqa and truma denote "belonging to in-laws." Note that Marshall (1957:23) recognized that these terms are connected, she thought possibly through a common root.

There are only three other affinal terms, and these are also compounds. The consanguineal gxa (when married to tsu) becomes tcutsu (‖'ùdshù: from gu = take/marry, plus tsu, hence "wife of tsu"). Parents of child's spouse are quntae (!úntãè: name, plus tãè = mother, hence "name-mother") and qunba (!únbà: name, plus father, hence "name-father"). Notice that these two affines were respectively already in the consanguineal qu-name relation with the same-sex parent of child's spouse: quntae was qunqa/ma to child's spouse's mother, and qunba was in the same relationship to the father. And, of course, opposite-sex parents of this offspring pair had been in the tru relation.

One further terminological distinction is relevant here; a set of actual brothers (sharing at least one parent in common) is designated by the reciprocal term qoakwe (!òakwe: !o = older brother, hence brother/[reflexive]/together), "brothers to each other." Symmetrically, a set of actual sisters is designated qwiakwe (!uiàkwe: !ui = older sister), "sisters to each other." It is from these sets of own and spouse's siblings in addition to own and spouse's parents' sets that a person's children receive their names. As Marshall (1957:7) noted, "Very rarely is a child named for another relative." Name-receiving children have special reciprocal rights with members of their name-giving sets, whose houses they enter and whose private property they use at will.

The set of coparents-in-law contains the four persons for whom their children's first children will preferentially be named and whose siblings will normally be namesakes of their younger grandchildren, hence the terms name-mother and name-father. They are "called so because the children you bear, you and your wife, you can give them names from both families . . . so if you do that you are going to use your parents' names for your children because those children are theirs."[11] These coparents-in-law apply the term quma (!úmà, literally younger name: "name receiver") to all their mutual grandchildren, by whom they are reciprocally called qunqa or mama. These same coparents-in-law also apply qunqa to own grandparents and grandparents of child's spouse's parents, thus encoding the intergenerational continuity of reciprocal name relationships within the kindred, for names pass from this older set of grandparents through them—the current parental generation—to their grandchildren. Marshall (1959: 340) was told of siblings of grandparents and more remote collaterals: "Those people would name their children for their own people. . . . We name our children for our people."

Lee (1986:97) captures the core of sentiment engendered: "'If your name is /Tontah,' he said, 'all /Tontahs are your !kun!as. All who /Tontah birthed are your children. All who birthed /Tontahs are your parents, and all who married /Tontahs are your wives.'" Thus the puzzling aspects of the name relation noted by (Marshall 1957:7–14) become clearer; this system operates in a straightforward way not to override consanguineal relations, but to recognize terminologically a bilateral consanguineal-affinal group, the qunqaakwe—that is, an intermarrying set of local descent groups.

This Zhu kinship group resembles the "regional band" identified among the Dene a quarter-century ago by Helm (1965) with its "chain of primary relative links, consanguineal and affinal, by which a person is tied once or several times into a community." It "may be likened to a set of nodes within a kinship field" (Shapiro 1981:152) wherein persons negotiate their relationships to a wider polity. Analytical attention to Zhu kinship has focused primarily on what Helm (1965) called local bands, that is, on "cores" with peripheral recruits; this has inhibited appreciation of the centrality of the kindred functions of local descent groups for individuals and the importance of affinity (cf. Shapiro 1973:363) in the reproduction of Zhu social relations. But the finding that kindred ties and close affinal ties (but not ties of fictive kinship) define those who are comparable is not surprising in this situation, where kindred membership and affinal ties structure living arrangements, social relations to land, and most reciprocal material relations (Wiessner 1984:206).

We may now consider Zhu marriage prescriptions. Any opposite-sex, same-generation descendant of ego's parent's parent's sibling (PPsCC) or parent's parent's parent's sibling (PPPsCCC) is called by a term (trugqa-truma) that connotes persons "belonging to in-laws," and such persons—and only such persons plus their terminological equivalents—are permissible marriage partners and sexual mates. "The only people you can marry are people you know; they are family. Or to marry a stranger, yes, . . . we cannot marry a stranger, just any woman who resides in a far-off place. We must marry only a woman of our family, or that is, a relative, or a very very close [one] like of your father or of begetters of begetters who comes here to this place." [12]

At another time, in idle conversation, I asked, "Really; if you want to marry, what do you do?" "Kù ůwá txůmà":"Go to my cousin." "What if you just want to fuck?" "Kù ůwá txůmà; žùsì kǎà tshǐ txůmàsì ò n|è'èsì":"Go to my cousin; people fuck only their cousins" (Wilmsen, n.d.b). Appropriately, Marshall (1957:21) notes that a joking relationship exists between these persons, and Lee (1986:83) discusses the appropriate behavior of potential mates with respect to each other. Marshall (1957:19) also records that persons in a joking relation who apply the reciprocal tru terms to each other are permissible marriage partners. Persons in this category will be ego's PPsCC or PPPsCCC or both. It is possible that the relationship may extend further collaterally, but I have found no acknowledged instances of marriage beyond these limits in family histories (these are presented in chap. 6). For the group, local descent solidarity, and for the individual, kindred solidarity would be diluted by further collaterality; this effectively constrains marriage to descendants of same great-grandparents. The already-noted need to specify *which* name sharer a person is lies in this constraint.

The name relation serves to reduce the probability of first cousin (PsC) marriages because both partners will have a primary name-relative pair (grandparents) in common. It does not eliminate such marriages, however; for example, in figure 5.1, ego's brother may have married his MBD, but he will more likely be considered to have married his MMBDD or perhaps his MMMBDDD or even his MMFMBSDDD—although, as noted above, this last calculation is seldom if ever made. Figure 5.3 delineates the alternative lines of reckoning; of course, there is also the set of possibilities (not shown in fig. 5.1) traced through father, for example, FFZSD. The lines of reckoned descent will be orchestrated by the principals to the marriage, primarily the parental sibling sets of prospective spouses, according to their perceived interests. In the attendant negotiations, ways out for those "sa ge a ‖emi":"they are in the middle"—those, that is, whose eligibility for marriage to each other has an impediment—may be found if other considerations are strong enough for both parental sets of the potential couple (cf. Lee 1986:91–97). Adjacent-generation primary kin of trumasi-trugqasi are never eligible mates for them, are also accorded respect, and after being directly linked through a mar-

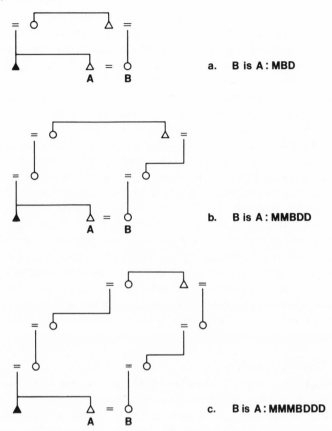

Figure 5.3. Different strategies for legitimizing marriage between the same two individuals.

riage, are addressed by an in-law possessive term (tcum or tcutsu) of respect by affinal ego.

In the next chapter I shall detail CaeCae family histories that reveal this marriage system in action. Marshall (1960:332–33) too provides some evidence that this is indeed the system operating among the people she studied. Her figure 3 is a chart of partial relationships among 108 persons in what she calls eight band segments. Among these persons there are fifty-eight spouses, of whom nineteen are without information regarding their kin; of the remaining thirty-nine, thirty-seven have at least one primary kin link (parent or sibling) in the group. Since this information is confined largely to a single generation (there are only eight living persons in the eldest of the three generations shown and only five marriages in the youngest) and is, no doubt, also incomplete (an unknown number of persons are said to have been omitted), this number of links is even higher than may have been expected. Furthermore, Marshall (1960:344) records that she has no data on second- and third-cousin relationships and therefore can say nothing about marriages among persons so related. In the single case she gives that can be worked out, 25-tsamgao (Samkao) is engaged to marry 54-kushay (Xushe) his MFBSD, as he should.

The anomalies Marshall (1957:23) thought existed in Zhu kinship and the failure of the system to "make much sense" (Barnard 1978:75) turn out to lie in the eye of the observer, not among the Zhu. It is now fully apparent that Zhu marriage takes place within a clearly defined descent coterie in which affines are simply recategorized kin. This overlapping of consanguinity and affinity distorts any assumption of a dichotomy between these categories. There are different lines for reckoning degree of kinship, and a person falls into one or another category according to contingencies of the moment. Kinship in Zhu society, rather than being a static straitjacket, is a dynamic keyboard on which individuals play variations on a theme of options. It is, as Comaroff (ed., 1980:164) notes, up to the individual to "create and manage an effective social network."

Zhu Relations to Land

Within this incorporative structure of Zhu kinship the corporate unity of Zhu landholding devolves from one generation to the next. In response to the question, "Is it good and just to say that people live in a defined country?" Ssao replied, "If a person stays with his relatives; if a person separates from his relatives it is not right to call that place his. Yes. This I will call my land. . . . this land is mine, the whole of it. That is to say it belongs to everyone, the community. Like when we are here, that is to say where these people stay . . . my land, it is that of the community." [13]

Property-right transfers consequent on marriage are, accordingly, largely matters of reshuffling priorities among latent claims by members of a descent consort. This is because the new married pair will already, as children of their related parents, hold a set of entitlements in common (because they have a grandparental or great-grandparental (or both) sibling pair in common); they will possess other entitlements that may or may not be held in common. Any proper (preferred) marriage, one between PPsCC will unite two strands of an entitlement (one each through a parent from an ascending sibling set of bride and groom). A more desirable marriage—to PPPsCCC—will unite two strands through each parent (from both sets of ascending sibling sets). Marriage strategy is directed toward bringing about this more desirable condition; this is why marriage of sets of brothers to sets of sisters is said to be ideal (Marshall 1959:345), even if seldom realized.

To the extent that the strategy is successfully employed by sibling sets from generation to generation, kindred ties are strengthened for individuals, and local group solidarity is passed on from grandparental through parental to current sibling sets. It is in the politics of implementing this strategy that relations of production are created. Negotiations for and legitimation of marriage ties are important moments in this creative process; they occupy much of the time and energy of descent-group elders. Wiessner (1977, 1986), Shostak (1981), and Lee (1986) portray vividly how several facets of the strategy are put into practice. The direction by elders of their descendants' kinship decisions, described by Lee as the "wie factor" (wī = "help"; Snyman 1975:87), and the channeling of haro obligations described by Wiessner are undertaken to ensure entitlement consolidation within descent groups. As we shall see in the next chapter, Zhu homestead 1 at CaeCae claims to have controlled its entitlements in this way for several generations, to its continuing benefit.

In this perspective, Zhu marriage service can be seen not in the decontextualized structural-functionalist terms usually offered (Lee 1979:240–42, 1982:42–43) but as a form of devolutionary marriage payment mediating conflicts over land that inevitably must occur among interdependent groups. San marriage service has long been recognized as marriage payment in traditional Tswana law and is specifically related to bogadi, the Tswana from of marriage payment. In 1930 Tshekedi, then regent of Bangwato, testified before the British resident commissioner: "Bogadi is a tradition and a right of Masarwa: bride service of one or two years or, if a man owns cattle, he can pay in stock" (BNA 1930).

Schapera (1970:138) notes that when in 1875, under missionary influence, Khama III abolished bogadi among Bangwato he specifically did not ban the practice among his other subjects, including San-speakers, who continued their traditional forms of marriage payment—as did, and do in practice, many Batswana as well as most Zhu and Ovaherero to this day.[14]

For Zhu, marriage service resolves the question of personal status and locates a marriage union with its offspring within the structure of relations between persons and places. The devolution of property begins with negotiations and prestations between principals to a future marriage, primarily future coparents-in-law. Wiessner (1986) shows this process in action through hxaro prestations (Snyman 1975:88 writes xàró, but to avoid confusion with the orthographic function of x in Setswana, I shall write haro), primarily of beadwork and other symbolically valued materials. This process may extend over a period of many years, as Marshall (1960:351–52) and Lee (1979:240–42) confirm. Devolution begins to take more concrete form with the establishment of a new household located in association with the woman's parents. The period of marriage service is measured in terms of offspring, its conditions having been satisfied when two or more children have been born to the union.

Children born during this period in the woman's nqore will have that locality as their primary country. This confers lifelong mutual obligations between persons in the woman's natal group and her children and, indeed, on the descendants of those children so long as kindred obligations are met. As we shall see in the next chapter, as many as six generations of continuity can be traced at CaeCae today. Lee (1979:240) stresses the surface features of hunting prowess during the period of service—he refers to it as a period of probation for the man, which in part it is—and thereby fails to comprehend its deeper significance. The activation of latent affinal rights to land by the man and the validation of primary inheritance rights for his children are at issue in this service, not the few pieces of meat that a newly recruited hunter may provide. Economics and nutrition are, of course, unassailable necessities in corporal and social life, but the large animal that the young husband is expected to kill and present to his parents-in-law does not just provide protein and calories; more important, it materially mediates the new relational status of families.

That it is not hunting ability per se that is specifically at stake is confirmed by the fact that domestic animals (either owned or obtained from employers—or even purchased with mine labor wages [Lee 1979:241]) are readily substituted for hunted animals. Such substitution does not, however, free the husband from uxorilocal residence obligations. This transferred animal, hunted or herded, should be seen as a signifier of commitment by the parties concerned (acceptance is as much an active act as is giving) and has its analogue in the transferred mokwele (betrothal) animal among Batswana (Comaroff and Comaroff 1981:34) as well as in the onjova (wedding) sheep among the Ovaherero (Gibson 1959a:7). An employed man may evade his commitment more easily (by moving away or hoarding easily hidden cash) than is possible for his hunting brother, but he knows this commitment is reciprocal. Half the social and material support for his household resides in his wife's social matrix, for not only does he share with them, they share with him. He may manage his end of the commitment differently, but ultimately his status devolves in the kinship-defined network of nqore relations. Without that base he has no status. Shostak (1981:240) vividly portrays the "far-reaching impact on the family's social and economic life, and often on that of the entire group" of Zhu marriage relations.

During the period of service in the wife's home nqore, devolutionary rights in the husband's nqore are kept open by visiting his primary kin who reside there and participating with them in production from their mutually possessed land. This is a labor process that revalidates entitlements through production relations; as Lee (1979:259) notes, visitors who stay longer than a couple of days are expected to contribute to the food supply. After the period of marriage service, if household residence changes to the husband's nqore, rights in the wife's nqore are kept open by visiting her kin who remain there. Such visiting is undertaken not only to enjoy each other's company but to ensure that entitlement devolves upon children. Lee (1979:377, 389–91) documents that nearly 70% of all homicides occur when groups are visiting each other and that a high proportion of fights and murders occur between affines. These risks are counterbalanced by the need to keep options open through fulfillment of obligations to participate actively in social relations to land. Expectably, many conflicts arise in disputes over the exercise of those options, although they may be masked as simple marital difficulties.

It is probable that the frequency—and perhaps the violence—of such Zhu disputes has increased under colonially induced disruptions of relations to land. But the source of these disputes—in the interpretation of rights and obligations—must always have been present in Zhu social relations of production. These relations, if they are to persist, must be unambiguously expressed even if they are ambiguously practiced. "Because the status of property holdings and exchanges conveys a range of messages concerning social linkages and individual rights, their definition and designation are always critical to the parties involved" (Comaroff and Roberts 1981:175). Disputes, conflicts, and their adjudication are inescapably entailed in such definitions and designations. It is in this dialectic of structure and practice that Zhu regulation of entitlement to land lies.

Continuity of Tenure

It is now possible to demonstrate that Zhu kinship and land tenure are stable in space. To begin with, most Zhu marriages take place between

people who live in contiguous nqoresi. Harpending (1976:161) plots
marital distances for a large number of married pairs who are parents,
that is, whose marriages have been stable. These data, regrouped into
intervals of 30 kilometers (following Lee's 1969 estimate of nqore
sizes),[15] are displayed in table 5.1. Harpending stresses the large distances over which marriages may take place, and indeed they are striking—especially as they occur among peoples who are said to be locally
isolated. Equally striking, however, is that 53% of all partners were
married within 30 kilometers of their birthplaces and 78% within
60 kilometers; in other words, more than half of all marriage partners
were born within the same nqore space as their spouses, and more
than three-quarters within the same or adjacent nqoresi. In addition,
Harpending (1976:161) states, without citing evidence, that parent-
offspring birthplace distances (distance between birthplace of respondent and that of respondent's parents or children) are even less
dispersed. Supporting evidence is provided by Lee (1979:338), who
found that 77% of his respondents inherited their nqoresi from one or
both parents. To this may be added that in the next chapter (see also
Wilmsen 1976:4–7) I document six-generation continuity of kin-
based entitlement at CaeCae.

Thus the probability of a Zhu's being born in parents' ancestral
land is at least 0.8. This is precisely the result one would expect under
a structural system that incorporates primary relatives into spatial entities and puts collaterals into contiguous units linked through reciprocal, bilateral marriage. A high degree of generational continuity of
tenured family groups is evident from these data. If anything, events of
recent history, which have introduced pressures from European- and
difaqane-induced movements, have reduced these probabilities. For ex-

Table 5.1. Distance between Birthplaces of Married Zhu with Children, and between
Haro Partners

Distance (km)	Birthplace		CaeCae Haro		Tchumqwe Haro	
	Number	Proportion	Number	Proportion	Number	Proportion
0–30	184	.53	247	.48	210	.55
30–60	87	.25	110	.22	44	.12
60–90	29	.08	102	.20	121	.31
90–120	24	.07	—	—	5	.01
120–50	13	.04	36	.08	—	—
150–80	7	.02	—	—	—	—
180–210	4	.01	12	.02	2	.005
Total	348		507		382	

Source: Data from Harpending (1976:161, table 7.1) and Wiessner (1977:246, table 2).

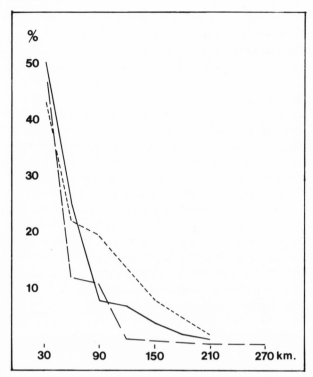

Figure 5.4. Frequency distribution of individuals engaged in social exchange at given distances. Solid line, between birthplaces of marriage partners; dashed line, between haro partners living at Tchumqwe and at other places; dotted line, between haro partners living at CaeCae and at other places.

ample, these pressures, in conjunction with ecological changes that may be linked to a more intensive pastoralist land use keyed to market production, are responsible for bringing half of the current rural inhabitants of western Ngamiland from elsewhere to their current places of residence. I shall return to these processes in chapter 6.

Exchange networks play important integrative roles in this social-spatial structure. Wiessner (1977: 119, 178, 1982) found that 62% of haro partners (persons who engage in preferential, reciprocal exchange) are traceable to same grandparents and 82% to same great-grandparents. Given the marriage prescription and spatial distribution noted, these people will be contiguous, consanguineal relatives among whom are potential as well as actual affines. Wiessner (1977: 246) gives the spatial distribution of haro partners by area and distance for a sample of people residing at CaeCae and at Tshumqwe in Namibia;

these data are displayed—also grouped in 30-kilometer intervals—in table 5.1. This table reveals that 48% and 55%, respectively, of haro in these two places is transacted within the home location, and 70% and 67% within 60 kilometers of that location, that is, within same or adjacent nqore. Wiessner (1980:111) finds that a high proportion of this exchange is associated with marriage negotiations.

Figure 5.4 combines these data and demonstrates graphically that kinship, space, and exchange describe an interlocking system of status relationships in which individuals are bound within a set of reciprocal obligations among persons and things. The internal boundaries within this system are zonal rather than incisional but are well known and are open to those with appropriate social ties. Entitlement—in the sense in which I have been speaking—is vested in all members of a group who apply a reflexive set of reciprocal terms to each other and refer to themselves as "those who have each other." It is these people who form the stable set of descendant tenure holders. They are the nqore kausi (kx'ào = "possessors"), "possessors of a place/country"; that is, they are those who have generationally continuous, inherent rights of tenure in their ancestral land.[16]

Convergence of Indigenous Systems

Other San Systems

Schapera (1943:5–7) speaks of "this system of land tenure characteristic of Bushmen" in exactly this way. The compatibility of other San tenure systems may be indicated quickly. Table 5.2 lists cognate terms for locational place in six San languages plus Nama; all these terms are clearly derived from a common root. Anthony Traill (personal communication) has confirmed the essential meaning to be locative, referring to a person's or a group's possessed country. Common origin and common meaning do not, however, guarantee that terms are parts of otherwise common systems; other evidence must be called in support.

Silberbauer (1981:99) records that Gcwi attitudes to land are centered on "the fact that the primary bond is between the individual and his band, whereas the link between the individual and territory is derived from the bond between community and land . . . rights . . . flow from band membership." Land tenure is vested in band members, for whom elders act as intermediaries when nonmembers enter and ask to use the land, "a formality that clearly indicates that the use of territorial resources and residence have to be granted before they are gained" (Silberbauer 1981:141). On the question of the social determinates of membership, however, Silberbauer is not so clear, although he recog-

Table 5.2. Cognate Terms for "Place in Land" in Six San Languages and Nama

Nama	n!u:s
Gcwi	n!ûsà
Nharo	n!û:bà
Kqoo	n!óle
Zhu	n!órė
Kwa	n´gū:
Gxanna	ngo

Source: Anthony Traill, personal communication.

nizes (1981:141–42, 147) Gcwi kindreds with cross-cousin endogamy. He applies a normative, rule-centered approach to his strictly ecological frame of reference. As we have seen, he recognizes that, inevitably, real and classificatory kinship links are established and there is a high probability of a kinship bond among members (Silberbauer 1981:142). It is apparent that this high probability is the product of Gcwi marriage arrangements in which bilateral cross-cousins are preferred mates, tenure entitlement is inherited bilaterally, and "brideservice" in the wife's natal country, measured in terms of offspring (Silberbauer 1981:154), is prescribed. Silberbauer (1981:151–52) describes the menarcheal ceremony in which a young woman's mother introduces her to the group's land: "This is the country of all of us, and of you; you will always find food here." And the father introduces her to the group: "See your people . . . see [them] wherever you go."

Cashdan (1977:22–24, 1980b:12) states that "among the Bagǁanakwe, a person has an automatic right of access to an area that is part of his 'lefatshe' (ngo) meaning 'place' or 'territory.'" She illustrates the process of land inheritance in which generational continuity is stressed in order to strengthen the validity of a claim: "This is my place—I was born here, and my father and father's father were born here." Thus Gxanna tenure rights, as among Zhu, are based upon "birth and/or residence and/or parentage," are negotiable, and are manipulated by individuals according to their perceptions of the needs of the moment. Marriage increases options, and visiting keeps these options open. This kinship matrix controls access to land, whether for resource exploitation or for residence; Cashdan notes that "the absence of [a claim to kinship] may prevent a person from choosing to use an area even if it is geographically convenient." Persons ask to use land "where they already have close relatives, and consequently permission is rarely if ever refused." Cashdan (1984:453) elaborates on this observation: "Since people will not normally go to a place where they have no rights of access, one rarely witnesses overt exclusion resulting from territorial trespass." She goes on to stress that "sanctions for trespass exist and are used when needed."

Heinz (1966, 1972, 1979) documents an equivalent system for the Kqoo, as does Barnard (1975, 1976, 1979) for the Nharo. Barnard (1976:72–75) details the devolutionary nature of transferal of rights among Nharo: "*Kamane,* or marriage and childbirth prestations, mark the change in the disposition of rights over individuals." Gifts are exchanged during negotiations for marriage, at marriage, and at the birth of the first child. People are said to be "owned" by their grandparents, ownership being inherited bilaterally. Kamane symbolically mediates transfer of sexual and residence rights at marriage and establishment of primary rights at birth. As among Zhu, Nharo marriage prestations enter the larger gift-giving cycle, where they reinforce the continuous association of persons and place. The case for the Ghanzi area of these people has historical documentation; Hahn (1895:618) concludes the report of his investigation for the imperial secretary, Cape Town, as follows: "*It can only be claimed by the Bushmen, who admittedly and indisputably from times immemorial lived on it and never left it.*" Heinz (1972:412) records that even today Ghanzi ranchers recognize Zhu and Nharo land divisions that intersect their own holdings and employ these people in relation to those land divisions.

Barnard (1986:8) confirms that "the deep structure of all the Khoe [Central Khoisan] kinship systems is essentially the same." This includes bilateral name relations, consanguineal-affinal term transpositions, reciprocal grandrelation and sibling-cohort terms, extension of relationship terms through namesake equivalence, and marriage to specific cousin categories. In addition, he notes (1986:11) that the Nama MB-ZS (‖nuri-‖as) relationship involves "obligatory cattle snatching on the part of the ZS, [and] exchange of the MB's good beasts, or indeed other possessions, for the ZS's poor ones." In 1925, Hoernelé had noted these relations and stated further that "the different water holes, or fountains, in the country were always thought of as belonging to certain specific groups" so defined. Hoernelé (1985:65) notes "the communal nature of land among the Nama," which was held in trust by the chief and could not be alienated; at the same time, "certain clans seem to have had greater control than others over specified pieces of land and local springs."

Identical systems for the Kwa (Hitchcock 1978, 1980) and Tsassi (Vierich-Esch 1982; Hitchcock 1978) are recorded in eastern Botswana, where Esch (1977:11) notes that kinship groups and their marriage networks are associated with overlapping but separately demarcated land areas and says "this is also true of intermarriage between Basarwa and Bakgalagadi . . . [where] there are created kin relations between the peoples." Hitchcock (1980:25–26) emphasizes that even today local Ngwato ward heads and cattle owners recognize Kwa tenure, if only to the extent of consulting Kwa headmen before using the land for their own purposes.

Herero Land Tenure

The relevant features of Herero land tenure will be summarized briefly. The principal residential unit is the onganda, a settlement constituted by a set of patrilineal affiliates with their wives and children; matrilineal kinsmen and affines may be included and may even be more numerous but are never organizationally dominant (Gibson 1959b). Vedder ([1928]1966:180) says of the onganda that it "only includes a community of relatives." Ozonganda have associated sections of land (omahimahi) for grazing, hunting, and gathering in which are located ozohambo (sing. ohambo), cattleposts conjoined to water sources of varying permanence.

Almagor (1978, 1980a) documents that an Omuherero's rights in land are traced exclusively through kin networks, real and fictive. Initial rights are ascribed at birth into an intersection of oruzo (patrilineal) and eanda (matrilineal) social units. Rights to land derive from the concept of locality; a person attached to a specific place cannot utilize another place except by activating the structural links among individuals (see also Luttig 1933:96–97). A person's identification with natal eanda household and oruzo locality is lifelong, but links to kindred households and localities may be invoked to change residence.

These links are materially mediated by the "bridewealth" (otjitunya) that legitimates the union into which a person is born. Ovaherero say otjitunya " 'is for children,' i.e. it establishes the husband's genetricial rights to the children subsequently born to the bride" (Gibson 1959a: 5, 1962). Marriage is preferred among bilateral cross-cousins, who apply the reciprocal term omuramuandje (Otjimbanderu)—Gibson (1956:131) gives omuramwe for Otjiherero—with a stated preference for FZD-MBS unions. Gibson (1956:133) found that in Ngamiland during the early 1950s, although relatively few then-existing marriages were between FZD and MBS, in nearly half the wife was from her husband's father's eanda, although he notes that maternal cross-cousins are now preferred. Citing Dannert (1906), he suggests that the Herero rationalization for patrilateral marriage bias—that it prevented excessive herd dispersal—may have been valid in the past, since thereby oruzo and eanda herds would have been reunited in alternate generations.

That same marital bias also restricts fissioning of land rights. Entitlement to land—again in the sense used here—is vested in the oruzo
group (Vedder [1928] 1966:193; Luttig 1933:96–97), and children
are born preferentially in mother's natal onganda to affirm the social-
spatial solidarity among generations of the eanda group (Luttig 1933:
69). Maternal kinship links are important in negotiating interpersonal
relationships, particularly between MB and ZS. Gibson (1956:132–
34, 1959a:6) describes the reciprocal rights and obligations of this relationship; especially important is okutuura, which permits a ZS "to
take any old thing, such as an aged beast or a worn article of clothing,
to his maternal uncle and to request that he 'eat' it, i.e., that he use it,
in return for which the uncle must replace the object with a new one."

Possessive particles are applied to persons closely related in the
oruzo-eanda intersection, and once established, rights to land, water
sources, and chattels remain in this group. The wells at CaeCae, for
example, are the current states of natural springs that have been progressively deepened since the mid-1930s; each well has passed in ownership through a set of patrilaterally related Mbanderu men. Alnaes
(1979b) stresses this obligatory reciprocity and points to its crucial
economic importance for the 1904 refugees from South-West Africa,
most of whom had relatives already in the Protectorate from whom
they obtained loan cattle to reestablish their herds (recall, p. 141, that
Nikodemus received such cattle at Qangwa).

Coherence in Concepts of Tenure Systems

Despite significant differences in details, the underlying principles of
affiliation and legitimation of land tenure among these systems are
compatible with Tswana institutions. Batswana permit cousin marriage of all types, with preference given to bilateral cross-cousins
(Schapera 1938; Kuper 1982) but with a strong bias, at least among
some groups, toward patrilateral parallel cousins, FBD (Comaroff and
Comaroff 1981).[17] The particularly strong relation of obligations between F/MB (molome) and B/ZS (motlogolo) among all Tswana groups
is well recorded (Schapera 1970:140; Comaroff and Comaroff 1981:
37). Schapera (1940:83–89) and Comaroff (ed., 1980) describe
the sequence of devolutionary payments attending betrothal and
marriage, culminating but not ending with the transfer of marriage
(bogadi) cattle or nowadays perhaps cash. Bogadi transfer may occur
at the wedding itself, but it more often is extended in installments that
frequently mark the birth and even the marriage of children resulting
from the union (Comaroff, ed., 1980:167). The main effect of bogadi

is to validate the claim of the husband's group to children the wife bears in the marriage. As such it is, in Schapera's phrase, "a kin obligation, not a private affair." Comaroff and Comaroff (1981) make clear the spatial correlates of these obligations.

Schapera (1943:46–59) encapsulates the essential determinates of place in Tswana customary law: the location of a Motswana's home is determined primarily by kin affiliation—ascribed at birth into a land-holding group or acquired by marriage or adoption into such a group—not by income, occupation, or social ambition. Tribal land is apportioned among social units constituted as wards—whose members were, in the past more than now, conceived to be related to an eponymous founder—under the administration of headmen. The basis for establishing a ward was initially kinship or ethnic identity, although this is no longer invariably the case. Areas mofatshe (rights to use specific sections of land) are allocated to members of a ward and may be passed to descendants, but the land remains the property of the morafe under the administration of the kgosi and his dikgosana. Entitlement inheres in membership in the morafi—through birth, marriage, or adoption—and is activated by application to the head of one's ward (Schapera 1938:195–213; BNA 1958). Schapera (1943:46) is clear that the possessor of land is entitled only to its use and not to absolute ownership. He further notes (1963:164–69) that in precolonial times fission as a result of tenure disputes was common among Tswana, for whom in such cases assassination and secession were the principal recourses. As a Motswana recently put it, "It's just that we moved around a lot looking for good land" (Kiyaga-Mulindwa 1980:85).

Regarding leadership in the past, Schapera (1963:160) quotes a letter from Bathoen I, Kgosi of Bangwaketse, written in 1885: "It is a basic principle of Tswana government that tribal affairs are directed not so much by the chief alone as by him and his brothers, his father's brothers and their sons, and also his own sons." This probably reflects an original situation in which leadership was based on economic differentials; it is pertinent that Burchell ([1824] 1953, 2:347) recorded that kgosi (chief) meant rich man. Schapera (1963:163) goes on to remark that the process by which chiefs became more centrally powerful during the period of first mercantile and then early colonial penetration was accelerated by the official demarcation of tribal reserves coupled with enforcement of the rule that all inhabitants of a reserve must submit to the authority of the Tswana dikgosi.

Thus it appears that, before direct colonial intervention, San, Herero, Nama, and Tswana tenurial systems had as much in common as they now superficially appear to lack. That this should be so is not really surprising, given the millennia-long history of associations of peoples whose descendants are now seen as different tribes. When Early Iron Age pastoralist economies were absorbed into southern Africa 2,000 years ago, the social groups involved in the process were almost surely not markedly differentiated.[18] Of one thing, at least, we can be quite confident (as the archaeological evidence has shown): both forager and pastoralist groups—if there was such restricted categorization—were distributed in small local residence units. We do not now know, perhaps can never know, how the kin-marriage arrangements of these groups were administered, but it is not going out on too thin a limb to posit that some form of filiation was a necessary, but not necessarily a sufficient, condition of group coherence. Given the economic and social scale of their lives, bilaterality was probably advantageous. Subsequently, strong hierarchical status structures did arise in the eastern half of the region of our concern; it may be that the historical roots of Tswana status ranking lie in these earlier formations. In the western half such status structures were much more weakly developed. Subsequent transformations in Khoe-speaking forager-herder social formations never developed strong hierarchical structures, but Barnard (1986:15) sees them as logical transformations of earlier forager formations.

In any event, we have Tshekedi's testimony that in the early eighteenth century there was little difference between San and Tswana social formations and their internal economic relations, at least that was discernible to the members of those formations at the time. In addition, we have eighteenth- and nineteenth-century Euroamerican accounts of Tswana polities (recall chap. 3); ethnographers today might describe those polities in terms we would recognize as applying to Herero, Nama, or even San peoples in our contemporary vocabulary.

The important thing to note is that—despite significant differences in specific kinship-marriage arrangements and in status hierarchies—there is an equally fundamental structural commonality underlying San, Herero, and Tswana land tenure: bilateral ascription of tenure entitlement and obligations by birth into a set of corporate, tenure-holding groups; cousin marriage as a mechanism for defining and restricting the extent of these groups; ritualized reciprocal uncle-nephew or grandparent-grandchild exchanges; preferential birth within tenurial bounds of mother's family; reinforcement of entitlement through marriage or adoption into a group; reciprocal obligations among members; inalienability of entitlements so long as membership in the kin-affine set is maintained; and inalienability of land.

Scheffler (1986:347) summarizes these conditions in which filiation

is the condition for inclusion in a group and exercise of filial obligations the condition for continuing inclusion:

It is possible for a person to maintain two or more affiliations by maintaining
more-or-less extensive and intensive social relations with the two or more
groups with which his father or mother, or both, were socially identified. Co-
residence with the local nucleus of such a set is not necessary for that purpose.
If a person participates in such social relations and thereby maintains for himself two or more such identities, that person's child has a right to do the same,
and through either or both parents. If the parent omits to maintain such relations with any one set, the child does not acquire that particular identity. What
the child acquires by virtue of filiation is not a single such identity but a set of
them, and that set may or may not be the sum of the sets acquired by his father
and mother. In short, the right possessed natally by anyone to participate in
the assets and affairs of any one group is the result of a series of parental natal
accumulations *and* of parental maintenances *or* losses. Continued possession
of that right is contingent on exercise of it.

This is precisely what I have described for the Zhu filiation-tenure
system and summarized for the other systems with which it has long
been in association. Status and tenure entitlements inhere in these conditions. The only conclusion we can reach is that San tenure has been,
and continues to attempt to be, generationally stable and sanctioned
by traditional rules that are congruent with other southern African
systems. The basis of entitlement to land is membership in a kinship
group whose history is associated with a specific parcel of geographic
space. That related persons are admitted to a tenure group's land in
order to share ecological resources reinforces rather than weakens tenurial right based in group sociality. For only persons who can claim
participation in the social polity are admitted, and then only after they
present their kinship credentials for examination.

Multitiered ownership of places and things has characterized the remembered and recorded past. Space associated with one particular
group was layered upon that of other groups. This was possible not
because of some altruistic urge for accommodation, but because the
tenure systems of the different competing peoples were mutually intelligible and ecological requirements were to some extent complementary rather than conflicting. Displacement and display were the usual
modes of defense of these tenures, with considerable negotiation based
on detailed examination of genealogies given an important part in the
process (cf. Comaroff 1973).

Fights over land did, and do, occur, of course; all the cases given by
Lee (1979:336–38) for the Zhu illustrate this, although he chooses to
interpret them as revealing paucity of structure rather than structural

articulations of persons in place. The literature on Herero conflict is vast (Vedder 1938; Tlou 1972, 1976; Estermann 1976), as is that for Batswana (Parsons 1983 gives an extensive summary). And the history of subjugation of San-speaking peoples by others was documented in chapters 3 and 4.

Nevertheless, a striking feature of current settlement in the Kalahari is its continuity—a continuity that transcends time and space and ethnicity despite some major displacements of peoples. The current distribution of groups in the region is clearly the product of a very long process of interaction involving congruent social concepts and complementary economic systems. If this were not the case, current debates within Botswana over the reallocation of tenure rights (Hitchcock 1980, Wilmsen 1982a, and Kerven 1982 give extensive overviews) would not be necessary. These systems were able to maintain their integrity until disrupted by the penetration of commodity capitalism at the beginning of this century. Even during the initial colonial period of mercantile capitalism in the nineteenth century, they were able to retain significant parts of their former structures, which—though constantly modified in relation to each other—continue to be realized today.

6

The Political Construction
of Production Relations

As the taste of porridge does not tell you who grew the oats, no more does
this simple process [labor] tell you of itself what are the social conditions
under which it is taking place, whether under the slave-owner's brutal lash,
or the anxious eye of the capitalist, whether Cincinnatus carries it on in
tilling his modest farm or a savage in killing wild animals with stones.

Karl Marx, *Capital,* 1865

Economic Correlates of Foraging and Food

Unlike Sahlins—who assured us that primitive reality was one of affluence based on trust in the abundance of nature—Richards (1983:38)
has come to the more reasonable conclusion that "hunter/gatherers do
not simply help themselves to natural abundance." Instead, Richards
continues, citing the work of Lee (1979) and Silberbauer (1981) as
having established this point, "considerable managerial skill is involved in getting a range to produce." This being the case, the social
conditions under which production takes place must also involve considerable managerial skill.

Nevertheless, articulated relations of property, production, labor,
and exchange are generally treated as being absent from San social formations. The decomposition of these relations into separate systems of
extraction and transaction continues to be a basic tenet of studies of
the economic life of these peoples. Indeed, it is just this analytical disarticulation that defines San-speakers as belonging among simple foragers. This division engenders a false sense of security about the
autonomy of what are considered the resource-exploitation functions of these peoples, in effect setting foraging—and especially food
production by foraging—outside the economic realm. The ways San-
speakers are able to reach beyond domestic kinship while orchestrating effective kin networks to participate in regional economies are lost
in that reduction.

195

It may seem ironic, and it is certainly contradictory, that those authors, Lee and Silberbauer, who illustrate most thoroughly the degree of resource management skill exhibited by San-speakers also conclude most emphatically that these skills evolved to restrain productive growth in order to sustain populations in environmental equilibrium. Equally inhibiting has been the failure to differentiate the study of San production from that of energetics. Associated with this orientation has been an identification of San economy with material culture and "primitive" technology.

Accordingly, in his study of Zhu production, Lee (1979:251) explicitly eschews a consideration of labor relations in favor of a study of work. He then defines work in terms of energy relations (the input and output of calories); for him these are the real relations "underlying . . . the ephemera of social life." It would be difficult to frame a clearer declaration: social relations are epiphenomena, secondary consequences of energy flow. Appropriately, Lee finds that the main work Zhu engage in is that necessary for subsistence, and he discusses this work in terms of implement manufacture and maintenance, resource procurement techniques, and transportation factors. Silberbauer (1981:256–57) too finds energy chains to be the economic measure of choice. Citing Dalton (1969:73), he sees Gcwi economy as "'embedded' in other community relationships and not composed of associations separate from these"; stability is achieved through mobility (Silberbauer uses the term lability) among loosely allied kin, itself an adaptation to the vagaries of the Kalahari productive base. We examined the flaws in this reasoning at the beginning of this book.

Most particularly, as was shown also to be true of relations to land, San relations of kinship to production are merely assumed to have a simple form and have remained unanalyzed. Here we see the failure that Clammer (1978:3, emphasis added) notes is all too common: there has been no systematic move "from the recognition that economics in small-scale societies (as presumably it is in all) *is* deeply embedded in the other forms of social life, *to an analysis of the actual articulation of such relationships of embeddedness.*"

Investigating these relations of production in the Kalahari will reveal that here, no less than elsewhere, they are not invariate, mechanical consequences of the priority of an ecological base (as Meillassoux and Lee insist) or transaction etiquette (as Sahlins would have it), still less of shared sentiment (as Marshall supposes). We will find significant production differentials to be a feature of contemporary San social units. These differentials in attained production are emergent results of the interplay of kinship status, land-tenure entitlements, propinquity to other peoples, investment opportunities, and so forth. They have been realized by virtue of the variable participation of generations of Kalahari peoples in the changing local and worldwide economic conditions that we have traced through two millennia of the region's history.

As we have seen in that history, neither San social formations nor their productive capacities are static. The political and ideological components of those social structures retain considerable autonomy, subject to independent—or at least not obligate—directions of transformation under conditions of ecological change or of alterations in the terms of exchange. Understanding the expression of these formations at any moment therefore requires a contingent analysis of the formative forces at that present moment. The first task, then, is to bring into focus the actuality of San relations of production. To accomplish this, I will turn initially to a description of Zhu, Mbanderu, and Tawana relations of production in Ngamiland today. This will serve as a scaffolding for an analysis of actual realized production of these groups in terms of their differentiated status with respect to each other.

Allocation of Access to the Means of Production

Zhu access to the forces and means of production resides in kinship practice. It is essential, therefore, to begin by moving away from the abstract format of kinship structure, which we have just worked through, to a detailed examination of realized kin relations among these people. In doing so, we move from the constraints imposed by the conditions of production—such things as variation in rainfall, the mechanical techniques used to make tools, and so forth—to the process of surplus extraction that enables relations of production to be reproduced. This will allow us to address directly the embeddedness of economics in the social life of Kalahari peoples. The analysis is centered on CaeCae but encompasses all those parts of Ngamiland-Namibia where we traced Zhu activities through the nineteenth century—that is, Ghanzi and Gcam to the south, the Tsau-Sehitwa area on the Okavango Delta to the east, and Tsodilo to the north.

Zhu residential arrangements distribute families among homesteads[1] within which household heads or their spouses, or both, ideally trace their ancestry to common parents in the first or second ascending generation; these are the people Lee identifies as a core group. As Lee (1979:61–67) points out, this ideal is not always realized today, but as we shall see, the bases of compromise for departures from it can be traced more often than not to identifiable displacements of individuals during the past century and a half. During the twelve years I recorded residence information, there were nine Zhu, six Mbanderu/Herero, and one Tawana homesteads at CaeCae. The number of residents varied, of course, as a result of births, deaths, and to a lesser degree movements of people. I use the median numbers of resident persons to characterize the period; these are 220 Zhu, 35 Ovambanderu/Herero, 2 Batawana, and 1 each Nama and Mbukushu. Wiessner (1977:284–309), using unpublished data made available to her by Lee, gives detailed histories of CaeCae Zhu households during the decade 1963–73; these offer valuable comparisons to the household histories I present below.

Genealogies of all Zhu adults resident at CaeCae between 1973 and 1980 who had contracted marriages or had had liaisons that resulted in the birth of a child are given in figures 6.1–6.8; these are composites compiled from individual genealogies elicited from the then-living adults shown who were more than about twenty years old at the time. The genealogies are organized according to the residential homestead of the persons identified in each. Six reproducing generations are represented; to direct readers' attention somewhat more easily, I have numbered them sequentially beginning with generation 1, the youngest now-reproducing generation. Applying an average generation span of about thirty years (Howell 1976:214, 335), we find that the oldest persons in the oldest generation, generation 6, would have been born in the 1820s and 1830s (a few perhaps slightly earlier, but in any case after 1800), whereas the oldest in the youngest generation began to be born in the early 1960s and were just beginning their reproductive careers about 1980. The arrangement of generational cohorts in horizontal tiers is of course a simplified schematic convenience; actual ages of the persons included are relatively continuous and sometimes overlap adjacent tiers.

It goes without saying that these genealogies are incomplete, especially in the ascending generations. Persons are missing either because they have no currently living descendants at CaeCae and thus are not directly relevant to this initial analysis (the descendants of many of these people live in other communities in the region) or because they either have been genuinely forgotten or have been suppressed for reasons of immediate social strategy. There are also a few uncertainties about actual relationships; these occur with increasing frequency in the more remote ascending generations, again owing to loss or suppression of memory. These are shown as broken lines on the figures and specified at appropriate moments in the discussion. When relevant to the current status of current CaeCae residents, disputes arising over strategy-selected memory are discussed when the genealogical histories of the parties involved are taken up. The principal kin connections of CaeCae residents to people living to the north in what is known as the Nqumsi (rocky) part of the Dobe area (Dobe, Qubi, Qabi, Magopa, Qangwa), to the west (now mainly at Tshumqwe), to the east (Tsodilo and the Tsau-Sehitwa area—Makaukung, Namanyani, Qonqa, Mahoeihoei, and Kowrie), and to the south (on the Ghanzi freehold farms) are summarized in table 6.1. Associated Tawana and Mbanderu genealogies are given in figures 6.3, 6.9, and 6.10.

In figure 6.1, the kinship relations of persons who are members of homestead 1 are given along with their extensions to other CaeCae homesteads as well as to other areas. These are the people who claim lineal inheritance of CaeCae nqore through either or both of their parents. Their claim is not challenged by others and is supportable to the limit of living memory, extending back at least to the latter part of the eighteenth century in the grandparents of Tcoma (C/100),[2] whose names are forgotten (but see below, p. 207); this is the T#omag!ai identified by Lee (p. 138 above) as the nqorekau who preceded Shexai (A/110). Figures 6.2 and 6.3 present a more detailed description of the connections between members of homestead 1 and those of homestead 2 and homestead 3, some of whose members are also direct descendants of CaeCae people.

To begin with, sometime after the middle of the nineteenth century three Zhu men from Ghanzi (who are said to have been brothers and cousins) married CaeCae women who were Tcoma's sisters (refer to fig. 6.1). The means through which these introductions were accomplished may be found in an aside made by an old woman, Xin (U/642), as she told me about her kinship relations. When speaking of her mother's father, who was born about 1840 at Gxogxanna in the Gcam area, where in adulthood he inherited the nqorekau position, Xin related this vignette, which apparently her grandfather had recounted many times: "People from elsewhere would visit Gxogxanna; these were friend Zhu (Zhu tcarakwe), usually from around Ghanzi. They would trade beads with these people. The Ghanzi people trading ostrich eggshell beads and necklaces for glass beads that Gxogxanna Zhu obtained through the CaeCae to Qangwa to the Mbukushu net-

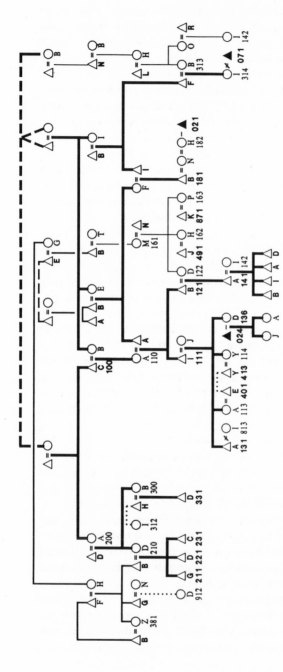

Figure 6.1. Genealogy of Zhu homestead 1. Dashed lines indicate presumed relationship; letters refer to the name code given below, numbers are the identification designations of CaeCae people; filled-in triangles indicate CaeCae people; — indicates visitor-spouse; ≠ indicates divorce; = indicates marriage; / indicates marriage. Filled-in triangles are Mbanderu and Tawana men; / indicates divorce; — indicates visitor-spouse. The name code is:

Men

A	Qam	H	Xau	O	Kanxa	V	Bo
B	Kao	I	Tcishe	P	Tcunta	W	Qoma
C	Tcoma	J	Tcwi	Q	Tcoka	X	Xoishe
D	Ssao	K	Tcashe	R	Tciqe	Y	Dam
E	Kaishe	L	Gcau	S	Tsaa	Z	Tcanqo
F	Homi	M	Kamtco	T	Kumtsaa		
G	Tcinxau	N	Tcu	U	Zotcoa		

Women

A	Shexai	H	Dixau	O	Ncaka	V	Cam
B	Bau	I	Tshwa	P	Tcasa	W	Wanxa
C	Shuqo	J	Nquka	Q	Tcuka	X	Hama
D	Xushe	K	Kalu	R	Tcabo	Y	Qu
E	Nqai	L	Ncisa	S	Be	Z	Gexai
F	Nqoshe	M	Koba	T	Tinqai		
G	Tcwa	N	Tcoshe	U	Xin		

work through Tsodilo." Xin's grandfather simply restates from an insider's point of view the conclusion reached in chapter 3 that trade networks have an ancient history in the region and provides context for local details (recall that T. Hahn recorded this same route in 1895; p. 116 above. The three Ghanzi men to whom we shall now be introduced simply followed the well-worn routes of this network long known to their fathers. We shall pick up these routes again when I consider kinship as practice.

The first of the Ghanzi men was the father of Qam, Shexai's (A/110) husband and the narrator of Lee's vignette about Zhu-Tawana relations in the 1890s. Qam's mother was a CaeCae women, Nqai, the cousin of Tcoma (C/100). Howell estimates that Qam (who died in 1971, shortly before I arrived at CaeCae in 1973) was born about 1895.[3] His father, Kao, arrived a decade or more earlier; whether he came as an independent trader, a guide for European merchants, or a herdsman of Tawana cattle at the many cattleposts in the area at that time is unclear (that is, I have been unable to determine this satisfactorily). According to several accounts, he, along with Tcoma, was herding Tawana cattle—and some of his own—by the time Qam was born.

The descendants of this pair, Qam and Shexai (A/110), along with those of Qam's mother's older sister Tshwa and her husband, who was a collateral of Kao, Qam's father (and also named Kao), along with the spouses of these descendants and some of their children, are the present residents of homestead 1.[4] Tshwa and Kao's grandson is Kao (B/181), who acquired the nqorekau position after Shexai's death; he is considered by Shexai's sons—Tcishe (I/111) and Kao (B/121)—as well as by some others to have held this position illegitimately (we shall return to this dispute after kin network identifications). All of these homestead 1 people trace their descent through CaeCae kausi to Tcoma (C/100) or his sisters, or both, and by inference to the seventh generation (not shown) and beyond. They do so because it is axiomatic to them that (even though they can no longer name those ancestors), since Tcoma was nqorekau, at least one of his parents (note that they claim both) and thus at least one of those parents' parents were CaeCae kausi. Indeed, they extend that reasoning indefinitely; Lee (1979:344) records that he was told that Shexai (A/110) "was a descendent of several generations of /Xai/Xai owners." They also argue that in the past there was far less moving about in the nqoresi, and people tended to marry relatives who lived next to each other. To a great extent, the genealogies bear them out.

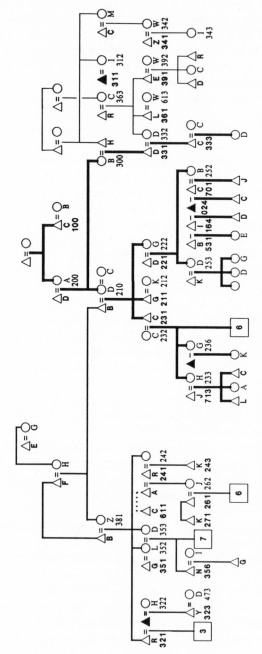

Figure 6.2. Genealogy of Zhu homesteads 2–3. Identification and name codes and legend as for figure 6.1; numerals in boxes refer to number of children borne by a couple.

The second Ghanzi man, Ssao, to marry into CaeCae during this period married a women named Shexai (A/200) who was the uqnqa (FZ, Tcoma's sister) of Shexai (A/110); in a moment we shall find their descendants in homesteads 2–3. The third Ghanzi man, Qam's father, Kao's brother Qam, will be taken up when homestead 4 is presented.

Shortly after these first three, two other Ghanzi men worked through CaeCae in the latter part of the nineteenth century (fig. 6.2); though they neither married nor settled here, they have many descendants in the community today. The first of these was Tshwa's husband Kao's older brother Homi, who is reported to have worked with Karuapa Katiti (Axel Ericsson); recall that Ericsson hunted elephants at CaeCae in the 1870s. Homi and his wife, Dixau, are the parents of Gexai (Z/381), whose descendants make up most of the members of homestead 3; of Kao, whose sons are the heads of several homestead 2 households; and of Tcinxau, whose daughter Xushe (D/912) will turn up in several homestead histories. Dixau's sister's son, another Kao, married a Gcam woman, Tinqai; they are the parents of Koba (M/161), one of whose three daughters, Xushe (D/122), is married to Shexai's (A/110) son Kao (B/121).

The second Kao referred to above, Tshwa's husband, the brother of Homi, that one who is Kao's (B/181) father's father,[5] later married Gexai (Z/381), his brother's daughter; together Homi and Kao are the progenitors of many of the members of homestead 3 (fig. 6.2). These people have spent most of their careers in the NyaeNyae and Gcam areas, residing periodically at CaeCae since the 1930s; even today they move frequently between CaeCae and Tshumqwe. They have two collateral links here, one through Gexai's brother's wife, the other through the present nqorekau, Ssao's (D/331), father.

Homi's son (Gexai's brother), also named Kao, married Xushe (D/210), the daughter of Ssao and Shexai (A/200). Their children—Tcinxau (G/211), Ssao (D/221), and Tcoma (C/231)—the spouses of these, plus the children of these people today make up all the members of homestead 2. Xushe's (D/210) mother was that Shexai (A/200) who was the uqnqa (FZ) of Shexai (A/110), thereby giving CaeCae nqore entitlement to these people.

We must return briefly to generation 5 to trace the final important CaeCae nqore line. Tcoma's (C/100) sister Shexai (A/200) is also the mother of Bau (B/300), who is the mother of Ssao (D/331), the current undisputed CaeCae nqorekau. This is the man whom Lee (1979:344) notes was already the spokesman to "outsiders" while his great-aunt (MMBD) Shexai (A/110), was still alive and nqorekau. He remained

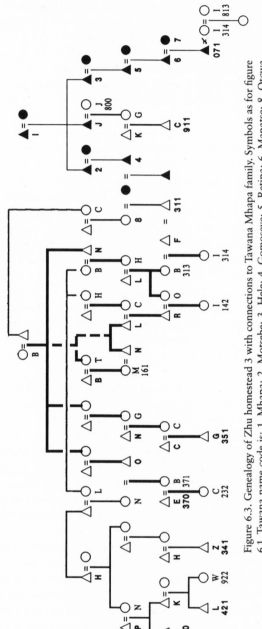

Figure 6.3. Genealogy of Zhu homestead 3 with connections to Tawana Mhapa family. Symbols as for figure 6.1. Tawana name code is: 1, Mhapa; 2, Motsebe; 3, Hele; 4, Gomoseye; 5, Retipa; 6, Mapatse; 8, Otcwa (a Cexai).

spokesman during the approximately ten years that his tsu, Kao (B/181), who was still living in 1985, claimed nqorekau status. Ssao (D/331) is a direct descendant of Tcoma's (C/100) parents, who were his mother's mother's parents; therefore he is a central CaeCae person and, as mentioned already, is currently nqorekau. He lives, however, in homestead 3; we shall presently learn why.

Finally, these CaeCae kausi have important links to the east in the Tsau-Sehitwa area (fig. 6.3), links that were created in the movements induced by events connected with Tawana and European activities in the region. These movements reverse the flow of the earlier nineteenth-century exodus that took some proportion of the previous San-speaking peoples of the Tsau-Sehitwa-Kwebe region into the western sandveld to escape Tawana domination (p. 101).

First, a daughter of one of Tcoma's (C/100) parents' siblings (which one appears genuinely to have been forgotten), a women named Bau, married a man who is now unknown but who was apparently from the east; she went to the Tsau-Sehitwa area sometime after the mid-nineteenth century. Extrapolating from the ages of this woman's current descendants, it seems likely that this happened in the 1860s or 1870s, in conjunction with either mercantile trade or cattle herding, as was the case with the Kaos and their kin whose careers we have just witnessed in cameo. The precise relationship of this women to CaeCae is disputed, but the connection is not denied. The strongest claim offered is as follows: Ssao's (D/331) mother, Bau (B/300), was the uqma (DD) of Tcoma's (C/100) and Shexai's (A/200) mother, who accordingly would have been named Bau; the parents of this woman and of the Bau who went east more than a century ago are thought to have been related. This presumed relationship is shown in figure 6.1. Although it is not generally disputed that a reasonably close connection exists among these Baus, that the relation between the older pair cannot be specified more closely than parent's sibling suggests that this particular relationship has become strategically controversial; its closeness is, expectably, argued most strongly by the eastern Bau's descendants, who spend as much time in the villages of the east as at CaeCae. Significantly, Ssao (D/331) recognizes the relationship and has given me plausible kin terms that he applies to the persons concerned.

At about the turn of this century, several men from the CaeCae-Dobe-NyaeNyae area are known to have gone east to the Tsau-Sehitwa area as herders of Tawana cattle; these were Gexai's brother Kao, her husband, Kao, the latter's son Homi, and Kao the father of Koba (M/161). This last-named Kao was the son of a man, Kaishe, who on some accounts was the brother of the father of the Kao first mentioned as the father of Qam, Shexai's (A/110) husband. The tale told to Lee by that Qam is set in this time. Some of these men remained in the east for extended periods, particularly during the decade or so after the resident magistrate at Tsau, Merwyn Williams, removed Sekgoma's cattle from the area in 1903. At least three of these men—Koba's (M/161) husband's brother Gcau, his cousin Tcu, and Homi, the uqma (BS) of the only other Homi we have met—married in the east, the younger Homi to Bau (B/313) (fig. 6.3). As already mentioned, Koba's daughter Xushe (D/122) is married to Kao (B/121) in homestead 1, her MMF(B)SSS on the basis of the assumed generation 6 relationship just delineated.

During the next three decades a constant flow of persons moved between CaeCae (as well as other communities in western Ngamiland-Namibia) and the eastern Tawana cattleposts, creating an eastern branch, as it were, of CaeCae kinship relations. All the Zhu in this eastern area consider themselves people from western Ngamiland, especially CaeCae (Biesele 1975; cf. Lee 1979:81 and Wiessner 1977); Harpending (1976:163) confirms these claims by gene-frequency analysis.

Two women from this eastern extension of CaeCae kinship have exercised their inherent options to marry CaeCae men and now live in the community. Tshwa (I/142) is married to her FFBDS, Kao and Xushe's son Qam (A/141), the uqma (SS) of Shexai's (A/110) husband in homestead 1 (fig. 6.1). Shuqo (C/232), the daughter of Bau (B/371), is married to her presumed MMM(s)DDS, Tcoma (C/231), in homestead 2 (fig. 6.2); but note that for this relationship to be correct some juggling of the claim to CaeCae legitimacy preferred by this group is required. A second Tshwa (I/314), the daughter of Homi and Bau (B/313), was married until 1980, when they divorced, to Bashile (/071), a Motawana whose family, Mhapa, was given the CaeCae-Gcam areas in lefatshe (use right) by Sekgoma in the 1890s as part of his policy to gain support from basimane commoners.[6] Bashile is his family's current overseer of their grazing rights in the CaeCae area. Bau (B/313) is herself now the junior wife (Homi having died) of Halengisi (/311), whose father, Gomoseye, was the grandson of Mhapa and nephew of Hele, the grandfather (FF) of Mapatse, the father of Bashile (/071). Through this connection, Tshwa (1/314) is Bashile's {FFFBS[S]D} (fig. 6.3).

Halengisi's mother, Otcwa, was a Cexai from east of Ghanzi around Karang, where the Mhapas (whose center is at Tsau) also have had cattleposts since at least the time of Sekgoma in the 1890s. Shuqo, the mother of Otcwa, was the cousin of the father (Tcu) of Bau's (B/313) mother, Dixau, though whether through one or two ascendant generations is forgotten. The sister of that man, Tcu, is the MM of Shuqo, the mother of Tcinxau (G/351). The mothers' mothers of Bau (B/313) and Bau (B/371)—Bau and Ncisa, respectively—are said to have been sisters from the Kareng area. Figure 6.3 shows their descendant relationships to other current CaeCae residents. This figure also displays relations through Bau's (B/371) mother's father's brother to Tcanqo (Z/341), Gcau (L/421), and Wanxa (W/922). These latter people have immediate relatives at Tsodilo, one of whom, Gcau's (L/421) uqnqa, Gcau (L/000), is indicated in figure 6.3. It seems, however, that as in the case of the Tsau-Sehitwa area, the Tsodilo Hills community is now composed of recent Zhu and Cexai immigrants; all these people trace their parents and parents' parents to the south or west of Tsodilo.

In his youth, Halengisi (who was seventy-four in 1976) returned his father's herds to the west (this was about 1918); he stayed for a time at CaeCae then settled at Gcam, where he married his senior wife, Tshwa (I/312). This woman's brother Xau is the father of Ssao (D/331). In turn, Ssao married this man's father's sister's daughter's (Shuqo [C/363]) daughter, Xushe (D/332); that is, Ssao married his FFZDD (fig. 6.2). In 1937 or 1938, soon after Moremi III became chief of the Batawana, Halengisi settled at CaeCae, having been forced to move frequently in the Gcam area by Union police in keeping with South African government policy of expanding Boer farming settlement of South-West Africa. Except for a brief period in the mid-1950s, when he participated in the attempt to resettle on old claims in the NyaeNyae-Gcam areas, Halengisi has lived at CaeCae.

A brief recapitulation and a comment are in order. All the members of homestead 1 trace their descent from CaeCae kausi demonstrably to the sixth, inferentially to the seventh, and plausibly to the eighth and beyond ascending generations from the youngest currently reproducing cohort in the community. Wiessner (1977:297) remarks of them that they are the most generationally stable group at CaeCae. In the fourth and fifth generations, a set of men from Ghanzi are known to have married women from this group. These men may have had prior kinship status in the community, acquired through their predecessors in the trade network; that certain names—some of which are not Zhu, or at least are now extremely rare among Zhu—are found among the descendants of these men and not elsewhere in the community suggests that kinship does extend into generations that can no longer be documented. Indeed, some members of the community willingly speculate about such statuses. Whatever they may actually have been, those

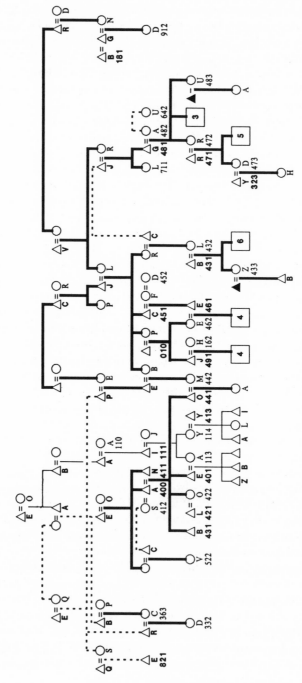

Figure 6.4. Genealogy of Zhu homestead 4. Symbols as for figure 6.1.

prior relations now enter into negotiations over status entitlements at CaeCae; I shall return to this when I consider kinship practice. Those marriages to Ghanzi men were legitimized through adjustments, possibly including the creation of presumptive kin ties if necessary, that brought them into conformity with the social and material needs of the parties to the unions (recall that one does not marry strangers). In a moment I will examine the mechanisms by which this may have been accomplished. Those adjustments are the fulcrum on which conflicting claims to nqore status at CaeCae now hinge, both by those current descendants of the Ghanzi men whose own parents remained at CaeCae and those whose parents moved to other areas.

The members of homestead 2 also have direct links to CaeCae, through Xushe (D/210), extending beyond the sixth generation. In homestead 3, however, only Ssao (D/331) has such a claim (through his mother, Bau [(B/300]). In addition, he is linked through his father to Gcausha and Gcam. Many of the people in homestead 3, as has been noted, are recognized to be appropriately associated with those latter areas; they are at CaeCae because of increasingly scarce surface water and political instability in Namibia. They have, however, in common with homestead 2 people, strong affinal links to CaeCae through Xushe (D/210), as well as to Bau (B/300), Ssao's (D/331) mother, and also to the paternal family of Ssao, the current CaeCae nqorekau. They are thus linked to Halengisi (/311), whose senior wife, Tshwa (I/312), is Ssao's father's sister. Wiessner (1977 : 297) notes that these two homesteads also enjoy a high generational stability.

Halengisi has been the principal channel through whom Tawana cattle (recall that his father was a Motawana of the Mhapa family) have passed in both mafisa and ownership to members of this homestead. Ssao, a consummate politician and, as Lee (1979 : 344) noted, an articulate spokesman, has manipulated these relationships along with his entitlement to CaeCae and his heritable right to the nqorekau position to considerable economic advantage, both for himself and for his homestead associates. Ssao exercises his paternal links to secure a substantial share of the economic assets of homestead 3, while investing his maternal connections to gain the leadership of CaeCae community. Appropriately, in 1976 he was "elected" chairman of the CaeCae Village Development Committee (VDC) when that program was initiated by the Botswana central government.

We must return, briefly, to generation 5 to trace the relationships of the members of homestead 4 (fig. 6.4). About the same time that the first Ghanzi Kao, Qam's (Shexai's [A/110] husband) father, settled in CaeCae, that Kao's brother Qam—the uqnqa (FB) of Shexai's (A/110) husband—married a Gcausha woman. Most of the descendants of this

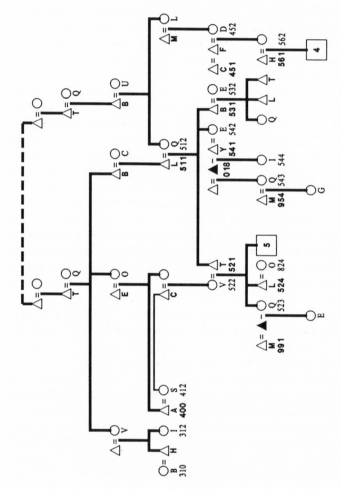

Figure 6.5. Genealogy of Zhu homestead 5. Symbols as for figure 6.1.

pair are now to be found in the Dobe and NyaeNyae areas; some of them live at CaeCae in homestead 4. Marshall (1976:181) mentions these people whose tie to CaeCae is the collateral one (Qam's brother Kao) in generation 5. More recently, Tcishe (I/111), of homestead 1, married a Gcausha woman descended from that Qam, his FFBDD. In turn, Dam (Y/413) married Tcishe's daughter Qu (Y/114), his FFFBSSD; Kaishe (E/401), Dam's older brother, subsequently married another of Tcishe's daughters, Shexai (A/113), the uqma of Shexai (A/110), of course also his FFFBSSD. These marriages have forged increasingly close ties between homestead 4 and homestead 1.

In the mid-1920s, a woman from this group, Tcasa, married Tautona ([/010]; his Tswana name: literally, male lion = king, given to him because he was a strict instructor of young men in choma [initiation rites; see p. 261 below]), the Nama man we met in chapter 4; their children—Tcwi (J/491), married to Dixau (H/162), and Nqai (E/462), widowed from Tcwi (J/461)—live at CaeCae closely allied with the senior homestead of the Mbanderu family, Tuvare, with whom Tautona's family has a long association. Be (S/412), a Zhu woman from the Andara area, married Qam (A/400), the uqma (SS) of the Ghanzi Qam; she and her children—among whom are the Dam and Kaishe just mentioned—are today the most numerous members of homestead 4. Both Qams worked for the Marenga family, as do their descendants today; all the people of this homestead settled in CaeCae in the 1920s and 1930s in conjunction with this Mbanderu family. As a result of this association, these homestead 4 descendants of Qam and Tautona own 15% of the Zhu livestock at CaeCae.

Homestead 5 (fig. 6.5) is made up of a single extended family: Gcau (L/511), his FFF[B]SSD and wife, Tcuka (Q/512), their children, and the spouses of these. Nqai (E/542), the daughter of Gcau and Tcuka, is married to Dam (Y/541), her FMBSS; she has a daughter, Tshwa (I/544), known as Tshwazho (Black Tshwa) because her biological father is Ismair Tuvare (/018). The son of Gcau and Tcuka, Kumtsaa (T/521), is married to his FFZDD, Cam (V/522), whose mother is the sister of Qam (A/400). These people are thus linked to homestead 4. They also claim a link to homestead 1 through Gcau's (L/511) mother, Shuqo, but this is not recognized by homestead 1 people. The people of homestead 5 often live at Qubi. During 1973–77 they lived in the Aha Hills about 6 kilometers from the CaeCae wells, and all their economic activities were conducted northwestward from the hills (that is, away from CaeCae). In 1977 they joined homestead 4 at CaeCae when their children began to attend the newly opened school.

Homestead 6 (fig. 6.6) was established at CaeCae in the early 1960s

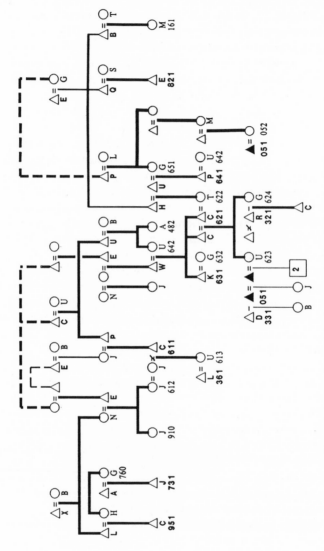

Figure 6.6. Genealogy of Zhu homestead 6. Symbols as for figure 6.1.

(Lee 1979 does not list it among his 1963 living groups but does list it in 1968); it is composed of households with multiple sibling and collateral links to each other in current generations. They claim many common links in generation 6 and above but do not now give consistent accounts of these. These people came from Gcam, where they have a long history. A CaeCae man said of them rather contemptuously in 1976, "Siqa za tsia gwatcna": "They came here yesterday." Homestead 6 people have no direct claim to CaeCae but have a collateral link to Ssao (D/331), whose father's father's father's brother's son married Tcwa (G/651); Tcwa is the mother and grandmother of several members of this homestead, but she has no surviving children by Ssao's collateral. During those periods of the year when surface water is available, these people live at XumXenni, a place within their home nqore range 35 kilometers to the south of CaeCae; to extend their stay at this place, they have invested in old 200-liter gasoline drums, which they fill with water from rain pools and save for use when the pan goes dry. This is not an insignificant outlay; each drum costs a heifer or its equivalent in cash (P60, about $40) or labor. Since these people own no livestock, they paid for the drums with labor and animal pelts. They have made persistent and strenuous efforts to dig deep wells at XumXenni in order to be able to remain there permanently, but they have not struck water. Until 1977, homestead 6 was usually situated about 2 kilometers south of the CaeCae wells, and all their foraging was done farther southward.

The shutcokau (homestead head) of this group, Tcoma Qumqosi (C/621), an ambitious and very capable man, has made a number of attempts to improve his economic position in the community. Particularly, he has tried to exploit his distant collateral tie to homestead 3 (his wife is the daughter of Ssao's [D/331] father's father's brother's son's widow) by promoting the marriage of one of his homestead kinswomen to Ssao's wife's brother, but this was unsuccessful. He has, however, negotiated the marriage of his wife's older daughter, Xin (U/623), to an Mbanderu man, Kondowra (/051), and this brought him the usual marriage payment of livestock, as well as a flow of goods from his son-in-law until the man died; we shall hear more of this shortly. He also placed his wife's younger daughter in a second-wife position with a Zhu employed on the border by Namibian police, which brought in substantial quantities of store goods until the arrangement dissolved.

The people of homestead 7 (fig. 6.7) are organized not as a single homestead, but as two. In the first, all are members of an extended family whose head, Ncisa (L/711), is the sister of Tcinxau (G/481). She

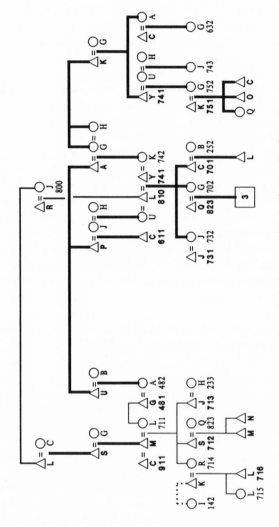

Figure 6.7. Genealogy of Zhu homestead 7. Symbols as for figure 6.1.

and her grown sons (and before her death, her daughter) live with the Herero family, Keharera (/061), with whom they came to CaeCae in 1957 after their forced return from Onyainya. They have an employment association of four generations or more with Keharera's family; they say they are like children of this family and eat its food. Through this association, they have acquired substantial per capita livestock holdings. The other set of homestead 7 people, many of whom were siblings or collaterals of homesteads 8–9 (through Gcau [L/810]), had died or dispersed, most to other areas, by 1979. Wiessner (1977: 307–9) details the steps in this group's dissolution. Of interest to us in this group is Tcoma (C/701), a half-brother of the head of the next homestead to be introduced; in 1978 this Tcoma married Bau (B/252) in homestead 2, to whom he is not obviously related.

The last group of Zhu who live at CaeCae told Lee (1976:94): "You know we are not /Xai/Xai [CaeCae] people. Our true n!ore is east at /Dwia [Dcwia]. . . . We think of the meat that will soon be hanging [there] thick on every branch. No, we are not of /Xai/Xai; /Dwia is our earth. We just came here to drink the milk." These are the people of homestead 8 and homestead 9 (fig. 6.8; see also fig. 6.3); their associations are, as they say, entirely to the southeast and include Cexai as well as Zhu ancestors. Wiessner (1977:304–7) chronicles the peripatetic existence of these homesteads, saying that they "lead a varied life." Whenever water conditions permit (as in 1974), the people of homestead 8 live in the home nqore of their shutcokau, Tciqe (R/811), at Dcwia. They have a long history of association with the Tawana family Mhapa; in the first decades of this century Tciqe's father, Gcau (L/810), tended Mhapa cattle, and in pursuit of his duties is said to have killed several Herero men in herding disputes. This history is expressed today in their close attachment to Bashile (/071), whose milk they drink.

Bashile has married Tciqe's daughter Tshwa (I/813), since he divorced that other Tshwa (I/314); this couple has had their first child. Notice that this is a classificatorily correct marriage; Tshwa (I/813) is Bashile's {FFFB[S]SD} by virtue of her FFF having been married to the same woman, Nquka (J/800), as had Bashile's FFFB. Tshwa (I/813) was previously married to Qam (A/131) of homestead 1, by whom she bore two children; this marriage was the source of considerable conflict in the community. Tciqe's other daughters have established liaisons with itinerant Tawana men; at present it seems unlikely that they will marry within the CaeCae community.

Tciqe's (R/811) wife, Koba (M/812), is the daughter of Kaishe (E/821)—actually, of his older brother whose widow he married in

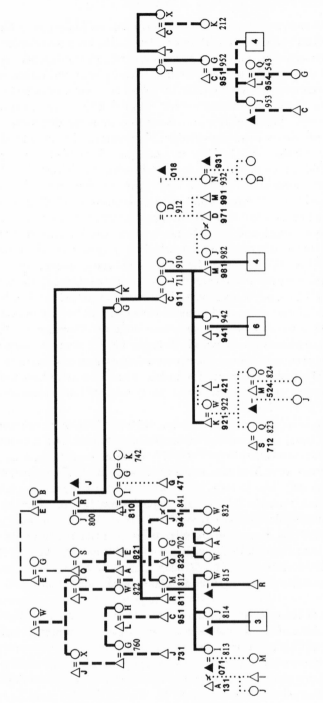

Figure 6.8. Genealogy of Zhu homesteads 8–9. Symbols as for figure 6.1.

levirate—and Wanxa (W/822), who worked for Halengisi at Gcam and first came to CaeCae with him in 1937–38. They move back and forth between this place and the eastern Mhapa cattleposts, as do many of the members of these two homesteads. Tciqe and Kaishe have worked out a connection between two Kaishes in generation 6 of their respective descent lines; they readily admit that they are not sure of this, because those Kaishes moved off into different directions and were not in direct contact thereafter. Tciqe asserts that his FFF (Kaishe) was Kaishe's (E/821) FF, but the latter demurs on this point. Nevertheless, they aver that a close relationship "feels right" to them after many long discussions. As Lee (1986:95) remarks, "the older you get, the more 'control' you have over your kinship." Wanxa, who was born between 1900 and 1910, says that her mother's father came from very far south and spoke Nama, a few words of which she herself retains. This man is said to have worked for a white man whose name they recall as "Dowtli"; if so, he would have been employed by one of the very first Europeans to enter the region.[7] Tcuka (Q/823), the son of Kaishe (E/821) and Wanxa (W/822), moved to CaeCae in 1976 from the Tsau-Sehitwa area, where he had been employed at Mhapa cattleposts. This move was in conjunction with his marriage to Tcwa (G/ 702), a half-sister of Tciqe (R/811) (see fig. 6.7) and thus—by virtue of the presumed connection between the generation 6 Kaishes—his FFF(B)SSD. Tcuka now works for Bashile, while his parents have moved to Mahoeihoei in the east. Spatially, this homestead has become an appendage of Bashile's residence.

The head of homestead 9, Tcoma (C/911), known as Tcomazho (Black Tcoma), is the son of a Cexai man, Tcashe, and a woman, Tshwa, whose mother, Nquka (J/800), was from the Karang area and whose father was a Motawana called by his Zhu name, Tcwizho (Black Tcwi) (fig. 6.8). Tcwizho was the younger brother of Motsebe, Halengisi's FF, and the older brother of Hele, Bashile's FFF (refer to fig. 6.3). That same Nquka (J/800), Tcoma's (C/911) MM, was married to a Zhu man, Tciqe, by whom she bore Gcau (L/810), the father of the current head of homestead 8, Tciqe (R/811). Tcoma (C/911) is thus the FMDS of Tciqe (R/811). Tcomazho came to CaeCae as a cattle herder for the Tawana Mhapa family along with Halengisi, his MFBSS.

None of Tcoma's three marriages were to traceably related women, nor are those of his daughters and sons. Tcoma attempted to gain a measure of CaeCae nqore rights by marrying a women with a tenuous CaeCae connection, Xushe (D/912), through whom he has made persistent efforts to press a claim to CaeCae status on the ground that her mother married Kao (B/181) in later life (thereby Kao becomes Xushe's

classificatory father). His claim carries little weight with the members
of homestead 1. Before she was married to Tcoma (C/911), Xushe
(D/912) was the visitor-spouse[8] of Ismair Tuvare (/018); their daughter Tcoshe (N/932), known as Tcoshezho (Black Tcoshe), is married to
an Mbukushu, Brown Makoeya (/931), from the Tsodilo Hills.

Tcoma's son Tcashe (K/921), has lived for about two decades with
Wanxa (W/922) whom he considers his wife, although Tcoma does
not recognize this as a marriage (Wiessner 1977:111 mentions this
couple). Tcoma's refusal stems from his earlier ambition for Tcashe to
marry into CaeCae, a marriage he could not arrange. Wanxa, who is
from the northeast in the Tsodilo area (fig. 6.3), is the sister of Gcau
(L/451), who was married before his death, to Qam's (A/400) daughter Ncaka (O/422) in homestead 4; through this connection both
Wanxa and Tcashe are employed by the Tuvares, with whom they now
live. With the exception of Tcashe (K/921), all the rest of Tcoma's children have gone, since 1979, to other places (Tshumqwe, Nqumsi, Tsau)
looking for paid employment, and this homestead no longer exists.

Table 6.1 summarizes the number of people living in each of these
homesteads and expresses these numbers as proportions of the total
community population. The table also lists the number and proportions of relatives now living in the other areas we have considered who
were identified by the members of each homestead. With only one exception, homestead 9, these proportions are highest in those areas
from which generation 4–5–6 homestead ancestors are said to have
come or to which they went from CaeCae. Many of the younger members of homestead 9 have been attracted to the administrative center of
Tshumqwe, thus accounting for the disproportionate western orientation of this eastern group. These numbers are in accord with the results
of Harpending's (1976:164) genetic distance analysis, which, as he remarks, places people right where they say they came from. This, in
conjunction with his (personal communication) finding only two pa-
ternity exclusion cases among progenitors claimed by Zhu (on the
basis of ABO, MNS, and Rh blood types), lends confidence to the
identifications of actual progenitors given to me, and to other anthropologists, by CaeCae residents. This is not really very surprising, for as
Marshall (1976:5) remarked, "Genealogies were a good beginning
with those people; they seemed to enjoy telling us who they were." Indeed, they want us to know exactly who they are and why they are
who they are; to them kinship is an indispensable ingredient of that
self-identification. Table 6.1 stratifies these homesteads in terms of
members' nqore entitlement or distance from collaterals with nqore
entitlement at CaeCae.

Table 6.1. Number of Residents in each Homestead and Number of Relatives Named by CaeCae Zhu Living in the Regions Indicated

Homestead	N	West	North	South	East	Total
1	34 (.15)	18 (.20)	7 (.08)	10 (.12)	53 (.60)	88
2	33 (.15)	4 (.09)	16 (.33)	5 (.10)	23 (.48)	48
3	33 (.15)	65 (.48)	27 (.20)	25 (.20)	19 (.13)	136
4	36 (.16)	42 (.27)	92 (.60)	0	20 (.13)	154
5	17 (.08)	30 (.66)	10 (.22)	0	5 (.11)	45
6	17 (.08)	49 (.65)	12 (.16)	2 (.03)	12 (.16)	75
7	13 (.06)	2 (.04)	33 (.69)	0	13 (.27)	48
8	24 (.11)	8 (.21)	3 (.09)	4 (.10)	23 (.60)	38
9	13 (.06)	23 (.37)	32 (.52)	0	7 (.11)	62
Total						694

Note: Proportions in parentheses. N is number of residents in homestead.

A brief synthesis of these homestead relations will be helpful at this point. Some readers will have been amused and others annoyed by the repetition of Kaos begetting Qams begetting Kaos, and such. Yet this detail is unavoidable in order to bring unequivocally to notice how the names form successions; those names we encountered first in homesteads 1–2–3 are almost absent among those we met last in homesteads 7–8–9. Recall that the premise underlying the name relationship is that persons who share a set of names have common ancestors. The importance of this circumstance was emphasized by Marshall (1957) years ago and is not taken lightly, as the following story illustrates.

When Bau (B/252) married Tcoma (C/701), she already had two living children; one by a visitor-spouse relationship was named for her father. The other, fathered by Simon Tuvare, was given (by Simon) his father's Zhu name, Tcoma; upon his marriage to Bau, Tcoma (C/701) gave this child his own (dead) father's name, Gcau, and became angry when people used the child's former name.

A second significant characteristic of the presentation is this: an adequate description of homesteads 1–2–3, and to a somewhat lesser extent of homestead 4, entailed detailed recitations of marriage relations; such is not the case for homesteads 7–8–9, in which there are very few marriages between identified kinspeople. This situation is reflected in statements made by people in the different homestead sets about their marriage practices. Tshwa (I/142) told me that, although many people nowadays married without regard to relationship, she and her husband, Qam (A/141), married properly. Tcinxau (G/211) said, "Yes, some people do just marry anybody, but if you have sense

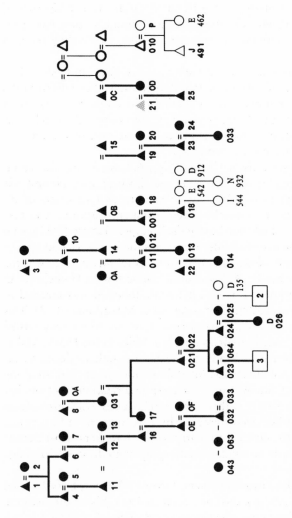

Figure 6.9. Genealogy of Mbanderu homesteads 1–2–3. Legend as for figure 6.1; filled-in symbols indicate Mbanderu (gray is European); heavy outline symbols indicate Nama; light outline symbols indicate Zhu; Herero/Mbanderu names are unique to individuals; only those mentioned in the text are listed here. People living at CaeCae are marked by their identification numbers. 1, Munjuku; 4, Kaverure; 6, Kehimemua; 8, Kwane; 9, Katittewe; 10, Hameja; 11, Nikodemus; 12, Kongareri; 14, Tuahukuje; 15, Katetee; 16, Keharanjo; 17, Kakura; 21, Venter; 25, Kamburu; OA, Katire; OB, Nanisee; OD, Retia; OE, Munjuku. The father of Munjuku (1) was Tjozohongo (see p. 141).

you marry who your parents tell you to." In contrast, Tcinxau (G/481), insisted that the only people one could marry were nonrelatives. Gcau (L/511) agreed with this but proceeded to describe kin visiting, cooperation, and haro in marriage negotiations identical to those related by Tshwa and Tcinxau (G/211), saying "it made their hearts feel like relatives." These differentials are the result of variant recent histories of the present Zhu members of the CaeCae community; they have profound economic consequences for these people, as we shall see in a moment.

The Tawana kin relations represented at CaeCae—in Bashile, Halengisi's father, and Tcomazho's grandfather—have been given in the discussion of Zhu kin relations to highlight the interlayered nature of these peoples' living together; figure 6.3 summarizes these relations graphically. I shall now turn quickly to a recitation of the relevant Mbanderu relations in the community.

Mbanderu homesteads at CaeCae (figs. 6.9, 6.10) are also as integrally related among themselves as are those of Zhu homesteads 1–2–3. The senior men of Mbanderu homesteads 1–2–3 are all direct descendants of the same Mbanderu woman, Katire (OA in figs. 6.9 and 6.10), who had four husbands. Tohoperi Tuvare (/011), who died in 1980 at the age of seventy-eight, was the son of Tuahukuje (14 in fig. 6.9), the fourth husband of Katire. Tuahukuje, in turn, was the son of Katittewee (9 in fig. 6.9) and his Mbanderu wife, Hameja (10 in fig. 6.9); this will interest us in a moment. Tohoperi was married to Katjateri (/012), his {FZD}; their daughter is Makadume (/013). This homestead is senior among Mbanderu at CaeCae, where they settled after having been forced out of South-West Africa in the 1930s. Makadume now functions as its head and is, since her father's death, by far the wealthiest person at CaeCae (in 1980 owning about a third of the cattle of this place). She was in a visitor-spouse relationship from her maturity into the 1970s with a cousin who lived with his wife in Magopa; her children were fathered by this man. By all accounts, Tohoperi refused to allow her to marry so as not to disperse the family herds. She is now in a similar relationship with Manuel Marenga (/041), her {MBS}.

The eldest of the Tuvare brothers, Jacob (/001), most often called by his Zhu name Samkao, died of old age in 1975; his mother was the same Katire, and his father was Nanise (OB in figs. 6.9 and 6.10), her third husband. Jacob was the father of Ismair (/018), whom we have met as the father of Tshwazho (I/544) and Tcoshezho (N/932) in Zhu homesteads 5 and 9. There are further connections here. Piet Venter and Retia will be remembered as channels, during the early 1920s, of Mbanderu attempts to undermine Tawana control over them (p. 149).

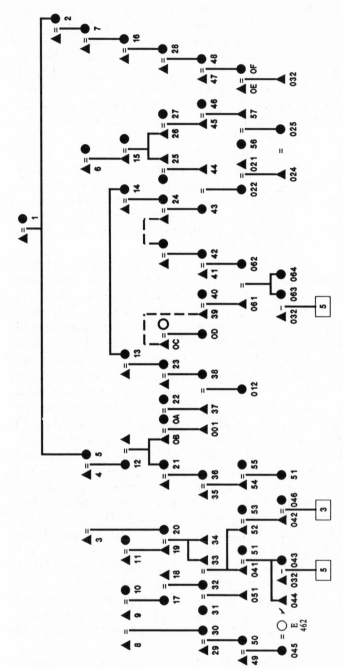

Figure 6.10. Genealogy of Mbanderu homesteads 4–6. Legend as in figure 6.9; the persons indicated by the letters OA through OF are the same individuals who appear with these designations in figure 6.9: 33, Katuwi; 34, Jacob; 37, Nderico; 52, Kaujumbo.

Now, Retia's mother was the daughter by a Nama women of Katittewee, the father of Tuahukuje who was the father of Tohoperi; thus Retia was the {FZD} of Tohoperi and, by extension, of Jacob. I should remind readers that Retia's mother's mother is also the mother—by a Nama man—of the mother of Tautona (/010), who married Tcasa in Zhu homestead 4 and is the father of Tcwi (J/491) and Nqai (E/462), who work for and live with this Tuvare family. Tautona died in 1977, aged eighty-three or eighty-four; for the last decade or so of his life, he was completely blind and feeble, utterly unable to care for himself. During this time he was housed and cared for by Katjateri (/012) and Makadume (/013), the wife and daughter of Tohoperi (/011), Jacob's younger brother, who became homestead head during Jacob's senility. These women, of course, also cared for Jacob during his last years, and then Tohoperi in his turn; there was no difference in their attention to this half-brother and half-cousin, the one called Mbanderu, the other Nama, of their husband and father.

Kahae Tuvare (/021) is head of the junior Tuvare house at CaeCae, which settled here along with the senior house after the removals from South-West Africa. He is also the son of Tuahukuje (14 in fig. 6.9) by a marriage to Pazikwane (/031), the daughter of Katire (OA) and her second husband, Kwane (8 in fig. 6.9). Kahae (/021) is married to Mariam (/022), whose MMMZDDD is Katjateri (/012) and whose classificatory cousin, Katandu (/062), is the wife of Haruvesa Keharera (/061) (fig. 6.10). Tjerire (/023), the son of Kahae and Mariam, is the visitor-spouse of his {MZD}, Anna (/064), the daughter of Haruvesa and Katandu, by whom he has three daughters. Kahae had in the past been the visitor-spouse of Dixau (H/182), the wife of Kao (B/181) in Zhu homestead 1, by whom he had several children, all of whom died as infants. His son by Mariam, Simon (/024), has an ongoing similar arrangement with Xushe (D/115) in Zhu homestead 1, who is his {[F]MBSD} as a consequence of his father's earlier relationship with Dixau, through which Kao (B/181) became Simon's classificatory father (indeed, Simon addresses Kao as mba, my father). The lasting nature of the union between Simon and Xushe is attested by their two children, whom Simon partially supports. Simon gave Xushe's name to his daughter borne by his Mbanderu wife, Reginah (/045), his MFFBSSD.[9] In the Herero custom of ovianda, a mother "lends" one of her children (a second- or later-born) to her sister, with whom the child resides for a period of years. Simon spent most of his childhood in Dixau's household under this arrangement; in essence, he was reared as much a Zhu as an Mbanderu.

The members of Mbanderu homestead 3 trace their descent in the male line through Kahimemua (6 in fig. 6.9), whom we witnessed being executed by the Germans in 1896 (p. 140). Kahimemua's grandson {[S]S} Keharandju (16 in fig. 6.9), recall, became his successor after the German-Herero war of 1904–5, but only after a factional struggle with Nikodemus (11 in fig. 6.9), his actual father who had raised seed for Kahimemua's son, Kangariri (12 in fig. 6.9), who had died in a German prison (cf. Schapera 1945:17–20). Keharandju's son Munjuku Nguvauva (OE) is currently head of the Mbanderu Council in Namibia; Munjuku's son Manuel Nguvauva (/032) lives at CaeCae to oversee the family herd maintained here as part of his family's claim to grazing rights at this place. Manuel's father's mother, Kakura (17 in fig. 6.9) is the sister of Kahae (/021); their mother, Pazikwane (/031), headed this homestead until 1985, when she joined her grandson at Epikuru after Manuel's marriage. A final contribution of Katire to the CaeCae Mbanderu: she is the FFM, by her first husband, Katetee (15 in fig. 6.9), of Monika (/033), the wife Manuel recently married.

A fourth Mbanderu homestead at CaeCae is headed by Manuel Marenga (/041), the pastor of the Okavango-Kavango Lutheran Church in this community; in 1981 he was appointed first village headman of CaeCae by the district council.[10] Marenga's father, Katuwi (33 in fig. 6.10), was the brother of Nanisee (OB) (same father, different mothers), the father of Jacob Tuvare (/001) and of Katjateri's father Nderiko (37 in fig. 6.10). It was Katuwi's older brother Jacob (34 in fig. 6.10) who was killed in the German-Herero war. Marenga's son John (/044) was the visitor-spouse of Nqai (E/462), John's {FF[F]DSD} traced through sibling and marriage links to Nqai's father, Tautona. John is now married to Irene (/045), his FMMZDD, {FZD}. Gideon (/042), the son of Marenga's older brother Kaujumbo, has recently established a separate homestead after marrying his {FFF[Z]SD}, a niece of Mariam (/022).

Kondowra (/051), the younger brother of Marenga (same father, different mothers), was married to Basana (/052), whose father, Omangemere, was Damara and whose mother, Koba, was Zhu, the MMZD of Xin (U/623) in homestead 6 (fig. 6.6). Basana died giving birth to premature twins in 1976; Kondowra subsequently married her cousin Xin. Ssao (D/331), Xin's {M[F]FBSSS} is the progenitor of the second child of this couple, whose social father is recognized, nevertheless, to be Kondowra. Kondowra slaughtered one of his goats for the birth feast in Xin's parents' homestead, where the child was born, thereby legitimizing his paternal relation to the child.

The final house to be documented is headed by an Omuherero, Haruvesa Keharera (/061), whose wife, Katandu (/062)—in addition to the connection to Mariam (/022) already noted—is the classificatory cousin {FF[s]MSD} of Marenga through his FF, Kakurupa (19 in fig. 6.10). Keharera's father was related to the father of Retia, but the degree of relationship is forgotten or suppressed; that it is remembered at all is grounds to speculate that it was reasonably close.

These Mbanderu people are members of extensive families with many relatives in Epikuru and Windhoek in Namibia as well as in the Tsau-Sehitwa area, Rakops, Pilane, and Mahalapye in Botswana. Aspects of the history of their—and Tawana—distribution in the region have engaged our attention at many points in the foregoing narrative. Here I wish to emphasize a concomitant of this history that becomes apparent in the recitation of kin relations, to which I will return at several points in the subsequent unfolding of this narrative. That concomitant is the structure of the interlayered discourse of encounter among these peoples—Zhu, Mbanderu, and Tawana—revealed on a close reading of their actual social relations. Those social groups whose kinship and tenurial integrity has remained intact through the upheavals of the past 150 years are today secure, within limits to be considered in a moment, in their political and economic standing in the community. This is true because they have been able to manipulate events to advantage—aided often, certainly, by accidents of geography and ecology. This advantage that kin-tenurial integrity carries in the competition for status enhancement, with its attendant control of economic resources, will be examined closely in association with an analysis of kinship practice. But first we must turn to the material consequences of the social relations just presented.

Production as a Function of Emergent Status

The CaeCae homesteads may be stratified according to their principal production activities; I have labeled these strata pastoralist, independent, forager, client, and reliant.[11] Those included among pastoralists derive more than half of their production from herds they themselves manage, through ownership or ownership combined with employment with other owners. All the Mbanderu/Herero and Tawana homesteads fall under this heading, of course; among Zhu in 1975–76, only that homestead 7 unit that lives "like the children" of Keharera was in this category. In 1979–80, homestead 1 and homestead 3 qualified; in 1975–76, these were two of the three independent homesteads, the other being homestead 2. The independent category includes those homesteads whose members own cattle and other domestic stock but who rely on foraging for more than half their income; in 1979–80, of the three earlier independents only homestead 2 remained in this cate-

Table 6.2. Total Meat Production in Kilograms by All Zhu Homesteads during
1973–76

	1973				1974		1975	
Species	09	10	11	12	01	03	04	05
Steenbok	67.0	36.4	23.2	14.4	8.4	8.4	21.0	5.4
Duiker	23.2	32.4	52.0	11.6	0.0	0.0	4.0	0.0
Kudu	430.0	320.0	548.0	0.0	0.0	0.0	0.0	0.0
Gemsbok	0.0	50.0	0.0	0.0	0.0	91.0	91.0	121.0
Wildebeest	0.0	115.0	0.0	0.0	0.0	0.0	0.0	0.0
Eland	0.0	70.0	0.0	0.0	0.0	218.0	0.0	0.0
Buffalo	0.0	0.0	0.0	0.0	0.0	244.0	0.0	0.0
Giraffe	0.0	0.0	250.0	0.0	0.0	0.0	740.0	740.0
Warthog	0.0	11.0	0.0	66.0	0.0	0.0	0.0	0.0
Aardvark	15.0	0.0	0.0	0.0	0.0	0.0	0.0	0.0
Porcupine	14.0	0.0	0.0	0.0	0.0	0.0	0.0	0.0
Springhare	0.0	25.5	43.5	12.0	31.5	0.0	1.5	0.0
Hare	0.0	0.0	0.0	0.0	1.0	0.0	0.0	1.0
Pangolin	0.0	12.0	6.0	0.0	0.0	0.0	0.0	0.0
Francolin	2.8	0.0	0.2	0.0	0.2	0.0	0.0	0.4
Guinea fowl	0.0	1.5	1.0	0.0	1.5	0.5	0.0	7.0
Bustard	5.0	0.0	0.0	0.0	0.0	0.0	0.0	0.0
Korhaan	6.0	2.4	5.5	0.3	0.6	0.0	0.0	1.5
Dove	0.0	0.0	0.0	0.0	0.1	0.0	0.0	0.0
Hornbill	0.0	0.2	2.4	2.0	5.8	0.0	0.0	0.0
Leopard tortoise	0.0	14.0	14.0	10.0	14.0	2.0	0.0	0.0
Starshell tortoise	0.0	3.3	9.6	3.3	2.2	0.6	0.8	0.0
Leguaan	0.0	3.0	1.0	2.0	0.0	0.0	0.0	0.0
Total	563.0	696.7	956.4	121.6	65.3	564.5	858.3	876.3

gory, and no others had joined it. Foragers own no stock (except a few donkeys and dogs) and derive 95% of their income from wild sources; homestead 5 and homestead 6 are in this category, although in 1979–80 they did little foraging and lived largely on food relief and district council wage labor. Client groups, as the name implies, are employed by local Mbanderu families; a number of members of the homesteads (4 and 7) in this strata own small stock and a few cattle. The reliant homesteads (8 and 9) are virtually wards of Bashile, for whose relatives they and their forebears worked in the past and for whom some younger members now work.

Foraging

The total amount of hunted meat, in kilograms, produced per month in all homesteads is tabulated in table 6.2 for 1973–76 and in table

	1975						1976			
06	07	08	09	10	11	12	01	02	03	04
22.8	36.0	39.6	17.4	17.0	6.0	17.0	0.0	5.6	5.4	5.6
4.0	11.6	33.6	8.0	0.0	12.0	0.0	0.0	11.6	0.0	11.6
0.0	0.0	0.0	0.0	280.0	0.0	0.0	160.0	160.0	110.0	110.0
0.0	91.0	0.0	0.0	91.0	0.0	0.0	91.0	91.0	273.0	222.0
0.0	0.0	0.0	0.0	0.0	0.0	0.0	40.0	115.0	230.0	0.0
0.0	0.0	0.0	0.0	0.0	0.0	0.0	0.0	0.0	0.0	436.0
0.0	0.0	0.0	0.0	0.0	0.0	0.0	0.0	0.0	0.0	0.0
1,580.0	0.0	0.0	250.0	250.0	0.0	0.0	0.0	0.0	0.0	0.0
66.0	22.0	33.0	22.0	0.0	0.0	22.0	66.0	33.0	0.0	0.0
25.0	0.0	25.0	0.0	0.0	0.0	0.0	0.0	0.0	25.0	0.0
21.0	0.0	14.0	14.0	14.0	30.0	5.0	12.0	0.0	21.0	32.0
0.0	0.0	0.0	0.0	3.0	33.0	13.5	31.5	36.0	33.0	1.5
1.0	0.0	0.0	0.0	2.0	1.0	0.0	0.0	0.0	1.0	1.0
0.0	0.0	0.0	0.0	0.0	0.0	0.0	0.0	0.0	6.0	0.0
5.4	12.2	11.6	10.6	4.2	9.4	0.0	0.0	0.0	0.3	0.8
17.0	17.5	6.0	1.5	5.0	2.0	2.5	0.5	1.0	7.0	2.5
0.0	5.0	10.0	5.0	5.0	0.0	0.0	0.0	0.0	0.0	0.0
8.1	19.5	52.5	22.5	6.6	6.0	1.5	0.6	0.9	0.6	0.0
0.0	0.1	0.7	0.1	5.2	1.6	0.0	0.0	0.1	0.2	0.0
0.0	0.6	0.6	0.2	0.2	0.0	0.0	2.0	2.4	2.2	3.2
0.0	0.0	0.0	2.0	4.0	2.0	4.0	8.0	6.0	16.0	4.0
0.0	0.0	0.3	1.0	3.3	5.9	2.9	2.6	3.4	1.4	0.3
0.0	0.0	2.0	0.0	0.0	2.0	2.0	0.0	0.0	3.0	0.0
1,750.3	215.5	228.9	354.3	690.5	110.9	70.4	414.2	466.0	735.1	830.5

6.3 for 1979–80. Table 6.4 summarizes the total number of each species killed and the methods by which these animals were captured. The ecological restraints on the production of this hunted meat and complete statistics of the production itself are detailed in Wilmsen and Durham (1988). In later tables the homesteads are grouped according to stratigraphy of production.

These data document marked and consistent skewness in meat production among the homesteads. All pastoralists at CaeCae—Batawana, Ovambanderu, and Zhu—hunt almost exclusively from horseback and partly with rifles, concentrating on high-yield, large species; all but four of the fifty-six animals taken by Zhu from horseback were killed by men of homesteads 1–2–3–7. These pastoralists realize the highest return on their efforts, consistently about 10 kilograms/person/month. Not all of this meat is consumed within the homestead of the hunters who acquire it. Some is shared with others; but this sharing

Table 6.3. Total Meat Production in Kilograms by all Zhu Homesteads during 1979–80

Species	1979								1980				
	05	06	07	08	09	10	11	12	01	02	03	04	05
Steenbok	0.0	0.0	8.4	27.6	11.0	0.0	0.0	0.0	0.0	0.0	0.0	0.0	0.0
Duiker	0.0	0.0	0.0	0.0	0.0	0.0	22.0	11.6	10.4	0.0	0.0	0.0	4.0
Kudu	0.0	0.0	0.0	0.0	0.0	110.0	0.0	0.0	0.0	270.0	320.0	0.0	0.0
Gemsbok	0.0	0.0	0.0	0.0	0.0	91.0	0.0	0.0	0.0	0.0	0.0	160.0	91.0
Wildebeest	0.0	0.0	0.0	0.0	0.0	0.0	0.0	0.0	0.0	0.0	0.0	0.0	0.0
Eland	2,499.0	1,090.0	981.0	763.0	218.0	327.0	654.0	0.0	0.0	0.0	0.0	218.0	0.0
Buffalo	0.0	0.0	0.0	0.0	0.0	0.0	0.0	0.0	0.0	0.0	0.0	0.0	0.0
Giraffe	0.0	0.0	0.0	0.0	0.0	0.0	0.0	0.0	0.0	0.0	0.0	0.0	0.0
Warthog	0.0	0.0	0.0	0.0	22.0	0.0	66.0	44.0	44.0	88.0	88.0	110.0	0.0
Aardvark	0.0	0.0	0.0	0.0	0.0	0.0	0.0	0.0	0.0	0.0	0.0	0.0	0.0
Porcupine	0.0	14.0	0.0	14.0	0.0	0.0	0.0	0.0	0.0	0.0	28.0	0.0	0.0
Springhare	0.0	0.0	0.0	0.0	0.0	35.0	0.0	0.0	0.0	0.0	0.0	0.0	0.0
Hare	0.0	0.0	0.0	0.0	0.0	3.0	16.5	0.0	0.0	1.5	0.0	0.0	0.0
Pangolin	0.0	0.0	0.0	0.0	0.0	0.0	0.0	0.0	0.0	0.0	0.0	0.0	0.0
Francolin	0.0	0.0	0.0	1.5	3.9	5.0	2.0	2.5	0.0	0.0	0.0	0.0	0.0
Guinea fowl	1.5	0.0	6.5	1.5	0.0	0.0	0.0	0.0	0.0	1.5	1.5	0.0	3.0
Bustard	0.0	0.0	0.0	0.0	0.0	0.0	0.0	0.0	0.0	0.0	0.0	0.0	0.0
Korhaan	0.9	1.8	1.2	2.7	2.4	3.6	1.8	0.0	0.0	0.0	0.0	0.0	0.0
Dove	0.0	0.0	0.0	0.2	0.0	0.0	0.0	0.0	0.0	0.0	0.0	0.0	0.0
Hornbill	0.0	0.0	0.0	0.0	0.0	0.0	0.0	0.2	0.0	0.0	0.0	0.0	0.0
Leopard tortoise	0.0	0.0	0.0	0.0	0.0	0.0	0.0	0.0	0.0	0.0	0.0	0.0	0.0
Starshell tortoise	0.0	0.0	0.0	0.0	0.0	0.0	0.0	0.0	0.0	0.0	0.0	0.0	0.0
Leguaan	0.0	0.0	0.0	0.0	0.0	0.0	0.0	0.0	0.0	0.0	0.0	0.0	0.0
Total	2,501.4	1,105.8	997.1	810.5	257.3	574.6	762.3	58.3	54.4	361.0	437.5	488.0	98.0

occurs strictly according to kinship ties. Marshall (1961) gives a vividly detailed account of this sharing, but her readers must bear in mind that she is describing sharing within units that are structurally like the homesteads I have described, not sharing among them. Lee (1979: 118) stresses this point: "The hunting band or camp [homestead in my terminology] is a unit of sharing, and if sharing breaks down it ceases to be a camp." Further on (1979: 336), he once again provides anecdotal color for a critical point: a CaeCae man illustrated the probable response of people who found relatives from elsewhere foraging without permission in their nqore. "Look we have given each other children and today we are *n!umbaakwe* ('affines') and the n!ore is ours (inclusive), but why when we weren't here did you come. . . . In other words, as long as you eat together it is all right. Or if they come to you first, it is all right too. It's when they eat alone and you come along later to find them there, that's when fights start."

Marshall (1961: 238) says that "a man wants sometimes to be the owner of the meat in order to start the distribution off in the direction of his own kin and affines. . . . close kinship is what sets the pattern of giving." She notes that a man selects the arrow he will use at any particular moment, and thus he determines who will be owner in the case of a successful kill (see below). Then, when the owner "makes his primary distribution, he is aware of where the meat will go in subsequent distributions and plans accordingly" (Wiessner 1977: 134–35). Given this degree of distribution planning, it is not surprising that, as Shostak (1981: 86) says, "distributions are emotionally charged events; the size of the portions depends not only on clear issues such as kinship, but on subtle ones." Both Marshall (1976: 297) and Lee (1979: 247–48) emphasize the tensions (and hostilities) engendered in the sharing process within homesteads; these tensions are heightened between homesteads. Thus meat sharing—the putative sine qua non of San egalitarianism— is thoroughly controlled to meet the political ends of the distributors. An anecdote will capture the actuality:

One day I chanced upon Xushe (D/121) striding furiously toward her home in homestead 1 from homestead 6, in which she has no relatives; after the required greeting, I asked a common follow-up:
From where are you coming?
From that Zhu dole place [dole = strange, undesirable, bad]. Those shit people! They got a lot of meat; they won't give me any. They say I'm not one of them. Me! Tcwi, see me! I'm a CaeCae person; that meat is mine! They don't belong here. Shit people!

Shostak (1981: 366) gives another example of the form that arguments over food (and other goods) routinely take: "Tell me, are you

Table 6.4. Capture Methods for Each Species

Species	Zhu (All Homesteads)													
	Sna	Run	Bow	Dog	Hor	Roc	Dug	Nes	Hoo	Pic	Unk	Total	Sca	Los
Steenbok	61	10	9	1	1	17					1	100	13	9
Duiker	13	8	4			4					1	30	7	1
Kudu	1		16	1	2							20	5	
Gemsbok			6	6	8							20		
Wildebeest			4		1							5	1	
Eland			3		29							32		
Buffalo					1							1		
Giraffe					7							7		
Warthog		2	2	26	7							37	1	
Aardvark						2	3					5		
Porcupine	3			1		18	12				2	36		1
Springhare									222			222		
Hare			2			3					4	9	1	
Pangolin						4						4		
Carnivores	3			6		9	9				3	30		
All mammals												558	28	11
Ostrich	1	1										2	1	
Francolin	326		2			4		5				337		11
Guinea fowl	150	26	9			28					2	215		
Bustard	6											6	1	1
Korhaan	568					4		2				574		67
Dove						31						31	19	
Hornbill						6		123				129		
Waterbirds						4						4		
Small birds	5					14		125				144	82	
All birds												1,442	103	79
Leopard tortoise										50		50		
Starshell tortoise							1			411		412		
Leguaan						25	1					26		
Snakes						3						3		
All reptiles												491		
Frogs										12		12		
Totals	1,137	47	57	41	56	176	26	255	222	473	13	2,503	131	90

Notes: Sna = snared   Nes = caught in nest
Run = run down   Hoo = hooked in burrow
Bow = bow and arrow   Pic = picked up
Dog = dog and spear   Unk = unknown
Hor = horse and spear   Sca = scavenged
Roc = rock (thrown) or club   Los = lost to scavenger
Dug = dug out of burrow

				Mbanderu and Tawana						
Sna	Bow	Dog	Hor	Roc	Nes	Dug	Pic	Gun	Total	Sca
								5	5	
				3				6	9	
								13	13	
		1	1					5	7	
								2	2	
			13					3	16	
									0	
			3						3	
		7						6	13	
									0	
	1	2		1					4	
				1					1	
	1	3							4	
									0	
		11				2		1	14	
									91	
									0	
22	1			4					27	
10	4			1					15	
									0	
20									20	
				18					18	3
				1	1				2	1
									0	
									0	3
									82	7
							3		3	
							14		14	
				1					1	
									0	
									18	
									0	
52	7	24	17	30	1	2	17	41	191	7

someone I don't know, perhaps not my kin?" Homesteads 2–4–5 receive substantial shares from homesteads 1–3; Zhu clients and reliants receive significant amounts from the Mbanderu and Bashile, depending on their association.

Some meat is dried for future use; tables 6.2 and 6.3 reveal very large monthly differences in production, and surpluses are stored for scarce times. Lee (1979:247) notes that dried meat also aids the process of reciprocity by allowing a hunter to retain the portion due the owner of the arrow that killed an animal if that owner is absent at the time of fresh meat distribution. This same principle, that the owner of the instrument of production is the owner of the product, applies to guns as well as to arrows.[12] CaeCae Zhu today own no guns but hunt often with guns lent by the Mbanderu and Bashile, with whom they are associated. They receive a substantial share of the kills they make under these arrangements. In the tables, all gun kills are entered in the Bantu account regardless of whether they are actually killed by Zhu. Nowadays some meat is sold. A small but significant amount feeds the dogs that help in the hunting.

Foragers, when they hunt, also have a high mean rate of meat production, over 8 kilograms/person/month. The equivalent Gcwi forager rate (table 6.5), taken from Tanaka (1980) and Silberbauer (1981), is 7.3 kilograms/person/month, which is in substantial accord with the CaeCae forager rate. It is tempting to speculate therefrom that something on the order of 8 kilograms is a general rate of return from hunting by indigenous means (bow and arrow, hand-thrown spear, snares) under present conditions in the region. Perhaps this is so, but if so it cannot be extrapolated into the past, for, as we have seen, animals were much more numerous and more assiduously hunted before Europeans and rinderpest intervened. In 1979–80 these forager homesteads hunted very little, relying instead on a combination of food distributed by the government under various relief programs plus council wage labor, allocated preferentially to persons who have few or no cattle, and contributions from their collaterals.

Independents and clients have moderate rates of hunted meat production. Their access to meat for consumption is enhanced, however, because they receive a portion of their kinsmen's and their patrons' kills. Reliants kill almost nothing at CaeCae because they have no usufruct rights in this place for that purpose. When at Dcwia or in the east, these people attain production rates approaching those of CaeCae foragers. The members of homestead 8, of course, receive substantial contributions of meat and milk from their in-law Bashile.

Table 6.5. Comparison of Return on Hunting Effort

	Total Edible Weight (kg)		
Species	CaeCae: 1973–80	Chadi: 1966–72	Chadi: 1958–65
Steenbok	404	202	369
Duiker	264	116	715
Kudu	2,818	160	1,820
Gemsbok	1,554	273	273
Wildebeest	500	1,150	2,300
Eland	7,474	872	1,962
Giraffe	3,810	125	500
Warthog	803	11	22
Springbok	—	125	800
Hartebeest	—	100	1,100
Total	17,627	3,134	9,861
Months of record	32	12 (estimate)	12 (estimate)
Kg/month	551	261	822
Number of hunters	18	10	16
Kg/month/hunter	31	26	51
	$\bar{X}$(Chadi 1966–72 + 1958–65) = 38.5		

Source: Data for Chadi 1966–72 from Tanaka 1980:63 (weights recalculated); data for Chadi 1958–65 from Silberbauer 1981:205 (weights calculated).

Note: Carcass weights for Chadi estimates are calculated with the same average carcass weights as used for CaeCae.

Marked variation in production among the strata is evident. Pastoralists, both Zhu and Mbanderu/Tawana, have the highest rates of return when measured either in absolute quantity of product or in product per unit effort. They also account for by far the largest number of large animals killed by the homesteads combined. Forager, independent, and client groups have intermediate values. Reliants, without tenure rights in the area, are confined to marginal productive activities with little return.

The differences observed are due in part to variation in time allocation; for example, foragers devote a greater proportion of their time to hunting than do clients. Clients. on the other hand, devote more time to this pursuit than do pastoralists and independents, so that time allocation alone is not a sufficient route to increased production from hunting. Then, time allocation is itself partly a function of status differentials—reliants devote little time to hunting at CaeCae because they have no hunting rights here—as is access to acquired means of production (rifles, horses, and to a lesser extent dogs) dominated by pastoralists. Acquiring these means depends on an ability to accumu-

Table 6.6. Forager Estimated Dietary Intake from Wild Plants, Daily per Person, 1975–76

Plants	J	F	M	A	M	J	J	A	S	O	N	D
Beans												
Grams	44	44	27	8	3	—						
Kilocalories	183	183	113	33	13	1						
Protein	11	11	7	3	1	—						
Fat	8	8	5	2	1	—						
Cucks												
Grams	746	874	780	415	249	109						
Kilocalories	224	262	234	125	75	33						
Protein	15	17	16	9	5	3						
Fat	—	1	1	—	—	—						
Nuts												
Grams			157	347	355	330	305	266	204	174	185	83
Kilocalories			1,005	2,221	2,272	2,112	1,952	1,702	1,306	1,114	1,184	531
Protein			44	97	99	92	85	74	57	49	52	23
Fat			80	177	181	168	156	136	104	89	94	42
Fruits												
Grams	272	121	140	69	51	146	165	173	545	568	591	366
Kilocalories	204	91	105	52	38	110	124	130	409	426	443	275
Protein	8	4	4	2	2	4	5	5	16	17	18	8
Fat	2	1	1	—	—	1	1	1	4	5	4	3
Berries												
Grams	509	518	517	399	245	160	141					450
Kilocalories	356	363	362	279	179	112	99					315
Protein	15	16	16	12	7	5	4					16
Fat	2	2	2	2	1	1	1					2
Roots												
Grams	34	24	24	10	3	3	10	16	29	30	33	31
Kilocalories	27	19	19	8	2	2	8	13	23	24	26	25
Protein	—	—	—	—	—	—	—	—	—	—	—	—
Fat	—	—	—	—	—	—	—	—	—	—	—	—

Beans: *Tylosema esculanta; Bauhinia macrantha.*
Cucks: *Acanthosperma naudinianus.*
Nuts: *Ricinodendron rautenenii; Sclerocarya caffra.*
Fruits: *Strychnos coccoloides; S. pungens; Ximenia caffra; X. americana; Adansonia digitata; Coccinia sessilifolia.*
Berries: *Grewia flava; G. flavescens; G. bicolor; G. retinervis; G. avellana; Ziziphus micronata.*
Roots: Species of *Vigna, Coccinia, Dipcadi, Eulophia, Ceropegia, Walleria,* and others.

late cash or barter capital, which, now as in the past, means access to labor opportunities or cattle or both. As I have already indicated, prices have been high for a very long time. Today, horses cost from P120 to over P200. Galton ([1853] 1971:243) gives a glimpse of what people were willing to pay for hunting dogs in 1851; "Hans sold two of his curs to some of the Damaras for two oxen each. . . . They were keen upon dogs, for they offered four oxen for another one." I shall return to the differential access to these means of production after examining the other forms of production in the community.

The technologies and techniques Zhu employ for gathering wild plants have been ably summarized by Lee (1979). These remain relatively unchanged regardless of economic strata. I shall be concerned only with the ways production varies among these strata. Daily per capita consumption of wild vegetables is summarized in table 6.6 for foragers in 1975–76; clients and reliants had similar food budgets except that they obtained almost all the indicated milk from their patrons, whereas foragers received much less. Table 6.7 presents comparable summaries for pastoralists and independents during the same period. Tables 6.8–6.9 summarize the contributions to diet of all the categories of food available to Zhu so we can set plant collecting in its overall production context. The data from which the information in these tables is extracted are tabulated more fully, and some of the uncertainty parameters associated with plant collecting are documented, in Wilmsen and Durham (1988). The single pastoralist group in 1975–76 had a diet essentially like that of Mbanderu (cultured milk, maize meal, and meat, with some fruits and berries); this group is not included in the following calculations.

Two observations deserve initial comment. First, the magnitude of seasonal variation in diet is apparent (fig. 6.11). Lee (1969:71) reports a daily per capita allotment of 2,140 kilocalories for a three-week period in July 1964 (he has now changed this to 2,355 kilocalories [1979:270–71]);[13] considering the margin of error inherent in calorie counting, either figure is in good agreement with my estimate of 2,294 kilocalories/person/day for foraging Zhu in July 1975. Lee (1969:65) selected July as the time for his input/output analysis of food budgets because he judged this to be the time of about average food availability. The average monthly consumption rate (2,100 kilocalories/person/day) of foragers obtained in my nineteen-month observation period in 1975–76 confirms his judgment.

Lee, however, extrapolates his data to infer similar levels of dietary intake throughout the year, and this is another matter. It is clear that such extrapolation is not warranted by data collected over a longer

Table 6.7. Pastoralist and Independent Estimated Dietary Intake from Wild Plants, Daily per Person, 1975–76

Plants	J	F	M	A	M	J	J	A	S	O	N	D
Beans												
Grams	9	39	6	2								
Kilocalories	38	162	25	8								
Protein	2	10	1	—								
Fat	2	7	1	—								
Cucks												
Grams	121	142	127	68	41	18						
Kilocalories	36	43	38	20	12	5						
Protein	2	3	2	1	1	—						
Fat	—	—	—	—	—	—						
Nuts												
Grams			155	247	254	310	301	266	214	202	169	63
Kilocalories			992	1,582	1,624	1,984	1,926	1,702	1,370	1,293	1,082	403
Protein			43	69	71	87	85	74	60	57	46	18
Fat			79	126	130	158	154	136	109	103	86	32
Fruits												
Grams	222	199	114	55	43	120	135	130	415	390	311	300
Kilocalories	167	149	86	41	32	90	101	98	311	293	233	225
Protein	7	6	3	2	1	4	4	4	12	12	9	9
Fat	2	2	1	—	—	1	1	1	3	3	2	2
Berries												
Grams	417	422	423	327	184	146	141					450
Kilocalories	292	296	296	229	129	102	99					315
Protein	13	12	13	10	6	4	4					16
Fat	2	2	—	—	—	—	—					2
Roots												
Grams	32	30	16	10	3	3	10	18	25	30	32	35
Kilocalories	26	24	13	8	2	2	8	14	20	24	26	28
Protein	—	—	—	—	—	—	—	—	—	—	—	—
Fat	—	—	—	—	—	—	—	—	—	—	—	—

Beans: *Tylosema esculenta; Bauhinia macrantha.*
Cucks: *Acarthosperma naudinianus.*
Nuts: *Ricinodendron rautenenii; Sclerocarya caffra.*
Fruits: *Strychnos coccoloides; S. pungens; Ximenia caffra; X. americana; Adansonia digitata; Coccinia sessilifolia.*
Berries: *Grewia flava; G. flavescens; G. bicolor; G. retinervis; G. avellana; Ziziphus micronata.*
Roots: *Species of Vigna, Coccinia, Dipcadi, Eulophia, Ceropegia, Walleria, and others.*

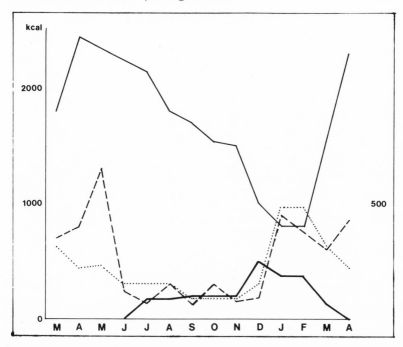

Figure 6.11. Average contribution to the daily diet of Zhu adults of the principal categories of foods in 1975–76. Light continuous line is foraged vegetables; dashed line is meat; dotted line is milk; heavy continuous line is maize meal. Scale on left vertical axis (kcal/person/day) pertains to vegetables; scale on right (kcal/person/day) pertains to meat, milk, and meal; horizontal scale is in months beginning with March 1975.

time span.[14] For foragers, single monthly means range between 1,408 and 3,114 kilocalories/person/day; gathered vegetables contributed a minimum of 60% and as much as 98% of monthly food budgets. For independents the range was 1,703 to 3,573 kilocalories/person/day, with vegetable contribution never exceeding 80% and falling as low as 28%. For both food dependencies, the variation in daily energy intake is high; for foragers this is 18% to 36% of monthly means, for independents 15% to 30%. I shall take up the consequences of this variation in the concluding chapter when I examine the political economy of physiology and physique. In 1979–80, after homesteads 1–3 had increased their cattle holdings and external food inputs (school lunches, drought relief, and aid to indigents—in the form of maize meal,[15] soybean oil, and beef) had reached substantial proportions, gathered vegetables declined to 11% of overall diet (table 6.8). No statistics upon which to base estimates of proportional contribution of foraged plant

Table 6.8. Sources of Dietary Contribution, Daily per Person, 1979–80

	July	September	December	April	Total	%
Grams						
Vegetables	60[a]	200[b]	320[a]	370[c]	950	16
Meat[d]	93	100	110	20	323	5
Milk	1,230	450	650	1,230	3,560	59
Meal	300	150	375	200	1,025	17
Sugar	47	47	47	47	188	3
Total	1,730	947	1,502	1,867	6,046	
Kilocalories						
Vegetables	42	100	224	537	903	11
Meat	233	250	275	50	808	9
Milk	858	297	429	858	2,442	29
Meal	1,071	535	1,339	714	3,659	43
Sugar	180	180	180	180	720	9
Total	2,384	1,362	2,447	2,339	8,532	
Kc/kg	51.8	31.7	53.2	50.8		
Protein (g)						
Vegetables	2	0	10	28	40	10
Meat	15	16	18	3	52	13
Milk	86	32	46	86	250	60
Meal	21	11	26	14	72	17
Total	124	59	100	131	414	
Fat (g)						
Vegetables	0	0	1	31	32	8
Meat	19	20	22	4	65	17
Milk	86	32	46	86	250	66
Meal	9	5	11	6	31	8
Total	114	57	80	127	378	

Note: Vegetables = all vegetable food; meat = all meat; kc/kg = calories per kilogram of body weight.

[a] Entirely fruits of *Grewia* sp.

[b] Mainly gums of *Terminalia, Acacia,* and others, plus roots.

[c] Composed of 120 g *Grewia*, 50 g mongongo, 200 g cultivated melons and maize.

[d] July and September mainly from wild animals, December entirely from cattle by government drought relief program.

foods to Herero diets are available for earlier decades; but testimony given above indicates that it was much greater than it is today, when it is about 9% for some Ovambanderu.

The second important aspect of the data is that components of diet are represented unequally between forager and independent Zhu (table 6.9). Vegetable foods constitute 85% of forager diet but only 65% of that of independents, while meat remains relatively constant for both groups. This is not a function of loss of access to plant resources, for pastoralists and independents are those who have inalienable rights of use of the CaeCae area. Rather, it is a result of production priorities and the ability to act on them. Average daily caloric intake is 9.5% higher for these people than for foragers, clients, and reliants, a condition that is reflected in the 10% greater average body weight of pastoralist and independent Zhu.

Herding and Farming

Government of Botswana veterinary service records for anthrax and brucellosis inoculation show that during the 1950s and early 1960s about ten thousand cattle were kept in the CaeCae-Qangwa valleys and adjacent parts of western Ngamiland, 98% of them owned by Bantu. This number fell, owing to drought and outbreaks of foot-and-mouth disease, to about six thousand in the late 1960s but had rebounded by 1974. The area in which these animals were kept is about 3,000 square kilometers, which indicates a stocking rate of about two to three head per square kilometer. Similar stocking rates are maintained in the rest of Ngamiland where water is obtainable—hence where people live.

The first accurate figures we have for Zhu stock ownership are provided by Lee (1979:411) for 1967–69. At this time, 27% (41) of the 151 adult male Zhu in his sample acknowledged ownership of 102 head among themselves for an average of 2.5 head per owning household, representing about 2% of all cattle in the area. Ownership of donkeys and goats was, respectively, 20% and 55% higher. Furthermore, Lee (1979:409) tells us that "many [of these] men had owned cattle and goats in the past." In addition, every one of these men was then, or had been (either at CaeCae or in their areas of origin), actively engaged in the care of cattle for others, Ovambanderu, Batawana, or European.

Not only are Lee's data valuable for what they document for the 1960s, they are also independently acquired confirmation of Zhu stockkeeping in earlier decades. They provide, furthermore, a basis for assessing more recent Zhu stockholding. Numbers of animals held by each CaeCae homestead in 1975–76 and 1979–80 are given in table 6.10,[16] which is stratified, as are previous tables, to allow convenient comparison of homestead production. Of the fifty-three Zhu households at CaeCae in 1980, thirty-five (66%) owned no cattle or goats; at the other extreme, six households (11%)—all in homesteads 1–3—held 64% of all cattle owned by Zhu at this place. With one exception, the remaining Zhu cattle are owned by members of homesteads 2–4–7. In comparison, a partial survey of CaeCae Zhu households

Table 6.9. Summary of Dietary Contribution: Daily per Person, 1975–76

	J	F	M	A	M	J	J	A	S	O	N	D	Total Kcal	%	Daily Average
							Forager								
Grams															
Vegetables	1,605	1,581	1,645	1,248	906	748	621	455	778	772	809	930			1,795
Meat	239	220	160	188	2	98	53	120	38	136	52	60			244
Milk	250	250	38												31
Meal					60				8	8	8	38			30
Total	2,094	2,151	1,843	1,436	968	846	674	575	824	916	869	1,028			2,100
Kilocalories															
Vegetables	994	918	1,838	2,718	2,572	2,370	2,183	1,845	1,738	1,564	1,653	1,146	21,539	85	1,795
Meat	502	462	336	396	4	207	111	253	79	286	108	126	2,926	12	244
Milk	165	165	136										370	1	31
Meal					40				29	29	29	136	359	2	30
Total	1,661	1,545	2,310	3,114	2,616	2,577	2,294	2,098	1,846	1,879	1,790	1,408	25,194		2,100
Kc/kg	40	37	55	74	62	61	55	50	44	45	43	36			42
Protein (g)															
Vegetables	49	48	87	123	114	104	94	79	73	66	70	47			
Meat	38	35	26	30	1	16	19	20	6	22	8	10			
Milk	18	18	3												
Meal					4				1	1	1	3			
Total	105	101	116	153	119	120	103	99	80	89	79	60			
Fat (g)															
Vegetables	12	12	89	181	183	170	158	137	108	94	98	47			
Meat	48	44	32	38	1	20	11	24	8	27	10	12			
Milk	18	18	2												
Meal					4							2			
Total	78	74	123	219	188	190	169	161	116	121	108	61			

Pastoralist and Independent

Grams												
Vegetables	801	743	841	709	529	597	587	414	654	622	512	848
Meat	189	133	124	213	615	24	19	18	19	10	22	25
Milk	1,000	1,000	1,000	750	750	500	500	500	250	250	250	500
Meal	300	300					150	150	150	150	150	300
Total	2,290	2,176	1,965	1,672	1,890	1,121	1,246	1,080	1,073	1,032	934	1,673
Kilocalories												
Vegetables	559	675	1,450	1,888	1,799	2,183	2,134	1,814	1,701	1,601	1,341	971
Meat	398	280	259	448	1,291	49	20	38	40	21	46	52
Milk	660	660	660	495	495	330	330	330	165	165	165	330
Meal	350	350					175	175	175	175	175	350
Total	1,967	1,965	2,369	2,831	3,573	2,560	2,659	2,357	2,081	1,971	1,727	1,703
Kc/kg	43	43	52	62	78	56	58	51	45	43	38	37
Protein (g)												
Vegetables	24	37	63	82	79	95	93	78	72	69	56	43
Meat	30	21	20	34	98	4	2	3	3	2	4	4
Milk	70	70	70	53	53	35	35	35	18	18	18	35
Meal	25	25					13	13	13	13	13	25
Total	149	153	153	169	230	134	143	129	106	102	91	107
Fat (g)												
Vegetables	6	25	8	127	130	160	156	137	112	106	88	36
Meat	38	27	25	43	123	5	2	4	4	2	4	5
Milk	70	70	70	53	53	35	35	35	18	18	18	35
Meal	13	13					6	6	6	6	6	13
Total	127	135	178	223	306	200	199	182	140	132	116	89

Note: Vegetables = all vegetable food; meat = all meat; kc/kg = calories per kilogram of body weight.

Table 6.10. Household Ownership of Cattle and Goats

Home-stead	N	Own	C76	G76	C80	G80	$\bar{x}$ HH	$\bar{x}$ Own
1	8	4	9	21	13	19	1.6	3.2
2	6	3	5	29	4	23	0.7	1.3
3	8	6	34	37	58	33	7.3	9.7
4	8	2	0	16	9	10	1.1	4.5
5	4	0	0	0	0	0	0	0
6	5	1	0	0	1	2	0.2	1.0
7	5	2	4	11	6	11	1.2	3.0
8	3	0	0	0	0	0	0	0
9	6	0	1	10	0	0	0	0
Total	53	18	53	124	91	99	1.7	5.1

Note: N, number of households in homestead; Own, number of households owning cattle in 1979–80; C76, number of cattle owned in 1975–76; G76, number of goats owned in 1975–76; C80, number of cattle owned in 1979–80; G80, number of goats owned in 1979–80; $\bar{x}$ HH, mean number of cattle for all households in 1979–80; $\bar{x}$ Own, mean number of cattle for owning households in 1979–80.

made by Wiessner (1977:336) in 1974 found that household cattle ownership was more than three times as high in homesteads 2–3 (homestead 1 was not sampled) as in homestead 7, the next highest in cattle wealth.

Six of the eight households in homestead 3 now (1980) own cattle, with 9.7 head per owning household. These related families pool their holdings and thus have a viable herd, from which they get twenty to twenty-five liters of milk per day in the rainy season and about half that in the dry season. The homestead 7 family living with Herero family 061 has 6 head. Cattle-owning households in homesteads 1–4 have an average of 4.5 head. Homestead 2 holdings are depressed owing to recent losses to disease and poison leaf, *Dichapetalum cymosum* (Zhu = mai, Otjiherero = omohau, Setswana = mogau, Afrikaans = giftblaar). Homestead 6 also lost one of its two head to mai; both of these animals, plus four goats, were the marriage payment Kondowra gave to her stepfather for Xin. Homesteads 5–8–9 have no cattle, or any other livestock, except one horse purchased by a man with wages earned from an anthropologist.

In February or March of each year, the veterinary service inoculates cattle at CaeCae. At this time a census of herds is taken as the animals pass one by one through the inoculating chute; about 90% to 95% of all cattle in the area are usually included in this count, the remainder being at distant cattleposts. In 1975 a total of 651 head were counted; of these, 53 (9%) belonged to Zhu. In 1980 the situation had changed somewhat. Zhu then owned 14% (91) of the 666 cattle counted; the mean number of beasts per owning Zhu household was 5.1, with a range of 1 to 29. The comparable mean for CaeCae Mbanderu and Tawana was 82, with a range of 38 to 130 (all these households have herds in other places which are not included in these figures). Zhu realized a net gain of 28 head during this period, while Mbanderu/Tawana holdings decreased by 13. These changes are attributable mainly to differences in herd-management strategies. Zhu were conserving breeding stock for herd growth and were purchasing animals when possible.[17] Mbanderu/Tawana, on the other hand, were aggressively seeking high cash returns and selling animals (mainly prime oxen to the Botswana Meat Commission and some calves locally). Tohoperi (/011), for example, bought a new Toyota Land Cruiser in 1977 with which he began itinerant trading; he sold 36 prime head during the next two years to pay for it. The other Mbanderu/Tawana homesteads also sold significant numbers of animals (Bashile told me he had sent 23 head to his family in the east to be sold). Thus, in terms of herd dynamics these people also realized a net increase in their herds, perhaps 100 head in aggregate. This estimate of offtake production should be added to the total number of Mbanderu/Tawana cattle in 1980. Doing so, however, still leaves Zhu with 12% of the CaeCae total in that year, a significant gain (from 9% in 1975) in five years—a gain that nevertheless leaves them, as a group, poor in stock, since they compose 93% of the community population.

The distribution of goats (table 6.10) and horses is skewed in a manner similar to that of cattle, with essentially the same homesteads owning the greater proportion of this stock. Goats are valued principally for meat; unlike cattle, they are slaughtered readily when other food supplies are low or when hunting has failed for an extended time. Horses—because they enable fast travel to distant commercial nodes and because they are the key to consistent success in hunting large animals, especially eland and giraffe—are highly valued. Male horses, because of their speed, are preferred even though they cannot be replaced by natural reproduction and must be purchased. The ownership of horses enabled homesteads 1–3–7 as well as Mbanderu homesteads and Bashile to wallow in eland meat during the very severe drought of 1979, when, among other things, not a single mongongo nut was to be found in most groves. All the horses that were the necessary means for this production (because eland remained too far from CaeCae to permit regular hunting on foot) were acquired by those Zhu whose advantageous position is secured by tenurial integrity. An analogous advantage has been constructed by Mbanderu and the Mhapa people here; they carefully restrict the numbers of their congenitors who are allowed to settle and graze stock in the area.[18]

Production from crop planting is very difficult to measure. Although the primary harvest of each crop takes place in a day or two, maize ears, melons, pumpkins, and even small quantities of sorghum and millet are often picked for an immediate meal as the fields begin to ripen. If these grab harvests occurred on days when I monitored food consumption they were recorded; otherwise they were not. Fields were not plowed in 1972–73 or in 1977–78 and 1978–79 because of drought. As with hunting return and livestock holdings, crop yields are highly skewed, with homesteads 1–2–3 realizing high returns; homestead 6 also realized a moderate yield. Of interest is that cultivated crops quickly displace gathered plant foods. Tables 6.6 and 6.7 demonstrate that even before relatively full pastoralist-planting economy is attained, the contribution of gathered vegetables to the diet of Zhu in a domestic food economy drops markedly. This change conforms to an observation made by Campbell (1986:88) regarding altered attitudes among Batswana toward wild foods, "many of which are now seen as being fit only for the very poor or those belonging to lower social strata." In 1979–80, a year of high mongongo yields, the only plant foods collected with any regularity in CaeCae were *Grewia* berries and fruits; these not only are sweet but are available within meters rather than kilometers of all homesteads. *Grewia* berries are also a basic ingredient of home-brewed kqadi (an alcoholic drink similar to hard cider), whose sale is a source of income to several women.

Wage Labor

In recent decades, income in cash and kind has been derived from wage employment as cowherds and milkmaids and from the sale of crafts (including the proverbial shirt/skirt off one's back/buttocks) to safari tour groups that frequented CaeCae and Dobe in the 1950s and 1960s, until prohibited by the central government after independence. Very little income from craft sales can have been realized during this time.[19] Beginning in 1974 Botswanacraft, a parastatal, not-for-profit marketing agency, has made regular buying visits to the area and has substantially raised the prices paid for craftwork (although these are subject to fluctuations in the world market where crafts ultimately are valuated).

I shall turn to craft sales in a moment, but first I want to draw attention to table 6.11, which lists the people of CaeCae who have been employed since 1973. The first thing to note is that all these employees are from the families whose histories of stock raising in as-

Table 6.11. CaeCae Zhu Employed by Mbanderu Cattle Owners

Employer	1973	1975	1976
01	J/491	J/491	J/491
	K/921		
02	B/111	B/111	B/111
	A/141	A/141	A/141
			K/171
			C/951
03	K/171	K/171	
	C/951	C/951	
		K/921	K/921
04	B/431	B/431	B/431
	O/441	O/441	O/441
06	S/712	S/712	S/712
	J/713	J/713	J/713

Note: K/171, K/921, and C/951 live with their Mbanderu employers rather than in Zhu homesteads; they and their families are designated households 51, 52, and 53.

sociation with Bantu peoples were recounted above; these are homesteads 1–4–7. Also notice that no persons from homesteads 2–3 (even those who are CaeCae nqorekausi) are included among the employed; these people have become independent stockholders and farmers who do not seek employment from other pastoralists, although some of them and their ancestors did so in the past. Four men in homestead 3 have worked as construction laborer, truck driver, and borehole pumper at Tshumqwe; part of their earnings at that place were invested in cattle there.

The general conditions of current wage employment at CaeCae are those obtaining between Zhu and Mbanderu. Tohoperi paid only in kind, milk and other food, and animals; in fact, Tohoperi claims that he does not hire labor, pointing out that the Zhu who work for him are his poor relations. Manuel and Marenga pay P4 per month plus food, clothing, and occasional stock. Kahae and Haruvesa pay P5 per month plus food, clothing, and stock. Actual compensation varies greatly, and payment of cash is sometimes delayed; the pay scales above, however, were fairly well adhered to during the 1970s.[20] In 1977 two new permanent jobs were added, borehole pumper (held by Simon [/044]) and cook for the school lunch program (held by Kalu [K/212]).[21]

Table 6.12 lists all wages in cash received from all sources in 1975–76. Production of crafts for commodity sale is a labor process; income from this source is listed in table 6.13. These tables are stratified, as were other tables of production, to aid comparison among the strata.

Table 6.12. Cash Wage Income of CaeCae Zhu, 1975–76

Household	Men	Women	Household Total	Homestead Total
		Homestead 1		
1	60.00*		60.00	
2	96.00*		96.00	
3	60.00*	2.50	62.50	
4	13.50	5.00		
	60.00		78.50	
5	13.75		13.75	
6	2.50		2.50	
7	19.50	2.50	22.00	
8	60.00		60.00	335.25
		Homestead 2		
9	24.60	15.00		
	20.00			
	20.00		79.60	
10	28.60		28.60	
11	5.75		5.75	
12	27.00	11.25	38.25	
13	25.00		25.00	
14	40.00		40.00	
15	16.50		16.50	233.70
		Homestead 3		
16	12.50		12.50	
18	14.50		14.50	
20	13.50		13.50	
24	11.25		11.25	61.75
		Homestead 4		
25	15.00		15.00	
26	60.00*	20.00	80.00	
27	60.00*	15.00	75.00	
28	15.00	5.00	20.00	
29	4.50	15.00	19.50	209.50
		Homestead 5		
30	2.50		2.50	
31	12.50		12.50	
33	5.40		5.40	20.40
		Homestead 6		
35	3.00		3.00	3.00
		Homestead 7		
39	15.00			
	15.50			
	60.00*		90.50	
40	36.00*	2.50	38.50	
42	10.00	6.25	16.25	
43	2.50	6.00		
	1.25		9.75	154.75

Table 6.12. (*continued*)

Household	Men	Women	Household Total	Homestead Total
		Homestead 8		
45	8.60		8.60	
46	3.25		3.25	11.85
		Homestead 9		
47	20.00	7.50	27.50	
48	14.50		14.50	42.00
51	50.00*		50.00	
52	48.00*		48.00	
53	60.00*		60.00	158.00
Total	956.70	113.50		1,070.20

Average wage of employed persons listed in table 6.11 = P59.00
Average earnings of persons with casual cash wage   =   10.20
Average for all employable persons   =   6.00

Household	Men	Women	Household Total	Homestead Total
		Mbanderu		
1	10.00			
2	242.00			
3	80.00			
4	65.00			
Total	397.00			397.00

Note: Household total, combined income for all members of a household; homestead total, combined income for all members of a homestead; * indicates regularly employed wage earners listed in table 6.11—most of the income for women in these households came from the same employer; most of the remaining income came from me.

The skewed cash income distribution from employment for 1973–76 matches that of livestock ownership and hunting production, with homesteads 1–2–3 receiving 88% of all compensation. Craft sales income, because it too is to a great extent dependent on tenurial rights for its raw materials,[22] is also skewed. We shall examine these income differentials more closely in chapter 7.

Structural Divisions in an Appearance of Equality

The structure of this complex situation lies in the historically realized and transformed social relations of production of the groups involved, along with their associated means of production. At CaeCae (a diversified community containing residential and kinship units that in the past would not have been settled together for many years at the same place), contradictions in Zhu social relations that are not easily observed in smaller aggregations become apparent. These contradictions, however, are inherent in those social relations and are not innovations emerging from Bantu or European influence.

Table 6.13. Income from Craft Sales by Household Residents, 1975–76

House-hold	Men	Women	Household Total	Homestead Total
		Homestead 1		
1	9.00	11.50	20.50	
2	1.80	2.00	3.80	
3		3.00		
		6.50	9.50	
4	1.35	6.50	7.85	
5	10.95	11.50	22.45	
6	11.00	6.00	17.00	
7	12.40		12.40	
8	20.00		20.00	113.50
		Homestead 2		
9	31.80	42.05	73.85	
10	16.60	9.80		
		10.50	36.90	
11	2.00	18.05	20.05	
12		8.25	8.25	
13	6.40	2.90	9.30	
14	4.95		4.95	
15	13.70		13.70	167.00
		Homestead 3		
16	7.40	1.85		
		7.25	16.50	
17		7.50	7.50	
18	25.90	15.50	41.40	
19	15.60	5.50	21.10	
20	39.25	4.50		
	2.00	10.30		
		7.25	63.30	
21	3.00	10.15	13.15	
22		4.60	4.60	
23		26.75	26.75	
24	13.00	9.40	22.40	216.70
		Homestead 4		
25	3.00	0.80	3.80	
26	4.00		4.00	
27	6.00		6.00	
28	8.00		8.00	
29	18.00	2.00		
	10.00		30.00	51.80
		Homestead 5		
30	6.80	2.50	9.30	
31	15.00	2.05	17.05	
32	3.20		3.20	
33	7.55	1.10		
		2.00	10.65	40.20

Table 6.13 (*continued*)

House-hold	Men	Women	Household Total	Homestead Total
		Homestead 6		
34	4.00		4.00	
35	12.20	12.00	24.20	
36	3.20	14.25	17.45	
37		12.00	12.00	
38	5.50	2.00	7.50	65.15
		Homestead 7		
39	6.00	29.90		
	15.00			
	15.50		66.40	
40	26.00	10.00	36.00	
41		31.60	31.60	
42	0.40	4.50	4.90	
43	8.00	27.20		
	5.00			
	2.00		42.20	181.10
		Homestead 8		
44	13.50		13.50	
45	8.80	2.00	10.80	
46	4.00		4.00	28.30
		Homestead 9		
47	9.00	23.00		
	8.00		40.00	
48	36.00	2.50		
		2.00	40.50	
49		20.85	20.85	
50	6.50			
	56.00	5.50	68.00	175.35
51	6.00	5.50	11.50	
52		28.00	28.00	
53		3.00	3.00	42.50
Subtotal	580.25	489.85		
Total			1,070.10	
		Mbanderu		
1		40.00		
		44.50	84.50	
4	2.00		2.00	
5	2.00	2.00	4.00	
Subtotal	4.00	86.50		
Total			90.50	
Total (all)			1,160.60	

That this is so may be seen in the fact that although Zhu producers retain control of their own means for carrying on their production activities, relations of extraction exist through which a surplus is appropriated by owners of the land. Such a relation of extraction is an explicit feature in the account of late nineteenth-century herding that Qam gave to Lee and is inherent in the histories of individuals recounted earlier in this chapter. Although such a lack of coincidence between the labor process and the relations of extraction is usually considered a characteristic of feudalism, Taylor (1979:110–11) stresses that it is also crucial in other noncapitalist forms of production, "since it *determines which of the practices in the social formation . . . structures the social formation within which each mode of production exists.*" Under these conditions in the combination of elements in the mode of production, the power to extract a surplus plays the larger role in structuring the processes of production. To anticipate for a moment, these dominant relations of production are the "basis for the class structure" of the social formation itself (Taylor 1979:151). In the Zhu instance we are examining, these dominant relations are those of kinship.

It is important to reemphasize that, with the single exception noted, all CaeCae Zhu who have fully entered the pastoralist economy in the later half of this century have the longest generationally validated history of residence and entitlement at their place. These people have retained effective control of local land-tenure decisions and have enhanced their status at the expense of others here. In the course of time, as part of their priority position with respect to imposed forces (Bantu or European), they have carried out a program of capitalization by investing in livestock. The same situation applies at Dobe (Gelburd 1978:101), where in 1975–76 Zhu with livestock or fields for planting, or both—39% of all women and 85% of all men (Gelburd 1978: 58)—exhibited significantly (33%) more material wealth, including European goods, than did those without stock.

There have been four channels of investment in livestock, three of them noted by Gelburd (1978:58) at Dobe. The first stems from the nineteenth century; this cannot be quantified or even given vital details at this time. But I have reviewed the operation in the area of Sekgoma's mafisa policy toward subjugated peoples and the involvement of named Zhu individuals in the realization of this policy and its aftermath. The generation 5–6 men who were engaged in cattle work are identified above in the recitation of CaeCae genealogies. We also have Andersson's eyewitness testimony (p. 112 above) that Zhu in the NyaeNyae area kept cattle in 1857 (but he does not specify who the owners were). As the history of the area reveals, one also cannot discount an increment of acquisition through theft at that time. Lee's report that many of the 151 men he interviewed—the oldest among them born in the 1890s—had owned cattle before the 1960s, and that 27% (41) still did at the time of his work, must trace its roots from earlier times through the nineteenth-century scenes we have witnessed (since they were already commonplace at the time Europeans recorded them).

The second channel is Halengisi, who does not disguise the fact that he passed many cattle to his wife Tshwa, beginning in the 1920s. Tshwa redistributed numbers of these cattle to her relatives, all of whom now own cattle—including Ssao. Halengisi insists that the past was better than the present—he once said to me, with a wave of his hand at the herds around us, "Gumisi ka kwarra kwinki" : "There are no cattle here now." He made this remark while we were standing together near the CaeCae wells surrounded by about a third of the more than six hundred cattle kept here; we were, in fact, leaning against his magnificent bull, in which he took justifiable pride. He was of course speaking rhetorically and went on to say that in recent years his homestead had suffered substantial losses due to the poisonous plant mai. But he is an excellent pastoralist, as are his relatives, and he does not deny that not many mongongo nuts are cracked in his homestead. A similar, if not identical, role was played by Isak Utugile at Qabi. Isak's father was also Tawana and his mother was Zhu, and he is known to have kept cattle in the Dobe and NyaeNyae areas "long before Damasi [Ovaherero] came here to stay" (Yellen 1985:16). His descendants own cattle at Qabi today.

The third channel of investment is employment with Mbanderu and Tawana cattle owners; this is a relatively slow accrual and likely to produce more goats and donkeys than cattle, but probably 20% of the cattle actually acquired (as distinct from those resulting from breeding increase) by Zhu came through this channel. For example, in December 1975 Marenga gave a heifer to each of his two principal employees and a goat to the third (these are all brothers in homestead 4). At the same time, Kahae gave a donkey each to two of his main employees and a goat to the son of one of these, who is also employed by him (these people lived in his homestead). In addition, he gave a horse to Qam, his third employee, in homestead 1. Also at that time, Haruvesa gave a horse, a cow in calf, and a goat to his "children" in homestead 7. Christmas has become the traditional time to make these yearly distributions.

The fourth channel is cash purchase. In the past this was of variable—usually negligible—importance, dependent almost entirely on external markets for cattle, mainly those belonging to Mbanderu, the income from which permitted low wages to be paid to a few Zhu. Since the 1960s, with the relative stabilization of the cattle market after independence, the creation of a moderately dependable craft market (since 1974), and the influx of wage opportunities with anthropologists, mineral explorations, and relief work programs, cash purchase has become much more important. By no stretch of the imagination, however, is it on a large scale, being constrained by the fact that average CaeCae Zhu household income falls in the lowest 5% of that of Botswana as a whole. I shall take this up in detail when I consider the conditions of the present in the final chapter.

The members of homesteads 1–2–3 constitute only 45% of the Zhu population now living at CaeCae, yet they own 90% of all Zhu-held livestock at this place; they received 88% of the wages (in cash and kind) distributed to Zhu in the community before the intervention of relief programs. Before that intervention, they captured and consumed 60% of the hunted meat killed within the area by Zhu at Cae-Cae, and after it, 85%. It is apparent that inherited tenurial rights carry with them privileged access to the means of production in all economic categories, not just those associated with traditional rights to forage. Productivity from hunting is itself enhanced for those with such privileged access. The data in table 6.14 show that Zhu pastoralists with horses and spears hunt about half as frequently as do foragers using

Table 6.14. Comparative Returns from Hunting

	D	H	HD	N	N/D	N/HD	N/Hh (hr)	Kg/hr (kg)
Bow and arrow								
Kudu	24	1	24	4	0.17	0.17	0.019 (9)	3.02 (160)
	31	1	31	4	0.13	0.13	0.013 (9)	2.08 (160)
	29	1	29	5	0.17	0.17	0.019 (9)	3.02 (160)
Total			84	13	0.16	0.16	0.018 (9)	2.88 (160)
Eland	2	2	4	1	0.50	0.25	0.019 (13)	4.11 (216)
Horse and spear								
Eland	17	4	68	26	1.53	0.38	0.038 (10)	8.28 (216)
Giraffe*	49	8	392	7	0.14	0.02	0.002 (10)	1.00 (500)
Giraffe	7		56		1.00	0.13	0.013 (10)	6.50 (500)

Note: D = number of days hunted; H = number of hunters working together; HD = H × D, number of hunter-days; N = number of kills; N/D = kills per day; N/HD = kills per hunter-day; N/Hh(hr) = kills per hunter-hour (number of hours worked); Kg/hr(kg) = kilograms return per hunter-hour (mean weight of kill).

* Upper row includes travel and meat-drying time, lower row is actual hunting time only.

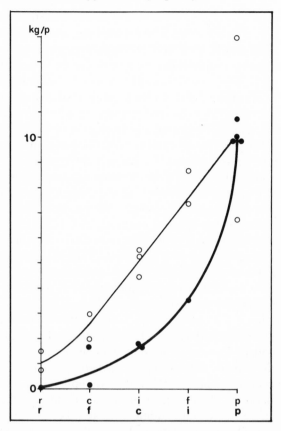

Figure 6.12. Differential hunted meat production by homesteads in different economic strata. Light line and open dots pertain to 1975–76, heavy line and solid dots to 1979–80; vertical scale is in kilograms/person/month; horizontal scale is in homestead economic strata: r is reliant, c is client, f is forager, i is independent, p is pastoralist (upper row, 1975–76, lower row, 1979–80).

bow and arrow on foot but realize about twice the return per unit effort and almost two and a half times as much total return. Mbanderu/Tawana pastoralists have similarly high rates of hunting production, for identical reasons of privileged access to productive means. Table 6.14, along with tables 6.2 and 6.3, attests to the dramatic consequences that are shown graphically in figure 6.12. It is evident that as economic differentiation increases, hunting production differentials change from a linear to an exponential form, indicating that here as elsewhere higher status brings disproportionately higher returns from effort.

Pastoralists—Zhu, Mbanderu, and Tawana—are the only groups who have gained secure access to the underlying means of this production; they thus produce not only the highest proportion of domesticated food product in the region but also by far the largest proportion of hunted meat. They are accordingly in an accelerating spiral of advantage. The dimensions of this advantage are readily apparent. While, during the decade 1969–80, the number of Zhu livestock-owning households increased only marginally, from 27% to 33% of all CaeCae Zhu households, the mean number of cattle per owning household doubled, from 2.5 to 5.1 head. We see here the continuing accumulation of economic advantage by those with intact tenure entitlement or a secure link thereto (homesteads 1–2–3, along with certain families of homesteads 4–7), who increasingly take on the initial characteristics of capitalists at the expense of those who, lacking local entitlement, are impelled to seek other locations where they may sell their labor (homesteads 6–7–8–9). Wiessner (1977 : 342) estimates that in 1974 the value of private possessions—including livestock—of the former set of households was nine times that of the latter set.

Given the relative inelasticity of readily usable land in western Ngamiland that has brought about a concentration of peoples at Cae-Cae, it is—as Smith (1984 : 10–11, citing Hyams 1970 : 21) suggests for early modern Europe—almost inevitable that development will proceed at the expense of the less protected groups, that is, those without strong claims to that land. Thus the assumption that resources are readily available to all Zhu under projected conditions of equality is inappropriate to the actual conditions of stratification that are a salient feature of Zhu social relations. Especially, as we have seen, those without descent-group land to return to and without secure kinship attachment to CaeCae (homesteads 6–7–8–9) are in a descending spiral of poverty, a legacy of their colonial disfranchisement that has left them landless, with only their labor to sell and no adequate market to absorb that labor. Indeed, almost all persons of employable age, women as well as men, of these homesteads have left the community, while (with one possible exception) none from homesteads 1–2–3 has done so.

Ovambanderu/Batawana have maintained their advantage, despite some severe setbacks during colonial domination, largely through management of large herds inherited through elaborate extended kinship networks, but also to a significant degree through external wage work on South African mines. In addition, as seen in chapter 4, Tawana have benefited because their hegemony over other groups was consolidated by colonial rule. Zhu, more thoroughly dispossessed during the nineteenth century, have until recently had to depend for disposable income almost exclusively on bartering labor with local Mbanderu/ Tawana cattle owners. Zhu access to these local labor markets is itself mediated by historical factors: those families who have been least displaced from hereditary tenures have retained virtual monopoly prerogatives with respect to local Mbanderu/Herero employers, with whom they have been—by virtue of being in longest continuous residence in a place—in longest association.

We must be clear, however, in our understanding that labor for wages is not a late twentieth-century innovation for Zhu. The concept of labor/work for others (xwua, pl. = xwuasi; Snyman 1975:137 writes ‖x'oà, "werk") is well entrenched in Zhu vocabulary. A man may say "Mi ku uwa nci tji gumi":"I'm going to water cattle" and mean by this that he is on his way to water his own animals, or to help with those of a relative, or to fulfill contractual labor obligations (that is, go to work). But he would say "Mi ku uwa xwua gumi":"I'm going to work cattle" or "Mi ku uwa gqunqi xwua":"I'm going to work at the well" only if he were "going to work" for compensation.

The Zhu word tcao (‖xào = "betaal," Synman 1975:100), glossed in English as "pay," does not seem to be derived from any other language. Neither does Zhu xama (‖'àmà = "koop," Snyman 1975:130), "purchase."[23] This is good evidence that a notion of compensated exchange distinct from reciprocity (haro, "prestate") is indigenous to Zhu understanding. In addition, a Zhu person does not enter into contractual employment relations on the basis of reciprocity (that is, of haro) but does so on the basis of negotiated compensation (tcao). Shostak (1981:41) illustrates this in her retelling of a dream Nisa had concerning employment with a Tswana man: "I'm not selling my labor for cornmeal. . . . I wouldn't do it because I wasn't getting paid." There is no reason to suppose that this attitude was different in the nineteenth century, where we have seen Europeans (and Bantu) negotiating for San (among these, Zhu) services. And since these nineteenth-century employments were entered into without seeming effort (except in those instances when gratuitous coercion was applied by those who wished to appropriate Zhu labor against the workers' will), there must have been already a sound idea of what this entailed. We do not know what the rates of compensation may have been; we have learned enough to appreciate that they were variable and negotiated and that they diminished with time. We also know, from accounts detailed in the history of the region, that agreements were struck with previously unknown Europeans for black ostrich feathers, tusks, meat, beads, cloth, guns, powder, and other valuables essential for the already well-established trade.

Current Zhu nqore kao advantage is thus acquired through historically mediated advantageous political position in place, which allows hereditary owners to appropriate economic opportunities for themselves to the nearly complete exclusion not only of nonkin but of collateral rivals as well.

A form of privatization is taking place at CaeCae in which kinship entitlement is still central for individual participation in its development, notwithstanding that this development is itself becoming more reliant on communitywide—indeed, extracommunity—cooperation among economically dominant persons irrespective of their kinship affiliations to each other. This is a phenomenon of the past two, perhaps at most three, decades, but it has its roots in long-standing Zhu, Herero, and Tswana concepts of private ownership of the means of production. Bows, arrows, snares, spears, nets, bags, distaffs—all of these and many more means of production, along with the products themselves—were and are privately owned. In Lee's (1979:119) words, "the [Zhu] 'worker' owns the means of production" (cf. Carstens 1983). Introduced means of production—guns, bullets, steel traps, plows, horses, donkeys—with far higher return potentials than indigenous means were incorporated through the existing ideology of private property and became the individual possessions of producers. Differential access to these introduced means simply multiplied the effects of existing hierarchical structures. Recall that the owner of the product is—and was as far into the past as we can know—responsible for its distribution; that owner thus holds the power to determine the value others receive. We have also seen that ownership of livestock is similarly private. The penetration of mercantile capital in the later nineteenth century, rather than separating direct producers from these private means of production, reinforced a preexisting nonseparation; that is to say, merchant capital reinforced existing private ownership of those means along with the structure for distributing the product of those means.

Production under these terms is, of course, private and individualized. It takes place within individual households, which look primarily to their own interests. "A household owns . . . the nuts in the pile at its doorway," and nonmembers may eat them only when specifically offered; even after the fruity outer flesh is sucked off, "the nuts revert to the one who collected them" (Lee 1979:200–201). Shostak (1981:242) adds that the woman of a household "determines how much of her gatherings, if any, will be given away. . . . from start to finish, her labor and its product remain under her control." Draper (1975:84) stresses the family orientation of this control: "The gatherer has the last word regarding the distribution of vegetable food, at least when it concerns anyone outside her immediate family."

Finally, a person is bound by kinship and affinal ties to share only with "parents, spouse and spouse's parents, and to a lesser degree siblings" (Wiessner 1977:132), any or all of whom are likely to be living in the same homestead. As Gibbon and Neocosmos (1985:171) point out, "This private nature of production makes possible . . . the specialization of productive activity and the consequent necessary interdependence of these private producers via exchange." Historically, this dialectic between independent private production and dependent community sociality formed the extensive exchange networks that wend their way through this narrative, tying together diverse, disparate goals and strategies—the political conditions of their labor—of families, homesteads, kinsmen, and neighbors. It was just the fabric of this interdependence, not the continuing need of it, that colonial administration destroyed, as Lord Hailey recognized. In some cases this destruction was purposeful, for reasons of policy, but just as often it was simply an accidental by-product of ill-informed actions.

Nevertheless, the result has been the same: dislocation of previous relations to land, and extraction of labor surplus. Taking a clue from Brenner (1976), we must therefore interpret not only the distribution of the immediate product of Zhu land but the prior questions of the distribution of landed property and—so far having only described them—the extraction relations that flow from this distribution. For the new social relations emerging at CaeCae are themselves the result of previous, relatively autonomous processes. I shall argue, as Trapido (1978:28) does for nineteenth-century Boers, that Zhu households do not and did not reproduce a single relationship for the appropriation of a surplus product because Zhu society is and was itself stratified.

Kinship as Practice

It is apparent in what has gone before that Zhu kinship is a form of conjectural history whose elements—both the positions potentially open to persons and the connections among these positions—are subject to manipulation in conjunction with wider social and economic concerns. Comaroff (1973) makes a similar point with considerable force regarding the Tswana polity, Barolong boo Ratshidi. As the individual histories testify, for some Zhu the scope of these manipulations includes the conjectural histories of those Ovambanderu and Batawana with whose actual histories they have been meshed, just as, of course, do the histories of the latter with those Zhu. Taking as a point of departure Wright's (1983) observation that political practice is that activity that produces and transforms social relations, it becomes evident that, among the people we have been examining, kinship is the arena in which political practice takes place. Shostak (1981:169), referring to the advantages of marriage for a Zhu man, spells this out with clarity: "He gains recognition and status in the community, and he extends his social and political influence to include his new in-laws, their village, and their foraging grounds." She goes on to show how polygynous marriage further enhances the status of a man. The family—Zhu, Mbanderu, Tawana—histories recited earlier in this chapter are records of the playing out of these processes.

I have already referred to Taylor's expansion of Marx's insight that in noncapitalist forms of production a practice other than the economic must structure the social formation because there is a disjunction between the labor process and the relations of extraction. In the formations we have examined, the intervening practice is political and is constituted in the kinship relations through which status is determined. This intervention is political because those with entitlement to land have defined rights to its product, both subsistence and surplus, at the expense of others. In addition, those persons within the entitled group who are hierarchically dominant (principally nqorekausi, but also anyone's own parents—particularly own father[24]—and parents-in-law) have a defined right to an extra portion of the surplus product, even if that extra portion may be momentarily intangible, as in the case of enhanced right to arrange a marriage (Wiessner 1977:102). This right, moreover, carries with it access to material and social resources—the reason Zhu parents strive diligently to reserve for themselves this potentially onerous right (cf. Shostak 1981).

Recall that "the cattle boys [young Zhu men] loaded the pack oxen with bales and bales of eland biltong and went east with it to collect the balls of shoro [tobacco] and sometimes corn. These they would deliver to [the nqorekau, Tcoma]." Of course Tcoma redistributed these goods, but we have seen that distributed portions are unequal and that the direction and volume of distributions flow along kin lines. Although we cannot follow this flow in the nineteenth century, we can be quite sure that Tcoma, and his family, were not the first to run out of tobacco before the next trip east.[25] It is also crucial not to lose sight of the fact that Tcoma gained access to this surplus product by being in a status position that he alone held, and furthermore, that he organized the men whose surplus labor he thus extracted.

This took place toward the end of the nineteenth century, before significant dislocations of persons from nqoresi. Thus the structural relations exposed cannot be the result of European intervention. Batawana, furthermore, who intervened earlier and more thoroughly, understood Zhu hierarchical structure and worked through it. All the

men mentioned in the homestead histories who were direct participants at that time in the two most significant economic activities of the
region, trading and herding, were central to their kinship networks,
and their descendants remain so today. Those who were not central
participated only indirectly through reciprocal obligations of collaterals (where these could be maintained), or through infrequent chance
opportunities (as when a merchant might be encountered while hunting), or not at all. The progression of these inequalities through this
century into the present has already been described.

It should be clear now that Zhu relations of production are not re-
ducible to relations of necessity or of distribution. Neither are they
communal; important differences exist among categories of economic
agents in their access to conditions of production. I have attempted,
first, to demonstrate that kinship is the intervening practice that results
in this differentiation, and second, that this intervention is not a mere
abstract "realization" of an economic level that is empirically absent
from the social formation (cf. Terray 1972). That is, this is a clear-cut
specific instance of the general proposition argued at the beginning of
this book. Zhu relations of production are not constituted through a
noneconomic intervention by kinship, a kinship that would then lack
independent identity apart from relations of production and would devolve to the minimum primordial dimension of Meillassoux.

But of course we have seen that Zhu kinship is anything but primordial, and relations of production are far from secondary. Zhu kinship
is instead, as Bourdieu (1977:36) says of all such relationships, "the
product of strategies (conscious or unconscious) oriented toward the
satisfaction of material and symbolic interests and organized by reference to a determinate set of economic and social conditions." It emerges
as relationships that can be read in different ways by their participants.
Harries (1982:145) has given us a detailed analysis of how kinship
and kinship ideology did not merely constitute superstructure but actively structured relations of production in nineteenth-century Delagoa Bay hinterlands. Marks (1982:13) observes that this was true for
all the societies of southern Africa. Zhu relations of production are
structured in the engagement of this kinship practice with the economic sphere. Peters (1984:4) says that, among Bakgatla, it was just
this "dynamic interaction between the solidarities evoked by 'kinship'
and the status inequalities of 'political' organization [that] facilitated
the slipping of collateral branches of chiefly lines into commoner status,
of impoverished individuals and families into servitude, . . . and, in reverse direction, facilitated the movement of the fortunate up through
the ranks." To which Werner (1980:66) adds of Ovaherero, "It is pre-

cisely in form of the cattlepost system that the chiefs could extract surplus labour from the commoners," to whom of course they were related
through oruzo and eanda lineages.

We can now understand the conflicting perceptions among Zhu
over what constitutes a "proper" marriage. On the one hand are Zhu
who say that to marry properly is to marry only specified kin, specifically second or third cousins. These are the people who have secure
entitlement in place. Their strategy aims to retain the advantage accruing in entitlement; it protects the undivided inheritance of descent-
group land. On the other hand are those who insist that one marries
anyone other than kin. Their strategy seeks entrance to entitled en-
titities; as Wiessner (1977 : 162, 266) says of them, those families "whose
membership has been dwindled by emigration or death constantly seek
alliances with others. . . . once attached to a large productive group, a
person has a much stronger base for developing reciprocal obligations." These conflicting perceptions are rooted in convergent interests
of persons who find themselves in contrasting circumstances and are
expressions of strategy options sought to fulfill those interests. The
strategies themselves are directed toward preserving or expanding access to material entitlements. The reason for this transformation in
Zhu marriage behavior is parallel to and inextricably associated with
the similar transformation observed by Gibson among Ovaherero.
Kuper (1987 : 138) states this reason succinctly for the Tswana, among
whom a similar change is taking place: "With the disappearance of its
political rationale, preferential marriage on kinship lines is rapidly becoming a thing of the past, although it still may be practiced more than
people themselves realize."

I must return at this juncture to the point Gibbon and Neocosmos
made concerning the necessary interdependence of private producers
via exchange. In keeping with this necessity, no local descent group
can independently reproduce itself within the parochial limits of a
single nqore. For this reason a significant number of marriage ties are
negotiated with strategically placed collateral affines in adjacent and
nearby nqoresi. Wiessner has revealed the crucial role played in this
process by reciprocal exchange, haro. She says that adults with mature
children choose to gain strength through intensified haro and other
forms of cooperation in specific nqore areas because they are concerned with finding spouses in those nqoesi for those children. "Finding a mate involves more than just locating one and in a competitive
situation, the person with the broadest social influence is likely to be
most effective in arranging marriages" (Wiessner 1977 : 185–86).

Haro chains serve as channels along which devolutionary marriage payments are made and premortem and postmortem inheritance flows. Wiessner (1980:11) says that productive partnerships between first cousins are passed on from parents to children. Such inheritance accounts for 45% of the haro links of Zhu individuals, and these links are the most secure and long lasting of haro partnerships, some of them spanning "many generations." This is another way Zhu "choose which kin they wish to 'remember' in reciprocal relations and which kin they prefer to 'forget'" (Wiessner 1980:17). Now, first cousins of parents are the parents of one's PPsCC—that is, of one's preferred marriage partner. Haro exchanges between parties to these partnerships begin in childhood, between a child and its PPsC (gxa:aunt/tsu:uncle); they intensify, in the parental generation as well as between the now-adult child and aunt/uncle, during marriage negotiations, then solidify during the period of marriage service and devolve incrementally upon the next generation as before. Thus haro partnerships are premortem inheritances that provide a person with working keys to the future. In consequence of the maturing of these haro cycles, the bulk of a person's private property will have been transferred to own children and collateral haro partners before death. Postmortem, children or siblings or both take a person's remaining possessions to those haro partners they want to remember—that is, with whom they want to retain future marriage options for themselves or their children—and ask that the relationship be continued (Wiessner 1983b:14). That this may be a structural characteristic common to Khoisan in general is suggested by Carstens's (1983:66) observation that similar "premortem inheritance while their children are establishing themselves as adults" is preferred by Nama.

There is also "foreign" exchange. Exotic products are transferred over distances far greater than those to nearby nqoresi in the Ghanzi to Gcam to CaeCae to Qangwa to Tsodilo network with its web of extensions within the region and beyond. This exchange has been present in varying degrees of intensity since the Early Iron Age. Xin's aside gives a glimpse of its operation: trade friends from different locations meeting to engage in haro exchange on a scale larger than simple gift giving.

Another description given to Lee (1976:89) captures the atmosphere in which these trade relations were conducted in the past. The speaker is Tciqe (R/811):

/Xai/Xai has always been a meeting place for people even before the blacks came. People came from the north, from !Kangwa and !Goshe, and from the south from G/am, and from the west from G/ausha, stayed here, did hxaro, drank n!o (a choice wild fruit [from which kqadi is made]), ate //"xa (mongongo nuts), and then went back. They asked Kan!o (one of the owners) for permission. They also asked #Toma!gain [C/100]. /Xai/Xai was favored because the water was so big. Choma (men's initiation ceremony) was danced here, but the main reason (to meet) was hxaro trade.

We do not know, of course, how far into the past Tciqe's "always" extends, but we can be sure that he is not describing a new event. Choma (dzxòmá = "weg kruip," Synman 1975:10), "keep out of sight,"[26] a Zhu incorporating ritual, is a rite of passage for bringing young men into adulthood. Its Herero counterpart, osukareka, is described by Gibson (1959a:4) as "a rite celebrating the collection of young men into discrete age groups and their preparation for marriage." Both choma and osukareka initiate a set of age-mates (Zhu, ≠àrà (tcara) = "vriend," Synman 1975:104, "friend"/"age-mate," Shostak 1981:131 also glosses "peer"; Otjiherero, ekura = "age-mate" Gibson 1959a:4) into adulthood and thus make them eligible for marriage. In currently living generations, numbers of men from both groups of people when in their youths underwent both initiations. Lee (1979:365) describes assemblages of large numbers of local groups that formed the initiation camps and says "the initiates and their families would often travel 70 to 100 km to join chomas." Older adults today can name several of their tcarasi/ovikura in numbers of distant places.

Choma thus, in addition to—or perhaps better, as part of—its ritual function of ushering sets of age-mates into adulthood, also cements ties to trade friends who become tcarasi by participation in the ritual. It does so by coupling of haro with the creation of tcara sets. Shostak (1981:131) stresses the strong and loyal bonds that last for many years among tcarasi, bonds that are formalized and strengthened by active exchange. Tcarasi say they "feel like" relatives. Indeed, although not all persons who are tcarakwe to each other are necessarily traceable kin, with few exceptions those also in a haro relationship are. Wiessner (1977:208) has demonstrated convincingly that more than 90% of haro is conducted between relatives; haro initiatives may be made to "any putatively consanguineal kin, close or very distant."

Such relationships stretch for hundreds of kilometers through many hands; Wiessner (1986:109) says, therefore, that any account of group interaction must take into consideration an area within a 200 to 300 kilometer radius centered on the locality of concern (cf. also Lee 1979: 365–66). Persons closer to each other in any direction along the network are closer relatives or affines; those farther away, both in geographical distance and along the links of haro chains, are progressively more tenuously related (Wiessner 1977:197). Marriage negotiations form part of the strategies employed to tie desirable haro partners more closely together and to give generational continuity to these arrangements. Haro partnerships are passed in inheritance from parent to child, and inheritors strive to solidify anew those partnerships that offer continuing advantageous access to material and social resources. It is through delicate, complex balancing of these interests in a fluid field of options that the parochial bounds of local groups are opened to a necessary wider social sphere. That is, to borrow the terminology of Dupré and Rey (1973:145), "The role of exchange in the reproduction of the conditions of production [takes place] at a different level from that of exchange itself." The early nineteenth-century Ghanzi men who married into CaeCae must have arrived and been incorporated into the local polity through routes of this kind.

Class Characteristics of Zhu Social Relations

In the same way that it is an error to look at Zhu outside the context of their participation in larger regional economic systems encompassing Bantu-speaking coresidents, the analytical isolation of individual homesteads in their separate nqoresi prohibits us from examining the integration of these homesteads within the overall structure of Zhu land tenure. We have already seen that neither individuals nor homesteads act as if such isolation were the case. It is important, therefore, to focus on relations among members of different nqoresi, for the extraction of a surplus is only one aspect of the resource relations we are examining. The other, prior, aspect is the guaranteed, impartable inheritance of productive land.

The impartability of descent-group land is ensured by the cooperation of homesteads in negotiating proper marriages, that is, marriages that protect the undivided inheritance of that land. Marriage negotiations, therefore, are not the simple prerogatives of single families but involve numbers of senior members of a kindred. Lee (1986:93–96) describes very clearly the ways seniority is the basis for "exercising authority [that is] crucial in determining who should choose the kin terms to be used." He says, in fact, that usage is *imposed* (my emphasis) by elders; "the older you get, the more 'control' you have. . . . [usage] depends on what the older person wants to do, but kin terms flowing out of marriage names, because they are reciprocal, are among the most popular of the name-relation kin terms." Shostak's (1981) retelling of Nisa's marital career captures better than any other account we have the roles of grandparents, aunts, brothers, affines, "my relative," and others in the contracting and dissolution of her marriages. As Shostak (1981:240) remarks of the generality of this particular case, "The choice of a spouse has a far-reaching impact on the family's social and economic life, and often that of the entire group." Except that the qualifier "often" should be deleted, this is an accurate assessment of the central importance of marriage in Zhu political life. Without strong kindred control of marriage, the impartability of descent-group land inheritance could not be perpetuated.

The stratification process is thus based on the capacity of some kin units to retain or expand family land at the expense of politically weaker fractions of the social formation. This is very clearly illustrated in the tightly delimited exchange of marriage partners between CaeCae and Ghanzi in generations 5–6; only the central families were involved (recall that excluded families either are no longer represented at Cae-Cae or have returned through marriage of one or more of their members to close kinspeople in the community). Consequently, as Berry (1985:7) observes for many peoples of sub-Saharan Africa, Zhu "invested [and continue to invest] considerable effort and resources to ensure or advance their status within kin groups or local polities." The nqore recruitment efforts noted by Marshall and Lee (p. 169 above) are interpretable in this context.

Some of the dynamics of the process are visible in a small drama that occurred at CaeCae in April 1976. Ncisa, the seven-month-old daughter of Dixau (H/152), died of a respiratory disease, one of three Zhu infants who succumbed to this malady in the same month. Although the other two deaths were attributed to the ordinary caprice of Gxanwa, the administrator deity, that of Ncisa was found through divination to be an act of retribution by that same deity. The transgression that brought this about was committed by Qam (A/131), Dixau's MZHBS and thus Ncisa's classificatory cousin, and Qam's then father-in-law, Tciqe (R/811), who together killed and ate a large python at a rainpool cattlepost, Gqo, some 20 kilometers east from CaeCae. Pythons are associated with rain and ought not be killed in ordinary circumstances. The location, Gqo, is generally conceded to have been within the descent-group land of homestead 8 in the past, but members of Zhu homestead 1 in association with Kahae's Mbanderu homestead have in recent years begun to station their cattle there during the rainy season. A dispute over ownership arose, of course, with Tciqe claiming rights to some of the milk from cattle kept there as a form of rent, which in fact he received. Since the infant Ncisa was present at Gqo when the transgression—killing the python—took place, a direct connection between that act and her illness, which commenced less than two weeks later, could be drawn by divination. Thus, Tciqe—along with Qam, as his son-in-law, not as a homestead 1 member—was implicated in Ncisa's death; it follows that their future presence at Gqo is threatening to others in her homestead (actually only Tciqe's, not Qam's as a homestead 1 member). Ssao (D/331), who through his relationship to homestead 1 has a direct interest in these proceedings, performed the divination. Shortly after Ncisa's death, Qam's marriage to Tshwa (I/813), Tciqe's daughter, dissolved, despite the fact that they had two young children, thus severing his relation to homestead 8; this is the only divorce of established parents that occurred at CaeCae between 1973 and 1985. Homestead 8 no longer presses its claim to Gqo, and homestead 1 (along with 2 and 3, of course) has effectively extended its range.

To invest resources, one must possess them to begin with, and to invest competitively there must be potential disparities of possession. I shall turn once more, therefore, to linguistic evidence to establish that a concept of unequal possession is inherent in Zhu ideology.[27] The verb xhai (‖'ái = "ryk wees," Snyman 1975:129), "to be wealthy" (Lee 1979:344 writes "//kai [wealth]"), is contrasted with gxaa (g‖àá, "to be poor"). The noun derivatives are xhaiha (‖'áixà = "heer," "rykaard," "leier," Snyman 1975:129), "master," "wealthy person," "leader," and gxaakwe (g‖àákhòe = "behoeftige," "armlastige," Snyman 1975:27), "poor person," "needy," "indigent." On a subjective level, Shostak (1981:41) records Nisa's use of this contrastive set in describing herself as "a poor person. Yes, grandmother, a poor person." Obviously, a notion of differential accumulation is part and parcel of Zhu ideology. Wiessner (1977:224) adds to this that those "who can regularly produce a surplus do have a broader sphere of hxaro than the average San." As we have seen, a broader sphere of exchange partners is associated with enhanced political influence—that is, power.

We have also seen that many Zhu households today are incapable of securing social reproduction and that this inability is grounded in the historical development of local social interaction as well as of production. Most starkly notable in this regard is the inability of households in homesteads 6–7–8–9 to gain footholds through marriage in the CaeCae nqorekau homesteads. This failure is not the consequence of a paucity of members of marriageable age or of the capabilities of such persons in the excluded homesteads. As Wiessner (1977:298, 306) notes, in the first half of the 1970s homestead 9 had several very attractive persons of both sexes but made no marriages in the community, while during the same period homestead 1 made four lasting marriages and realized eight births. I have already noted that homesteads 6–8 were unable to place their daughters (with the exception of Tshwa [I/813]) within the community. These otherwise desirable persons were thoroughly dispossessed and could offer no security—in access either to cowherd jobs or, now of secondary but still significant importance, to foraging grounds; they are therefore of no interest to landholding households.

Nor is success in biological reproduction in itself of any consequence. One man, Gcau (L/810), has a greater number of descendants than any other person at CaeCae (not all his children and grandchildren continue to live here, however); none of them, save one possible exception who is in an early stage of trial marriage, has gained a secure, permanent place in the community independent of Tawana patronage. Tcomazho (C/911), with five sons and two daughters, has made no lasting mark on the community. The persons of homesteads 6−7−8−9, especially the men (for whom there is a potentially wider range of job categories), have become freed labor in Marx's sense of being dispossessed from land; except for the homestead 7 family associated with Keharera, they are seeking markets for their labor elsewhere. It is also significant that all of the eleven children fathered by transient Tswana mine exploration company and government workers in the early 1980s were borne by unwed and unbetrothed teenage and young adult Zhu women in homesteads 6−8−9. While this confers neither opprobrium on the mothers nor illegitimacy on the children, neither the mothers nor the children will derive any social or material support from the fathers. It would be perverse to see the conditions that formed this unbalanced situation of social reproduction in anything but class terms. Furthermore, the children have no claim on their paternal family or its land; this places them at a severe disadvantage with respect to those children in the community who can call upon full kindred support. While a few of these "fatherless" children may overcome their disadvantage, most will probably live a life of poverty.

I turn now to leadership among Zhu, a question that has taken very curious turns in the literature. In chapter 3 I cited numbers of references to San leaders made by nineteenth-century European observers; the terms these observers used were usually headman or chief or Häuptling. Many other examples could be included. We need not waste time trying to decode what they meant by applying these terms to San leadership, because they were applied loosely and inconsistently not only to San-speakers but to many other peoples of southern Africa.

But neither can we entirely ignore these early observations; the following passage from Passarge (1907:114) merits very close attention:

The Bushmen of the middle Kalahari are divided, as is well known, into two great peoples, these again into individual branches/clans and the clans into kindreds. Previously, these clans formed complete political organizations. At the head of each of them stood a "Grootkapitain," as the Dutch-speaking Bushman expressed it, who was supported by the "⁴áichadji" [xhaihasi], the family heads. . . . In the Xaudum Valley, I came upon a band of Zhu whose leader's name was Kumtsaa. But the headman of the clan was named "² Auka" [Xauka] who formerly kept a valley called Tsanni for himself; this must lie westward from Tshocanna.²⁸

If we read "local descent group" for "clan," we find that Passarge here gives a reasonable description of Zhu political divisions with their leaders; he uses the term "xhaiha" in an appropriate manner and suggests the existence of nqoresi. Furthermore, he specifies as leaders two men whose names match those of the grandfathers of CaeCae Zhu homestead 5 heads Gcau (L/511), whose FF was Xauka, and his wife Tcuka (Q/512), whose FF was Kumtsaa. These men would have been in their mid- to late fifties in 1896–98 when Passarge met them. Both are known to have had nqoresi to the northwest of Tshumqwe, Kumtsaa at ǂeni (which could have been written Tsanni by a German-speaker), and Xauka at !ama, the Zhu name for Karakuwisa. All of this matches what is known of the ancestors of homestead 5, and it seems that Passarge has given us a very valuable firsthand glimpse of Zhu leadership in place a century ago.

It is cogent that modern anthropologists have treated the question of San leadership rather loosely. Silberbauer (1981:134), for example, says, "There are some social concepts included in the vocabulary for which the G/wi have no cultural equivalent, for example, //*xeixama* (chief)."²⁹ Now, it is difficult to imagine how a language could come to include a lexical term for an abstract position such as "chief" unless speakers of that language had a conception of what "chiefliness" is for them. Another brief linguistic excursion will shed some light on the matter. Lee (1979:344) recognizes that the Zhu "word for 'chief,' //*kaiha*, [is] derived from the word //*kai* (wealth)." Recall that Snyman derives xhaiha ("master," "leader," "wealthy person") from xhai ("to be wealthy") and that this is contrasted with gxaakwe ("poor person"), from gxaa ("to be poor").³⁰ Thus, leadership is associated with wealth—as among Batswana and Ovaherero.

The basis for that wealth resides in nqore entitlements and the productive benefit they entail; these entitlements are inherited by all members of a descent group. But it is apparent that leadership positions are passed through a smaller subset of families within the nqore entitlees. Some examples will make this clear. Lee (1979:344) tells us that Shexai (A/110) "was the descendent of several generations of /Xai/Xai owners, and though she was a soft spoken person she was the acknowledged leader of her camp." We have traced Ssao's (D/331) inheritance through four documented generations and cited Zhu extensions of this generational depth by logical argument. Lee (1979:350) says of

Ssao's leadship powers, "Because his kin ties to past n!ore owners gave Tsau a strong claim to legitimacy, he did not elicit from his own people the same degree of hostility and criticism that other !Kung leaders suffered when they tried to deal with outsiders." Remember that Ssao is the nephew of Shexai and that she is the daughter of Tcoma (C/100), the first CaeCae nqorekau we met. It is for this reason that Ssao—before he became chairman, the honorific by which he is now addressed—was called xhaiha.

Two other examples given by Lee will illuminate the issue more brightly. He recounts (1979:349) the selection by the people of Dobe of their representative to the Northwest District (Ngamiland) Council Land Board; they chose "a quiet and unaggressive man named ≠Dau, whose main claim to the role was the fact that he was the descendent [of the previous] senior owner of Dobe." Kalahari Peoples Fund representatives unsuccessfully promoted another more articulate and forceful man. Lee interprets this to mean that the people of Dobe "were not yet fully aware of the threats to the security of their land and thus were not able to mobilize fully against it." But of course they are more fully aware of the balance of threats to and possibilities for their land than anyone else; the history we have rehearsed prepared them for that. They are also fully aware of the locus of power in their social relations; Dcau, a soft-spoken person like Shexai, may have been an unwise choice, but he is of the set of families from which the next nqorekau will come. And it is abundantly clear to all that nqorekausi accumulate disproportionately more than others do; a wise person wants "to be felt good about in the hearts" of these people. The Dobe Zhu were simply following the quite rational strategy of acting with thought for the future.

In acting thus they were no more victims of their own naïveté then were CaeCae Zhu in recognizing soft-spoken Shexai as their nqorekao, or were Batawana in 1906 when they rejected as their new chief to replace the deposed Sekgoma a candidate put forward by the British administration in favor of Mathiba, who had a legitimate claim to succession, even though they did not like him and he was known to drink heavily (Tlou 1974:67). Comaroff (1973) and Motzafi-Haller (1987) offer instructive analyses of these decision-making processes in other Tswana cases like this.

Finally, Lee (1979:347–48) relates conversations with two Kaos at Dobe who appear to suggest that Zhu ridicule the notion of Zhu headmen. In fact, many do so. But they do so with irony, recognizing that the structure of nqore relations has been broken forever. Just as with Halengisi's rhetorical dismissal of the cattle standing around him, it is mistaken to take these anecdotes at face value. While making fun of

headmanship and of themselves, these Dobe Kaos place all the prominent persons they mention—and they cover much of the Ngami-
Namibia region—precisely in their proper nqoresi and say, "If X were
a headman that is where he would be headman." That is, they are saying, "If things were as they were in the time of our grandfathers, these
persons would be nqorekausi in their proper nqoresi."

In similar vein, but with no trace of humor or irony, Dam (Y/741),
a very old man from Gcam, told me that there are not even nqorekausi
anymore, much less xhaihasi. He told me this in the presence of Ssao,
who was rather embarrassed, but neither of us wanted to challenge the
old man on the point. Dam was speaking as an exile at CaeCae, with
no chance of ever returning to his kindred land, his homestead melting
around him; he knew that on his death the remnant members of his
family would disperse to all sorts of places. Which they did. Dam did
not mean that Ssao was not a legitimate nqorekau. He meant that the
structure had been torn apart by forces beyond his control. He feared
that no Zhu center could hold. Dam's was an apocalyptic view, the
Dobe Kaos' perhaps more resigned; but they were all speaking structurally, not superficially.

Challenges to the structure also occur from within. Two men during the past two decades, Tcomazho (C/911) and Qumqosi (C/621),
made strong, well-conceived attempts to gain real—that is, structurally integrated rather than peripheral—prominence in CaeCae.
Tcomazho is a decade older than Ssao, Qumqosi slightly younger.
Both are extremely able, intelligent men with forceful personalities;
both are renowned curers. Neither has nqore entitlement to CaeCae.
We saw, in the recitations of their homestead histories, a brief summary of their efforts at marriage manipulations and economic interventions aimed at establishing entitlement claims. Neither achieved
more than notoriety. Power and decision making remained in the
hands of Ssao and his nqore relations. While not a foregone conclusion, this was a highly likely outcome, for as Shostak (1981:245) says,
"The most crucial aspect of the balance of power [among Zhu] is the
process of leadership and decision making." This leadership is accomplished through the exercise of power to dictate each person's dimensions of kinship and marriage. Clearly, nqorekau families are able to
reproduce the conditions of their xhaiha dominance over numbers of
generations.

Also clearly, xhaihasi are able to mobilize labor and to extract a
surplus product. Tcoma (C/100) was doing just that when he organized men to herd Tswana cattle and to return their earnings in tobacco and maize to him for redistribution. Not all of these men were
younger than he; a brief perusal of the worker inventory (given in the

family histories at the beginning of this chapter) will reveal that some were Tcoma's own generation second and third collaterals. Thus this is a case not of age-set oligarchy but of central family authority. Similarly, Samkao was able to mobilize a considerable raiding/fighting force in the 1920s, as were other leaders at the turn of this century (recall the rustling of Sekgoma's cattle) and before.

The structure of Zhu class relations in the regional economy is rooted in these specific conditions of production and accumulation. These relations have been defined in a particular history of political struggle over access to land resources and their products and to the attendant power conferred by recognized legitimate entitlement to manipulate the disposal of these products. It should be clear that this structure is inherent in Zhu social relations and has not been imposed by external forces in recent decades.

Present conditions of political and economic asymmetry visible at CaeCae are, of course, a result of the colonial era and its aftermath—that is, of the particular modern history of the region. But particular histories engage underlying structures to produce visible results, and these structures—though not deterministic in the sense that the conjunction of certain variable events will have a fixed outcome—do *structure* the outcome in terms of their own logic. For example, if Zhu ideology were in fact egalitarian, its structural logic would distribute entitlements and leadership positions among individuals on an unbiased, perhaps random, basis. Yet the evidence—drawn, I wish to stress, from every author who has worked among these peoples—demonstrates unequivocally that quite the opposite is the case. Clearly, nqorekausi homesteads reproduce the conditions of their exclusive entitlements, and those families from which the nqorekau leader is drawn reproduce the conditions of their dominance. Equally clearly, the nqorekau leader, the xhaiha, is able to extract a surplus labor value not only from members of his kindred but from members of his wider descent group and beyond as well; such extraction is similar in effect to the extraction of ground rent in the form of a labor levy. These fundamental conditions of class reproduction are endemic in Zhu social relations.

If, nonetheless, even to careful observers Zhu may superficially appear classless today, it is because they are incorporated as an underclass in a wider social formation that includes Batswana, Ovaherero, and others. The same may be said of San peoples in other parts of the Kalahari region. But that appearance is itself illusory. Zhu exhibit sufficient class characteristics—differential accumulation of wealth, asymmetrical extraction of surplus product, exclusionary control of social reproduction—to say that class is an inherent feature of their, and probably all San, social relations. That Zhu in present circumstances, though an underclass, are not an undifferentiated underclass is itself evidence for endemic class structures in their social formation.

Some will argue that if this conclusion is correct then it must be because of interactions with pastoralists. I cannot quarrel with that argument; to the contrary, I have striven to show that all the peoples examined here are, in varying transitory combinations, as much pastoralists as foragers, as much foragers as pastoralists. I have documented at length the extent to which neither Zhu particularly nor San-speakers generally provide a basis for seeing "foragers in a world of foragers." To assert an argument of interaction is to accept the kind of interactive history documented in this and the preceding chapters, a history to which Zhu, and all San-speaking peoples, have contributed as richly as have any of the other peoples of the Kalahari. To see Zhu and their fellow San-speakers as astute political persons with competing economic goals and social strategies is to see them not as ahistorical residues of ancient foragers but as coproducers, along with their Bantu-speaking cohabitants, of a history they helped form. It is also to see them as real people, not as a category.

7

What It Means to Be Excluded

I [see] no reason whatever for preserving Bushmen. I can conceive no useful
object to the world in spending money and energy in preserving a decadent
and dying race, which is perfectly useless from any point of view, merely to
enable a few theorists to carry out anthropological investigations and make
money by writing books which lead nowhere.

   Col. Charles F. Rey, Resident Commissioner, 1936

By no stretch of the imagination was Rey's reaction (BNA 1936a) to
the few initiatives to alleviate the plight of "Bushmen" that followed
the Tagart Report representative of majority opinion among British
administrators, no matter how much most of them wished to get the
"Bushmen" off their backs. Many realized the necessity for at least a
show of equality of opportunity for San-speaking peoples and an official end to serfdom, perhaps mainly to present a favorable image of
empire to the world, but also out of a sense of fair play. To the high
commissioner (BNA 1936b), "it seemed a little cold-blooded to ac-
quiesce merely and indeed to facilitate their [Bushman] extinction."
Rey replied, "I did not see what we could do about it." At the same
time, policy direction required a close definition of the units being administered. Yet even in this self-serving atmosphere, as Gadibolae
(1985 : 28) has remarked, "there was a discrepancy between the policy
on paper and practice."

   The net effect of government proclamations defining free conditions
of "Bushman" life and labor was to reinforce existing disfranchised
"Bushman" status. This came about partly through the administration's neglect of its own directives, but more through inconsistent,
sometimes contradictory, measures aimed at turning "Bushmen" into
a kind of peasantized labor force (Gadibolae 1985 : 30). This, of course,
meshed very well with long-standing Tswana policy. Among Batswana,
as we have seen, only those San-speakers who were at any moment
surplus to immediate labor needs were considered useless; the rest
were valued as an indispensable subservient labor source. Had this not

been so, the question of serfdom would never have arisen. But the policy of indirect rule never contemplated taking administrative control of minorities out of the hands of Tswana chiefs. Consequently, the continued subjugation of these peoples was guaranteed.

Rey's blatantly racist outburst thus brings sharply into focus the nadir to which relations among categorized peoples had sunk at this time, when colonial authority lay heaviest upon them. Since Sir Charles (as Rey subsequently became in His Majesty's service) wrote, opinion in Botswana—both public and private—regarding Basarwa (as San-speakers are now called within the country) has improved considerably. Equality of rights of all citizens is protected without distinction in the country's constitution. Still, D. Kwele (RADW 1980:9–10), then assistant minister, local government and lands, found it necessary, in his opening address to the Remote Areas Development Workshop of 1980, to allude transparently to the ethnicity of remoteness—that is, of being "Bushman":[1]

Ensure that feudalism is relegated to its rightful place in the annals of history and not a daily embarrassment to the government of the day as well as to all normal thinking democratic-minded modern day Batswana. I need not delve in depth on this one for it is not unknown to anyone of us that Remote Area Dwellers are hardly treated as partners by fellow Batswana in everyday life. I wish Mr. Chairman at this point to remind everyone of us that labour should be reasonably rewarded, whatever form that labour may take, and that there are laws specifically meant for this, but I am afraid they continue to either discriminate against or disregard fellow Batswana referred to for our purposes here today as Remote Area Dwellers. The definition of Remote Area Dwellers is well known to all of you and it is therefore your duty to disseminate it to Botswana at large.

The issue is blurred along ethnic lines. For example, Lethlakane—with a large operating diamond mine and a well-developed service infrastructure on an excellent all-weather road, but with a significant resident "Bushman" component in its population—is officially designated a remote area, while Orapa—also with a diamond mine and similarly developed infrastructure about 25 kilometers farther down the same road but with no ethnic "Bushman" minority—is not. Furthermore, northern Kgatleng District, on the border of the Republic of South Africa, with resident "Bushmen" (few of whom are found in the rest of the district), is a tiny "remote" pocket in an otherwise standard rural area, even though it is adjacent to the main highway of Botswana served daily by several scheduled bus services between Gaborone and Francistown and is on the railroad line, with two daily passenger trains in each direction. A remote area development officer, K. Mara-kanyane (RADW 1978:34), speaking of his work in this district, re-marked that Basarwa there "are not very remote."

Clearly, remoteness has three dimensions: geography, economics, and ethnicity. Geographic distance is not even a necessary, let alone a sufficient, criterion of remote status. Equally important are ethnic dis-tance (with San-speakers being the most remote) and, to a lesser de-gree as defining variable but almost invariably as consequent factor, economic status. Thus some Batswana may be assigned to the remote category if they are sufficiently poor and far away from a town center. As the intersection of any two of these dimensions decreases from the (Tswana) norm, a designation of remoteness becomes more likely; in the intersection of all three stand San-speakers, who are generally con-ceived to be the most remote from Setswana society even if not from settled villages.

The Emergence of Ethnicity as a Central Logic

Two initially separate but ultimately converging processes combined to create these ethnic distinctions. The first lies on that trajectory of social relations with ancient roots in the region that we saw clearly in operation during the difaqane in the early nineteenth century, when a large proportion of southern Africa's peoples became realigned so-cially and politically. Marks (1982:10) has called attention to the manifest fluidity of political boundaries in the region at that time, when the objective of leaders and societies was to "secure a certain degree of control over people, followers, not units of wage labour. In this situation, amongst Africans ethnicity would appear to have been of relatively little significance." That is, historically constructed as-sumptions about individual and group identity associations were, in practice as well as in ideology, what Worsley (1984:242) has labeled "relative, situational categories." The spectacular growth of Sekgo-ma's and Sechele's merafe in mid-nineteenth century was accomplished by just such recruitment of followers (p. 98).

At the time there was no overarching Tswana category, only several independent polities whose chiefs were descendants of eponymous Tswana founders. Then Barwa/San was an economic epitaph, and group signification either followed self-designated usage or referred to a local leader, as with other peoples. We have seen how the consolida-tion of power in a few chiefly hands coincided with, and was in large measure stimulated by, the insertion of mercantile capital into the re-gion. It was as a consequence of struggles to control commodity production—that is, to control labor units—and to channel access of the resultant product to its market that "secondary rationalizations" (Worsley 1984:235) were invoked to first concretize ideologically then stigmatize in practice those groups that became progressively more disfranchised. In this atmosphere the native category Barwa (which in its root connotation of aboriginality was neutral, or perhaps positive) acquired negative ethnic connotations.[2] These connotations became reciprocally marked in symbolic ordering, with Barwa "Bushmen" increasingly consigned to a peripheral "wild, uncontrolled 'nature'" in Tswana ideology, while in much, but by no means all, San ideology Batswana took on the central attributes of overlordship.

The second process that brought about the ethnicization of San-speaking peoples was that "self-fulfilling . . . colonial prophecy that foretold the existence of 'tribes' and, through an administrative order, created what it could not discover" (Galaty 1982:1; Gutkind 1970). This was also essentially a labor process that relegated stigmatized peoples to lower echelons in the labor pool while insulating—through the legal structure erected by colonial administration—hegemonically higher strata from lower-echelon competition. Official policy "announced that if Basarwa were allowed to leave their masters they should do so only in a recognized and controlled manner" (Gadibolae 1985:28).

The resultant constructed ethnicities rarely conformed to a people's prior self-identification (cf. Wolf 1982:380–81); for example, all ten mutually unintelligible San languages spoken in the Kalahari region were lumped undifferentially by Setswana under a single term, Sesarwa—the language of Bushmen—while the speakers of these languages became undifferentially labeled Basarwa.[3] Jones and Hill-Burnett (1982:218) argue that it is just this homogeneous treatment of diverse peoples that brings about the formative stage of ethnicity. This categorization process remains in practice in Botswana today.

The cumulative effect of these congruent processes was to consolidate a generalized ethnic inequality inserted into precolonially existing structures of inequality. These preexisting structures were overridden when local group autonomy was subverted by the stereotyping recategorization that was a salient feature of Tswana hegemonic consolidation begun with the kgamelo system. As Cooper (1977:4) remarks, "this itself reflects the ethnio-politico 'state formation' [of the Tswana polity]." "Such ethnicities are therefore not 'primordial' social relationships. They are historical products of labor market segmentation under the capitalist mode" (Wolf 1982:381).

Some examples will illuminate the process that perpetuates this segmentation. The first is taken from Worby (n.d.: 46). In 1977 a Mosarwa man (whose group of origin is unidentified) employed by a Motswana in that part of Kgatleng District designated remote applied to the subdistrict land board for a field to plow; after questioning by the kgosi and land board chairman designed to undermine his credibility, he was told, "As you are not a Mokgatla you cannot be allocated land in Kgatleng District."[4] Now, one of the first pieces of legislation passed by newly independent Botswana, the Land Act of 1968, forbids "tribal" injections into land board deliberations; this is intended to make land democratically available to all. If land is available and an applicant appears capable of husbanding it, he is to be granted registry regardless of his place of origin within the country.

In the case described by Worby, the land board resorted to dubious measures to discourage—but not go so far as to deny—an application from a stigmatized class cum ethnic person in order to safeguard increasingly scarce Kgatleng land for a more centrally perceived Kgatla constituency. It is clear, therefore, as Hitchcock (1978, 1:110) remarks concerning a similar series of cases in Central District, "that without reference to the ethnic composition of the region it would be impossible to understand the composition of the land tenure system." Earlier, Syson (1973) had noted that land allocation continues to follow the precolonial pattern of land control. Cooper (1980b:130) points to the mutually reinforcing nature of this practice in which established social divisions are partly reproduced because land allocations based on them are continually partly reproduced. Roberts (1982: 118, 129) cautions, however, that precolonial forms are only partly reproduced and that a gradual privatizing of interests in land predates the Tribal Grazing Land Policy (TGLP) of 1975 and has been a feature of land transfers since the 1930s; Peters (1984) details this process in Kgatleng. This process has allowed the same ascendant aristocracy to retain almost all the benefits it has arrogated to itself since the nineteenth century at the expense of the rural poor, among whom ethnic minorities are now doubly dispossessed.

Motzafi-Haller (1987) goes into considerable detail to document a similar perpetuation of advantage accruing to historically sanctioned elites in nearby Botswapo in Central District (as Gangwato is now called). There, however, it is not San-speaking peoples but Setswana-speaking Batswapo (Bapedi, Bakaa, and other minorities) who are disadvantaged. Earlier she documented (Motzafi 1986) a three-generation reproduction of socially isolated and economically depressed Sarwa households at Tamasane in eastern Central District. All but two of these households are female headed. This has come about because adolescent and adult Sarwa males are forced to seek labor opportunities in the only places available to them, almost invariably at distant cattleposts. Sarwa men are rarely present in the village, and the women say of themselves, "we are born alone," that is, without men.

Consequently, these women are vulnerable to the demands of other men (Motzafi-Haller lists eight "ethnic" identities among those at Tamasane), who father their children but seldom acknowledge or support either the mothers or their progeny. There is only one instance of "marriage" and another of bonyatse (a Tswana form of visitor-spouse relationship) among the nineteen adult Sarwa women in the village.[5] Motzafi (1986:308–9) records that, with the exception of these two cases plus five others no longer in the community, the children of all nineteen women are "fatherless" in the sense of having no social or material link to their paternal families. These are acted-out instances of the saying, "Mosarwa ke yo motonanyana yo monamagadi ke Mongwato":"The real Bushman is the male one; the female one is a Mongwato" (Gadibolae 1985:26). What is meant here is that sexual pollution is not part of the stigma of female lower social class; on the contrary, Tswana (and other) men are granted cost-free access to still another service of the submerged class. The result is a truncated Sarwa household development cycle that reproduces social marginality, with its attendant economic poverty coupled with stigmatized group identification. In the process the unserviced, voiceless labor pool is kept full and available at little cost to the ruling class, which thus reproduces itself—in both dimensions of the term.

To a large degree these conditions of class poverty are shared with poor Batswana irrespective of ethnic labeling. Ethnicity merely functions as one of a constellation of markers to assign class status to individuals. But these ethnic categorizations are today, as in the past, neither homogeneous nor immutable, and as earlier, they mask underlying class conflicts. On the negative side, those CaeCae children with itinerant Tswana fathers who were recently born to disadvantaged Zhu women face a probable Sarwa future parallel to that experienced by the current generation of Tamasane Basarwa. On the other side, the children of those CaeCae Zhu women who have married Tawana and Mbanderu men will likely escape both Sarwa ethnic and underclass stigma and take on the identity of their paternal (Tawana and Mbanderu) groups;[6] Silberbauer (1965:128) found cases of this form of identity transferral during his 1959 survey. The members of CaeCae nqorekau homesteads will probably continue to wear Zhu (but not Sarwa) identity as an emblem of pride, as they do today. These people have already escaped underclass status with its subservience; indeed, through the chairmanship of Ssao, they have gained a foothold in the administrative hierarchy.[7] Barring economic catastrophe, they will, perhaps in the next generation, gain a place among the rural bourgeoisie of Botswana.

Nor are CaeCae nqorekausi the first San-speakers to make this transition. Cashdan (1986:313–14) says of the Bateti (Remember those Botletli from whom Sebetwane twice restocked his raid-depleted herds in the early nineteenth century?): "The Bateti are today wealthy cattle owners" who employ Lake Xau Basarwa as herders on the same terms as do their Kalanga and Tswana neighbors. Bateti also give out to the Lake Xau people, who are generally poor and own few cattle, nearly half the animals the latter keep in mafisa. In keeping with their wealth, Bateti "do not like to speak of themselves as Basarwa" (Cashdan 1986:312), and a Mokalanga told Cashdan that they become angry if called Basarwa by others. He added significantly, "The Bateti are only rich because they had land." Joyce (BNA 1938:15) did not include Bateti among the "Bushmen" of his survey because he said that economically they could not be distinguished from their Tswana and Kalanga neighbors, though "in appearance and language they were Masarwa."

Zhu also do not refer to themselves as Basarwa, except when they decry their downtrodden state. This denial of "Bushman" status has historical depth. Every Zhu and Mbanderu person with whom I have discussed the matter rejects the notion that Zhu are now, or ever have been, Ovatua ("Bushmen"); such people are impoverished and are to be found far to the west and south. Zhu have always been people of substance and status, Ovakuruha ("aborigines"/"ancestors"); recall that Marshall in the 1950s and Carl Hugo Hahn a century earlier recorded this Herero term for Zhu.

As class interests of the peoples labeled Basarwa/San become more explicitly aligned with those of others of Botswana's rural poor, these ethnic labels are likely to become submerged and ultimately replaced by self-designated terms that are more meaningful to the bearers. It is not possible to predict how these terms may be selected, but the process can already be observed. Cashdan and Chasko (n.d.:1) reported to the then-named Basarwa Development Office: "The ethnic status of these Bakgalagadi [in the eastern Central Kalahari Reserve] is not clear-cut. While the Bakgalagadi distinguish themselves from the Bushmen who live in the same area, they refer to all the inhabitants of the area, including themselves, as G‖anakwe." (These are the Gxanna "San" who have appeared regularly in this narrative; recall that John Moffat said of central Kalahari "Bushmen" that "their appearance, their walk and their language at once mark them out as Bakhala-hardi.") Also recall that Esch found that marriage creates close ties between Basarwa and Bakgalagadi in Kweneng. In a subsequent investigation of "the needs and aspirations" of the peoples of the entire reserve, English et al. (1980:8) found "that today there does appear to be a definite Central Kalahari identity that transcends ethnic origins. . . . This is not to suggest that there is now no cultural differentiation between groups but that ethnicity has at least overtly taken second place to a shared common plight." Sheller (1977) alludes to this as well. Childers (1976:25), however, finds strong Bangologa animosity toward Nharo and Zhu on the Ghanzi farms. On the other hand, he found that marriage between Herero men and Zhu women was not uncommon, and that congenial relations between these peoples were expressed in the saying, "We can drink together from the same cup."

At a meeting held at my shutco in 1975 to discuss plans for drilling boreholes in the vicinity of CaeCae and to draw up a petition to the district council for a school, speaker after speaker affirmed, "Yes, we here are both Zhu and Mbanderu, but we are all CaeCae people." Although this declaration rhetorically overlooks the fact that at CaeCae some people are more equal than others, the speakers made it clear that any government development scheme would have to serve them as a group, not as fragmented units. This is neither some newly discovered altruism on the part of advantaged CaeCae people nor a residual, aboriginal egalitarianism, but the current expression, in terms of perceived present political realities, of attempts to redefine their social order; it also reflects a growing awareness of the value of a united front in negotiations with the district council.

Zhu, Mbanderu, and Tawana will doubtless remain significant terms in the construction of individual identities for a long time to come, but among the emerging bourgeoisie identification as a member of CaeCae community is already taking precedence over ethnic specification. Although there is a current trend—on the part of CaeCae nqorekausi—to reinforce land entitlement criteria in marriage negotiations as a means to further consolidate control of local conditions of production, as this transformation in identity construction matures it is probable that other assets will become equally sought after. For example, should one of Tcomazho's homestead 9 sons secure a permanent wage-paying job in a town (say as gardener or as guide in a Maun safari camp), he might well find that homestead 1–2–3 people could then "remember" a generation 7 connection to him in order to clear the way to a proper marriage, should he wish to negotiate one.

An appreciation of this dynamic flux in identity construction is essential to a prescient understanding of Kalahari relations of production as they have been historically formulated and are realized today. A situational understanding that assumes the sort of cafeteria model, to use Worsley's (1984:246) scathing term, in which individuals are served-up in preestablished order, is incapable of grasping the dynamics of practices in a social formation structured by class. Yellen (1985, n.d.) has recently reiterated just such a model for the Kalahari and, not surprisingly, is at a loss when confronted by persons who refuse to call themselves Sarwa.

The intersection of ethnicity and class in the Kalahari lies in the creation of what Wolf (1982:380) has called "a 'disposable mass' of laborers out of diverse populations." In this creation, the basic relation between capital and labor is reproduced at the same time that the heterogeneity of labor sources is reinforced. This is accomplished "by ordering the groups and categories of laborers hierarchically with respect to one another, and by continuously producing and re-creating symbolically marked 'cultural' distinctions among them" (Wolf 1982: 380). It was in just this intersection that native and colonial European concepts of ethnic divisions converged to create the class structure found in the Kalahari today.

A brief recourse to redundancy will refresh memories on the history of bushmanizing terminology traced at the beginning of this book. Recall that the extended sense of Bushman, Barwa, and San applied as undifferentiated category labels to peoples of many different languages and social allegiances has a history of just more than a century and a half. Previously, native—and early European—usage was more restrictive, applied to specific groups practicing various forms of lifeways that, though not initially so, became progressively more stigmatized. Nowhere was it used in a generic sense of community self-reference. It is worth repeating Parkington: "It seems certain too that Harry did not intend the word *Soaqua* [San] to have been capitalized, in the sense of referring to named communities, but meant it as a reference to a particular, and widespread, life-style. Soaqua seems not to be a word of equivalent status to Namaqua [Nama]" (Parkington 1984:158). In similar vein, Elphick (1977) traces "Bushman" to Dutch *Bossiesman*, which meant any number of ways of making a living, not the name of any people.

As an ethnic label, Bushman/Basarwa/San, alone or in combination, has a history of barely half a century. I have traced the colonial policy, applied between the two world wars, of deliberate "retribalization," with its system of indirect control in the hands of "traditional" African authorities and its emphasis on ethnic and cultural separatism.

The anthropology of this period codified this collective separatism of "all the Bushmen in their native condition" (Schapera 1930:75) and was intended, in Schapera's words, to provide the scientific tools with which "the administrator, the missionary, the economist, and the educationist, each in his own way now moulding the life of the Native into conformity with the standards of European civilization," could proceed. Native African, administrative, and anthropological interests converged to create a monolithic "Bushman" image and persuaded the creators that the image was real.

Accounts that ignore this convergence and that "have taken ethnicity as an artifact of precolonial tribal structures have been little more than pseudohistories" (O'Brien 1986:905) of the sort we have come to expect of ethnographies of San-speaking peoples. Yellen (1985) carries this thinking to its logical conclusion, predicting the imminent assimilation of Basarwa into an unproblematic, undifferentiated Setswana metabeing. This thinking is the intellectual residue of a disarticulated conception of the social world, a logical inversion of the notion that in the past people interacted through segregated channels. In this scenario the future holds the ultimate segregation, achieved through social and biological elimination. "Such impoverishment of theory leaves us incapable of contending with the complex dynamics of modern ethnic processes, and of finally transcending the apologetic tribal atavism thesis that ascribes contemporary political fragmentation in African countries to the effects of primordial ethnic loyalties" (O'Brien 1986:906). The future foretold with such atavistic vision is as unlikely to be realized as the view of the past on which it is predicated has been exposed to be false.

Subordinate Tiers in the Labor Reserve

The study of labor migration in Botswana begun by Schapera (1947) continues in currently active investigations of the labor reserve concept and of the creation of labor reserves at both a subnational and a subcontinental level (Palmer and Parsons 1977; Kerven 1979a; Cooper 1979; Massey 1978; Parson 1979, 1980). I (Wilmsen 1982b) adopted this discourse to reveal that a multitiered system of reserves was required in the Bechuanaland Protectorate in order to free Tswana men from otherwise inescapable duties in domestic production and allow them to take advantage of cash income opportunities on the mines and farms of South Africa that were denied to others in the Protectorate. One subordinate tier in this system is the female-headed household, which is especially prevalent in the southern and eastern parts of the

country whence the greater proportion of migrant labor is drawn. Research is well advanced on such households, upon which falls the
major burden of reproducing labor migrants' social relations of production (Kerven 1979b; Cooper 1980b; Parson 1981; Izzard 1982). A
second subordinate tier is composed of ethnic minorities, among whom
San-speakers are prominent but hardly alone. The essential role of this
group in maintaining the labor system within Botswana is only now
coming to be appreciated.

A brief recapitulation of history is in order to set the discussion in
perspective. As we have seen, when Batswana entered what is now
Botswana, they began a slow process of disruption of indigenous land
tenure and economic production; the process operated simultaneously
along two interrelated trajectories. At first, coercive means were seldom available and were rarely needed to recruit autonomous, self-
sufficient foragers and pastroforagers into commodity production
through hunting ivory and feathers, while resident pastoralists were
apparently readily induced to take on the daily maintenance of Tswana
cattle. This transfer of livestock work to other groups by ruling Batswana took two forms. In one, cattle were taken to distant water
sources and left in the care of resident people; this seems to have been
a form of mafisa. Subsequently, young men and women were taken
from their homes and transported to established Tswana locations,
where they were used as herdboys, milkmaids, domestic servants, and
hunters. This transposition of labor appears to have initially been mutually agreed to and perhaps mutually useful. After a time, however, in
the southern part of the Protectorate, it often amounted to kidnap-
ping; in the northern areas it continued usually, but not exclusively, to
be included in labor negotiations.

The entire material relations of production of those persons displaced by force were thereby appropriated by their masters, as indeed
were substantial proportions of those displaced by negotiation—at
least while the latter were away from home. Those groups who were
retained at remote water sources—now effectively transformed into absentee cattleposts—were not, however, fully dispossessed of their previous relations to property. Tswana "ownership" and use of land was
layered upon these tenure systems already in place and added an economic product to those present indigenously, all of which continued to
be available at least to some degree. Parson (1980:6), citing Marx,
points out that the dissolution of persons to laborers in the employ of
others does not presuppose the disappearance of previous conditions
of property, but only entails transformations in their mode of existence. It was precisely this form of transformation that took place,

subverting autonomous social control to effective servitude. The initial stages of this process were completed in their essentials by the middle of the nineteenth century. Necessary to this process of subordination was an undermining of self-sufficiency; due not so much to a loss of indigenous productive capacity by the natural environment (although loss, particularly of animal species, did occur) as to a reorientation of relations of production stimulated by competition for favored positions in the only available labor market. That market—limited and exploitative as it was—provided the only means for acquiring investment capital and the exotic goods that were coming to be demanded and available in greater quantity at that time.

It is essential to pause here and remind ourselves of the processes by which particular class structures, with their attendant property and surplus extraction relations, were established in the region, initially in the institution of the kgamelo system. Through this, older forms of property relations were replaced by stronger suzerainty of Tswana royals and a new class structure that for the first time expanded the formerly bipartite royal/commoner division to include an intermediate administrator class and an underclass of malata, or serfs (Mautle 1986: 23). Whereas exchange relations between minorities and Batswana appear to have been reasonably balanced previously, from the second quarter of the nineteenth century direct force was increasingly applied to extract ever-larger levies of "ground rent" (in the form of tusks, feathers, hides, and livestock) from increasingly dispossessed San-speakers and other non-Tswana peoples. As part of this process, the mobility of minorities became a function of the wishes of Tswana administrators and masters, thereby preventing the growth of a free labor market that might have given minorities some advantage. In retrospect, it seems clear that the form subsequently taken by the labor reserve in the Protectorate during the twentieth century was conditioned by these earlier developments. The large economic differences found today between patron villages and remote-rural client settlements can be traced directly to this historically developed ecologic-ethnic pattern.

Thus there came into being a kind of propertyless class. A fraction of that class was not completely divorced from its property but was dispossessed from managing it in its own interest. The CaeCae nqore-kau homesteads, for example, and the Bateti did not lose entitlement to their lands but were, during the first half of this century, now tied to location in a new manner. They were no longer autonomous agents with administrative control over their place; rather, they had become servants responsible primarily for the interests of the minority that had dispossessed them. Most San-speakers, along with many Bakgalagadi, lost entitlement and were enserfed—most severely in those areas where, and at the time when, labor drain on the Protectorate was heaviest, in the southern and eastern reserves and between the two world wars. In places like western Ngamiland where labor pressures were not so heavy, dispossessed Zhu became clients rather than serfs.

The dependency of Batswana developed as the obverse of that of dispossessed minorities and was one over which they retained a large measure of control within their own political sphere while becoming, in their turn, subjugated to the labor needs of industrializing South Africa. Batswana—because they became dependent for their freedom of action, with regard to wage-labor opportunities, upon the enforced labor of others—had a vested interest in maintaining a system of labor control or at least deflecting its transformation into directions likely to be favorable to them.

Batswana imposed a straightforward form of native colonialism upon the indigenous peoples of the region by expropriating the productive capacity of their land as well as their labor and by pursuing a policy of relative underdevelopment of facilities for the subordinate majority. The transferred value for labor, usually in the form of payments in kind, was thus less than the cost to indigenous minority laborers of their social reproduction, forcing them deeper into varying degrees of serfdom or clientship. As we have seen, foraging offered an option to escape this dependency, but it was an incomplete one and not open to all.

The contradictions inherent in serfdom keyed to land-based relations of extraction came to a crisis with the opening of South African diamond and gold mines, with their demand for an ever-larger labor force. Serfdom—in its very essence—inhibited the creation of a labor reserve in the Protectorate. Serf ownership, like that of other forms of productive ownership, was concentrated in the hands of a few wealthy families who were mainly of the royal class. Most middle-level and commoner farmers were dependent entirely on kin-network labor, augmented at times by paid casual workers; they frequently were shorthanded. As Schapera (1947:119) stated, "Serfs remained permanently attached to their 'masters,' they were not free to work as and for whom they liked." This situation was tolerable so long as labor was primarily in local demand; there was enough slack in the system to keep things going. But when wide-scale commercial demands on labor, followed shortly by mining demands, grew as the nineteenth century neared its end, the system could not stretch to cover all needs. The direct control of serf mobility meant constriction of the industrial labor force. As Brenner (1976, 1985) points out, the restriction of labor mobility was a type of unequal exchange that had to be eliminated, and this could be done only through a change in the balance of class forces. It was in this atmosphere that Khama "freed" serfs.

"Once the European demand for Native labor developed, serfs began to desert from the cattleposts and make their way abroad" (Schapera 1947:119). "Abroad" was, however, not always very far away; Resident Commissioner Panzera (BNA 1903d) testified in 1903 that about 1,000 Basarwa were employed on the Ghanzi farms. Panzera's estimate may not have been far off; in 1975, Russell and Russell (1975: 87) counted 675 farm-employed Basarwa, and a year later Childers (1976:47) enumerated 679. This European demand exacerbated already-pressing Tswana demands as early as the late 1880s; for example, the missionary Wookey (BNA 1887; Mautle 1986) reported the forcible removal of Bakgalagadi and Basarwa children from their homes to be raised as servants. The court cases involving the confiscation by Tswana men of San children and their mothers (p. 181, 338) are to be understood in this light; it was not children (or their parents) as such that were at issue, but their labor potential.

The situation reached its lowest point in the 1920s and 1930s—just how low may be seen in some available data (Wilmsen 1986:419–22). In his 1936 survey, Joyce counted 3,092 adult San-speaking men (excluding Bateti) in Central District and noted that the census register for that year listed 486 cattle owned by them. He remarked on the difficulty of obtaining accurate information on stockownership from anyone in Botswana (on the well-founded grounds that tax collectors often received this information) and estimated, therefore, that this number represented no more than about a quarter of Sarwa-owned cattle at that time. Using only the actual numbers recorded and assuming (on the basis of an age distribution of fifteen to sixty-five years) that two-thirds of the men were heads of households, we obtain a crude estimate of about 0.2 head of cattle per Sarwa household.[8] Joyce recorded individual Sarwa ownership of as many as 40 head, but his data also reveal that fewer than 10% of all Sarwa households owned any cattle at all. In comparison, Schapera (1938) found an average of 10 head per household on the Tlokwa Reserve, with 43% of all households owning at least one animal. Although these figures are limited, they do show that San cattle ownership, while surely not high, was not entirely nonexistent in 1936.[9]

These figures may be compared with those reported a decade later from the same district, when a total of only 98 head (0.01 per household) were reportedly owned by San-speakers. Almost all of this reduction took place in the 1930s and was intended to force those San-speakers who retained a degree of self-support into the labor market. The Molele and Mobusetse family removals as well as the other cases of coercion we have reviewed are examples of this effort.

Massey (1980:11) has stressed that, while there is no decisive record from which to argue that the imposition of a hut tax in 1899 was primarily intended to force labor migration to the South African mines, "colonial officials were well aware that the introduction of such a tax would necessitate such a movement." This was especially true after 1909, when the tax was doubled (to £1) and a heavy monetary fine (£5) for nonpayment was imposed. Tswana household heads found themselves in need of immediate cash, which the poorer among them could obtain only by migrating to jobs. At least part of their consequently absent domestic labor had to be replaced. As Parson (1984:25) observed, this "quickly created a pattern of oscillating migratory labor that touched almost all the people who lived in the protectorate." Thus began the transformation of the rural poor, among whom serfs and clients were among the very poorest, into what Parson (1981:240) has called a peasantariat, a proletarian industrial working class with a retained agricultural base (see also Kerven 1977, 1979b, and Cooper 1982). In this transformation Sarwa and Kgalagadi serfs, who had nothing to offer but their labor, increasingly found their place in this partly proletarianized agricultural base; they filled the homestead labor gap created by absent Tswana migrants. As a result, Joyce (BNA 1938:14) reported of western Central District, "There are hundreds of cattleposts at most of which Masarwa are found."

Force was sometimes necessary to keep them there. Tshekedi (BNA 1930) testified in the trial of a Mongwato accused of killing his runaway Sarwa serf that "Masarwa were deserting their lords and masters in Bangwato Reserve and finding work or squatting in Northeast District [Francistown]"; he said that Bangwato go on "slave hunting" tours to return them and sometimes kill them if they resist too much. Less harsh, perhaps, but at least equally effective was the decision taken ten years later to confiscate all Sarwa firearms in Central District, thus forcing the men to seek out work on cattleposts (Gadibolae 1985:29). These measures were taken because "all Tswana are agreed that migration [of labor to the mines and farms of South Africa] has led to deterioration in the herding of cattle, and that losses due to straying and neglect are far more numerous than before" (Schapera 1947:164; see also authors in National Migration Study). Hiring casual labor to replace men absent on the mines became "fairly common" for those who could afford to do so (Schapera 1947:178). Kerven (1979b:11–12) documents evidence that this practice continues today. The only peoples available to be hired in any numbers were Basarwa and Bakgalagadi; in large measure this is why they are to be found on almost every cattlepost in the region today, rather than only those of the wealthy. Ethnic minorities, San-speakers in particular, played a critical role in providing a second-tier labor pool, thereby releasing for labor migration Tswana men who would otherwise have been indispensable for immediate household production.

A major consequence of this historical development was that Tswana men were able to respond in large numbers to wage-labor opportunities on the South African mines and farms when these opportunities were made available to them. In Cooper's (1979:35) term, the structural transformation into a labor reserve was now complete. A look at some of the dimensions of this structure is revealing. Schapera (1947: 32, 222) tabulates the numbers of Protectorate men away from home on labor contracts for every year 1910–40 inclusive; there was an increase in 1925 of 48% over 1920, and in 1935 of 119% over 1930. The pressure on secondary labor sources was correspondingly intensified during these periods, and it is just in these years that court and kgotla records contain by far the highest proportion of all cases involving abuse of Sarwa labor; Stigand (BNA 1929) remarked near the middle of this period that all Masarwa had become sophisticated enough to appeal to British courts for relief from Tswana labor infringements.

Other statistics shed even more light on the processes at work. First, an unequal drain on the manpower of different sections of the Protectorate took place; Schapera (1947:34) found that, in 1943, 60% of taxpayers and 42% of all adult men in the southern and eastern districts were away on contracts, while only 12% and 8%, respectively, were away from the northern and western Tawana, Ghanzi, and Kgalagadi districts. Furthermore, 90% of all those men who were absent were fifteen to forty-four years old (Schapera 1947:40). These are the age cohorts most active in domestic production; their absence placed a severe strain on that production. It was also in those districts of highest labor demand that the most sustained and severe abuses of Basarwa and Bakgalagadi were reported[10] Finally, there were different forms of opportunities; from the south and east, only 8% of migrants went to jobs within the Protectorate, while 30% of those from the north and west (where Basarwa made up 20% or more of the population) did so. Schapera (1947:40–41) says of the latter, "Most are employed as herdsmen, etc. by farmers and traders in adjoining districts." In other words, San-speakers along with Bakgalagadi were filling in for labor lost to migration from southern and eastern districts to South Africa.

Increasing demands for mine and agricultural labor in South Africa brought about changes in recruitment practices during the 1940s; now even remote cattleposts were routinely canvassed by recruiters, and for the first time Basarwa were specifically sought out. Taylor (1978 : 108 – 10) quotes a Native Recruitment Corporation agent as saying, in 1955, "Exploitation of Bushman potential is the only likely way of increasing Crown Lands [mainly Kgalagadi District] output" of labor for South African farms and mines. By that time recruiters had been making regular trips to sandveld cattleposts for a decade. There continued to be a prohibition on recruiting "wild Bushmen," however, and the Native Recruiting Corporation was unwilling to leave the definition of "wild" to attesting officers, who received a commission on recruited men (BNA 1957:9). All recruitment of "Bushmen" was officially suspended for a time in 1957, but this does not seem to have had much effect on actual recruitment practice. British policy regarding such recruitment was sometimes couched in liberal development terms; in 1954 Forbes-Mackenzie, the resident commissioner (BNA 1960), echoed Tagart:

Unless the Bushmen were given the opportunity of developing side by side with the rest of the indigenous inhabitants they could hardly be expected to survive for any length of time. . . . the development of the Bushmen could only take place where they were able to acquire those material possessions (livestock, etc.) which are vitally necessary to the African in establishing himself in permanent self-supporting communities. To obtain these possessions the Bushman would have to be given the opportunity, in fact encouraged, to become a wage earner for at least part of his life.

Sandveld recruitment met with considerable success; in 1955 at least ninety-eight Basarwa were recruited from the remoter sections of Central and Kweneng districts alone (Taylor 1978:109). In some areas of the western districts, it seems that by 1958 as many as 50% of married Sarwa men were at times away on the mines (BNA 1958). Hitchcock's (1978:325) survey of 486 Kwa households at cattleposts in the western sandveld of Central District revealed that 45% of Kwa men had been on the mines. Lee (1979:416) estimates that 10% of the Zhu men he interviewed in the Dobe area had been on the mines, an estimate that agrees with my own finding (at CaeCae, none of these men were from nqorekau homesteads). All of these men went to the mines during this period of intensified recruiting in the late 1950s to early 1960s. Kerven (1979a:72−73) and Solway (1979) have noted that migrant labor had then become the major cash income producing option for all ethnic minority labor on cattleposts, not only Basarwa. The depletion of cattlepost labor became such that Tshekedi Khama and Kgari Sechele (the then-sitting Kwena kgosi) complained that too many "boys" were being taken away. Some of those "taken away" were indeed teenage Tswana boys; most others were Basarwa. All were herdsmen vital to the care of cattle.

From 1909 to Botswana independence in 1966, "British rule in Bechuanaland saw a transformation of the Protectorate into an element on the periphery of an economic system which had its centre in the Union of South Africa and was dominated by the interests of the mining industry" (Taylor 1978:111). British officials, perhaps unwittingly, maneuvered themselves into a symbiotic relationship with those interests. Parson (1984:114) has recently said of these developments, "The effective integration of Bechuanaland into the South African economy stripped the African society of Bechuanaland of its autonomy. Political relationships were frozen in a rigid colonial and tribal form." While this may be said of the decades 1910−60, it is too strong as a generalization; relationships were not forever frozen, however rigid colonial intentions may have been. Serfdom, and its mirror image "parasitism," in the emergent common Kalahari social formation has an antiquity of just over a century and a half, barely more than fifty years in its most severe colonial form. Its remaining vestiges in modern Botswana are being eliminated, although clientage continues in places and underclass disadvantage is deepening. From a San perspective, we have seen that these peoples were indeed subordinated, but we have also seen that this subordination did not occur automatically or uniformly throughout the region. Rather, it came about through episodic transformations in power relations involving political and economic struggles among many peoples, spanning centuries in an encompassing historical sense and decades in a more restricted colonial sense. Thus, in the political economy of the region—certainly for the past two centuries or so, arguably for much longer—we cannot reasonably speak of a social formation particular to any entity called San, or Tswana, or any subdivision of these. The material and social histories of the people involved are too inextricably intertwined for that.

Contemporary Relations of Production

The material and social lives of these people continue to be inextricably intertwined. To see how far this is so, let us examine data. Again,

CaeCae Zhu will serve as the paradigm for San-speakers; data for others of these peoples in other areas—because they are less detailed—will be interposed at appropriate points in the narrative. Data for Botswana as a whole are taken from a number of sources; chief among these are the Rural Income Distribution Survey of 1974–75 (RIDS), the fifth National Development Plan for 1979–85 (NDP5), the Remote Area Development Workshops of 1978–80 (RADW), and the National Migration Study of 1981–82 (NMS). Much of the following discussion is extracted from my contribution to NMS (Wilmsen 1982b:337–76).

Cash income received by all CaeCae homesteads and households during 1975–76 was listed in tables 6.12 and 6.13.[11] These tables reveal that the mean annual cash wage received from local sources by employed Zhu at CaeCae was P59 in 1975–76. Mean casual cash wage from external sources was P10.20 in these years; almost all of this increment of income came from me, and I made an effort to distribute it relatively evenly through the community. The average per capita cash wage income for all Zhu adults in the CaeCae community was P6 during 1975–76. This cannot be considered typical, since only 15% of the CaeCae Zhu labor force was locally employed (this rate, incidentally, compares favorably with that for all rural employable persons in Botswana as a whole).

Table 7.1 lists the average cash wage paid to Basarwa in other districts; from these data an unweighted average of about P5 is apparent as annual cash wage compensation for San-speaking peoples in the country as a whole.[12] Hitchcock (1978 1:27, 2:205–9) records that about 10% of Central District Kwa are employed, with an average annual cash wage per employed person in this district of P66; he notes that these laborers also receive payment in kind and that about half receive only compensation in kind. Schwatz (RADW 1978:97) estimates 6% employment on the Ghanzi farms, with an indicated average annual cash wage paid to employed San-speakers on the farms of P82. Childers (1976:47) gives P74 as the Ghanzi farms annual cash wage; two years later, Kjaer-Olsen (1978) calculated an almost identical P72. In comparatively wealthy Kgatleng, where Caye and Koitsiwe (1976:9) found an unusually high rate of Basarwa employment (76% of all household heads), just over half of employed Tsassi received a regular cash wage; this amounted to P5–P8 per month. Later, in this same district, Cooperman (1978) found the modal and mean Tsassi cash wage to be P7 per month, P84 for the year.

These data document clearly the homogeneity of payment for equivalent work that prevails over all that portion of Botswana classified as

Table 7.1. Basarwa Cash Wages in 1978, by District (Pula)

District	Average Wage	Range
Kgalagadi		
General	0	None given
Bere	6	5–8
Molopo farms	20	2–60
Ngamiland		
Sehitwa	4	0–6
Haina	6	3–11
Ghanzi farms	5	0–12
Ghanzi nonfarm	0	None given
Kgatleng	6	None given
Central	6	2–30

Source: RADW 1978:96–99.

remote. Indeed, overall San average annual cash income from local rural labor, at P5–P6, appears to fall just off the lower end of the range, P8–P16 per annum, for all the poorest rural workers in Botswana regardless of ethnic classification (NDP5 1980:22), thus underscoring the underclass conditions of local employment shared by all rural citizens of Botswana today. These figures have not changed significantly for perhaps a decade (as of 1981); the RIDS (1976:94–97) survey, estimates obtained by remote area development officers (RADW 1978; 96–99), and the NMS (Kerven 1982:526–626) all report similar figures. Jackson (1970:559) noted a mean annual income for agricultural laborers and herders of R90 [13] in 1969, but this includes the cash value of all receipts in kind (Native Labor Statistics, quoted in Jackson 1970:559). Gadibolae (1985:32) was told by informants that in the 1950s herders on Colonial Development Corporation (CDC) ranches north of Nata were paid R5 per month plus rations, but overall average annual rural income within the Protectorate in 1965 was estimated to be R28 (Native Labor Statistics, quoted in Jackson 1970: 560). Many Bangwato chose not to compete with high CDC wage scales and in consequence lost a substantial number of their Basarwa herders—who were no longer subjected to the same degree of coercion—to that labor market (Gadibolae 1985:30).

Income from craft sales realized by CaeCae people in 1975–76 was listed in table 6.13; estimates for the other districts are given in table 7.2. Mean sales income for CaeCae Zhu who sold anything was just over P11; since most persons sold something, the mean craft income distributed among all adult Zhu residents is reduced only slightly, to P10. The mean for San-speaking peoples in other districts was about

Table 7.2. Estimated Craft Sales of Remote Area Dwellers, 1978

District	Number of RADs	Sales Value (Pula)
Kgalagadi	2,870	8,860
Ghanzi	6,800	4,010
Northwest	2,450	47,810[a]
Southern	1,500	1,100
Central	4,360	8,050
Total	17,980	69,830
$\bar{X}$ = P3.90		

Source: RADW 1980:100. All figures are rounded.
[a] About 90% of this amount went to Mbukushu and Yei basketmakers in the Okavango Delta.

P4. By 1979 the world market for ostrich eggshell beads, glass beadwork, and exotic leather crafts had collapsed. As a result, Botswanacraft drastically curtailed its purchase of these items and in 1979–80 paid out a total of only P10,862 in all of the remote area, an average of less than P0.50/person/year (Egner 1981b:31). Prices offered at Cae-Cae in September 1979 were so low that people refused to sell, and the buyer did not return there at all in 1980.

Average annual per capita cash income from all sources (except kqadi sales, which I shall take up when I consider expenditures and cash flow) for CaeCae Zhu in 1975–76 is obtained by summing mean wage and craft sales receipts; this comes to P16 per adult. Undifferentiated household average was thus P32, while for households with a wage earner the average was P79.[14] For the rest of the remote areas, overall San per capita cash income from wages and crafts was P9 in the mid-1970s, with employed persons realizing between P64 in Central District and P86 on the Ghanzi farms. Thus, undifferentiated average household cash income in these areas was P18; for households with a wage earner the range was between P72 and P94. On the Molopo farms, the average annual wage per unskilled employed person was P110 on cattleposts and about P275 for agricultural labor (Wiley 1982:418). Both of these figures apply to people of several ethnic classifications, not just Basarwa; there are no figures for craft sales in this area.

RIDS attempted to estimate real rural income, recognizing that cash returns in themselves were inadequate indicators for this purpose. Accordingly, cash market values were determined for payments in kind and for foraged products; table 7.3 displays the calculations of these values for CaeCae Zhu households in a livestock economy (those in

Table 7.3. Income in Kind, CaeCae Zhu, 1975–76

A. Forager: Summary of Daily Consumption per Person (g)

	J	F	M	A	M	J	J	A	S	O	N	D
Vegetables	1,065	1,581	1,645	1,248	906	748	621	455	778	772	809	930
Meat	239	220	160	188	2	98	103	120	38	136	52	60
Milk	250	250	38									
Meal					60				8	8	8	38

Mean Daily Consumption (J–D/12) and Equivalent Cash Value

Vegetables	1,008 g	×	5t/kg	= 5t/day
Meat	118 g	×	60t/kg	= 8t/day
Milk	47 g	×	10t/kg	= 1t/day
Meal	8 g	×	11t/kg	= 1t/day

Total = 15t/day

365 days per year × 15t/day = P54 per annum

B. Pastoralist and Independent: Summary of Daily Consumption per Person (g)

	J	F	M	A	M	J	J	A	S	O	N	D
Vegetables	801	743	841	709	529	597	587	414	654	622	512	848
Meat	189	133	124	213	615	24	19	18	19	10	22	25
Milk	1,000	1,000	1,000	750	750	500	500	500	250	250	250	500
Meal	300	300					150	150	150	150	150	300

Mean Daily Consumption (J–D/12) and Equivalent Cash Value

Vegetables	655 g	×	5t/kg	= 3t/day
Meat	117 g	×	60t/kg	= 7t/day
Milk	604 g	×	10t/kg	= 6t/day
Meal	138 g	×	11t/kg	= 2t/day

Total = 18t/day

365 days per year × 18t/day = P65 per annum

Source: Prices from RIDS 1976.

Note: J–D heads refer to months of year, January–December; data are based on 20% random sample of all days in the year and calculated for adult equivalents (children counted as one-half adult). P = pula; t = thebe (100t = 1P).

homesteads 1–2–3) and for households in a foraging or reliant economy (those in homesteads 6–7–8–9) in 1975–76. Data for all households in 1979–80 were obtained but are not used here.[15] Per capita income in kind for adults in homestead 1–2–3 households had a calculated value of P65 per annum in 1975–76; for adults in homestead 6–7–8–9 households that value was P54. These per capita values multiplied by three yield the standard household value; the results are P195 and P162, respectively. Thus, in those years average total income in cash and kind from all sources for CaeCae Zhu pastoral and independent households was P274, 70% of that being in kind. The comparable mean for foragers and reliant households was P182, 85% being in kind.[16] For Ghanzi farm labor households, the annual mean was P289, 65% in kind (Childers 1976:49, 52). Hitchcock does not calculate cash value of payments in kind in Central District, but the average appears to fall within the range above.

These figures may be compared with statistics compiled by RIDS and utilized in NDP5 (1980). Average annual value income in 1974–75 for the lowest tenth percentile of rural households throughout Botswana was P160; 70% of this was in kind, and 25% came from foraging (RIDS 1976:102). For lower-middle-income rural households, average value income was P430; 50% was in kind, about 12% from foraging.[17] RIDS (1976:76) set median annual rural household income for 1974 at R630. NDP5 (1980:20) assigned an average 1978 gross domestic product (GDP) share per capita of P420 for the country as a whole but noted that this figure would be about 40% lower (P252) in 1974 because of ensuing inflation; this implies an average household income of about P1,008 within all sectors of the country, rural and urban, in 1974. Thus most San-speakers fell within the lowest 5%, and the most fortunate just escaped the lowest 10% of income levels in Botswana.

To a great extent these calculations are simply a laborious game concealing the raw truth of deprivation. The vast majority of San-speaking Basarwa in areas not so fortunate as CaeCae fall well below the means just given, a fate they share with an equal or greater number of remote area dwellers of other ethnic codification. RIDS (1976: 211–13) calculates a poverty datum line (PDL) income for the standard rural household of five persons to be P555 per annum. That was, in 1974, the minimum amount of cash plus cash equivalency necessary to maintain an average rural family of five persons on what RIDS defined as a modest but adequate standard of living. Even the most well-off Zhu households at CaeCae—those that have entered the cattle economy and have a local-wage earner—fall well below this mark;

the estimated mean household income for this group is 50% below the PDL minimum needed to avoid poverty. CaeCae forager and reliant households realize at best only 33% of PDL needs. Other San-speaking Basarwa are not even as well off as this, a distinction they share—along with a 90% to 94% local unemployment rate—with rural poor of other ethnic definitions. It is this shared deprivation that contributes the principal incentive for making ethnic identity of secondary importance to many members of this rural underclass. Add to this that employment growth rates in the unskilled formal sector of the national economy are projected at 7% per annum, with little of this growth to be realized in the rural sector (NDP5 1980:35), and one needs little further arithmetic to grasp the scope of the problem.

That small economic growth in the rural sector "will directly benefit only those households already engaged in livestock"; for the rest of the rural population, prospects for improvement in their living standard are "based on optimistic assumptions," and the "decline of migrant opportunities is likely to affect poor households most" (NDP5 1980:45). Since 1974 South Africa has pursued a policy of increasing mine employment from its internal "Bantustans" and correspondingly decreasing its recruitment from neighboring countries. Cooper (1980a: 1) notes that this policy has already led to a 50% decrease in migrant labor from Botswana. This reduction has a compound effect; migrant wage-earning opportunities are directly cutoff, thereby curtailing replacement jobs on the former migrants' homesteads. RADs, at the end of this chain, have nothing to fill the void; this contributes directly to the "free" labor plight of persons in the position of Tcomazho's sons.

One of the important results of the 1974–75 RIDS survey of rural income is that within Botswana the distribution of cattle ownership is more skewed than is that of cash income (RIDS 1976:112). The Cae-Cae data presented in table 6.10 confirm that this is so for this community as well; these data are summarized here for convenience in reference to the following discussion. At CaeCae, thirty-five (66%) of all fifty-three Zhu households own no livestock other than a few donkeys; on the other extreme, six (11%) households own 64% (fifty-eight) of all Zhu cattle at this place. Mean number of cattle per Zhu household at CaeCae is 1.7; among cattle-owning households the mean is 5.1. Medians are, respectively, less than one and approximately four.

Information on stockkeeping by San-speaking peoples in other parts of the remote areas is not so detailed but is in agreement with the CaeCae data. In the western districts, Dikgale (RADW 1979:23) notes that a few Kqoo in Kgalagadi District have purchased small numbers of cattle, goats, and donkeys with money obtained from sales to Botswanacraft. Kqoo and Gcwi at Bere are reported to have over two hundred cattle (RADW 1979:34), which suggests that these people, with nearly two head per capita (and therefore an overall household average of about eight head), are now as a group the wealthiest cattle owners among peoples classified as Basarwa (excluding San-speaking Bateti from the category Basarwa). The Kqoo community at Kagcae also has a growing herd (RADW 1979:35), as does Dobe.[18] Childers (1976:58−62), in a survey of 236 of the approximately 990 San house-holds on the Ghanzi farms (these are not identified according to lin-guistic community—Zhu, Nharo, Gcwi, etc.), records that 56% (132) of his sample owned 1,290 goats, an average of 5.5 animals overall and 9.8 per owning household; 18 households owned over 20 goats each, and 3 had over 50. Of these same 236 households, 33 (14%) owned 185 cattle, for an overall average of 0.8 head and an average of 5.6 head per owning household. Two households owned over 20 head each, and 1 owned 57; among them, these 3 households owned slightly more than half (57%) of all San cattle on the farms. Ghanzi San stock-holding seems to have some generational depth; in his 1959 survey, Silberbauer (1965:128) found that "most Bushmen have their own herds of small stock and many also have cattle and even horses."

The vast majority of other San-speaking RADs own no cattle, and few possess small stock. In Kgatleng, while 39% of Tsassi own cattle (it is not clear if these are individuals or households), none own more than 5 head (Caye and Koitsiwe 1976:11). Cashdan (1984:461−62) reports an average of 3 head per owning Tshukhwe household on the Nata River; the average for all households is half that number or less. Hitchcock (1978, 1:280−83) found that over 76% of Kwa in Central District own neither cattle nor goats; he counted 379 cattle owned by 652 Kwa households for an overall household average of 0.6 head (1978, 2:173−204); 84 (12%) households owned all the cattle, with an average of 4.8 head per owning household. Two of these house-holds owned 30 head each (16% of the total). An additional 84 house-holds, for a total of 168 (24%), owned 816 goats; this is an average of 4.9 animals per owning household and 1.3 for all households. One household owned 50 goats, and 3 others owned 20 each (a total of 110, 13% of all goats). One of the households with 20 goats is also one of those with 30 cattle. English et al. (1980:24) recorded 221 households in the Central Kalahari Reserve; about 70% of these were Gcwi and Gxanna, and the remainder were Kgalagadi. These authors note that cattle are not normally kept year round in the Reserve, but goats are. Of the 221 households in their 1979 survey, 120 (54%)

owned no goats and 49 (22%) owned fewer than 5 each, but the remaining 24% owned more than 5 each. English et al. (1980:24) note, "This maldistribution takes on an ethnic look"; 72% of households without goats are San-speaking. Put another way, 66% of Gcwi and Gxanna households own no goats, while only 30% of Kgalagadi households are without these animals; most of the latter appear to be female headed. On the other hand, two of only three households holding more than 100 goats are headed by Gxanna men; one has 181 and the other 146 of these animals. These people are among those of whom Tanaka (1980:xi, 50) said, on the basis of his work that ended just five years earlier, that goats were a recent and relatively insignificant acquisition, "parasitic" on their Bakgalagadi neighbors. In contradistinction, Murray (1976:9) documents a generations-long and important history of these animals for the Gcwi and Gxanna in the Central Reserve area.

Compare these data with those accumulated by RIDS (1976:110–12), which show that 45% of all rural households in Botswana are without cattle. The Government of Botswana "constraints study" (GOB 1974) had an identical result, and NMS found that 55% of all rural households owned no cattle in 1981. Solway (1979) and Cooper (1980b:48–50) think these proportions may be too high, with Cooper "guesstimating" that 30% is closer to the true proportion of cattleless homesteads. RIDS data also indicate that the "median number of cattle owned among all rural households, including those who do not own any cattle," was 3 in 1974–75, while the median among owning households was 16. NMS determined a mean of 12 and a median of 12 cattle per owning household, with 56% of all households in its rural sample of Ngamiland having none. For the remainder of the rural areas of the country—except Chobe and Ghanzi districts, which were not sampled—the comparable figures are a mean of 19 and a median of 20, with 55% of all rural households owning no cattle in 1981. These data were obtained from locations most nearly like remote areas in conditions of life. Table 7.4 summarizes the distribution of cattle by numbers held per household for all sectors within Botswana.

By these measures, CaeCae Zhu are three to four times worse off in livestock ownership than is the rural sector of Botswana generally. Other San-speakers, those at Bere and also the Bateti, are substantially better off than this. By the same token, the vast majority of San-speaking peoples today are as economically depressed as they were a half-century ago. A pattern of San cattle ownership similar to that of rural Botswana as a whole is emerging: a third or fewer of the households in a language group own any cattle at all, and a handful, typically less

Table 7.4. Distribution of Cattle Owned by Rural Households, 1974

N/HH	HH	All	% HH	Total	% C
0	40,454	45.0	—	0	0.0
1	1,209	46.4	2.5	1	0.1
2	2,217	48.9	7.1	4.5	0.4
3–4	5,120	54.6	17.5	18.5	1.5
5–7	4,874	60.0	27.3	29	3.4
8–10	4,921	65.5	37.3	44	6.2
11–15	5,541	71.6	48.4	73	10.9
16–20	7,458	79.9	63.5	132.5	19.4
21–25	3,480	83.8	70.5	80	24.5
26–30	3,082	87.2	76.7	85	30.0
31–35	1,990	89.5	80.9	65.5	34.2
36–40	873	90.4	82.5	33.5	36.4
41–45	1,446	92.0	85.5 *	61	40.3
46–50	448	92.5	86.4	22	41.7
51–60	2,080	94.8	90.5	115.5	49.1
61–70	724	95.7	92.2	47.5	52.1
71–80	702	96.4	93.5	53	55.5
81–100	758	97.2	94.9	68.5	59.9
101–25	696	98.1	96.5	77	64.9
126–50	414	98.5	97.3	55.5	68.4
151–75	113	98.6	97.5	19	69.7
176–200	188	98.9	98.0	36	72.0
201–50	372	99.3	98.7	84	77.3
251–300	116	99.4	98.9	31.5	79.4
301–400	181	99.6	99.3	58	83.1
401–500	136	99.7	99.5	61	87.0
501–750	142	99.9	99.8	89.5	92.8
751–1,000	46	99.96	99.93	40.5	95.4
1,001–1,500	15	99.98	99.96	16	96.4
1,501+	22	100.0	100.0	56	100.0

Source: RIDS 1976:111.

Note: N/HH, number of cattle owned per household; HH, estimated number of rural households owning this many cattle; all, accumulated percentage of all rural households; % HH, accumulated percentage of rural households owning cattle; total, total number of cattle owned by all households in each interval; % C, accumulated percentage of cattle owned.

than 10%, own more than half of all the animals held by their group. These disparities in wealth distribution conform to the general situation in Botswana, where differential cattle ownership is the single most important factor in total household income (Colclough and Fallon 1983:143). Thus, economic disparities among San-speakers appear to be solidifying in a manner reminiscent of the rest of rural Botswana, and class distinctions are being correspondingly enhanced.

Egner (1981b:5) spelled out the imperative behind this process to the Presidential Commission on Economic Opportunity. The real rate of return on investment in cattle is higher than that on any other investment available to the average person in any sector of the economy. Those with the largest investments continue to try to expand their holdings, at the cost of further dislocating and eventually eliminating weaker and smaller holders. Zhu, and presumably the other San-speakers where they have established herds, are active within this arena and subject to its terms. There is no egalitarian impediment to their participating at the expense of their congenitors, any more than verbal advocacy of social justice inhibits attempts by Tswana elites to garner advantage for themselves.

But these things have been known before, even if the details have been hidden in comfortable statistics and academic rhetoric. NDP5, a very frank document, makes it all explicit: "At present the most productive employment opportunities are available only to a privileged minority; the work opportunities available to the remainder often offer people such a low return for effort that it is not worth their while to put in all the labour of which they are capable" (NDP5 1980:23); and, "Paradoxically, while there is a shortage of work for unskilled Batswana there is a dearth of trained and skilled people" (NDP5 1980: 43); so that, "Since income distribution is undoubtedly very unequal as in most developing countries, GDP per capita greatly overestimates the living standards of the typical Motswana" (NDP5 1980:43); and finally, "As might be expected, the poorer households receive only a small proportion of their income in cash. These households tend to be old people neglected by their families, Basarwa, or households where there is no supporting adult man" (NDP5 1980:45). For San-speaking Basarwa, who make up according to various estimates a third to a half of Botswana's poorest of the poor, now called Remote Area Dwellers, this is simply an echo of Tagart, of Joyce, of Forbes-Mackenzie, and of Gcaunqa, who said, "God made Zhu with fuck-all."

Value Flow in an Uncertain Cash Economy

Quantitative estimates of the consequences of the depressed income and competitive disadvantage documented in previous pages are the real constituents of assessments of the status of personal and social well-being currently experienced by San-speaking citizens of Botswana. Some of these consequences can be examined directly. Table 7.5 lists the categories of goods and the cash amounts expended on them for which all cash income available to CaeCae residents was allotted in 1975–76; these categories are those established by RIDS. Average expenditure by CaeCae Zhu for short-term durable goods, clothing, and personal care was P8 (rounded from P7.90). Expenditures in these cate-

Table 7.5. Cash Expenditures by CaeCae Zhu Residents, 1975–76 (Pula)

	January	April	July	October	Sum	%	Average per Person
Food	35	55	43	169	302	10	1.40
Clothing	245	151	220	255	871	30	4.00
Personal items	157	101	144	74	476	16	2.20
Durable goods	21	71	51	179	322	11	1.50
Kqadi sugar	42	13	29	33	117	4	.50
Kqadi	100	100	100	100	400	14	1.80
Livestock	0	230	220	0	450	15	2.00
Total	600	721	807	810	2,938		
Average per person	2.70	3.30	3.70	3.70	13.35		

Note: Expenditures categories are those of RIDS 1976:216–20; kqadi sugar is purchased to make kqadi beer for home consumption and sale. Expenditures exceed income because a proportion of income is circulated within the community (as debt repayment, loans, and such) and thus is available for expenditures by more than one person. Kqadi expenditures are for the preceding quarter.

gories represent 57% of total available cash. Compare these figures with those compiled by RIDS (1976:216–18), in which minimum annual cash requirement for one adult's needs for clothing, personal care, and short-term durable goods is calculated to have been P55 in 1974–75. Add to this an estimate for long-term durable goods (for example, increments for the eventual replacement of iron cooking pots) needed to supply the entire household of P7 per annum (RIDS 1976:220), and an annual minimum expenditure level for personal needs is set at approximately P56. It is important to note here that the discussion that follows these calculations in the RIDS document stresses that the "standard of living that results from Poverty Datum Line [calculations] is very harsh." These are minimum figures required to maintain a "very low standard of living." A desirable minimum cash expenditure to achieve a "humane living level" was set by RIDS at 150% of the level given above (RIDS 1976:221).

Thus, simply to maintain personal needs, an average yearly minimum cash expenditure might be set at P84 per individual. This figure makes no allowance for simple amenities (for example, RIDS excludes socks from basic needs and allots a single pair of underpants per year to a man; women are allowed four), not to mention investment in capital inventories. Yet that figure is nearly three times the total average annual cash income of most CaeCae Zhu *households,* not of the individuals in them. Zhu at CaeCae fall below this minimum "humane" PDL by a factor of ten; they were able to spend less than 10%

of the cash required to achieve minimum Botswana standards of personal maintenance.[19] They could, of course, have spent a greater proportion of their cash for such purposes, but even spending all their cash for personal needs would leave them 80% below PDL minimum.

It is remarkable that they did not make such expenditures but chose instead to allot 15% of disposable income to capital investment in the only way open to them, the purchase of livestock. An added component to this investment was derived by three members of homestead 3 from selling the meat of cattle they owned and butchered at Tshumqwe;[20] a large part of the profits realized were reinvested in cattle and horses in CaeCae. These investments contributed significantly to the increase in herd size realized by households able to make such investments.

Equally remarkable is that only 10% of cash expenditures went to the purchase of immediately consumable food.[21] The seasonal pattern of food purchase is apparent in table 7.5; food was bought mainly when needed—that is, when foraged food was scarce and milk production was low during September to December (fig. 7.1). Lee (1979: 440–41) speculates that time devoted to craft production cut into subsistence effort, to the detriment of food production; in other words, he

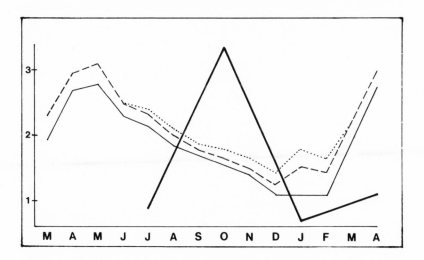

Figure 7.1. Expenditure for food (heavy continuous line) plotted against average daily caloric intake (light continuous line, calories from foraged foods; dashed line, caloric increment added by milk; dotted line, caloric increment added by maize meal). Vertical scale for foods in calories × 1,000, for expenditure in pula × 50; horizontal scale in months beginning with March 1975.

suggests that CaeCae Zhu were so eager to acquire cash that they allowed themselves to go hungry to get it. Furthermore, he attempts to argue that seasonal hunger at CaeCae is a function of a failed cash economy in the community, asserting that "by spending only R144 on store-bought food (less than 5 percent of their total income), the /Xai/ Xai !Kung could have compensated entirely for their lost weight and could have reduced their seasonal fluctuation to zero." Aside from being spurious (R144 would have bought about twenty servings of maize meal for each adult),[22] this assertion is incongruous—coming from a professed Marxist—for it lays the root cause of their predicament at no other place than on the shoulders of those who suffer.

But the blame is misplaced. CaeCae Zhu spent 56% of their total food expenditure in October and 68% during October through January combined; this was enough to purchase only 13% of their caloric requirement for this period (while their monthly average caloric shortfall was about 19%). A glance back at table 6.9 will reveal that 11% of pastoral and independent household calories came from purchased maize meal during October–January. Only 4% of forager calories came from this source even though their caloric shortfall became progressively greater during this period. By contrast, very little purchased food was eaten from March through June, the time of abundant local production (tea, coffee, and sugar were the main food purchases at this time). Clearly, budgetary planning took place. Equally clearly, pastoral-independent households were better able to compensate for production shortfalls than were foragers.

Lee, however, is not alone in finding Zhu unable to manage household budgets; Childers (1976:61) thinks that Ghanzi Sarwa farm laborers do not build up larger herds from animals given to them in payment for work because "the recipient is often too lazy or negligent to properly rear the animal." All the while this Sarwa laborer properly rears his employer's animals without negligence. These pronouncements played into the hands of the official view that "the unhappy state [of Basarwa] could not be laid at anyone else's door and was, to be blunt, their own fault" (Wily 1979:64).

These are dislocations of cause and effect that deflect attention from the underlying structure of rural poverty that Zhu—along with other San-speaking peoples—are struggling to transcend. As Gulbrandsen (1980:80) remarks, such stereotypical thinking explains nothing. The reasons behind the economic behavior of Zhu and Ghanzi persons— which Lee and Childers imply is less than optimum if not irrational— lie instead in each person's evaluation of the "subjective equilibrium between the disutility of labor drudgery and the utility derived from the returns to labour" (Haarland 1977). It is not a cash economy that has failed, certainly not Zhu management of their part of it. Rather, inequities in the overall political economy of Botswana reproduce the structural deprivation of a rural underclass deprived of a market for its labor, thus of the means of exchange necessary to achieve balanced household budgets. These inequities, themselves a modern legacy of the history of deprivation we have witnessed, have brought about current poverty at CaeCae and throughout those areas called remote.

The data on CaeCae expenditures document clearly that Zhu at this place dispose of their tiny incomes rationally and with considerable skill, belying the prevailing prejudice that assigns to them an ethnographic bewilderment when confronted by the present and an accompanying incapacity for managing more rapid incorporation into the national socioeconomic framework. These data, however, also imply deep frustrations; frustrations that are made explicit when one is speaking with Zhu. At present these people must spend disproportionate amounts to maintain barely tolerable standards of dress, comfort, and hygiene. They are forced to limit investment in longer-range security in favor of immediate needs. The next section condenses some of the consequences of these limitations for Zhu health and physical well-being.

The need to set priorities for expenditures and to defer desired investments is by no means restricted to the remote areas of Botswana, of course. But the government has announced its commitment to eliminating extremes in the terms for such decision making and to setting not minimum, or even simply humane, but equitable standards of living for all citizens. If this commitment is to be realized in tangible terms, significant changes in planning and implementation must be instituted.

The Political Economy of Physiology and Physique

The analyses of depressed income and competitive disadvantage that have so far been made express the social conditions of reproduction of the relations of production that now exist in the Kalahari. The extent of Zhu and other San-speaking peoples' deprivation has been exposed in the descriptions of income and livestock ownership inequalities already presented. Some of the immediate consequences of these inequalities, relative in the first instance to rural Botswana and then to the country as a whole, have also been documented. These relative consequences, however, are closely associated with absolute measures of deprivation, which are the real constituents of personal and social well-being.

Access to critical social measures, in terms of class conflicts over equitable shares of the gross domestic product (schooling, health care, transportation, and such), will be analyzed in the final section of this book. Personal measures are those that help determine physiological growth, development, and reproduction; of these, I will first consider diet and nutrition as they contribute to attainment of mature physique, body composition, and accomplished fertility.

Let us begin with a brief examination of conventional notions about Zhu and, more generally, San-speaking peoples' dietary adequacy. Lee (1979) appears to modify his (1969:47) earlier challenge to Truswell and Hansen (1968, 1976:190, 194), who concluded that "chronic or seasonal calorie insufficiency may be a major reason why San do not reach the same adult stature as most other people" and that a shortage of calories was a periodic weakness of their diet. Lee (1979:291) now concedes that the relative short stature of adult Zhu "probably indicates some degree of undernutrition in childhood and adolescence . . . [and that those Zhu] who have been raised on cattle posts on an essentially Bantu diet of milk and grains grow significantly taller" than do those on a foraging diet; he also recognizes (1979:308) seasonal variation both in the availability of food and in weight differentials.

Lee (1979:289–90), however, attributes this undernutrition and seasonal hunger not to objective conditions of Zhu existence—their productive capacities within a specific structure of social relations—but to subjective Western standards of observation. He repeatedly contrasts Zhu favorably with their Bantu-speaking coresidents as regards physique (1979:290), suggesting that "small body size and stature may be positively selected for in marginal environments." And he concludes (1979:437–38) that Zhu do in fact—despite juvenile undernutrition and seasonal hunger shared by all—enjoy "abundant food . . . sufficient to their needs." This is, of course, Sahlins's pristine affluence, albeit one of reduced needs rather than enhanced wants.

But let us look further. In contrast to this recent position, Lee's (1965:189–90) own initial conclusion was that in the lean months of the year, Zhu "must resort to increasingly arduous tactics in order to maintain a good diet. . . . it is during the three lean months of the year that Bushman life approaches the precarious conditions that have come to be associated with the hunting and gathering way of life." In what is probably the first recorded dissent from pristine ease, Marshall (1968:94) had this to say about the "original affluent society" when it was discovered during the Man the Hunter conference: "This is a *bon mot* but it does not add to understanding. . . . The !Kung we worked with are all very thin and . . . constantly expressed concern and anxiety about food."

Subsequently, several close observers of San peoples have made the same point. Harpending and Wandsnider (1980:16) are unequivocal: "Lee's (1968, 1969, 1979) studies of !Kung [Zhu] diet and caloric intake have generated a misleading belief among anthropologists and others that !Kung are well fed and under little or no nutritional stress." Tobias (1970:104) says flatly that "as nutritional level improves, San peoples grow taller, just as do other disadvantaged peoples of the world" (see also Tobias 1962, 1975). Konner and Shostak (1986:73) sum up neatly: "Data on !Kung fertility in relation to body fat, on seasonal weight loss in some bands, and on the slowing of infant growth after the first six months of life all suggested that the previously described abundance had definite limits. Data on morbidity and mortality, though not necessarily relevant to abundance, certainly made use of the term 'affluent' seem inappropriate."

Konner and Shostak (1986:72) make it very clear that all this is not simply in the eye of the observer: "Deprivation of material things, including food, was a general recollection [of Zhu adults], and the typical emotional tone in relation to it was one of frustration and anger." This same tone, with reference to the immediate present, was voiced to me many times: "Tcwi, ahe, ka se eqa; zjam za gu eqa":"Tcwi, you, look at us; thinness has taken us." Gcaunqa's God, who "made Zhu with fuck-all," stares down on all this.

Lee (1979:458) himself, after revealing to us that Zhu—despite all that he has said to the contrary—are indeed poor (1979:454), says that "when we are brought into closer contact with their daily concerns, we are alternatively moved to pity by their tales of hardship and repelled by their nagging demands for gifts." Here are hardship and begging, which Guenther (1980:137) also finds appalling. There seems to be some misplacement of trust in the abundance of nature (Remember Sahlins's easy primitive reality?); affluent, well-fed people seldom speak of dietary hardship, nor do they beg much. Mr. B. Mogome (RADW 1980:35), a Remote Area Development Officer who worked among Kqoo, spoke of these habits of begging found among San destitutes as the negative side of transformed relations between San minorities and Tswana elites. If it is the failure of a cash economy that has brought this about, that economy is itself the product of ideological practice that structures material existence and enters into the lived relations of individuals.

We can now turn to the effects this practice has on people's bodies.[23] Mean weights of CaeCae Zhu in 1968–69, 1975–76, and 1979–80 are given in table 7.6 and, along with parallel data for CaeCae Ovambanderu in 1975–76 and 1979–80, displayed in figure 7.2.[24] The first thing to notice about these data is that mean Zhu weight has

Table 7.6. Seasonal Mean Weight Fluctuations of Adult
CaeCae Zhu

Month/ Year	N	Mean	SD
Men			
4/68	20	48.9	5.36
7/68	22	50.2	5.17
10/68	30	50.2	5.55
12/68	29	48.6	4.93
4/69	15	48.8	4.73
4/75	27	49.7	4.23
6/75	26	50.8	4.54
10/75	38	49.9	4.53
12/75	41	48.9	4.78
2/76	40	49.1	4.21
4/76	32	50.6	4.94
6/79	35	50.7	4.93
9/79	36	49.6	5.24
12/79	37	50.6	5.40
2/80	35	50.7	5.05
5/80	38	50.6	5.00
Women			
4/68	17	37.7	4.75
7/68	19	37.9	4.87
10/68	21	39.1	5.02
12/68	23	38.3	5.27
4/69	15	39.1	5.38
4/75	25	36.9	4.18
6/75	24	38.1	4.25
10/75	32	37.6	5.17
12/75	33	38.3	6.28
2/76	33	38.4	5.46
4/76	27	38.4	6.03
6/79	38	40.6	6.42
9/79	38	40.1	6.48
12/79	38	40.1	6.86
2/80	36	40.5	7.01
5/80	42	40.4	6.72

Source: Data for 1968–69 based on individual values provided by
N. Howell and R. Lee.

a clear, constant seasonal periodicity, reaching its low point at the time
when food is minimally available and its high point coincident with
food abundance (tables 6.6, 6.7, 6.8, 6.9). In contrast, CaeCae Herero
weights are only negligibly lower during the hot, dry season. The second thing to notice is that this periodicity of Zhu seasonal weight fluctuation has remained constant during the decade over which it has

been systematically observed. The slight difference in the shape of the curves for 1968–69 and 1975–76 is well within the range of expectable annual variation. The difference in amplitudes of the curves, 3% overall variation between highest and lowest mean weights in 1968–69 and 6% in 1975–76, is attributable entirely to differences in attained highest mean weights during the observation periods. Maximum mean Zhu weight rose by approximately a kilogram or slightly more during

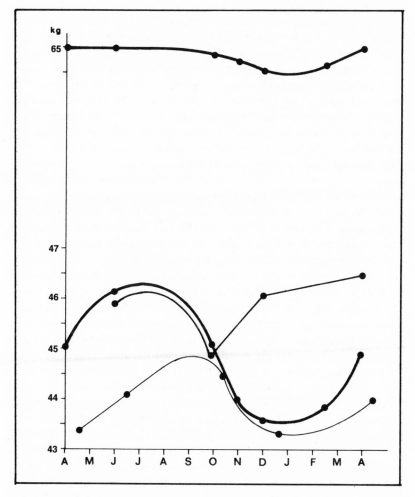

Figure 7.2. Mean adult weights. Lower curves pertain to Zhu, upper curve to Ovambanderu; light line, 1968–69, heavy lines, 1975–76, medium line, 1979–80; vertical scale in kilograms, horizontal scale in months beginning with April.

the seven years between Lee and Howell's observations in 1968–69 and my own in 1975–76; this appears to reflect the increased live-stock economy documented for this period. This higher maximum was maintained into 1979; recall also that mean weight, at all times, of in-dependent and pastoral Zhu is 10% greater than that of foragers.

Most dramatically, the data demonstrate the effect of food interven-tion and its implications for Zhu dietary adequacy. From mid-1979 a severe drought set in, and both wild and domestic foods were in ex-tremely short supply by September; at this time food-relief interven-tion was initiated by the government, and by late October refined carbohydrates (maize meal), CSM (corn-soy-milk; 85% maize meal combined with 10% soy flour and 5% milk powder), fats in the form of cooking oils, and government-purchased slaughter beef were over-abundant. Some families had stored reserves of 360 kilograms of maize meal and CSM. Zhu responded to this largesse by eating to satiety during a time of year when they normally expected to be hungry. The results are obvious in figure 7.2; mean weight rose rapidly from its normal September level to a point in November somewhat above pre-vious maxima and then began to level off. Mean annual Herero weight became constant, even though its former variation was hardly notice-able. Quite clearly, Zhu seasonal weight fluctuation (whether 3% as in 1968–69 or 6% as in 1975–76) is a function of food availability—in terms of the relations of access to realized production in the total so-cial formation—and nothing else. The apportionment of use of prod-ucts for consumption in the articulation of production relations lies, for Zhu no less than anyone else, in the class structure of the social formation in which they find their material existence.

The class-determined ability to respond to environmental perturba-tions in scarcity and abundance is distinctly expressed in that weight loss due to drought-inflicted scarcity is proportionately twice as great for foraging Zhu as for independent and pastoral Zhu. This is true for both men and women; Lee's (1979:295) data for women are of ex-actly the same order, although his data for men do not show the same tendency.[25] Lee (1979:304) does say, however, that eastern cattle-keeping Zhu (at Gqoshe) are heavier, "probably as a result of dietary changes." Midtriceps skin folds (table 7.7) display this differential even more clearly, and in this case it is obvious that independent and pastoral Zhu experience subcutaneous fat loss in relatively low pro-portions similar to those of Ovambanderu, while foraging Zhu are losing proportionally far more (as much as three or four times) than pastoralists. Foraging Zhu demonstrate this condition by pinching the skin of the upper arm between thumb and forefinger to give force to

Table 7.7. Mean Adult Triceps Skin-Fold Measurements
(mm), 1979

	June	September	% Change	February 1980
Zhu men				
Forager	5.9	5.0	15	
Pastoral	6.6	5.9	10	6.1
Zhu women				
Forager	12.4	10.7	14	
Pastoral	14.1	13.6	4	12.8
Mbanderu				
Men	8.7	7.9	9	8.1
Women	28.9	28.2	2	29.1

Note: February 1980 values include all Zhu.

their demand: "Look at us; thinness is taking us." In this regard it is cogent that foraging Zhu adults have weight-for-height ratios that are only 75% of those of local Bantu-speakers, while independent and pastoral Zhu ratios are 83% those of Bantu-speakers. While this higher ratio is brought about partly by increased adiposity (seen in greater skin-fold thickness), it probably also represents increased bone size (or density, or both) and greater muscle mass.

The same pattern is seen in blood chemistry. Serum cholesterol values in the forager stratum are low, while those of independents and pastoral strata are high, presumably because they ingest large quantities of saturated fats in milk (table 7.8). Steroid metabolism is also highly differentiated between the two groups, with foragers ($N = 17$) displaying very low mean values for testosterone (11.3 mg/100 ml) and estradiol (111.4 mg/100 ml) while independents and pastoral Zhu ($N = 60$) (and Ovambanderu) display values comparable to laboratory levels of these reproductive hormones in other populations (testosterone at 31.9 mg/100 ml, estradiol at 137.7 mg/100 ml). Seasonal changes in these parameters disappear with stabilization of diet. I shall take up the implications this difference has for fertility performance in a moment.[26]

This is not the place to argue the relative merits of short or tall stature, of lean or heavy body build, of low or high cholesterol levels, as has been done (Wilmsen 1985a cites the conflicting views of many of the adversaries as regards Zhu in this debate). The point is that, whether peoples are lean or fat, regular seasonal weight fluctuation—especially when accompanied by a regular flux in body chemistry—such as Zhu experience implies that periods of severe hunger are recurring features of life. Demonstrating that rapid seasonal gains and losses in body

Table 7.8. Mean Serum Cholesterol Values (mg/100ml)

	June	September	December	N
Forager	127	138	133	22
Pastoral and independent	200	225	181	14
All Zhu in 1979–80	183	—	165	38

composition disappear in the presence of regularly available adequate food provides compelling evidence that Zhu dietary needs and wants converge in a stable somatic image. That this convergence stabilizes at the former high point of their annual weight cycle rather than its mid-point shows that Zhu have had to contend more with scarcity than with abundance. These and other phenotypic expressions of deprivation—loose and inelastic skin beginning in late middle age, progressive vision impairment beginning about the same time, and a high rate of tuberculosis are the most obvious—distinguish foragers from pastoralists (Herero, Tswana, and Zhu), who only rarely suffer these afflictions.

That dietary and somatic differentials are disproportionately felt by some fractions of Zhu society underscores the internal class divisions of Zhu polity. That only certain ethnic minorities—Zhu, in our immediate interest, but also others of Botswana's rural ethnic poor, whether San-speaking or not—routinely experience these deprivations exposes the encompassing class structure of the overarching national social formation in which the structural conditions of disadvantage are imposed. I shall return to this, but first it is essential to pause for a glance at child growth, with its implications, as well as to note comparative data for the rest of Botswana's rural poor.

Truswell and Hansen (1976:178–80) devoted particular attention to child growth among Dobe-area Zhu. Their findings clearly show that, although Zhu neonates are comparable in weight to their Bantu counterparts (indeed, to American newborns), by the age of six months they have fallen significantly behind these other children. By six years of age Zhu children have attained only 63% of the weight of their Bantu counterparts, although they have achieved 86% of the height of these children. Thus the weight-for-height ratio of Zhu children is considerably below that of others in their age class and points to reduced rates of skeletal and muscular growth. Furthermore, Truswell and Hansen note that most Zhu children have subscapular skin-fold thicknesses below the fiftieth percentile of British children. They conclude (1976:178), "Low weight for height and thin skinfolds with normal serum albumins suggest an energy (calorie) deficit throughout the growing period which could reasonably account for eventual short stature in adults." They note further that during the season of food abundance growth returns to normal clinical expectations.

Truswell and Hansen had no prospective data by which to judge the validity of their conclusions. A twelve-year record of Dobe Zhu is now available, however, and Hausman (Hausman and Wilmsen 1985) has subjected it to rigorous analysis.[27] As a result (table 7.9), she has been able to show that food regimes that ameliorate seasonal fluctuation and caloric deprivation favor increased Zhu child growth—height, weight, and weight-for-height all increase—and that "San morphology achieves more of its genetic potential for growth" under these conditions. The greatest increase in growth performance was achieved by the youngest cohorts, who have had greatest access to a reexpanded pastoral economy as well as to drought-relief supplementation. Most especially, "The dramatic growth response of the girls may also suggest that nutritional equality did not exist with the traditional hunting and gathering economy" (Hausman and Wilmsen 1985:570). From these findings, Hausman predicts taller adult Zhu when the current in-

Table 7.9. Percentages of Children below the Fifth NCHS Percentile

Age Group (years)	1967–69				1975–76				1979–80			
	Height		Weight		Height		Weight		Height		Weight	
	N	%	N	%	N	%	N	%	N	%	N	%
1–4												
Boys	10	60.0	8	37.5	6	16.7	4	25.0	7	28.6	10	40.0
Girls	10	70.0	9	55.5	4	25.0	7	28.6	6	16.7	4	50.0
Total	20	65.0	17	47.0	10	20.0	11	27.3	13	23.1	14	42.8
5–9												
Boys	10	50.0	7	42.8	3	33.3	2	0	11	54.5	14	64.3
Girls	14	71.4	12	50.0	7	71.4	3	66.6	8	25.0	10	50.0
Total	24	62.5	19	47.4	10	60.0	5	40.0	19	42.1	24	58.3
10–16												
Boys	20	90.0	11	100	11	81.8	5	80.0	7	100	7	100
Girls	22	81.8	17	94.1	14	78.6	7	100	8	62.5	8	75.0
Total	42	85.7	28	92.8	25	80.0	12	91.6	15	80.0	15	86.6
Total												
Boys	40	72.5	26	65.4	20	55.0	11	45.0	25	60.0	31	64.5
Girls	46	76.1	38	71.0	25	68.0	17	64.7	22	36.4	22	59.1
Total	86	74.4	64	68.7	45	62.2	28	57.1	47	48.9	53	62.3

Note: Infants (one year old or less) are not included in height-for-age percentages; NCHS = National Center for Health Statistics.

Weights are average of April and October weights.

fant cohort reaches physiological maturity in about the year 2000. The extent to which this prediction is realized will depend on the degree to which dietary adequacy persists through the growth period of these children; for individuals among them, this will depend on their class-based differential access to a full diet.

All of this is not, of course, to argue that San morphology is entirely environmentally determined. There is genetic variation among San- and Bantu-speaking groups, although these can hardly be identified as separate gene pools (Nurse and Jenkins 1977). It is likely that this variation plays a role in shaping the realized physique of individuals. But we have seen in earlier chapters that the groups we segregate today as being distinct are themselves constructed by historical processes of political differentiation in altered relations of production. In these processes, individuals were recruited into different polities according to criteria structured by those relations and appropriate to the social formation in which they were realized at any particular moment. These criteria have as often as not ignored the biological attributes of persons—and indeed of entire polities—in favor of social attributes. And the visible somatic attributes of persons may not always have been so distinct; recall Andersson's stout, well-fed Zhu and Livingstone's six-foot-tall "Bushmen." Indeed, there is at least one Zhu man living on cattleposts in the Dobe area today who is six feet tall; Marshall (1957: 349) mentions another. It appears indisputable that we cannot blame the particular morphology of San peoples on the Kalahari Desert and that their growth achieves more of its genetic potential with improved diet (Tobias 1964, 1975). Nor does "available evidence entitle us to say that their small size is mainly determined genetically" (Truswell and Hansen 1976: 191). Rather, their bodies express their structural position as an ethnically encoded underclass in the political economy of the Kalahari. Today this position is revealed in the results of the National Nutrition Survey of 1978 (Kreysler 1978), which found that nationally 23% of children under five years old were below 80% of Botswana standard weight for age (note that this is an indigenous scale, not one from Harvard or London); the comparable figure for children in periurban slums was 33%, while 50% of remote rural dwellers (including two samples of Basarwa) fell into this "at risk" category. The class basis of physique could hardly be more sharply delineated (cf. Mushingeh, n.d.).

I will close this discussion of physiology with a very brief overview of Zhu demographic reproduction. Howell's (1976) work is the most careful consideration of this topic and should be consulted for its thorough coverage of its parameters. Others have contributed significant

Table 7.10. Age-Specific Fertility of Zhu Women in 1963–73 and 1976–80

Age Group (years)	f(a)		m(a)		f(a)/m(a)	
	1963–73	1976–80	1963–73	1976–80	1963–73	1976–80
15–19	.063	.179	.56	.50	.113	.358
20–24	.208	.263	.90	.82	.231	.321
25–29	.238	.325	1.00	.90	.238	.357
30–34	.183	.290	.94	1.00	.195	.290
35–39	.107	.280	.79	1.00	.135	.280
40–44	.043	0	1.00	1.00	.043	0
45–49	.013	0	.93	.94	.014	0
Total	.855	1.337			.969	1.644
TFR	4.275	6.685				

Source: 1963–73 entries from Howell 1976: 139, 234.
Note: f(a) = age-specific fertility rate; m(a) = proportion of women currently married; TFR = f(a) × 5, the total fertility rate.

analyses; Konner and Worthman (1980) present results of studies of lactation practices, Bentley (1985) investigates energy expenditure, and I consider dietary influence on hormone differentials (Wilmsen 1985a). All authors agree that both Zhu fecundity and realized fertility were unusually low in the recent past; completed fertility was about 4.5 live births per woman in what is loosely termed their traditional mode of foraging existence and becomes dramatically high, about 7 live births per woman, after adoption of agropastoralism and sedentary village life (table 7.10). Needless to say, as the bulk of this book stresses, the assumptions this division is based on can no longer be held, and the principal authors, as already quoted several times, recognize that this fact forces reevaluation of their earlier work.

The principal competing hypotheses that purport to describe and explain this charge in Zhu birthrate attempt either to relate body weight to fertility or to see fertility as controlled primarily by lactation. The body-weight hypothesis, however, actually addresses fecundity, and the lactation hypothesis addresses fecundability. Furthermore, as I have pointed out (Wilmsen 1985a: 72), both hypotheses, because their mechanisms are set ultimately in body composition, are subspecies of an encompassing body-composition model; the alterations in body chemistry described above are significant in this regard. I do not intend to repeat these arguments here, because our interests at this point are with realized fertility, to which I now turn.

As is apparent in figure 7.3, foraging Zhu women experience marked seasonality in births, with 36% of their children born nine months after their diet-induced peak weights are attained in July and August.

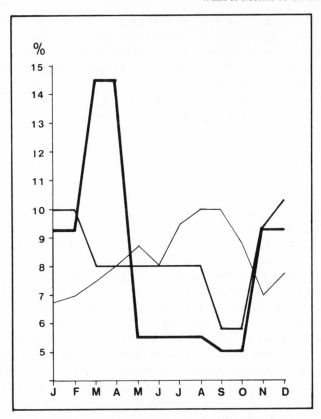

Figure 7.3. Percentage of all births to Zhu women occurring in each calendar month. Heavy line, births to women in a foraging economy (N = 127); medium line, births to women in agropastoral economies (N = 140); light line, comparative frequencies from Maun hospital records for 1953–80 (N = 7,113).

These women also have fewer children than do pastoral Zhu women, accounting for most of the very low completed fertility rate noted above. Independent and pastoral Zhu women, and all women in 1979–80, when food supplements were abundant, experience no such seasonality but give birth in more-or-less equal proportions throughout the year; in this they resemble Batswana women in general, as comparison with Maun hospital maternity records reveals. Independent and pastoral Zhu women also have much larger completed families, some with as many as nine surviving children, thus accounting for the very high current fertility rate. However these differences in realized fertility may eventually be explained biochemically, the transformation in family formation and reproduction is clearly associated with production and consumption of the products of labor and thus is a function of the political economy of the social formation in which it takes place. Zhu women have an intuitive understanding of this, for they say it is foolish "to catch a child" (become pregnant) when food is scarce and thinness takes them. They say that there is then a high probability of miscarriage, stillbirth, or early infant death.

The Direction of Intention

It is abundantly clear that Basarwa/"Bushmen"/San, no matter how distant in space, have never been historically remote from economic and social processes operating in the larger political entities of southern Africa but have functioned intimately within these processes. It is their relative position in a colonial hierarchical system—not their geographic or evolutionary distance—that makes them "remote" today. It is to the credit of all Batswana that they have renounced the validity of these historical impositions and have incorporated in their constitution the intent to redirect the course of subsequent development.

That intention is not called into question when we examine continuing discrepancies between its goal and the strategies employed to attain it—discrepancies between rhetoric and reality. Rather, such examination is essential in that it can clarify nostalgia for the positive values of the past through rational confrontation with the conditions of the present. Only in this way can those values form the basis for the future. In this regard it is important to recognize that the most pointed criticisms have come from within Botswana itself, as Minister Kwele's admonition at the opening of this chapter made clear. In an evaluation commissioned by the government of the Remote Area Development Programme, Egner (1981b:37–38) concludes that "the programme has to date had little or no impact upon its intended beneficiaries . . . because it has not yet secured substantial and coherent support at the national level" and has lukewarm support at best at all ministerial levels. Egner (1981b:5, 12) opened his evaluation with the observation that "such rights to land, water, and wages as RADs have gained since 1974 are by no means entrenched and could well prove to be ephemeral in the absence of the firm political support which will be needed in the next decade. . . . Until Basarwa are more fully integrated into the society and assured of their full political rights as citizens, as tribesmen and as employees their participation in many staged consultative exercises will remain something of a charade." Gadibolae (1985:30) ends his survey of colonial Bushman policy up to the time of independence with a pointed paraphrase of Sir Charles Rey: "The Government could not afford to spend money and energy on a useless, decadent, and dying race." Neither does Gadibolae exonerate subsequent policy, noting that in most respects at the end of the 1970s "Basarwa were still in the same position as they were in the 1920s."

Since the beginning of the postindependence planning process in Botswana, the government has realized that many of the problems facing the country are the result of previous colonial neglect; that essential heavy investment in urban centers during the immediate postcolonial period has created a marked disparity in living standards between urban and rural sectors that has led to social disorder; and that strong compensatory measures are necessary to right the balance. Among Botswana's principal planning objectives, social justice ranks high (NDP5 1980:61; RADW 1979:13). To realize this objective, Lipton (1978, 1:xvi) emphasizes that "a larger share of public sector resources [must be allocated] for *small villages, lands, and remote areas,* where the poorest live."

But little meaningful action has followed. Although national planning policy is repeatedly described as aiming to redirect investment from urban to rural areas and provide comparable amenities to the latter (NDP5 1980:61–62; RADW 1980:139), subsequent discussion has invariably led to the revelation that such declarations are largely rhetorical (NDP5 1980:90–91; RADW 1980:140–41). Even Hitchcock's (1978:11) modest proposal for "service centres" to cater to Basarwa needs in commercial areas met with little success. Parson (1981:252) says of this fallback position, "It is a comment on the strength of the movement toward dispossession that this solution had the effect of an assisted proletarianization rather than an argument for the retention of the means of production already held" by peoples on the verge of eviction from their lands.

Several weaknesses of RADP procedures that have hampered the program's effectiveness are readily apparent. First, people in the program have consistently worked from a set of assumptions about relations among person, land, and production in remote parts of Botswana that can provide no foundation for persuasive arguments. In other words, those who have been responsible for formulating and implementing policy toward Basarwa have relied on a functionalist equilibrium model derived from ethnography grafted onto a residual colonial construction of a static San social condition. These adopted assumptions preclude any demonstration of traditional San legal institutions for allocating land and regulating production relations that are comparable to those of other Batswana. I have shown these assumptions to be false.

Adopting these false assumptions forces the equally false view that any qualitatively original introduction into that assumed static "forager formation" (which I have argued has not been a fully independent social formation for more than a millennium) requires change in its processes of goal attainment, integration, and adaptation. Integrative mechanisms for incorporating such introduced features are defined to be absent from San social structures; without these, San peoples are incapable of transition to the higher levels of equilibrium progressively attained by the Tswana national polity. Relations with other peoples are shaped in this expectation of change, which because of the postulated stasis in San society, can only work to the detriment of the reproduction of San social relations and accounts for the disadvantaged position of San peoples today. This is the nineteenth-century view of "savages" that we saw at the beginning of this book and is the instrumental basis for the gradualist ideology that governs current Basarwa policy. It is an ideology that serves to solidify existing class structure and denies San expression of the class contradictions in which they are enmeshed. A key element in this ideology is the mystification of San uniqueness, a condition that Egner (1981b:12) rightly sees as having been imposed on them by other, hegemonically dominant ethnic groups. Among these hegemonically dominant groups—I urge that we not forget at this point—are ethnographers, whose work serves as scientific sanction for this mystification.

The resulting policy attitude rests in a notion that traditional institutions for cooperative endeavor are nonexistent among Basarwa; this supposed deficiency is then said to hinder development of those skills necessary for participating in the national present. Self-realizing interpolations of history are employed tautologically to justify this notion. It becomes both possible and comfortable to turn this attitude into a rationalization for limited, piecemeal, and conscience-easing policy by "letting the community determine its own rate"—a rate that is confidently projected to be slow. The prediction will be self-realized under low expenditure inputs and will serve as renewed justification for continued neglect. Its inevitable result is stagnation clothed in values that no longer are traditional but are pale reflections of invented tradition.

That reification of invented tradition is precisely the ground upon which gradualist policy toward San is founded. The Egner Report (1981a) called upon just those arguments to recommend significant scaling down of expenditures for ethnic minority programs because expected returns could not justify diversion of funds from more vocal Tswana constituencies. This recommendation (in an otherwise hard-hitting evaluation) was made despite the finding that "the prospects of meeting the basic social service needs of the smaller RAD communities (including an estimated 10,000 cattlepost residents) appear to be poor" (Egner 1981a:28). In these proceedings, distorted readings of anthropological abstractions and an ahistorical traditionalism are consciously employed to reinforce contemporary perpetuation of San dispossession. Guenther (1980:137) states the matter clearly: "Excessive emphasis of [an] overly abstract and idealized . . . image of Bushmen qua pristine innocent" jeopardizes the future of these peoples.

Kerven (1979:13) and Cooper (1982, n.d.:27) explode one facet of this mystification, that of the stereotyped Basarwa ambivalence toward wage work. They document that employment for the bulk of the rural poor labor force—not only those of Sarwa classification—is oscillatory and sporadic and that it is erroneous to speak of "a worker's full year-round employment in *one* job." In other words, so-called ambivalence about uncertain, underpaid employment is not a congenital ethnic trait but a function of the labor market in which all rural poor workers—irrespective of ethnicity—are captives. That ambivalence is, as Jones and Hill-Burnett (1982:236) insist, the result of "common treatment of a population, so defined, by the major institutions of power [and] is the most important source of the *common experience* all members of that population share." Mogome (RADW 1980:35) put it this way:

These groups have various relationships amongst themselves, some are social and some are economic, but whatever the case ethnicity plays an important role in determining one's socio-economic position and one's access to opportunities which can improve one's living conditions. Unfortunately the Basarwa and Balala (RADs) are not favoured by these relationships. They have come to take this as a way of life and in most cases will want to preserve it because they do not know what the future as pronounced by the programme has in stock for them. This presents a formidable challenge for the programme.

Koma (1984:114) has stated unequivocally that this situation will not change so long as dominated ethnic groups are denied access to equal education opportunities so that they can begin to participate as framers rather than followers of development programs. This denial of access to education is rationalized by rural poor parents as the fault of their children, who do not attend school because they are "not clever enough" (Case 1982:515; Kann 1984:91). Thus the common experience of deprivation is too often seen by ethnic minorities in Botswana as evidence that their condition—sometimes along with, sometimes separate from that of other rural poor—has objective validity.

Nonetheless, specific Zhu labor histories along with general narratives of other Sarwa wage labor that have featured prominently in earlier chapters are eloquent testimony that these peoples seek secure, compensated employment. One final anecdote expresses the attitude. During 1976, as it became clear that a borehole would be installed at CaeCae, a mixed anxiety arose among those Zhu men employed by Mbanderu; they asked, "Ka de pumpa ku nci shi gumi, eqa ku howa xwasi kore": "When the pump waters the cattle, where will we find work?" These Zhu men thus express a thorough understanding of the labor process that reduced cattlepost jobs at the beginning of this century (p. 132). Hitchcock and Nkwe (1986:98) identify the process in current terms: "As commercialization of the livestock industry proceeds, fewer *badisa* (herders) are needed, and those that are used tend to be ones with more skills." This is a contemporary intensification of the scale economies that reduced rural employment opportunities at the beginning of this century when commercial ranching displaced commodity hunting (recall chap. 4). There is another dimension; as cattle are more rapidly fattened for the cash export market, calves will be allowed to suckle longer, thereby reducing the amount of milk available to feed herders.

Within this framework, Remote Area Development Officers have been sincere and dedicated people who have worked hard against strong odds. But policy directives have relegated their activities largely to holding actions minimally designed to pass the current adult generation of RADs through life in a way that will not be embarrassing to the government, in the very way that Minister Kwele warned against. From this perspective, it is significant that the political objectives of RADP—of bringing San-speakers into full citizenship participation in the nation—have never been adopted as national policy. To call upon Egner (1981a:5) one last time, "The political/legal objectives of the RADP must be regarded as not feasible for attainment by public servants acting on their own without political or legislative backing." In practice, succeeding generations of Basarwa are given some additional attention—schools, child health care—but again in minimal, low-level, step-by-step increments. The situation is reminiscent of the 1930s of Tagart and Joyce, of the 1950s of Forbes-Mackenzie, and—more recently—of Gcaunqa.

It is worth spending a little time here on examining the basis upon which RADP was founded; the words are taken from Wily's (1979: 64–65) frank and unsparing retrospective evaluation of her role in establishing the program (she was the first Bushman Development Officer):

320   What It Means to Be Excluded

Bushmen generally retain (in the face of changes) the attitudes and philosophy of a hunter-gatherer way of life. It is this more than anything that makes their survival today problematic and precarious. . . . Progressive attitudes which expect and deal positively with changes were not necessary and therefore have not been cultivated or embedded in their society, unlike agricultural, pastoral and later societies." . . . There was a purpose to this view other than avoiding antagonizing Batswana who might fear they would be blamed for the plight of the San: "Thus" the BDO [Wily] logically concluded, "it would be futile to force San to adopt settled agriculture; the emphasis must lie on transitional rather than radical changes.

This gradualist philosophy was, and is, compatible with government priorities expressed in tangible actions (such as appropriations for remote area expenditures) even if not in pronouncements of policy. In the passage quoted above, Wily's citation from one of her earlier memoranda (written at the time the Bushman Development Office was being formed) documents quite unambiguously that the anthropologically "scientific" notion of "Bushmen" as evolutionarily prior peoples—"unlike agricultural, pastoral and later societies"—was established from the beginning as a tenet of policy.

This notion continues to have academic and administrative advocates. Yellen (n.d.), for example, reasserts the nineteenth-century ideology we found wanting at the beginning of this book. For him, "San although they incorporate livestock in their subsistence repertoire still act more as foragers than as traditional pastoralists" (Yellen, n.d.: 23). In Yellen's (n.d.: 25) eyes, to these peoples "a cow counts as just another large mammal," despite the fact that both he and Lee—and Marshall before them—aver that Zhu strive to acquire and increase herds of their own. He now, however, wishes to reverse the logic by which the idea of isolation has been sustained until now in order to accommodate the evidence that San history is one of neither stasis nor isolation. It now appears that "change may serve as anthropological ally" (Yellen, n.d.: 26), where before changelessness was required in order for San-speaking peoples to serve as evolutionary models. But even such a radical shift in logic does not shift his perspective; we are assured again that we need only follow Lee's (1979: 2) reiteration of Pitt-Rivers's 1875 prescription: "To understand the evolutionary significance [of San] the effects of recent change must be carefully peeled away." Sir Charles's useless objects of anthropological research are thus revivified.

Ethnography—not the peoples it purports to describe—has been isolated and unchanged for the past century. But to peel away millennia of material relations, centuries of production for social exchange, and decades of deprivation and to turn a blind eye to the inconvenient persistence in modern form of these social relations is—as Howell makes so eloquently clear—to be left with a parody of both the past and the present not only of San-speaking peoples but of everyone in the region.

Scientific inquiry, of evolutionary direction or any other, does not require such misrepresentation, and policy based upon it is doomed to compound the errors. Indeed, Egner (1981b:11) calls for more development-oriented anthropological research precisely to strengthen the case for Sarwa equality in Tswana ideology and practice. Only by contributing to the dialogue necessary to this project can anthropological discourse serve as other than an academic forum. Heretofore in that discourse, the principal vehicle for carrying knowledge of Clammer's "anthropological" peoples to the public has been ethnography, an ethnography that in its now classical, particularist form is an anachronism in the postcolonial world. To the extent that this world is also neocolonial, such ethnography serves the same purpose as did its colonial predecessor.

Given this congruence of purpose among scientists, administrators, development planners, the ruling elite, and an untutored public, it can come as no surprise that from the beginning the Remote Area Development Office has been forced to accept very low-level budgets funded mainly by external donor countries and has not been able to build a strong case for reliable, recurrent, incrementally growing, internal funding under National Development Plan authorization. NDP5 allocated a constant expenditure of P1 per RAD person per year for remote area development (Wilmsen 1982b:367) for the period 1979–85; in contrast, P69 per city dweller was allocated for urban development. NDP6, for 1985–91, allocates P3/RAD/year for remote area development (NDP6 1985:7.5); in real monetary terms, this is no different from the previous expenditure level and represents a smaller proportion of total gross domestic product than allotted under NDP5.

Nor has a strong case been forged for true political and social parity for RADs, let alone the San-speaking component of this underclass. The then head of RADP, M. Giddie (RADW 1979:12; RADW 1980:12–13), voiced dismay at this situation and pointed to the resulting chaos in RADP; he attributed this state of affairs to the lack of central government support for or even understanding of the program. In addition, he stated (RADW 1980:2) that a gradualist approach has been forced on RADP but that it will not work. Wily (1979) concluded that RADP was never intended to be more than a token welfare program reflecting little other than patronage toward RADs.

But the picture painted in this book does not support a notion of institutional backwardness. Social relations, in all their ramifications, among San-speaking peoples and other minorities have been shown to be fully developed in indigenous terms and to be compatible in essentials with those of Tswana and other dominant groups. Furthermore, as we have seen, relations of production among all groups were integrated until colonial disruptions realigned interests. What is realistically to the point is that tradition is not static. From a policy perspective, the current state of traditional practice is important, not some past state of tradition reimposed upon a society that has outgrown that state. The precolonial conditions with lopsided but nonetheless mutual mafisa and kinship relations identified by Nangati no longer exist as unifying principles. These relations—which formerly guaranteed usufruct rights in land and transferred cattle from rich elites to poor kinspeople and clients—were first weakened and then demolished by policy actions (cf. Hitchcock and Nkwe 1986:98).

The history of the region shows clearly that the contemporary state of all traditions in the region have incorporated much from each other. These traditions have undergone dynamic transformations in the process that have been by no means uniform, linear, or unilateral. Fluctuating economic fortunes have been equally characteristic of all the peoples we have met, the rapid fall and subsequent slow rise of livestock ownership by San-speakers in this century being an immediate example. This is the heart of the matter. San-speaking peoples have not always been as they are now, not even recently, nor have they been as ethnography has depicted them. Their current state is the result of transformations in relations of production involving many other peoples in a social formation that has itself undergone transformation of profound proportions during the past two centuries, and that during the past two millennia has experienced other transformations that we are only now beginning to comprehend. There is nothing to be peeled away to reveal an evolutionary residue that does not exist.[28] This is the point of departure from which future anthropology and administration must approach these peoples.

There is a positive side to the process that transforms San traditions. The most tangible aspects are manifest in the expenditure strategies and investment programs being followed by Zhu and other ethnic minorities. Where circumstances are favorable, these peoples realize reasonably balanced accounts, formulated both in customary terms and in innovative initiatives. Clearly, it is not tradition that is inhibiting change. Rather, historically realized relations between dominant and subordinate segments of society have acted to relegate dispossessed minorities to archaic economic forms while the actions of some individuals in those minorities have proceeded in modern terms.

Permanent commitment of person to place is essential if rural production is to be sustained. Yet as conditions of production change, conditions of land tenure and of kinship also change; commitments to person and place acquire different meanings in the process. The anxiety in the question "Ka de pumpa . . . where will we find work?" expresses this in all its ramifications, and alternatives are actively being sought, as we have seen (Ramatokwane 1987 has emphasized some of the more undesirable alternatives, such as migration to farm work in Namibia). This is an aspect of the "negative employment effects through scale economies" (Colclough and Fallon 1983 : 147) being realized in localities throughout Botswana.

In the communal past, the link to land was through kinship association with persons. But the communal past has passed. People in remote areas (in common with those in other sectors) now leave their traditional tenures to seek economic opportunity beyond kinship obligation. To say that this trend will accelerate is no sagacious prediction; the capital of Botswana, Gaborone, is the fastest-growing city in Africa today. Its growth must be fed from the countryside, or by the expenditure of foreign exchange, or by unpredictable largesse of external donor countries following their own agendas.

There has been a tendency in Botswana to treat unemployment as an urban problem, but rural unemployment is its reciprocal; it simply remains more hidden, especially in remote areas. When NDP5 was published in 1980, the urban sector and the remote sector held approximately equal numbers of people. Among remote persons, however, the proportion of unemployed was far higher, and the amount of disposable income was many times lower. It is this polarity that drives the imperative to urban in-migration, underscoring a point made by Parson (1981b : 1): "Concern about inequality emanates from more than moral imperatives" and is set in the extent to which it restricts socially useful activity. Matlhare (RADW 1980 : 79) decries this destitution-driven "going from one place to another with the hope of getting paid jobs" that is a daily reality for many rural Batswana today.

A process similar to that observed earlier in this century is operating—an accordion effect that allows remote dwellers to stand in for rural migrants, who move to an urban squatter existence, leaving both stand-ins and squatters on the margins of the national economy. We have witnessed how San-speaking peoples sought outlets for their "freed" labor in the 1920s, sometimes at great personal and social cost. It is important to reiterate that they were not alone in doing so;

mine labor migration of other peoples—and later of San-speakers—in the Protectorate carried equally great costs. Indeed, the two forms of labor search were carried out in concert; it is doubtful if one could have come into being without something like the other. Today, similarly "freed" Zhu labor at CaeCae seeking similar outlets is only one example of many to be found among the rural poor of Botswana. This process will be amplified in proportion to the extension of the social network along which movements take place. Typically, rural-urban food transfers are needed to sustain migrants to town and urban centers during probably long periods of job search (CSO 1974; Colclough and Fallon 1983 : 145). The vast majority of San-speaking peoples do not now have the requisite urban anchors for such a network. In the short term this may shield them from the harsher realities of current urban squatter existence: in the long term it will simply add another dimension of disadvantage, depriving them, for example, of an active, direct voice in the centers of decision making.

I do not wish to argue that reliance on inplaced kinship networks is an absolute, unchangeable requirement for facilitating the mobility of RADs or, particularly, of the Basarwa component of this category. Quite the opposite. It will be possible for these peoples to participate fully in all sectors of the national polity only when reliance on such networks is rendered irrelevant by a person's ability to cope as an independent entity within the national social milieu—rather than in some local fragment of that milieu.

Ssao eloquently voiced the need at an election rally in Maun in 1979 when he challenged Sir Seretse Khama, the founding president of Botswana and a man of awesome esteem in the nation, to articulate an unambiguous policy of equal opportunity for his people. But in reality, San-speaking peoples are today little more privileged in this struggle than they were a half-century ago. That a few among them are transcending their poverty underscores the fact that it is a class rather than an ethnic condition they are escaping. As Worby (1984 : 151) points out, this class position has been maintained through the reinvestment of profits by the ruling elite to its own benefit as well as through continuing control by that elite of the jural and ideological institutions of the state.

The thrust of my argument has been that it is useless to speak about "Bushmen"/Basarwa/San as a separate category unless we realize that these terms are class categorizations having nothing to do with ethnic entities or persons and only occasionally relating to a particular, restricted way of life. The first step to this realization leads away from a fascination with a fixed forager image, a fascination that sets the present of peoples so labeled out of focus and circumscribes any vision of their future. It is this step that I have hoped to help anthropologists, administrators, and the public to take.

Notes

Chapter One: The Evolution of Illusion

1. Some San-speaking peoples, the Bateti, for example, are usually not included among "Bushmen" because of their known history of pastoralism and their present large herds; details are given in chapters 3 and 7.

2. For example, in their introduction to *Politics and History in Band Societies*, Leacock and Lee (1982:10) assert the anomaly that in societies free from fundamental conflicts of interest (as they say foragers are), techniques for decision making and conflict resolution are necessary; however, as with Steward's (1938) earlier *Basin-Plateau Aboriginal Socio-political Groups*, no clear analysis of these techniques is attempted, and few of the papers included in the book address political structure.

3. Citations to Tlou (1972) are to his original Ph.D. dissertation; this dissertation has since been published (Tlou 1985) and is also listed in the References.

4. Lubbock is generally credited by English-speaking scholars with introducing the term prehistoric, but it seems to have been in use in Germany at least by 1845, twenty years before Lubbock's book. For example, Marx and Engels ([1846] 1977:49) rebuke their German critics, who, they say, accuse them of speculating about "not history at all, but the 'prehistoric era.'"

5. But in the *Ethnological Notebooks* Marx has extensive entries on Lubbock (Krader 1972:43–45, 339–51).

6. In a footnote to this passage, Marx ([1867] 1906:366–67) says, "Linguet is probably right, when in his 'Theorie des Lois Civiles,' he declares hunting to be the first form of cooperation."

7. This is an interpretation with which I thoroughly disagree. Ethnography does not play that sort of central or centralizing role in Marx, whose great merit continues to be that his critique of civilization was constructed from within, not upon others he knew little about.

8. These ethnographic studies were carried out without any illusions about their primary beneficiaries, as the following *Circular Memorandum* (Botswana National Archives 1940b) makes clear:

27th.June 1940
To all District Commissioners, the Chief Veterinary Officer and the Chief Agricultural Officer.
Subject: *Revision of Professor Schapera's Handbook on Tswana Law and Custom, Land Tenure, etc.*

I am directed by the Resident Commissioner to inform you that Professor Schapera is expected to arrive in Mafeking on the 30th.June and to leave Palapye on Monday the 8th.July. He will probably stay in Ngamiland for about six weeks, then go to Serowe for a month and then work southwards. More precise information as to his movements after leaving Maun will be communicated to each District Commissioner by Professor Schapera but it is requested now that the following arrangements be made for him at each centre in turn:

  (a) arrangements for his accommodation;
  (b) arrangements for the services of one, or preferably two, literate young natives who can be employed as full-time assistants while Professor Schapera is in the district concerned. These natives, if satisfactory, will be paid at the same rate as school teachers.
  (c) The Chief to be informed before hand of the date of Professor Schapera's arrival so that there will be no delay in his commencing work as soon as he arrives.

                                                                    V. Ellenberger
                                                                    for GOVERNMENT SECRETARY

9. "Unsere Leute nennen die Buschmänner Ozombusumana (Sing—Ombusumana), eine Verstümmelung des Holländischen Namens. Der eigentliche Name, unter welchem sie sonst bei den Ovaherero bekannt sind, ist Ovaguma. Der neue Name wird sicher den alten verdrangen und die Etymologie wird vielleicht später den Philologen Kopfbrechen machen" (*Petermanns* 1859: 299, reprinted in Moritz 1980:2).

10. The source of the element sa in Basarwa (and Masarwa) is not known; it is not a noun prefix in Setswana. My own hypothesis is that it is the Nama noun Sa(n), incorporated into Barwa when Batswana first encountered peoples referred to by this term when they entered the western Kalahari in the mid-eighteenth century. The evolution may have been something like Masa → Masarwa, with the attachment of the root *-rwa possibly an accompaniment to reduction in status of peoples called Masa. Rainer Vossen has pointed out to me that Köhler (1975:305) proposed a similar hypothesis more than a decade ago: "Und es liegt nahe anzunehmen, dass diesem Namen der Wortstamm *Sa* zugrunde liegt, mit dem die Rinderhirten die nomadischen Jäger bezeichneten und der vielleicht in Ma-*Sa*-rwa wiederlebt, einem Namen, den die Tswana die hellhäutigen Jäger gaben."

11. I employ self-referents in all appropriate cases. One of these needs special mention: those people of Botswana and Namibia known as !Kung in the literature refer to themselves as žu|'õasi (žu = person, |'õa = finished or complete, si = plural suffix; hence, completed people). !Xũ, which is the source of the term !Kung, is the self-referent name of a people who live in Angola and speak a dialect very similar to žu|'õasi; the name has been applied to both languages indiscriminately, since it was used this way by Bleek, who worked with a few prisoner !Kung or Zhu informants at the Cape in the 1880s. I have also adopted Setswana spelling of Khoisan words to reduce orthographic obstructions in the text; in this orthography, the dental and alveolar clicks (usually represented by | and ≠ are written as c, the lateral click (||) as x, and the palatal click (!) as q. When necessary to give more precise phonological representa-

tions of words, I employ Snyman (1975 and to a lesser extent 1969) for Zhu, Traill (1974) for Kqoo, and Barnard (1985) for Nharo. I use Zhu instead of the longer form, a practice in keeping with these people's own usage. I use the term Bushman and rwa/tua forms only when their historical or connotational aspects are clear. I use San only to indicate that set of peoples who speak what used to be called the "Bush" languages of Khoisan. Although it is sometimes a bit awkward, this usage takes the form of San-speakers or San-speaking peoples except when used adjectivally.

A note is also in order regarding Bantu-language words. Until this century, there was no unified Tswana polity; rather, several independent polities of Tswana-speakers were known by their eponymous names; the Bakwena, Bangwato, and Batawana will concern us most. The geographical space of each such polity takes the locative prefix (Class 9) ga-; hence Gakwena, Gangwato, Gatawana. The locative (Class 7) bo- is applied to both the conceptual landed space and the actual geographical space of all the people conceived to be associated in language and culture (as in Botswana, the true place of all peoples who speak Setswana—that is, people with Tswana culture). All, or any plural fraction, of these people are Batswana; those identified with a specific smaller polity are Bakwena, Bangwato, Batawana, and so forth. A single individual takes the prefix (Class 1) mo-; thus Mokwena, Mongwato, Motawana. An individual Sarwa person is a Mosarwa; two or more are Basarwa. Otjiherero has a parallel structure: ova- is the equivalent of ba-, omu- of mo-; hence Ovaherero, Ovambanderu, Ovakuruha, and so on, and their singulars Omuherero, Omumbanderu, Omukuruha. Ovambanderu are the eastern branch of Herero in general; there are slight differencs in speech, beliefs, and practices between the two groups. As adjectives, these roots take no prefix; thus Tswana agriculture, Mbanderu cattle, Sarwa hunters. For the spelling of geographical names in Botswana, I follow the *Third Report of the Place Names Commission* (GoB 1984).

Chapter Two: The Poverty of Misappropriated Theory

1. This is the period we now live in. Diamond also sees it as transitional.

2. Harpending (1976:155), however, notes a very wide range of economic activities, including pastoralism and plow agriculture, in which all Zhu took part to some extent during the course of the Harvard group's fieldwork in the 1960s.

3. Konner and Shostak (1986:70–75), in a thoughtful meditation, put it this way: "The !Kung have also been called upon to remind us of Shangri-La. . . . Most of us have participated to one degree or another in the dissemination of utopian ideas about the culture." But they also point out that this has been a participation of the profession as a whole, "not a flaw of certain investigators," and that the resultant textbook notions of other cultures as Shangri-Las are tenacious and difficult to erase. Just how tenacious may be judged by this admonition from Leacock (1972:17–18) regarding the pervasiveness of ethnographic isolation of foragers for evolutionary studies: "It

[is] ridiculous to treat such societies as isolated self-contained enclaves that can be described without a theory of economic effects on social and political structures." My purpose in this book is not to expose, as an academic exercise, the weaknesses of previous work, but to strip away those weaknesses so the real strengths of that work can be freed and thus become useful in a search for a better standpoint than Shangri-La from which to engage the real world.

4. I think we may assume that Lubbock saw his liberal political activity in the same light as his efforts to enlighten the past. His success in guiding the bill establishing the first secular national holiday (August Bank Holiday) through Parliament can be so interpreted (cf. Stocking 1987:151).

5. The numbers here correspond to those applied to Durkheim's list of characteristics of mechanical solidarity.

6. Helm (1965) was, however, at this same time demonstrating that such groups did in fact exist among the Dogrib.

7. In this regard it is hard to know what Marx ([1867] 1906:198) meant by "We are not now dealing with primitive instinctive forms of labour that remind us of the mere animal." Possibly he had in mind something like the notions about Neanderthals that were becoming current at that time.

8. Three seminal works have helped shape my thinking in this area, and I draw heavily upon them in the following discussion: Ted Benton, *The Rise and Fall of Structural Marxism* (1984), John Taylor, *From Modernization to Modes of Production* (1979), and Joel Kahn and Josep Llobera, "Towards a New Marxism or a New Anthropology?" (1981).

9. Lee, as we have seen, holds that this typicality is being eroded only now in the "contact" situation.

10. The heading of this section is taken from a stimulating honors paper, "Anthropology Comes to 'Class,'" written at McGill University by Eric Worby, which led me to think of some of these issues in new ways.

11. Disconcerting because, as Foster-Carter (1978a:77) says in a footnote, the great merit of this paper is that Brenner "unambiguously restates the analytical primacy of class and of class struggle in the study of development and underdevelopment."

Chapter Three: The Past Recaptured

1. It has been commonly assumed that agropastoral peoples were unable to settle the Kalahari until about 250 years ago (Schapera 1952; Sillery 1952; Tlou 1972), or even until the nineteenth century (Kuper 1969:45; Lee 1979:76, 404), because it was thought that the environment was unsuitable to the domestic economies of such peoples (Phillipson 1969:24–49). This notion persists; Gordon (1984:197) says that the land "is not especially suitable for pastoral activities for either white ranchers or Ovaherero cattle raisers. . . . the presence of lungsickness and horse-sickness served to inhibit any permanent predatory expansionist tendencies of ranchers." It is true that Europeans throughout southern Africa often recorded that they lost cattle to "lungsickness," but this occurred in many parts of the subcontinent and prohibited neither indigenous nor European herding. Andersson ([1875] 1967:239–49)

describes the disease and preventive measures against it in detail, including vaccination by inserting a piece of infected lung, obtained from a dead beast, into a cut made in an animal's dewlap or tail. Earlier, Alexander ([1838] 1967, 1:203) had referred to dewlap cuts as being "brands" of Herero cattle. Andersson prefaces his account with the remark, "And I speak with some authority, as during my long sojourn at Otjimbingue, I myself have possessed very large herds of horned cattle, and unfortunately lost upwards of two thousand of them by 'lung-sickness.'"

Otjimbingue is in the heart of the country where Ovaherero are known to have kept vast herds of cattle for generations and from which ten thousand or more head were shipped annually to the Cape during the 1860s and 1870s (Esterhuyse 1968:13). Chapman (1971:231; see p. 118), in fact, indicates that lungsickness was not in the area during the 1860s. The epidemic of this disease that ravaged Namibia in 1861–65 was centered at Otjimbingue; it seems to have affected Ngamiland far less severely. Indeed, this was the principal refugium from which the herds of Ngami-Namibia were restocked after the rinderpest epidemic of 1896–97 killed 75% of the cattle in all of southern Africa. Passarge (1907:123), who was at CaeCae and nearby cattleposts in 1897–98, mentions that the trader Müller's oxen escaped the rinderpest at Qubi.

In fact, respiratory diseases of cattle, malignant catarrh and others, are not as serious factors here as elsewhere (Botswana Society 1971), and the foot-and-mouth epidemics that ravaged Botswana in the 1970s did not affect the area. Lord Hailey (1953:260), for these reasons, went so far as to recommend increasing the number of cattleposts in the sandveld. In the second half of this century, Botswana Veterinary Service records indicate that at any one time six thousand to ten thousand cattle have been kept in the Qangwa and CaeCae valleys alone, with comparable numbers in the rest of the Ngamiland sandveld (Wilmsen 1976). This has been done with water available only in surface pans and hand-dug wells. Even today the two boreholes in the area supply only the domestic needs of people; cattle continue to be watered from lift wells.

2. Early Iron Age hardveld ceramics in Botswana are of types called Bambata, with thin walls and charcoal temper in a friable paste, and Gokomere-Kumadzulo, which is thicker, has a variety of tempers and is generally more elaborately decorated.

3. Kraals are cattle enclosures. The word is Afrikaans, probably from Portuguese; through a Spanish cognate it came into English as corral.

4. Divuyu ceramics are unmistakably different from those that preceded them in the area. Charcoal temper is often mixed with calcrete. Elaborate design elements are applied in alternate bands of comb stamping and incising in parallel, hatched, and herringbone patterns, often separated by undecorated bands.

5. Nqoma ceramics are uniformly charcoal tempered with few other inclusions; decoration is mainly in bands of interlocking triangles or pendant triangles filled with hatching, comb stamping, or linear punctating, and false-relief chevron designs are common.

6. Bryan Kensley identified the mollusks.

7. Matlapaneng ceramics have affinities to the Kumadzulo-Dambwa complex defined for the Victoria Falls area by Vogel (1971).

8. Mary Beaudry identified these nineteenth-century materials.

9. This is another form of extended identity. Manchatees, more usually written Mantatees, was a term derived from a group of Tlokwa in what is now the Orange Free State who had a woman chief whose name was Ntatisi; thus they were called the Batlokwa ba ga Mma Ntatisi. They were reputed to be highly mobile and successful raiders but never ranged north of the Vaal River. Their reputation was such, however, that any group of Tswana raiders, even in the western Kalahari, might be called Mantati, "People of Mma Ntatisi" (Thompson 1969:391–446). The "Manchatees" referred to here may have been Sebego's Bangwaketse; alternatively, they may have been Barolong, who were active in the area at the time.

10. Otjiherero takes the term from Nama, kwe (meaning people); some Nama groups referred to themselves as Kwekwe (or Khoinkhoin), "true people"; to avoid confusion with the Tswana group, Bakwena, who are entirely different, I use Ovakwena (Nama) sparingly.

11. Unabhangige Namaquas, Buschmänner, und Bergdamaras finden sich im Omuhererolande.

12. Die Rinderhaltung zeigt sich auch in einem alten Oraltext, in dem die Kxoé berichten, wie die Mubukushu die Rinder der Kxoé raubten. (Oraltext 2.6.1–2; see Köhler 1986:256).

13. Die Buschmänner leben von Wild. . . . da, wo sie in kleinen Werften unter einem Haüptling zusammenwohnen, haben sie auch etwas Kleinvieh, Ziegen und Schafe.

14. This appears to be Alexander's attempt to write "ovandu" = people, but he has omitted a qualifier indicating "white."

15. Dort finden sie auf der anderen Seite portugiesische, wie es scheint reisende Händler, welche das Elfenbein, und ich denke auch Rindvieh, für Glasperlen etc. erhandeln. Eisen ist ihnen wertvoller wie Kupfer.

16. Eine Vergleichung von Wörtern dieses Dialektes mit solchen, die ich bei späterer Gelegenheit bei uns besuchenden Buschleuten sammelte, zeigt, dass der Stamm der !Kun San nicht nur im ganzen unteren Omuramba ua Matako verbreitet ist, sondern sich auch in östlicher Richtung bis in die Nähe des Ngami-See erstreckt.

17. It is not certain, of course, that this was Livingstone, although it most likely was. The point is that news networks covered very great distances.

18. Die Herero haben auf Stellen, wo die Kalkschicht noch nicht allzu hart oder auch nicht allzu dick ist, Löcher in den Boden gemacht, aus welchen sie Tag für Tag ihre grossen Heerden tränkten. . . . Die meisten der auf der Karte verzeichneten Namen in der Omaheke oder Sandfeld sind solche Stellen und Senkungen, an welchen sich oft bedeutende Herero-Werften befinden. Schinz (1891:438) refers to the Omaheke as "Nordostern des Hererolands": "the northeastern part of Hereroland."

19. Als Schmuck dienen ²Chore-Ketten, sowie weisse, rote, blaue Glasperlen, die in Ketten um den Hals getragen werden oder in die Haare geknüpft sind und in Form eine Schlinge auf der Stirn geabhängen. (The superscript numeral two is Passarge's notation for the alveolar click consonant; his other notations are: superscript one, the dental, three, the lateral, and four, the palatal clicks.)

20. Mehrere ihrer Handels-Karawanen kamen an uns vorbei und sobald sie uns bemerkten, setzten sie sich in kriegerische Position. . . . Diess ist nicht zu verwundern, da sie durch Räuberbanden der Namaqua Vieh verloren haben.

21. Unsere Herero kauften eifrig Strausseneierschalen, die bei den Ovambo ein sehr gesuchter Handelsartikel sind. . . . Auch bereiten andere Buschmänner Salz auf den Salzpfannen in der Form von Zuckerhüten und bringen es zum Verkauf nach Ondonga, von wo es weiter zu den anderen Stämmen geht, so dass der Salzhandel wohl eben so wichtig oder noch wichtiger ist wie der mit Kupfer.

22. Sehr hohen Wert und, wie wir sehen werden, spielten sie in früheren Zeiten als Handelsartikel eine grosse Rolle.

23. This extremely inflated price came down in a matter of days.

24. Am 6.Mai erreichen wir Karakobis. . . . diese Etappe war für uns von Wichtigkeit, als wir nun der angenehmen Heerstrasse in Bett des Flusses verlassen mussten, um den nach rechts abzwingenden Wagonspuren folgend, Südostrichtung einzuschalgen.

25. The number of elephants that must have been killed to produce twenty thousand pounds of ivory can be estimated from tusk weights published at the time. Average tusk pairs declined in size as elephants were hunted out, but forty pounds per pair is a reasonable mean. Therefore, about five hundred elephants were required to yield twenty thousand pounds of ivory.

26. Zoodat de manner verplicht waren in het buitenveld bij de Boschjesmans water te gan ruilen om toch maar met hunne huisgezinnen in het leven te blijven. De Boschjesmannen moesten al het water uit den grund zuigen met rieten, en voor een kallebas, vijf bottels water houdende, moest men vijf pond kruit betalen.

27. By ondersoek het ons gevind dat daar 'n Boesman-pyl in die perd se lyf steek, en ons was dadelik baie onrustig. Ons wis dat dit die Boesmans se werk was, Oom Willem was die middag weg om wild te gaan soek., want wildvleis was al waarvan ons moes lif. Die aand kon ons in die donker niks kry nie, maar die volgende more heel vroeg is vyf van ons te perd weg om Oom Willem te gaan soek. Ons moes die perd se spoor volg, en nadat ons vir geruime tyd gesoek het, hoor ek Faan roep: "Hier le arme Oom Willem!" Ons ander het daarheen gejaag, maar vind toe dat Oom Willem lankal reeds moet dood wees, met 'nvergiftigde Boesman-pyl in sy sy. . . . "Kom, Faan," het ek verontwaardig uitgeroep, "kom ons gaan die ongedierte opspoor en doodskiet. Faan was dan ookgou by my, en nog een van die ander, terwyl daar twee by Oom Willem agterbly. Ons het na 'n uur se ry 'n hele paar Boesmans gesien en soveel ons kon kry doodgeskiet. Ons kon egter nie baie van hulle kry nie. Hierdie Boes-

mans had vir hoof of kaptein 'n "Berg-Damara" wat listiger en gevaarliker was as 'n slang.

The presence of a "Berg-Damara" is evidence that Nama-speaking persons visited or lived in the area; several Nama place-names are still in use there (e.g., Karakobis, Hakobis, Eiseb; Nienaber and Raper [1980] list others). In chapter 6 we shall find that several Zhu living at CaeCae have Nama ancestors.

28. Der Handler Franz Müller, ein guter Beobachter und ausgezeichneter Kenner der Kalahari, versicherte mir, das die Zahl die Buschmänner seit seinen Reisen im Anfang der achtziger Jahre auffallend abgenommen habe. Früher hatten sie sich zu Hunderten um die Wagen gesammelt und mancherlei Felle zum Handeln gebracht, jetzt aber sehe man an denselben Plätzen immer nur wenige, oft keinen einzigen. Besonders im Chansefeld war ihm das aufgefallen. Die Ausrottung des Wildes und die Abnahme der Melonen hatten seiner Ansicht nach so ungünstig eingewirkt. . . . Handelsstrassen scheinen durch das Gebiet der Buschmänner nicht bestanden zu haben, vielmehr erfolgte der Austausch von Stamm zu Stamm.

29. But we do not really know what value San workers received for their labor; during the early years of the merchant traders, it may have been reasonable, as Andersson's elephant, Baines's negotiations, and Chapman's black ostrich feathers suggest. As time passed, however, value for labor paid to San workers surely decreased.

Chapter Four: The Past Entrenched

1. Die Buschmänner haben auf das Vieh aufzupassen und es beim Beginn der Trockenzeit wieder richtig abzuliefern. Dafür haben sie ihrerseits das Anrecht auf die Milch, soweit die Tiere ohne Schädigung der Kälber sie abgeben können. So lag z.B. im Januar 1897 ein Ziegenkraal Killitibwes lediglich unter Aufsicht von Buschmännern an den Makabana-Bergen, im Februar weiter südlich im Sandfeld. Der Oberhäuptling der 2Aukwe von 2Garu hatte in Djarutsa einen Viehkraal des Batauanahäuptlings Ssekumi während der Regenzeit 1897/98 und zog mit dem Vieh mit dem Beginn der Trockenzeit ins Debrafeld.

2. Accounts given to Alnaes (1979a, 1979b) say that young Herero men knew southern Ngamiland well from having lived there in the past. Schinz (1891:400) found Ovaherero at Rietfontein in 1881.

3. Der Kapitain der Kungbuschleute suchte Graeff auf. . . . über das Eintreffen einzelner Hererobanden, die er als unbefugte Eindringlinge betrachtete, schien er wenig erbaut; daher versprach er willig seine Unterstützung . . . wurde der Vormarsch auf Gautscha, im Herzen der Oase, angetreten. Dort hatte noch eine grössere Hererobande gesessen; doch zeigte sich, dass der Feind, wohl durch den früheren überfall Graeffs erschreckt, das Weite gesucht hatte. Damit war auch selbst jener entlegene Teil der Kolonie vom Feinde gesäubert.

4. Note that the official records cited in these pages bear out Marenga's memory. Note also that Herero were in the attacking party.

5. These names are found on the *Kriegskarte von Deutsch-Südwestafrika*

([1904] 1987), Blatt Andara; these maps are compilations of earlier merchant and missionary maps and records.

6. The accounts given in Sundermeier ([1976] n.d.) differ somewhat from those given here, but the two versions are not incompatible.

7. This is firm evidence that Ovaherero had already returned to their cattleposts in the Dobe-NyaeNyae area by 1914.

8. There are rumors that the Germans buried a cache of arms at Onyainya in 1914, but there is no reason to think the rumor is true. There are, however, a few World War I British Enfield rifles still in use in the area.

Chapter Five: The Ideology of Person and Place

1. Snyman (1975) formulates a standardized orthography in which to couch the discussion; he also provides independent confirmation for my glosses of the lexical items to be considered. In this discussion of technical terms, Setswana spelling of Zhu (and other San language) words will be used as in the rest of the text; in addition, on first use of a term in the text, Snyman's orthographic form will be given. This form will also be used in the notes to retain phonetic distinctions.

2. I should note here that Cashdan (1986) has now moved beyond her earlier position and has begun to analyze San-Bantu interrelations.

3. In August 1980, in Gaborone, when I was preparing the first version of the paper that has evolved into this chapter in order to present it to the Botswana Society Symposium on Settlement, Pauline Peters suggested that I look at Gluckman's work on land tenure; I am much in her debt for that suggestion. Earlier I had posed the issue of tenure rather than territoriality as being important in San social relations to the First National Migration Study Workshop, Gaborone, in July 1977 (Hitchcock, Vierich, and Wilmsen 1977).

4. *The Compact Edition of the Oxford English Dictionary* gives for "entitlement": "II. From Title = 'right to possession.' 4. To furnish (a person) with a 'title' *to* an estate. Hence *gen.* to give (a person or thing) a rightful claim *to* a possession, privilege, designation, mode of treatment, etc." This concept of entitlement seems to capture Gluckman's "relations to property" as well as the specific systems to be discussed in this chapter, although in neither theory nor praxis is its use entirely unproblematic. For present purposes— seeking a deeper understanding of a social system—we must heed Carstens (1983:60): "All conceptions of 'ownership,' 'property,' 'estate' etc. are essentially socially related concepts . . . [that] . . . can never be studied independently of the social system of which they are a part." Thus, in native context, the English word "own" does not convey a meaning agreeable to a San-speaking—or Setswana-speaking or Otjiherero-speaking—person of being in a condition of possession of something such as land. But as I have taken pains to stress, those persons also live today—and have lived for some time—in a wider world context of national states that have encoded legal institutions that have borrowed heavily from European systems. In this world possession may be "nine points of the law," but it is—as Marx and Engels ([1846] 1977:79) claim of "tribal" property relations in general—*mere possession,* not owner-

ship. It is essential in this wider context to speak of rights of possession in land, chattels, or whatever in terms intelligible to interpreters of those national legal systems. Readers of *We Are Here: Politics of Aboriginal Land Tenure,* a collection of essays I edited (Wilmsen 1989) addressing the legal rights of what we now call former foraging peoples in modern national states, will be aware that *ownership* is used in that book. That usage is employed to stress the legitimacy of those peoples' rights in land under the legal systems of the states they now live in. This is not a contradiction of the usage employed here but is a contextual imperative emphasizing the substantive dimensions (those concerning "ownership" of landed property) of the entitlement domain. Indeed, this need to respect context should alert us to temptations to mystify the conceptual schemes we intend to convey by reifying the incommensurability of the terms employed by different peoples. The domains of concepts such as "ownership" are not monolithic among Euroamerican systems, yet we are able to accommodate our discourse to take the differences into account. We now need to recognize that this is also possible for other systems of thought. Bennett (1985:183) sounds a warning about using a term such as possession that must be given very careful attention: "Because, in the common law, this is notionally a question of fact and not of law, the courts are then free to apply remedies to assist the person who has been dispossessed and, at the same time, the courts can evade the issue of investigating the question of title to property." In this chapter I am addressing the issue of San title to real property in the context of native African systems. This seems to be the necessary first step to arguing the case before national courts in Botswana and, eventually, Namibia. By exploring more deeply concepts of entitlement—which subsume possession and at least some attributes of ownership—we can clarify somewhat the commensurability of different notions concerning rights to land. Similarly, Myers (1989:16) voices "discomfort with [Gluckman's] notion of property as being too concrete and specific for the meanings that Pintupi give to 'objects.'" I share this discomfort with respect to San—and Tswana and Herero—notions about land, although it seems to me to be compatible with those peoples' notions of personal private property, as does, indeed, ownership with respect to this latter kind of property. Here I adopt the distinction Myers traces from Mauss, that of real property as distinguished from personal property. Carstens (1983) has recently illuminated this distinction in a southern African context, and I shall call upon his work at several points in the ensuing discussion.

5. Hitchcock documents Botswana officials' use of ethnographic accounts in their attempts to rationalize continued dispossession of San. He quotes (1978:242) the litigation consultant for the attorney general's chambers, "Opinion in Re Common-Law Leases of Tribal Land," 23 January 1978: "As far as I have been able to ascertain, the Masarwa have always been true nomads. . . . it appears to me that (a) the true nomad Masarwa can have no rights of any kind except rights to hunting." In that same year, the commissioner of lands argued in parliamentary council that anthropologists had established that "Bushmen had no territories" and demanded of Hitchcock

(who was then rural sociologist in the Ministry of Agriculture), "Why then are you trying to tell me that they do?" (Hitchcock 1980:24).

6. Let me emphasize that in no sense do I suggest there is no difference in being a Motswana and being an Omuherero or a Zhu or what have you. I merely wish to point out what has been overlooked—by anthropologists and by Euroamericans in general, not by peoples who qualify for the labels just listed—that there is as much in common within the variation attached to this labeling as there is difference. Furthermore, what does inhere in that difference is not the product of "adjacent evolutionary stages."

7. To move more deeply into the meaning of n!òrè, it is necessary to recognize that the term is associated with a group of etymologically allied words carrying the primary sense "belonging or being inside defined limits." Placing the word n!òrè within its etymological group will help clarify the conceptual connotation it has for Zhu. The noun n!àm is translated into Afrikaans as "plek" by Snyman (1975:57); plek, in turn, is rendered "place/position" in English by Bosman, van der Merwe, and Hiemstra (1982:592), who associate it with the sense of location ("plaas"). The verb n!àng is glossed "vasmaak" (Snyman 1975:57); Bosman, van der Merwe, and Hiemstra (1982:817) translate this as "attach/secure." As an adjective or preposition, n!àng is given as "binnekant" (Snyman 1975:57), "inside" (Bosman, van der Merwe, and Hiemstra 1982:91); for example, g!ún!àng combines g!ú (water) plus n!àng, literally "waterinside" = waterplace or pan/well. All these words have the connotation of attaching or securing something inside or within the limits of its place. Thus n!òrè may be glossed "a place in land" or "country" and has the primary connotation of attaching persons properly inside tracts of land. Snyman (1975:62) captures this sense in n!òrè!xáiyàsi, "landgrens"—"land frontier/border" (of a country) (Bosman, van der Merwe, and Hiemstra 1982:407). N!òrè has both an inclusive—in the sense of the geographical region within which all Zhu live—and a restrictive meaning. In the restrictive sense, a Zhu refers to some locality—some demarcated land—as n!òrè mimà (n!òrè, plus mi = self, plus mà = possessive: "my country," meaning the place where I belong/was born). This meaning is also present in Setswana glosses of n!òrè: "lehatshe/lefatshe" = "a country," both in the inclusive sense of the geographical space inhabited by Batswana and in the restricted sense of a person's or household's allocated area of use right (plural = mofatshe); lehelo = "a place"; lehelong = "a certain place." Otjiherero glosses n!òrè in a similar fashion: omahi = "land possessed by residentially localized members of an oruzo" (patrilineal inheritance group with spouses); and ehi, the country of all Herero. Brincker ([1886] 1964:21) gives omahi = "Länder" ("landed property, estates") and omahimahi = "verschiedene Länder" ("differentiated lands"), Gegenden ("regions, districts, tracts of country"). Clearly these terms are conceptually similar if not identical. Indeed, they are employed interchangeably in bilingual conversations and are used by native speakers to specify for nonnatives (such as me) exactly what is meant.

8. Harold Scheffler and Warren Shapiro gave me crucial insights that are

incorporated in this discussion. Alan Barnard has constantly sharpened my understanding of its contents.

9. CaeCae Texts, tape 2, lines 479–84: "Lone lefoko le ke gore lelengwe fela, ko maheleletsong a teng, ka gore tsotlhe di a go fela ka bo *mà*, ke gore a difetsa ka bo *mà* jaana go supa gore ka selo same; kana sengwe same. Kana motho yo ke eng same. Eh." (This and the other texts presented in this section were recorded in Zhu, Setswana, and English. Anthony Traill recorded this set of interviews with me at CaeCae. Leonard Ramatokwana assisted with the questioning; Ssao Xau, Dam Qam, and John Marenga were the respondents. Mpho Molomo transcribed the Setswana portion of the tapes; he and Katherine Demuth helped clarify some English glosses. Alex Matseka and Alinah Segobye did the basic translation into English of the Setswana portion of the tapes.)

10. CaeCae Texts, tape 2, lines 458–60, 477–78: "Jaanong a ke re motho yo ene e le mogwagadi wa me, ene e le molome, a ke re, a be ke nyala ngwana wa gagwe a ke re. Ke tshwanetse gore ke mmitse ke re ≠xùm ka gore ke mo nyaletse. . . . Le supa gore o a motlotla. Yaa! Le supa go tlotla mo teng. Yaa."

11. CaeCae Texts, tape 2, lines 499–502, 514–17: "Ke gore ga ba bidiwa jalo ke gore bana ba wena o tla a bong a ba tshotse wena la mosadi wa gago, le ke nna la ba raya maina a bone batho ba. . . . Ao le ba bitsa jalo ke gore letlile go bitsa bana ba bone ka maina a bone, a batsadi ba lona. Bana ba bone, ba bone bana ba."

12. CaeCae Texts, tape 1, lines 327–36: "Go nyalana batho ba e leng gore le a ba itse; ke masika. Kampo go nyalana e le batho fela, eh, . . . ka rona ga re kake raya go nyala motho o sela fela, mosadi o sela fela o o nnang kgakala kwa. Ke gore re tshwanetse go nna le mosadi wa lesika. Kana ke lesika lagago, kana hela hela jalo, le wa ga rre kana wa botsala kwa botsala bo tewang teng."

13. CaeCae Texts, tape 1, lines 251–58, 337–42: "A go seame, go lebagane gore o re batho ba nna mo lehelong?" . . . "Ha e le gore motho o nna le ba lesika la ga bone; e le gore o kgaogane le lona go sekaa a go seame a go a tshwanela gore motho o ke re ke lehelo le gagwe. Yaa. Ha ke re lehatshe lame ke tlaa bo ke re. . . . Ke gore ke tlaa bo ke re . . . ke lehatshe lotlhe jaanong, lame. Ke gore ke la . . . yotlhe, batho botlhe . . . ke gore jaaka re le mahelelo jaana, go tewa gore ke lehatshe kwa ntseng teng . . . lehatshe lame, e le la batho botlhe."

14. Testimony taken in dispute cases during the 1920s and 1930s sheds light on the way bogadi was perceived and used at that time and on how seriously it was taken. In 1927 (BNA 1927) a Mokgalagadi man defended himself against charges brought by a San man, Charlie, that he had forcibly taken the latter's children, whose mother was a San woman, by claiming that he had paid bogadi (eight sheep and four goats) for the woman to be his wife; she subsequently left him to live with Charlie, by whom she bore the children in question. The Mokgalagadi claimed the children on the ground that Charlie had not paid bogadi to him for the woman. In another case (BNA 1930), a

Mongwato defended himself against a charge of murdering a San man, claiming that the killing was justified because the man had failed in his bogadi obligations; in support of this claim he cited Masarwa tradition to pay bogadi: "Perhaps ten goats or ten ship [sheep] is what Masarwa pay." (That both San and Bakgalagadi children were widely sold and that competition for labor was strong at the time are of central relevance in these cases and will be returned to in chapter 7.) The number of animals given in these cited transactions appears to have been about average for relatively poor families; goats, especially, were given by people whose holdings of other stock (cattle and sheep) were small or nonexistent.

15. This is, of course, only a convenient abstract measure; actual nqoresi vary in size and shape.

16. For a diametrically opposite view, compare Yellen (1977:51), who dismisses both my earlier (Wilmsen 1973) hypothetical model and Lee's (1972) empirical model of Zhu social integrity, noting—correctly—that for these formulations to be valid, Zhu social groups must be stable in space. He sees instead (1977:37, 43) "random" movements and invokes ecological stress to doubt that a mechanism of social cohesion could operate among Zhu. The evidence he offers for this doubt are his figures 1 and 2, which he asserts illustrate incommensurable individual dispersion of Zhu. His figure 1 diagrams the areas of resource exploitation and visiting of four men living at Dobe during his period of fieldwork in 1968–69; Yellen does not give the kin relationships of these men, but from other evidence in his text they appear to be a set of father, sons, and brothers. Of these diagrams, Yellen (1977:41) says, "one can see that in no two cases do they coincide." It is true that the shapes and sizes of the areas are different, but if the diagrams are superimposed with the location of Dobe as the common reference point, and the areas of overlap calculated, by overlaying a millimeter grid on them and counting the number of square millimeters contained in each, it can be calculated that 70% of the total area was utilized in common. Specifically, 61%, 73%, 100%, and 65% of the area used by each man individually was also exploited by the other men as a group. One could hardly say that these men were using exclusive patches of land. Thus Yellen's conclusion is not supported by his evidence.

17. Perhaps this is why Marshall was misled by her Tswana interpreter, who might have responded to questions phrased in terms of cousins in general that anyone who does not marry first cousins, as his group does, does not marry cousins.

18. Motzafi-Haller (1987), on the basis of oral histories she collected, describes various Sotho-speaking groups in Transvaal and the eastern Kalahari region as being small groups composed of agnatically related families whose leader was the most senior man in the agnatic cluster. These groups often fragmented, but they still acknowledged the seniority of the original group from which they had separated. The head of the agnatic cluster that had the longest history of occupation of an area was called the "mong wa lefatshe": "owner/ master of the land."

Chapter Six: The Political Construction of Production Relations

1. I use the term "homestead" as a gloss for Zhucoasi shutcoh, Otjiherero onganda, and Setswana lolwapa to refer to the primary place of residence of a family or set of families. This usage is in keeping with that of Tlou (1974:58), who glosses lolwapa as "homestead." Lee (1979) and Yellen (1977) use "camp" for shutcoh to stress a temporarily occupied residence; this is appropriate in many instances, especially when applied to rainy-season residences. In the past I have also used camp. There are compelling arguments, however, in favor of homestead, especially in the context of the present discussion. First of all, the term is in keeping with the tenurial basis of nqore entitlement; it situates Zhu dwellings as homes in "land adequate for the residence and maintenance of a family" (*Compact Edition of the Oxford English Dictionary*). Second, during all of the time anthropologists have observed them, Zhu have maintained stable, primary residences at which they lived for half of each year or longer and to which they returned from temporary trips undertaken for a number of purposes (foraging, visiting, trading); Yellen (1977:64–77) vividly portrays this, referring to Dobe and Qangwa as base camps (as distinct from temporary foraging camps). These, plus CaeCae and other places in Ngamiland, are known to have been occupied for generations. Cashdan (1984:450) notes that the same is true of Gxanna residences at Metseamanong and Molapo in Central District; indeed, it is true of dozens, if not hundreds, of inhabited places in the Kalahari. Often such short trips for limited purposes as described by Yellen are, and were, undertaken by only some members of a homestead, with the others remaining in residence. Zhu have told me that as long as they can remember (that is, stories told them by grandparents) this has been their pattern. Third, those familiar with Tswana and Herero residence patterns are aware that similar seasonal and social mobility to cattleposts (Setswana = matseka, Otjiherero = ozohambo) and farms (Setswana = bolemo), as well as for hunting and gathering, from the village homestead is as characteristic of them as of Zhu. As Silitshena (1982:220) says, "Until recently, Batswana were characterized as people with three homes: 1. a permanent one in the village: 2. a temporary one used during the agricultural season at the cultivated lands areas; and 3. a make-shift one used by herd boys at the cattle posts" (see also Silitshena 1978, 1979).

The following equivalent designations for my homesteads and Lee's living groups (LG) are offered to allow future researchers to use the two data sets in conjunction (consult Lee 1979:59–63).

	In 1964	In 1973
Homestead 1	LG 31	LG 30
Homestead 2	LG 27	LG 24
Homestead 3	?	LG 23
Homestead 4	LG 30	LG 29
Homestead 5	Most members at Qubi with LG 19	
Homestead 6	?	LG 26
Homestead 7	Not recorded	LG 24/68 *

	In 1964	*In 1973*
Homestead 8	LG 25	LG 25
Homestead 9	LG 32	LG 31

* This is the 1968 identification of this group (Lee 1979:345).

2. In this and following chapters, I use several conventions to present genealogical information for persons. Each CaeCae person is assigned a three-digit identification number in which the first digit designates homestead, the second household, and the third the individual; 0 in the homestead field indicates Bantu, 0 in the household field indicates the person has no fixed household residence, 0 in the individual field indicates the person is dead. Zhu names are assigned a letter (these are listed in the legend to fig. 6.1). Kinship designators are M, mother; F, father; P, parent; S, son; D, daughter; C, child; B, brother, Z, sister; s, sibling. Presumed ascribed kinship relations are shown in parentheses, ( ); those acquired through intermediary connections are shown in braces, { }, and the acquired link is shown in brackets, [ ].

3. Nancy Howell (1976), who has graciously allowed me to use her unpublished data, estimated ages by asking people lined up to be weighed if they were older than, younger than, or the same age as the person in front of them; after many reiterations of this procedure, she entered the data (along with known ages of young children) in a life table, MW5-F (Coale and Demeny 1966), and extracted ages for individuals. I made use of the age-mate system (tcarakwe) by which Zhu associate themselves with others (including, of course, ranking with respect to relative age). Ovambanderu with whom Zhu live are incorporated into this system. The cognate Mbanderu system, osukareka, includes Zhu in conjunction with the oviuondo calendar by which birth years are known; these can be converted to Gregorian calendar years. I made use of these to arrive at individual ages. A comparison of my method and that of Howell (confined to persons for whom we both estimated ages) produces an average difference in age estimate of only 1.6 years, almost all of which is attributable to discrepancies in estimated ages of persons over sixty. It is perhaps expectable that our age estimates should agree, for—although Howell and I worked independently, at different times, and without knowledge of each other's efforts—we both based our approach on the importance to Zhu (and to Ovaherero and Batswana) of seniority—and thus of knowing who is senior or junior to whom—that Marshall observed years ago.

4. All persons living at CaeCae since 1973 are entered in my censuses of the community; each person is identified by number as well as by name. Richard Lee, Nancy Howell, Patricia Draper, Henry Harpending, Polly Wiessner, and John Yellen have all generously shared their genealogical data with me; these data have been most useful in cross-checking my own interview data and in pointing to leads for investigation. Schapera (1945) was helpful in checking my interview genealogies of CaeCae Ovambanderu.

5. Readers will begin to sense a bit of the flavor of the interviews in which these kinship data were acquired. At some point the conversation would re-

duce to something like this exchange: "Which Kao was that?" "That one who is the father of Tcishe, the father of Kao." "Ah, that one whose father is Kaishe. . . ." "No; I don't remember his father's name." "Oh, so that one who was married to Nqai, whose older sister was married to Kao, who is the uqnqa of Kao, the one sitting there who is the father of Qam." "Yes, that one." And so it went. I could have mentioned that Qam is the father of Kao, who is too young to be the father of anybody—but in about ten years this Kao can be expected to become the father of Qam, who after all is not only his father but also his father's father's father and his father's father's father's father's older brother.

6. The Mhapa family had large cattle herds in western Ngamiland-Namibia during the time of the rinderpest, 1896–97 (p. 331); from these Sekgoma was able to acquire seed stock to rebuild his herds.

7. In Zhu, *d* and *t* are interchangeable in certain phonetic environments, and a terminal particle ending in a vowel is usually added to words introduced from European languages. Thus, "Dowtli" may have been James R. Todd, "who was engaged in copper mining in Hottentot country [in the mountains south of present-day Windhoek] during 1855–58" (Tabler 1973:111–12). Todd was the trading partner of Robert Lewis (Karobbie) and hunted with Axel Ericsson (Karuapa Katiti) throughout northern Namibia and Ngamiland; in July 1878 he—in company with Lewis and three other European traders—is known to have been "standing at Leeupan [in the vicinity of Samungaigai] to trade with the Dorsland Trekkers" (Tabler 1973:68; p. 120). Todd was married to a Herero woman.

8. Herero custom recognizes a category of legitimate conjugal unions in which the partners are not "married"; that is, between whose families marriage payments have not passed. These unions are often stable and longstanding. The usual reason for this arrangement, which is formal and negotiated, is to produce children for the woman's homestead without incurring the obligation of dispersing family wealth upon the death of the family head. The Herero word for persons in this relationship, otjiwateka, is glossed "concubine" by Gibson (1959a:20), and indeed concubine is used by Herero themselves as an English gloss. I use visitor-spouse to avoid the negative connotations that concubine has for American readers. Zhu custom has a parallel relationship, n‖ǎèakwe (nxaiakwe); persons in such a relationship are n‖ǎèha (nxaiha) to each other. Gift exchanges with many of the undertones of haro are features of this relationship (both Zhu and Herero), and some of the privileges of marriage are attached to it. As Gibson (1959a:27) states for Herero, "The preferred relative for a concubine is . . . [FZD] . . . or her classificatory equivalent—she who is also the preferred relative for marriage." Similarly, Zhu nxaihasi should be in the tru relationship, that is, PPsCC or PPPsCCC to each other. Since Ismair and Tautona have the same classificatory grandfather and Tautona was married to Tcasa, the FFZDD of Xushe's father, Ismair and Xushe can be considered trumasi (marrying cousins). The continuing affection of this pair for each other was apparent in their behavior when together; until

Xushe's death in 1978 they continued to exchange gifts. Tanaka (1980:106) mentions a similar relationship, which he called za-ku, among the Gcwi.

9. Reginah genealogy:

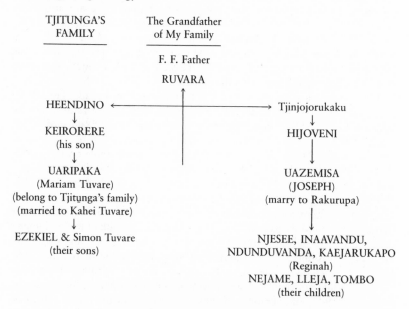

| TJITUNGA'S FAMILY | The Grandfather of My Family |

F. F. Father
RUVARA

HEENDINO ←——————————→ Tjinjojorukaku
↓   ↓
KEIRORERE   HIJOVENI
(his son)   ↓
↓
UARIPAKA   UAZEMISA
(Mariam Tuvare)   (JOSEPH)
(belong to Tjitunga's family)   (marry to Rakurupa)
(married to Kahei Tuvare)
↓   ↓
EZEKIEL & Simon Tuvare   NJESEE, INAAVANDU,
(their sons)   NDUNDUVANDA, KAEJARUKAPO
                                              (Reginah)
                                       NEJAME, LLEJA, TOMBO
                                          (their children)

REGINAH TUVARE (Simon's wife)

1. My mother who is Rakurupa was born of the family of NANGORO. NAN-GORO & NGUVAUVA were brothers. the Elder brother was NANGORO. NGUVA-UVA was strong enough to be a king, so the people chose NGUVAUVA to be their chief. thus why NGUVAUVA became a chief. Joseph Hijoueni married Rakurupa who's my mother at the family of NANGORO. JOSEPH belong to the family of Tjitunga. Mariam Tuvare is my aunt because she is the sister of my father. Mariam Tuvare went to his brother JOSEPH and asked for the child who is suppose to be married to Simon Tuvare. We are cousin.

10. The village headman position, held by Manuel Marenga, should not be confused with the position of chairman of the Village Development Commit-tee (VDC), held by Ssao Xau. The latter position was created as part of the Village Development Programme—funded largely by external donor coun-tries—and is intended to mobilize local initiative in planning community im-provement projects; the VDC chairman is elected by popular vote supervised by the district council. The village headman is appointed by the district coun-cil. The post is created when a settlement is officially raised from cattlepost to village status; this happened at CaeCae in 1980. The village headman is a magistrate who hears local disputes in kgotla and administers government policy in the community. Ssao and Marenga consult each other on all aspects of their duties.

11. Income, in all its forms, is given by household to facilitate later comparisons with studies of Botswana as a whole, especially the *Rural Income Distribution Survey* and the *National Migration Study*. Households are grouped according to homesteads so that comparisons among these are also easily made. Wiessner (1977) also provides income data by household.

12. This principle also extends to bullets. I once gave Marenga a handful of rifle shells that I chanced to find in Maun; sometime thereafter, his young son appeared at my camp with a very large piece of kudu haunch, explaining that one of my bullets had killed the animal.

13. It is not clear on what basis this new calculation is made. Lee (1979: 270) says he now uses the more accurate calculation of caloric value, 650 kilocalories/100 grams, for mongongo nuts rather than the 600 kilocalories/100 grams that he used for his initial calculation. The new figure seems to be rounded from 654 kilocalories/100 grams, found in the table on his p. 480; this is fair enough. However, this latter value is attributed to Wehmeyer, Lee, and Whiting (1969: 1530), and there we find a value of 641 kilocalories/100 grams; this is the value I used in my calculations. There is, moreover, an omission from the input budget; Lee (1979: 407) notes that people of Dobe "made frequent trips to Mahopa to pass the day and drink the milk of Katjambungu's cattle. In July 1964 [during the period of Lee's input-output study] they spent 20 person-days there." The caloric and nutritional value of the milk they drank is not included in Lee's calculation of overall consumption in that period.

14. I should note here that when Lee's original input/output study was carried out in 1964, ethnography was in what, in the present context, might be called its Stone Age of statistics. Within anthropology at the time, Lee's procedure was considered not only adequate in itself but ample in its results as grounds for constructing grand generalities, most notable among these being Sahlins's (Lee and DeVore 1968: 85–89) "original affluent society." Lee therefore should not be singled out for censure on this basis. His subsequent response to criticism, however (1979: 254 ff.), aims mainly to rationalize his methods. As Johnson (1975: 301–3) says, this is really quite beside the point; a researcher's belief that a single sample is intuitively representative does not substitute for adequate sampling.

15. The maize meal was more often CSM (corn-soy-milk), which is composed of 85% maize meal, 10% soy flour, and 5% milk powder.

16. The numbers entered in this table for 1979–80 refer to February 1980; not counted are twelve head that I had agreed to pay from my herd for services performed by five men (nine head to three Zhu, three head to two Ovambanderu) but did not transfer until later in the year.

17. This is not to say, of course, that Zhu sold no animals at all. In 1973 Halengisi sold a surplus ox (useless for breeding or draft power) to me for my Christmas party. He told me he would use the money he received to buy a young heifer. As I was short of cash at the time, he gave the animal to me on credit, payable when I returned. In January 1975 I paid him with 20% interest to cover inflation in the price of heifers.

18. For example, in 1979 a Herero man who had moved to Qangwa from

CaeCae in 1976 after his wife's death was refused permission to return on the grounds that grazing pressure would become too high with the addition of his cattle. Bashile, as representative of Tawana authority, was the spokesman for the community of stockowners who made the decision after consulting among themselves. Marenga, as village headman, now performs this role of spokesman in such matters.

19. Tourists took outrageous advantage of Zhu, even to the point of giving them coins worthless to them (French francs, German marks, and others). All Zhu can count and carry out addition and subtraction easily in their own system, and most of them can also do so in Otjiherero or Setswana or both and some in Afrikaans. In 1973 many were fully aware of the denominational differences of South African rand and British pound notes. In short, these people were ignorant neither of numerical nor of monetary systems, but none could do sums quickly enough to forestall dishonest tourists. Shortly after I arrived in 1973, a man came to me to confirm his suspicion that he had recently been cheated at the Namibian border (along which tourists continued to come into the area for some time into the 1970s). He had a piece of paper money he felt sure was a one-rand note, which it was; he said he had agreed to sell a bow-and-arrow set for R10 and had been given this. When he protested the group drove off, and of course the Boer tour guide refused to translate his objection. I offered to teach him to read and pronounce English numbers (which turned out to be beneficial to me, for to do so I had to learn the numbers in the three local languages). Shortly, thirty or more people were attending daily hour-long arithmetic lessons; Dam (whom I taught) taught numeral 0–9 recognition, Simon (literate in Otjiherero) taught 10–99 and place recognition, and I taught simple number manipulation.

20. An indication that low-level cash flow did take place is found in the following anecdote. In August 1975 Botswana established its own currency, the pula; the South African rand, the previous currency, could not be spent in the country after that time. Numbers of CaeCae persons brought their rands to me for exchange; several told me these represented their accumulated savings from herding wages. Some had more than R80.

21. During the first half of 1980 the Geological Survey of Botswana had a base camp at CaeCae from which geological mapping of the area was carried out. At the same time, the Northwest District Council instituted a relief work program in the area, in the form of clear-cutting the vehicle track to Tsau. Virtually every able man who was not already employed (and also a few women) acquired a job for three to five months at a pay of P30 a month. For nine months of 1983, a mining survey station was maintained at CaeCae, again employing—as bush cutters and camp attendants—a large proportion of the unemployed here. These injections from external sources provided brief but dramatic inputs of cash income into the community.

22. The following case illustrates the extent to which rights to products of land are enforced. In 1976 Tcashe (K/921) of homestead 9 was seen carving beads from a stick of kowi, Cape sandalwood (*Spirostachysis africanus*), intending to sell to Botswanacraft the necklace he planned to make. He was,

however, forced by the members of homestead 1 to relinquish the wood on grounds that he had no right to take it from a tree in their nqore. Other raw materials for commodity craft production, principally animal skins and ostrich eggshells, are by-products of hunting and thus are available in proportion to the ability to hunt. Glass beads for embroidery must be purchased initially (when not obtained as gifts from anthropologists or Botswanacraft), even though they subsequently circulate in the haro networks; again, this gives advantage to kin groups having some members with access to cash.

23. This form is found in other San languages. Barnard (1985:131, 152) gives Nharo ‖ámá = "buy"/"sell," "barter" and notes that Vossen writes ‖’ámá; I suppose, therefore, that this is a common form in Khoe languages.

24. For example, from puberty until midadulthood (usually specified as being reached at the birth of one's second child) both men and women are forbidden to eat steenbok; when captured, those animals are given to parents or parents-in-law. A person's father must release him or her from this prohibition. Tcomazho told me he thought this restriction was imposed by elders to ensure their meat supply in the hot, dry months when little other meat was available.

25. Tobacco distribution is a very anxiety-producing event. Herero folklore even has tales of Zhu killing people in order to suck the tobacco stains from their windpipes. Thus it can be entrusted only to the nqorekau. Ssao, who is one of my principal assistants at CaeCae, made certain that he distributed tobacco on those occasions when I didn't feel like walking several kilometers to hand some 260 people their weekly shares. When I suggested we appoint someone else to do it and pay for the job, Ssao would say, "Ehn ehn, people will fight." People agreed that only their nqorekau could carry out the distribution without conflict.

26. "To keep out of sight" refers to the month-long isolation of the initiates in the bush while they are instructed in the requirements of manhood. Recall that Tautona was said to have been a stern disciplinarian of young men in this context.

27. The concept of unequal possession is also inherent in other San ideologies. Barnard (1985:119) gives Nharo |kāna = "poor" and notes its relation to Nama |gā(sa). Cashdan (1980a:118) says that among the Gxana "inequality in total wealth is considerable"; her data indicate that 95% of "wealth items" (domestic stock and water drums) are owned by 25% of Gxana individuals, who are concentrated in a limited number of homesteads (bands). Gibson (1962:623) says of Ovaherero, "It was the common practice for a poor man to herd cattle for a rich chief or relative, being compensated with the milk of the herd and an occasional animal for his own." Recall (p. 167) the Otjiherero terms for wealthy and poor persons. Burchell ([1824] 1953, 2: 347) says kosi (kgosi) means chief or rich person. Also, Guthrie (1970, 3:322) associates the proto-Bantu-X stem for wealth with chief.

28. "Die Buschmannrasse zerfällt in der Mittle-Kalahari, wie bekannt, in zwei grosse Völker, diese wiederum in einzelne Stämme und die Stämme in Sippen. Früher bildeten die Stämme geschlossene politische Organizationen.

An der Spitze eines jeden Stammes stand ein Grootkapitain, wie der holländisch redende Buschmann sich ausdrückte, der von den ⁴aichadji, den Familienoberhäupten, unterstüzt wurde. . . . Im Schadumtal traf ich auf eine Horde Ssu²gnassi, deren Häuptling Gumtsa hiesst. Aber der Oberhäuptling der Stammeshiesst ²Auka und hielt sich seinerzeit an einer Vley Tsanni auf, die westlich von Sodanna liegen muss."

29. This Gcwi term, ‖xeixa(ma), appears to be cognate with Zhu ‖'áixà, the suffix ma being a gender marker in Gcwi. Hitchcock (1980:25) gives ‖kaiha for the Kwa who live in Gangwato. Barnard (1985:82) derives Nharo !khû = "'master' in the secular sense" from the same form applied to God, but one wonders if the ‖'xài form may not be present. Elphick (1975:46) glosses Nama !khu-khoi-b as rich man and says this term is the source of khoeque, chief.

30. Although Marshall (1976:191) retracts her earlier attribution of headmen to Zhu, she does so on a peculiar basis—her gloss of the word kx'ào (she writes k"xau), which she correctly gives as "owner" (or, as I say, "possessor"). Marshall says she felt that "owner" could be extended to encompass "headman." But in her earlier work (1960:348) she gives n‖iha and gaoxa as the principal words for "headman" and "chief," with kxau (as she then wrote kx'ào) having this meaning only secondarily. Gao derives from the name for God in his earthly manifestation, while n‖iha appears to be an attempt to write ‖'áixà. Thus it appears that Marshall's retraction is unwarranted.

Chapter Seven: What It Means to Be Excluded

1. The Remote Area Development Programme (RADP) is a unit in the Ministry of Local Government and Lands charged with carrying out policy directives in those rural areas classified as "remote"; by definition, such areas are not supposed to have registered villages, schools, or public services, but this definition is not strictly adhered to. RADP was established in 1974 and was initially concerned only with "Bushman" projects; it was then called the Bushman Development Programme. The name was soon changed to Basarwa Development Programme, and later—after documentation by the Rural Income Distribution Survey of extensive poverty common to a number of ethnic groups in rural parts of the country—Basarwa became first Extra-Rural and finally, in 1978, Remote Area to give the program its current name (Giddie and Maakwe, in RADW 1979). Throughout these name changes and up to the present day, "The programme as operated by its own staff continues to deal with the same issues and the same target group in the same way as in 1974" (Egner 1981a:2). That target group is, of course, ethnic San-speaking Basarwa. Initially, RADP was charged with contributing to policy formulation; annual workshops brought field officers and central administrators together for this purpose (Wily 1979). These prerogatives have, however, been taken from the program, which now has little more than pro forma paperwork functions, what Egner (1981a:7) calls "a passive watching brief." I examine the reasons for this change in the last section of this chapter. RADO is the acronym of Remote Area Development Officer, the principal field representatives of

RADP; RADW is the acronym of Remote Area Development Workshop, an annual meeting of RADOs and other ministries' representatives.

2. Gordon (1984) approaches this issue from a different perspective but arrives at very similar conclusions.

3. An indication of the pervasiveness of this categorization is apparent in this anecdote. In 1983, when I visited Pnina Motzafi in Mokokwana, she introduced me to the Setswana-speaking villagers as having worked with Basarwa for many years. But the San language spoken in that area, Kwa, is as different from Zhu as English is from Greek or Czech; I could not reply to the phrases of Kwa that were addressed to me but offered some Zhu phrases to underscore the differences in the languages. Numbers of people ridiculed my words as gibberish, saying I wasn't a Mosarwa after all but a Lekoa (white man, with class 3 prefix), just as I appeared. One older man upbraided me for making fun of Basarwa, who are, he said, people not baboons. It took a bit of demonstration to convince these Setswana-speakers, most, but not all, of whom were unaware that there are different "Sesarwa" languages.

4. The full text of this passage reveals "the way that the chief [C:] is able to 'constitute' the applicant [A:] as a special kind of ethnic subject" (Worby, n.d.: 46–47); notice also the use of the term "master":

C: As you are not a Mokgatla you cannot be allocated land in Kgatleng District. Before we can allocate land to you, you must go back to your headman in Lephephe District (*sic*) and get a letter from him; then you must have it stamped by paramount chief in Kweneng District and bring that paper to me in Mochudi. We can then make you a tribesman and you can apply for land like any other Mokgatla.
A: I left Lephephe a long time ago; will they remember me?
C: Do you still have relatives there?
A: Yes.
C: Then they will help you to go to the headman. You say that you moved around before you settled in Polokobatho; you people move around a lot. Are you not going to leave this field and move somewhere else when you feel like it?
Wife of A: We move Kgosi (Chief), when we are ill treated—then we go and look for work somewhere else where we will be treated better.
C: What will happen if you are ill-treated and you have a field? Will you move and leave it?
A: I think if we have a home and a field of our own we will be able to eat from this field so we will stay and look after it.
C: What will happen if your master says to you: "O.K., now that you have your own field you can leave my employment and go?"
A: I would not agree to go.

Wily (1979:183) states that this was not an isolated case. She says that local land boards routinely claim that Basarwa are Bakwena and not Bakgatla, even when the person involved speaks no San language. Only two of thirty-nine Basarwa ever received the "no objection" letter that would allow them to pursue their application for a plot of land to plow.

5. Although these people are categorized as Basarwa, none can be called "San"; almost all have a Tswana father, and most have at least one Tswana grandfather. All speak Setswana rather than a San language.

6. Although most "interethnic" marriages involving Zhu in Ngamiland are between Zhu women and Bantu men, two Zhu men (whose ancestry is in CaeCae) living at Mahoeihoei have Tswana wives with whom they have established households and borne children.

7. In the face of the uncertainties that are a feature of the future, I expect that this foothold will be maintained. Two candidates seem to be available. The brothers Kaishe (E/414) at age forty-nine and Dam (Y/413) at age thirty-two, each with three living children, are securely married to the sisters Shexai (A/113) and Qu (Y/114), the daughters of Shexai's (A/110) oldest son, Tcische (I/111). These women are Ssao's (D/331) MMZSD, and the younger Shexai is the uqma of the now-dead nqorekao Shexai (A/100). Kaishe's and Dam's FFF was the uqnqa (FB) of Shexai's husband Qam. Both men have traveled widely, are comfortable with the modern world as it is represented in Botswana, and have an articulate, projective manner. They are thus in prime position to become nqorekau, and chairman, upon Ssao's retirement. Ssao's son Tcoma (C/333) is of an age (twenty-six) and disposition to follow Kaishe or Dam.

8. Joyce's estimate that Masarwa owned four times as many cattle as reported in the census seems too high, although there is no firm evidence on which to reject it. Presumably Joyce based this estimate on observations he made during a year of very extensive travel throughout Central District when he saw Masarwa with sole charge of herds, but it is probable that many of the animals belonged to Batswana who gave them out in some form of mafisa or servitude. Joyce (BNA 1938:12–13) did find several villages of fifty and more Masarwa who owned cattle, sheep, goats, and donkeys and who plowed for themselves on a large scale; he says of these people that many of the young men had been away on employment but does not say where they had worked. He also referred to these people as having masters; thus it is unclear whether some of the animals they kept may have belonged to these masters. Even if we should use Joyce's higher estimate, for the sake of assessing what may have been the maximum Sarwa cattle ownership, average household ownership would still be only 0.8 head.

9. Joyce did not include Bateti among Basarwa but gave them separate ethnic status. Forty years later, Hitchcock (1978:218–20) also separated Bateti from Basarwa.

10. This is not to say that severe abuse did not also occur in other districts, but records of such mistreatment are not so common there as for southern and eastern districts. This could be a function of underreporting and underrecording in those districts, where administration was more lax. I should note also that in 1943 one-third of the men listed as being away from home were in the British army.

11. A few figures given here differ slightly from those in my NMS report (Wilmsen 1982b). This is due partly to different stratification of households, and partly to the fact that not all of my data had been compiled in 1981 when the NMS report was written. Average values have not changed.

12. Some summary statistics for Molopo farms are included in the text but are not used in other calculations of either San or RAD averages. This is be-

cause this block is not classified as remote, there is no census of San-speakers living there, available data apply to the aggregate ethnic groups contributing labor to the farms, and wages there are in part competitive with those on adjacent South African farms (Wiley 1982).

13. The South African rand (R) was the currency of Botswana until August 1975 when the pula (P) was issued; for calculations here, these currencies are essentially at par.

14. Obtained by adding mean wage, P59, plus two mean craft sales incomes (rounded to P10).

15. Massive inputs of drought-relief food and onetime make-work employment render income figures for these years completely atypical, and they are not used in any calculations.

16. Averages for households without a wage earner were obtained by summing the general cash wage and cash sale means and multiplying by two. Averages for households with a local wage earner were obtained by summing the mean local wage plus twice the mean cash sales. A single wage mean per household was used in the latter case because in every such household, while almost all wives and adult daughters of the male wage earner also were "employed" along with the man, no woman received a regular wage in cash, although all received payment in kind—sometimes comparatively generously. Cash equivalency averages were obtained by the formula: payment in kind times three (2 adults plus 2 mobile children times 0.5 plus 1 suckling child not counted) plus cash receipts. Thus, for local wage-earning households, 3 × P65 = P195 + P79 = P274; for nonlocal wage households, 3 × P54 = P162 + P20 = P182.

17. That rural poor Batswana gained on the average 25% of their subsistence from foraging in 1974–75, about the same percentage as pastoral Zhu in those years, raises again the question of what is meant by bushmanizing terminology and the classification of foragers.

18. Bere is a development settlement established by Hans Heinz; Kagcae was established by Anthony Traill. Both of these communities received relatively large amounts of external donor funding. The Dobe development is a Kalahari Peoples Fund project that has been successful largely through the efforts of Megan Biesele and Charles Rochardt. Leonard Mathlare (1979:71) underreports Dobe ownership and does not give distribution data (see also Lee 1979:427). A similar project in Namibia initiated by John Marshall and Claire Ritchie promises to have success.

19. Personal maintenance is, of course, more than a matter of cosmetics. Bar soap, laundry detergent, and body oil (usually ordinary Vaseline) are in great demand because with these in constant supply lice, skin eruptions, and conjunctivitis, ubiquitous conditions of deep poverty in the recent past, are all but eliminated. There is a strong social component to this need as well, for presenting the self to others is as important as maintaining hygiene and satisfying hunger.

20. These three men worked as laborers on buildings and roads construction in the Tshumqwe area; with their earnings they purchased eight, six, and

five head of cattle respectively. As the political situation in Namibia deteriorated, they butchered these animals for sale and reinvested the profits in higher-priced Botswana animals.

21. In addition, 14% went to kqadi purchases. Kqadi brewing is the principal source of cash income for women. A typical ten-liter bucket of kqadi costs about P0.50 in ingredients (mainly brown sugar) and perhaps P0.25 in labor collecting the *Grewia* berries, firewood, and water needed in the brew. At P0.10 per half-liter cup, a bucket of kqadi has a potential sales value of P2.00, but some is given away (a portion of this as haro, so that a return will eventually be forthcoming). Rarely a day passes that some woman has not made kqadi; as often as not this will be an Mbanderu woman. I did not keep accurate records of these sales and their intricacies of deferred payments, but it is likely that a dozen CaeCae Zhu women realize about two or three pula per month from kqadi sales; three Mbanderu women probably earn two or three times that amount.

22. The argument is spurious because very little time was required to make the craft items that were sold. Lee ignores his own data—and mine, which he cites. A mean daily time expenditure required to produce the value realized from crafts sales can be calculated as 3.6 minutes per person per day, at the hourly rate of return Lee implies in the prices for items he gives (this hourly rate is obtained by dividing the price of an item by the number of hours to make it). Thus, P1,093 ÷ 101 craftspersons ÷ P0.50/hour ÷ 360 days × 60 minutes/hour = 3.6 minutes per day needed to manufacture all the items sold. Lee also assumes constant prices, but the figures he used are too high for 1975–76; for example, a quiver set went for P10.00 in those years, down from the P20.00 that obtained a few years previously when Lee worked in the area. Other prices were depressed similarly—this yields a return of P0.25/hr. The actual effort required is thus double that thought necessary by Lee: P1,093 ÷ 101 ÷ 0.25 ÷ 360 × 60 = 7.2 minutes per day. We can also take the average individual income from sales and calculate effort required. The average crafts income, as we saw (table 6.13) was P11.00 for those who sold anything; this required an average 44 hours of labor, 7.2 minutes per day, as above. The person with the highest sales realized P56.00, for which he would have expended 224 hours in the year, or an average of 37.3 minutes per day; this person was, incidentally, one of the two most diligent and successful hunters at CaeCae, who also harvested over three hundred melons and about that many maize ears in 1975. Thus Lee's supposition that craft manufacture for sale inhibited food production is incorrect.

Lee's food cost estimate is also optimistic. R144.00 is an average of about R0.65 per person per year; in 1975 that would translate into 12 kilograms of maize meal per person (calculated from prices, R5 per 90 kilogram bag, for 1974 given in RIDS 1976:92), or about twenty days' minimum energy supply (12 kg × 3,600 kcal/kg ÷ 20 = 2,160 kcal) for each adult-equivalent person. This is hardly enough to offset observed caloric shortfalls: table 7.5 shows that Zhu spent more than twice Lee's estimate, and still they experienced seasonal weight loss. Furthermore, the disaggregated data that have been presented reveal that expenditures were not uniformly distributed among households, as they could not be, given the high disparity in income. Homesteads 1–2–3 spent three times more than others; correspondingly, they had higher average body weights and experienced less seasonal fluctuation. They could not have done this without higher income.

Lee's argument is also disingenuous. Though he has now (1979:228) returned Zhu from the utopian eighteen-hour workweek that he previously (1969) envisioned to a more realistic world of forty-two-hour workweeks, this is still just six hours per day in a seven-day week and leaves ample time for even the maximum half-hour per day of craftwork that we have seen to have been expended by the most craft-productive person in the community. But Lee alters his criteria to suit his argument and contradicts himself; two quotations will suffice: we read that "there is a rhythm of steady work and steady leisure throughout the year" (Lee 1979:118), and—just fifteen pages after asserting that craft manufacture may have eroded necessary subsistence effort and immediately after speaking of the casual requirements of quiver-set manufacture—Lee (1979:456) says, "Because of the ease with which articles can be made during the abundant leisure time, there is no lack of duplicate items." Lee's argument in these regards are simply ad hoc ecology, insensitive to the crucial importance of cash, and the consequences of its absence, in the local economy.

23. Complete protocols, statements of hypotheses, and results from which the following discussion is extracted are found in Wilmsen (1982c, 1985a) and in Hausman and Wilmsen (1985).

24. Janis Diring collected many of the data this discussion is based on. Alice Hausman, while holding a National Institutes of Health postdoctoral fellowship, supervised the data reduction and carried out the analysis; she was assisted by Keith Adams and Irene Good.

25. Lee's presentation is not exactly comparable because he does not break his sample down by economic strata.

26. A. van der Walt and D. Mendelsohn, South African Institute for Medical Research, assayed the blood samples.

27. The data are now available thanks to the generosity of John Hansen, Nancy Howell, and Richard Lee, who provided copies of their field records to Alice Hausman and me.

28. This is not to say that nothing useful to the study of human evolution can come from investigating certain aspects of San culture, but only those aspects of knowledge and technique employed in foraging itself are relevant to a study of foragers. Furthermore, unless one insists that there is, after all, a Paleolithic residue in San-speaking populations, there is no reason to single out these peoples for such investigations. One might as well select any of Botswana's rural poor who employ the same knowledge and techniques to acquire 25% of their sustenance from foraging.

References

Alexander, J.
1967 *An expedition of discovery into the interior of Africa, through the hitherto undescribed countries of the Great Namaquas, Boschmans, and the Hill Damaras.* Cape Town: Struik. Facsimile reprint of 1838 original.
Almagor, U.
1978 Locality and the regulation of grazing among the Herero of Botswana. SSRC conference on land tenure in Botswana, University of Manchester.
1980a Pastoral identity and reluctance to change: The Mbanderu of Ngamiland. *Journal of African Law* 24:35–61.
1980b Some notes on the Mbanderu calender. *Botswana Notes and Records* 12:67–82.
Alnaes, K.
1979a Oral tradition and identity: The Herero in Botswana. Postgraduate seminar in the societies of southern Africa in the nineteenth and twentieth centuries, Institute of Commonwealth Studies, University of London.
1979b Research findings. NORAD and Rural Sociology Unit, Ministry of Agriculture, Gaborone.
Alonso, A.
1988 The effects of truth: Re-presentations of the past and the "imaging of community." *Journal of Historical Sociology* 1:33–57.
Althusser, L.
1969 *For Marx.* London: Allen Lane.
1970 The object of *Capital.* Part 2 of *Reading "Capital,"* ed. L. Althusser and E. Balibar. London: New Left Books.
Amin, S.
1974 *Accumulation on a world scale.* New York: Monthly Review Press.
1976 *Unequal development.* Sussex: Hassocks.
Andersson, C.
1854 A journey to Lake Ngami, and an itinerary of the principal routes leading to it from the West Coast; with the latitudes of some of the chief stations. *South African Commercial Advertiser and Cape Town Mail,* 22 May.
1861 *The Okavango River: A narrative of travel, exploration, and adventure.* New York: John Murray.
1967 *Notes of travel in South Africa.* London: John Murray. Facsimile reprint of 1875 original.

Asad, T.
1978 Equality in nomadic social systems? *Critique of Anthropology* 11: 57–65.
1986 The concept of cultural translation in British social anthropology. In *Writing culture: The poetics and politics of ethnography*, ed. J. Clifford and G. Marcus, pp. 140–64. Berkeley and Los Angeles: University of California Press.

Athanassakis, A.
1983 *Hesiod: Theogony, Works and Days, Shield*. Baltimore: Johns Hopkins University Press.

Baines, T.
1864 *Exploration in South-West Africa*. London: Longman, Green.

Balibar, E.
1970 The basic concepts of historical materialism. Part 3 of *Reading "Capital,"* ed. L. Althusser and E. Balibar. London: New Left Books.

Barnard, A.
1975 Australian models in the South West African highlands. *African Studies* 34:9–18.
1976 Nharo Bushman kinship and the transformation of Khoi kin categories. Ph.D. thesis (anthropology), University College, London.
1978 Universal systems of kin categorization. *African Studies* 37:69–81.
1979 Kalahari Bushmen settlement patterns. In *Social and ecological systems*, ed. P. Burnham and R. Ellen, pp. 131–44. ASA Monographs 18. London: Tavistock.
1985 A Nharo word list. Department of African Studies, University of Natal, *Occasional Papers* 2.
1986 Kinship, language, and production: Aspects of Khoisan history and ethnography. Fourth International Conference on Hunting and Gathering Societies, London.

Bayer, M.
1909 *Mit dem Hauptquartier in Südwest-Afrika*. Leipzig: O. Spamer.

Beach, D.
1983 The Zimbabwe plateau and its peoples. In *History of central Africa*, ed. D. Birmingham and P. Martin, pp. 245–77. London: Longman.

Beinart, W.
1982 Production and the material basis of chieftainship: Pondoland, c. 1830–80. In *Economy and society in pre-industrial South Africa*, ed. S. Marks and A. Atmore, pp. 120–48. London: Longman.

Bennett, T.
1985 Terminology and land tenure in customary law: An exercise in linguistic theory. *Acta Jurdica*, pp. 175 ff. (University of Cape Town Law School).

Bentley, G.
1985 Hunter-gatherer energetics and fertility: A reassessment of the !Kung San. *Human Ecology* 13:79–109.

Benton, T.
1984 *The rise and fall of structural Marxism: Althusser and his influence.* London: Macmillan.
Bernstein, H., and B. Campbell
1985 Introduction. In *Contradictions of accumulation in Africa,* ed. H. Bernstein and B. Campbell, pp. 7–24. Beverly Hills, Calif.: Sage.
Berry, S.
1985 *Fathers work for their sons.* Berkeley and Los Angeles: University of California Press.
Biebuyck, D.
1963 *African agrarian systems.* Oxford: Oxford University Press.
Biesele, M.
1975 Folklore and ritual of !Kung hunter-gatherers. Ph.D. diss. (anthropology), Harvard University.
Birmingham, D.
1981 *Central Africa to 1870.* Cambridge: Cambridge University Press.
1983 Society and economy before A.D. 1400. In *History of central Africa,* ed. D. Birmingham and P. Martin, pp. 1–29. London: Longman.
Birmingham, D., and P. Martin, eds.
1983 *History of central Africa.* London: Longman.
Bley, H.
1971 *South-West Africa under German rule, 1894–1914.* Evanston, Ill.: Northwestern University Press.
Bloch, M.
1983 *Marxism and anthropology.* Oxford: Oxford University Press.
BNA. *See* Botswana National Archives.
Bohannan, P.
1957 *Justice and judgement among the Tiv.* Oxford: Oxford University Press.
1965 The differing realms of the law. In The ethnography of law, ed. L. Nader, *American Anthropologist* 67.6, pt. 2:33–42.
Bollig, M.
1988 Contemporary developments in !Kung research: The !Kung controversy in the light of R. B. Lee's *The Dobe !Kung. Quellen zur Khoisan Forschung* 7. In press.
Bosman, D., I. Van der Merwe, and L. Hiemstra
1982 *Tweetalige woordeboek: Afrikaans-Engels.* Kaapstad: Tafelberg-Uitgevers.
Botswana National Archives (BNA)
1887 HC153/1 High Commission for South Africa.
1897 HC140/6 RM, Tsau to RC, Mafeking, 20 August.
1903a RC10/10 RM, Tsau to RC, Mafeking, 2 September.
1903b RC10/10 HC, Johannesburg to CO, London, 2 November.
1903c RC10/10 RM, Tsau to RC, Mafeking, 5 November.
1903d RC10/10 RM, Gaborones to DC, Mafeking, 7 December.

1904a RC10/18 RM, Tsau to RC, Mafeking, 14 October.
1904b RC10/18 RM, Tsau to ARC, Mafeking, 31 October.
1905a RC11/1 RM, Tsau to RC, Mafeking, 25 April.
1905b RC11/1 HqGSWA to War Office, London, 26 June.
1905c RC11/1 AM, Tsau to RC, Mafeking, 31 June.
1905d RC11/1 AM, Tsau to RC, Mafeking, 30 December.
1906 RC 11/2 AM, Tsau to RC, Mafeking, 2 March.
1907a RC10/10 Sekgoma Letsholathebe states, 18 September.
1907b RC10/10 RM, Gaborones to DC, Mafeking, 21 September.
1907c RC 2/45 Officer of the German army on supposed expedition to N'gami.
1914a S28/3 Anglo-German & European war (1914–).
1914b S28/3 Dispatch found on a German soldier (Carl Hespe).
1922a S5/1 M, Gobabis to RM, Ghanzi, 19 August.
1922b S5/1 RM, Ghanzi to GS, Mafeking, 1 September.
1922c S5/1 M, Gobabis to RM, Ghanzi, 22 September.
1922d S5/1 Statement taken from a native named Samson, 28 December.
1922e S5/1 RM, Maun to AGS, Mafeking, 28 December.
1923a S5/1 Herero Samuel Karcho alias Samuel Sheppard, 4 April.
1923b S5/1 RM, Ghanzi to GS, Mafeking, 4 June; GS, Mafeking to RM, Ghanzi, 15 June.
1926a DCS45/7 Disclosing some of the serious facts for the first time to the administration of the Bechuanaland Proctectorate: How the Masarwa became slaves and why the chief's word is law.
1926b S3/1 Statements of Kuruman and Moses Malata.
1926c S3/1 Nettleton, History of the Batawana up to 1926.
1927 S43/7 Slave trade, slavery, and similar conditions.
1929 S47/1 Stigand, RC 28 December.
1930 DCF2/12 Marsarwa ex Bamangwato Reserve: Hunting of by Bamangwato masters.
1933 C/3/360 Bamangwato Administrative Records, R1-M1: Masarwa, 1933–40.
1934 S360/1 Notes of a meeting held at Serowe on the 18th January 1934, 6:30 A.M.
1935 C/8/725 Bamangwato administrative records. Chiefs Tshekedi and Bathoen vs. Rex.
1936a S469/1/1 RC, Mafeking to government secretary, 6 November.
1936b S469/1/1 Interview with high commissioner, November, 1936, 18 November.
1938 S360/1 Joyce, Marsarwa report.
1940a V14/2 Monthly report, general veterinary officer, Maun (V806).
1940b Revision of Professor Schapera's handbook on Tswana law and custom, land tenure, etc.
1944a DCF9/12 Notes of a meeting at Mafeking on 11th October 1944 re Masarwa on crown lands.
1944b DCS31/4 Damaras in Ngamiland: Discussion at Serowe.

1946 V3/1/1 Livestock improvement center for Basarwa.
1957 S279/60 Minutes "Control of recruitment," 29 November.
1958 S387/7/3 Recruiting of native labour in B.P.
1960 5031/7 Recruiting: NRC general file.
n.d. BNB2041 Z. Nguvirue, The external factor in nineteenth century Herero-Nama politics.

Botswana Society
1971 Proceedings of the conference on sustained production from semi-arid areas, Gaborone.

Bourdieu, P.
1977 *Outline of a theory of practice*. Cambridge: Cambridge University Press.

Bradby, B.
1975 The destruction of natural economy. *Economy and Society* 4:127–60.

Brenner, R.
1976 Agrarian class structure and economic development in pre-industrial Europe. *Past and Present* 70:30–75.
1977 The origins of capitalist development: A critique of neo-Smithian marxism. *New Left Review* 104:25–92.
1985 The agrarian roots of European capitalism. In *The Brenner debate*, ed. T. Aston and C. Philpin, pp. 213–28. Cambridge: Cambridge University Press.

Brincker, H.
1964 *Wörterbuch und kurzgefasste Grammatik des Otji-Hérero*. Ridgewood, N.J.: Gregg Press. Facsimile reprint of 1886 original.

Brooks, A.
1982 Changing subsistence and settlement patterns among northwest Kalahari foragers: Acculturation, development, and politics. American Association for the Advancement of Science annual meeting, 7 January.

Brown, T.
1979 *Setswana-English dictionary*. 3d ed. Braamfontein: Pula Press. Originally published about 1875.

Burchell, W.
1953 *Travels in the interior of southern Africa*. London: Longman. Facsimile reprint of 1824 original.

Campbell, A.
1982 Notes on the prehistoric background to 1840. In *Settlement in Botswana*, ed. R. Hitchcock and M. Smith, pp. 13–22. Marshalltown: Heinemann.
1986 The use of wild plant foods, and drought in Botswana. *Journal of Arid Environments* 11:81–91.

Carstens, P.
1970 Problems of peasantry and social class in southern Africa. Paper presented at Seventh World Congress of Sociology, Varna, Bulgaria.
1983 The inheritance of private property among the Nama of southern Africa reconsidered. *Africa* 53:58–70.

Case, J.
1982 The effects of migration on primary education. In *Migration in Botswana*, ed. C. Kerven, pp. 498–525. Gaborone: Government Printer.
Cashdan, E.
1977 Subsistence, mobility, and territorial organization among the G‖anaque of the northeastern Central Kalahari Game Reserve, Botswana. Report to the Ministry of Local Government and Lands, Gaborone.
1980a Egalitarianism among hunters and gatherers. *American Anthropologist* 82:116–20.
1980b Property and social insurance among the ‖ganna. Second International Conference on Hunting and Gathering Societies, Quebec City.
1983 Territoriality among human foragers: Ecological models and an application to four Bushmen groups. *Current Anthropology* 24:47–66.
1984 G‖ana territorial organization. *Human Ecology* 12:443–63.
1985 Coping with risk: Reciprocity among the Basarwa of northern Botswana. *Man* 20:454–74.
1986 Competition between foragers and food-producers on the Botletli River, Botswana. *Africa* 56:299–317.
Cashdan, E., and R. Chasko
n.d. Report on the Bakgalagadi settlements of Molopo and |o≠we in the Central Reserve. Report to Basarwa Development Officer.
Caye, V., and S. Koitsiwe
1976 Report on a survey of Basarwa in western Kgatleng District. Ministry of Local Government and Lands.
Central Statistics Office (CSO)
1974 Social and economic survey in three peri-urban areas of Botswana.
Chapman, J.
1971 *Travels in the interior of Africa, 1849–1863*. Ed. E. Tabler. Cape Town: Balkema.
Childers, G.
1976 *Report on the survey/investigation of the Ghanzi Farm Basarwa situation*. Gaborone: Government Printer.
Chirenje, J.
1973 The European impact upon northern Tswana chiefdoms, 1850–1910. Ph.D. thesis (history), University of London.
1977 *A history of northern Botswana: 1850–1910*. Rutherford, N.J.: Fairleigh Dickinson University Press.
Clammer, J.
1978 Concepts and objects in economic anthropology. In *The new economic anthropology*, ed. J. Clammer, pp. 1–20. New York: St. Martin's Press.
Clarence-Smith, W.
1979 *Slaves, peasants, and capitalists in southern Angola, 1840–1926*. Cambridge: Cambridge University Press.
Clarence-Smith, W., and R. Moorsom
1975 Underdevelopment and class formation in Ovamboland, 1845–1915. *Journal of African History* 16:365–81.

Clark, D.
1968 Further paleo-anthropological studies in northern Lunda. *Publicaçoes Culturas do Museu do Dundo* 78 (Lisbon).

Cliffe, L.
1977 Rural class formation in East Africa. *Journal of Peasant Studies* 4: 195–224.

Clifford, J.
1983 On ethnographic authority. *Reflections* 1:118–45.

Coale, A., and P. Demeny
1966 *Regional model life tables and stable populations.* Princeton: Princeton University Press.

Cohen, G.
1978 *Karl Marx's theory of history: A defense.* Princeton: Princeton University Press.

Colclough, C., and P. Fallon
1983 Rural poverty in Botswana: Dimensions, causes, and constraints. In *Agrarian policies and rural poverty in Africa,* ed. D. Ghai and S. Radwan, pp. 129–53. Geneva: International Labour Office.

Cole, D.
1975 *An introduction to Tswana grammer.* Cape Town: Longman.

Colson, E.
1953 Social control and vengeance in Plateau Tonga society. *Africa* 23: 199–212.

Comaroff, J.
1973 Competition for office and political processes among the Barolong boo Ratshidi. Ph.D. thesis (anthropology), University of London.
1978 Rules and rulers: Political processes in a Tswana chiefdom. *Man* 13: 1–20.
1980 Class and culture in peasant economy: The transformation of land tenure in Barolong. *Journal of African Law* 24:85–113.

Comaroff, J., ed.
1980 Bridewealth and control of ambiguity in a Tswana chiefdom. In *The meaning of marriage payments,* ed. John Comaroff, pp. 161–96. New York: Academic Press.

Comaroff, J., and J. Comaroff
1981 The management of marriage in a Tswana context. In *Essays on African marriage in southern Africa,* ed. E. Krige and J. Comaroff, pp. 29–49. Cape Town: Juta.

Comaroff, J.
1981 *Rules and processes: The cultural logic of dispute in an African context.* Chicago: University of Chicago Press.

Cooper, D.
1977 Some preliminary perspectives on social stratification in Selebi-Phikwe. Sociology Department, Birmingham University.
1979 *Economy and society in Botswana.* National Migration Study Working Paper 2. Gaborone: Central Statistics Office.

1980a An overview of the Botswana urban class structure and its articulation with the rural structure. Background paper for Symposium on Settlement in Botswana.

1980b *How urban workers in Botswana manage their cattle and lands*. National Migration Study Working Paper 4. Gaborone: Central Statistics Office.

1982 Socio-economic and regional factors of wage migration and employment. In *Migration in Botswana: Patterns, causes, and consequences*, ed. C. Kerven, pp. 297–336. Gaborone: Government Printer.

n.d. A socio-economic-geographical perspective on the causes of migration. National Migration Study Topic 3.

Cooper, F.

1981 Peasants, capitalists, and historians: A review article. *Journal of Southern African Studies* 7:284–314.

Cooperman, J.

1978 Report on the northwest of Kgatleng. Ministry of Local Government and Lands, Gaborone.

CSO. *See* Central Statistics Office.

Dalton, G.

1969 Theoretical issues in economic anthropology. *Current Anthropology* 10:63–80.

Daniel, G.

1950 *A hundred years of archaeology*. London: Duckworth.

Dannert, E.

1906 *Zum Rechte der Herero*. Berlin: Dieter Reimer.

Deimling, O. von

1906 *Südwestafrika: Land und Leute*. Berlin: R. Eisenschmidt.

Denbow, J.

1984 Prehistoric herders and foragers of the Kalahari: The evidence for 1500 years of interaction. In *Past and present in hunter gatherer studies*, ed. C. Schrire, pp. 175–94. Orlando, Fla.: Academic Press.

1986 Patterns and processes: A new look at the later prehistory of the Kalahari. *Journal of African History* 27:3–28.

Denbow, J., and A. Campbell

1986 The origins of food production in southern Africa and some potential linguistic correlations. In Proceedings of the International Symposium on African Hunters and Gatherers, Sankt Augustin, ed. F. Rottland and R. Vossen, pp. 83–103. *Sprache und Geschichte in Afrika* 7.1.

Denbow, J., D. Kiyaga-Mulindwa, and N. Parsons

1985 Historical and archaeological research in Botswana. Botswana Society Symposium on Research and Development.

Denbow, J., A. Manima-Moubouha, and N. Sanviti

1988 Archaeological investigations along the Loango coast, Congo. *NSI: Bulletin de Liaison des Archéologues du Monde Bantu* 3:37–42.

Denbow, J., and E. Wilmsen

1983 Iron Age pastoralist settlements in Botswana. *South African Journal of Science* 79:405–8.

1986 The advent and course of pastoralism in the Kalahari. *Science* 234: 1509–15.

Diamond, S.

1974 *In search of the primitive.* New Brunswick, N.J.: Transaction Press.

Dikole, W.

1978 Sekgoma Letsholathebe's rule and the British administration. B.A. thesis (history), University of Botswana.

Draper, P.

1975 !Kung women: Contrasts in sexual egalitarianism in the foraging and sedentary contexts. In *Toward an anthropology of women,* ed. R. Reiter, pp. 77–109. New York: Monthly Review Press.

Drechsler, H.

1980 *"Let us die fighting": The struggle of the Herero and Nama against German imperalism (1884–1915).* London: Zed Press.

Driberg, J., and I. Schapera

1930 Introductory note. In *The Khoisan peoples of South Africa,* by I. Schapera, pp. v–vi. London: Routledge.

Dubrow, S.

1987 Race, civilization, and culture: The elaboration of segregationist discourse in the inter-war years. In *The politics of race, class, and nationalism in twentieth-century South Africa,* ed. S. Marks and S. Trapido, pp. 71–94. London: Longman.

Dupré, G., and P.-P. Rey

1973 Reflections on the pertinence of a theory of the history of exchange. *Economy and Society* 2: 131–63.

Durkheim, E.

1964 *The division of labour in society.* New York: Free Press. Reprint of 1893 original.

1966 *The rules of sociological method.* New York: Free Press. Reprint of 1895 original.

Egner, B.

1981a *The Remote Area Development Programme: An evaluation.* Gaborone: Economic Consultancies.

1981b *Submission by Mr. E. B. Egner to the Presidential Commission on Economic Opportunities.* Gaborone: Economic Consultancies.

Ehret, C.

1967 Cattle-keeping and milking in eastern and southern African history: The linguistic evidence. *Journal of African History* 8: 1–17.

1982 The first spread of food production to southern Africa. In *The archaeological and linguistic reconstruction of African history,* ed. C. Ehret and M. Posnansky, pp. 57–65. Berkeley and Los Angeles: University of California Press.

Ehret, C., and M. Kinsman

1981 Shona dialect classification and its implications for Iron Age history in southern Africa. *International Journal of African Historical Studies* 14: 401–42.

Eich, X.
1899 *Berichte Rheinischen Missionsgessellschaft.* Barmen (Wuppertal): Rheinischen Missionsgesellschaft.

Elphick, R.
1975 *Khoikhoi and the founding of white South Africa.* New Haven: Yale University Press.
1977 *Kraal and castle.* New Haven: Yale University Press.

Emmett, T.
1986 Popular resistance in Namibia, 1920–1925. In *Resistance and ideology in settler societies,* ed. T. Lodge, pp. 6–48. Johannesburg: Raven Press.

Engels, F.
1972 *The origin of the family, private property, and the state.* New York: International. Ed. E. Leacock from 1884 original.

English, M., B. Clauss, W. Swartz, and J. Xhari
1980 *We, the people of the short blanket.* Ghanzi: District Council, Remote Area Development Office.

Ervedosa, C.
1980 *Arqueologia Angolana.* Lisbon, Edições 70.

Esch, H.
1977 Interim report on Basarwa and related poor Bakgalagadi in Kweneng District. Ministry of Local Government and Lands.

Esterhuyse, J.
1968 *South West Africa, 1880–1894: The establishment of German authority in South West Africa.* Cape Town: Struik.

Estermann, C.
1976 *Ethnography of southwestern Angola.* Trans. and ed. from [1957] *Ethnográfia do sudoesteo de Angola,* Lisbon, Junta de Investigaçoes do Ultamar by G. Gibson. New York: Africana Press.

Evans-Pritchard, E.
1940 *The Nuer.* Oxford: Clarendon Press.

Evers, T.
1981 The Iron Age in eastern Transvaal. In *Guide to archaeological sites in northern and eastern Transvaal,* ed. E. Voight, pp. 65–109. Pretoria: Transvaal Museum.

Fabian, J.
1965 !Kung Bushman kinship: Componential analysis and alternative interpretations. *Anthropos* 60:663–718.
1986 *Language and colonial power: The appropriation of Swahili in the former Belgian Congo, 1880–1938.* Cambridge: Cambridge University Press.

Fodor, I.
1983 *Introduction to the history of Umbundu.* Budapest: Akadémiai Kiadó.

Foster-Carter, A.
1978a The modes of production controversy. *New Left Review* 107:47–77.
1978b Can we articulate "articulation"? In *The new economic anthropology,* ed. J. Clammer, pp. 210–49. New York: St. Martin's Press.

Frank, A.
1967 *Capitalism and underdevelopment in Latin America.* New York: Monthly Review Press.
1969 Sociology of development and underdevelopment of sociology. In *Latin America: Underdevelopment or revolution,* by A. Frank, pp. 21–94. New York: Monthly Review Press.
Frankenberg, R.
1967 Economic anthropology: One anthropologist's view. In *Themes in economic anthropology,* ed. R. Firth, pp. 47–89, ASA Monograph 6. London: Tavistock.
Freeman-Grenville, G.
1962 *The East African coast.* Oxford: Oxford University Press.
Gadibolae, M.
1985 Serfdom (Bolata) in the Nata area. *Botswana Notes and Records* 17:25–32.
Galaty, J.
1982 Being "Maasai"; being "people of cattle": Ethnic shifters in East Africa. *American Ethnologist* 9:1–20.
Galton, F.
1971 *The narrative of an explorer in tropical South Africa.* New York: Johnson Reprint. Facsimile reprint of 1853 original.
Garlake, P.
1973 *Great Zimbabwe.* London: Thames and Hudson.
Gelburd, D.
1978 Indicators of culture change among the Dobe !Kung San. M.A. thesis (anthropology), George Washington University.
Gibbon, P., and M. Neocosmos
1985 Some problems in the political economy of "African socialism." In *Contradictions of accumulations in Africa,* ed. H. Bernstein and B. Campbell, pp. 153–206. Beverly Hills, Calif.: Sage.
Gibson, G.
1956 Double descent and its correlates among the Herero of Ngamiland. *American Anthropologist* 58:109–39.
1959a Herero marriage. *Journal of the Rhodes Livingstone Institute* 24:1–37.
1959b Levels of residence among the Herero. Paper read at the American Anthropological Association annual meeting, Mexico City.
1962 Bridewealth and other forms of exchange among the Herero. In *Markets in Africa,* ed. P. Bohannan and G. Dalton, pp. 617–39. Evanston, Ill.: Northwestern University Press.
1977 Himba epochs. *History of Africa* 4:67–120.
Giddens, A.
1971 *Capitalism and modern social theory.* Cambridge: Cambridge University Press.
Gilman, S.
1985 Black bodies, white bodies: Toward an iconography of female sexuality

in late nineteenth-century art, medicine, and literature. In Race, writing, and difference, ed. H. Gates, Jr., pp. 204–42. *Critical Inquiry* 12.

Gluckman, M.

1965 *The ideas of Barotse jurisprudence.* New Haven: Yale University Press.

1971 *Politics, law, and ritual in tribal society.* New York: Basil Blackwell.

GOB. *See* Government of Botswana

Godelier, M.

1966 Système, structures, et contradiction dans le *Capital. Les Temps Modernes* 246 : 828–64.

1970 *Sur les sociétés pre-capitalistes.* Paris: Editions Sociales.

1973 *Horizon, trajets Marxistes en anthropologie.* Paris: Maspero.

1975 Modes of production, kinship, and demographic structures. In *Marxist analysis and social anthropology,* ed. M. Bloch, pp. 3–27. London: Malaby.

1977 *Perspectives in Marxist Anthropology.* Cambridge: Cambridge University Press.

1978 The object and method of economic anthropology. In *Relations of production,* ed. D. Seddon, pp. 49–126. London: Frank Cass.

Goodman, N.

1967 Uniformity and simplicity. In *Uniformity and simplicity,* ed. C. Albritten, Jr., pp. 93–99. New York: Geological Society of America.

Goodwin, A., and C. van Riet Lowe

1929 The Stone Age cultures of South Africa. *Annals of the South Africa Museum* 27 : 1–289.

Gordon, R.

1984 The !Kung in the Kalahari exchange: An ethnohistorical perspective. In *Past and present in hunter gatherer studies,* ed. C. Schrire, pp. 195–224. Orlando, Fla.: Academic Press.

Gordon-Cumming, R.

1904 *The adventure of a lion hunter in South Africa.* London: John Murray. Facsimile reprint of 1850 original.

Government of Botswana (GOB)

1974 Report on a study of constraints on agricultural development in the Republic of Botswana. In association with UN/FAO, Rome.

1984 *Third Report of the Place Names Commission.* Gaborone.

Gray, R., and D. Birmingham

1970 *Pre-colonial African trade.* Oxford: Oxford University Press.

Green, F.

1857 Narratives of an expedition to the northwest of Lake Ngami, extending to the capital of Debabe's territory, via Souka River, hitherto an unexplored portion of Africa. *Eastern Province Monthly Magazine* 1.12 : 661–69.

Guenther, M.

1980 From "brutal savages" to "harmless people": Notes on the changing Western image of the Bushmen. *Paideuma* 26 : 123–40.

1981 Bushman and hunter-gatherer territoriality. *Zeitschrift für Ethnologie* 106 : 109–20.

Gugelberger, G., ed.
1984 Nama/Namibia: Diary and letters of Nama chief Hendrik Witbooi, 1884–1894. Boston: Boston University African Studies Center.

Gulbrandsen, O.
1980 Agro-pastoral production and communal land use: A socio-economic study of the Bangwaketse. Gaborone: Ministry of Agriculture.

Guthrie, M.
1970 Comparative Bantu: An introduction to the comparative linguistics and prehistory of the Bantu languages. Ridgewood, N.J.: Gregg.

Gutkind, P.
1970 The passing of tribal man in Africa. Leiden: Brill.

Haarland, G.
1977 Pastoral systems of production. African Environment (London). Special Report 5.

Hahn, C.
1857 Grundzüge einer Grammatik des Hereró nebst einem Wörterbuche. Berlin: Wilhelm Hertz.
1984 Carl Hugo Hahn Tagebücher, 1837–1860. Part 2. 1846–1851. Ed. B. Lau. Windhoek: Archeia.

Hahn, T.
1895 Who are the real owners of Ghanse? C.O. 16669, Public Records Office, London.
1971 Tsuni-‖goam: The supreme being of the Khoi-Khoi. Freeport: Books for Libraries. Reprint of 1881 original.

Hailey (Lord)
1953 Native administration in the British African Territories. Part 5. The High Commission Territories: Basutoland, the Bechuanaland Protectorate and Swaziland. London: Commonwealth Relations Office.

Hall, M., and J. Vogel
1980 Some recent radiocarbon dates from southern Africa. Journal of African History 11:431–55.

Harbsmeier, J.
1978 History and evolution. Telos 39:5–44.

Harpending, H.
1976 Regional variation in !Kung populations. In Kalahari hunter-gatherers, ed. R. Lee and I. DeVore, pp. 152–65. Cambridge: Harvard University Press.
n.d. Alphabetical code of place names: N!ori list. Manuscript.

Harpending, H., and L. Wandsnider
1980 Population structures of Ghanzi and Ngamiland !Kung. Manuscript.

Harries, P.
1982 Kinship, ideology, and the nature of pre-colonial labour migration: Labour migration from the Delagoa Bay hinterland to South Africa, up to 1895. In Industrialisation and social change in South Africa, ed. S. Marks and R. Rathbone, pp. 142–66. London: Longman.

Hausman, A., and E. Wilmsen
1985 Economic change and secular trends in the growth of San children. *Human Biology* 57:563–71.

Heikkinen, T.
1987 An outline of the grammar of the !Xũ language spoken in Ovamboland and west Kavango. *South African Journal of African Languages* 7.

Heine, B.
1973 Zur genetischen Gliederung der Bantu-Sprachen. *Afrika un Übersee* 56:164–85.

Heine, B., H. Hoff, and R. Vossen
1977 Neuere Ergebnisse zur Territorialgeschichte der Bantu. In *Zur Sprachgeschichte und Ethnohistorie in Afrika*, ed. W. Möhlig, F. Rottland, and B. Heine, pp. 57–72. Berlin: Dieter Reimer.

Heinz, H.
1966 Social organization of the !Ko Bushmen. M.A. thesis (anthropology), University of South Africa.
1972 Territoriality among the Bushmen in general and the !Ko in particular. *Anthropos* 74:405–16.
1979 The nexus complex among the !Xo Bushmen. *Anthropos* 79:465–80.

Helm, J.
1965 Bilaterality in the socio-territorial organization of the Arctic Drainage Dene. *Ethnology* 4:361–85.

Hendrickson, A.
1986 Early Iron Age ceramics from northwestern Botswana: The evidence from Matlapaneng, N!oma, and Divuyu. M.A. thesis (anthropology), New York University.

Herrenkirchen, A. von
1907 *Meine Erlebnisse wärend des Feldzüges gegen die Hereros und Witbois nach meinem Tagebuch.* Berlin: Eisenschmidt.

Herskovitz, M.
1962 *The human factor in changing Africa.* New York: Alfred Knopf.

Hill, R.
1983 *The Marcus Garvey and Universal Negro Improvement Association papers.* Berkeley and Los Angeles: University of California Press.

Hill, R., and G. Pirio
1987 "Africa for the Africans": The Garvey movement in South Africa, 1920–1940. In *The politics of race, class, and nationalism in twentieth century South Africa*, ed. S. Marks and S. Trapido, pp. 209–53. London: Longman.

Hilton, R.
1985 Introduction. In *The Brenner debate*, ed. T. Aston and C. Philpin, pp. 1–9. Cambridge: Cambridge University Press.

Hindess, B., and P. Hirst
1975 *Precapitalist modes of production.* London: Routledge.

Hirst, P.
1975 *Durkheim, Bernard and epistemology.* London: Routledge.

Hitchcock, R.
1978 *Kalahari cattle posts: A regional study of hunter-gatherers, pastoralists, and agriculturalists in the western sandveld region, Botswana.* Gaborone: Government Printer.
1980 Tradition, social justice, and land reform in central Botswana. *Journal of African Law* 24:1–34.
Hitchcock, R., and T. Nkwe
1986 Social and environmental impacts of agrarian reform in rural Botswana. In *Land policy and agriculture in eastern and southern Africa,* ed. J. Arntzen, L. Ncgoncgo, and S. Turner, pp. 93–99. Tokyo: United Nations University.
Hitchcock, R., H. Vierich, and E. Wilmsen
1977 Basarwa mobility and migration patterns. Paper presented to First National Migration Study Workshop, Gaborone.
Hobsbawm, E.
1983 Introduction: Inventing traditions. In *The invention of tradition,* ed. E. Hobsbawm and T. Ranger, pp. 1–14. Cambridge: Cambridge University Press.
Hoernelé, W.
1985 *The social organization of the Nama and other essays.* Ed. P. Carstens. Johannesburg: Witwatersrand University Press.
Howell, N.
1976 *Demography of the Dobe !Kung.* Orlando, Fla.: Academic Press.
1986 Images of Tasaday and the !Kung: Reassessing isolated hunter-gatherers. Manuscript.
Huffman, T.
1982 Archaeology and ethnohistory of the African Iron Age. *Annual Review of Anthropology* 11:133–50.
Hyams, P.
1970 The origins of a peasant land market in England. *Economic History Review* 23:18–31.
Iliffe, J.
1979 *A modern history of Tankanyika.* Cambridge: Cambridge University Press.
Irle, J.
1906a *Die Herero: Ein Beitrag zur Landes-, Volks-, und Missionskunde.* Gütesloh: Bertelsmann.
1906b *Was soll aus den Herero werden?* Gütesloh: Bertelsmann.
1917 Deutsch-Herero-Wörterbuch. *Abhandlung der Hamburgischen Kolonialinstitut* 32. Hamburg: Friederichsen.
Isernhagen, H.
1982 A constitutional inability to say yes: Thorstein Veblen, the reconstitution program of *The Dial,* and the development of American modernism after World War I. *REAL: The Yearbook of Research in English and American Literature* 1:153–90.
Izzard, W.
1982 The impact of migration on the roles of women. In *Migration in Bo-*

tswana: Patterns, causes, and consequences, ed. C. Kerven, pp. 654–718. Gaborone: Central Statistics Office.

Jackson, D.
1970 Income difference and unbalanced planning in the case of Botswana. *Journal of Modern African Studies* 8:553–62.

Johnson, A.
1975 Time allocation in a Machiguenga community. *Ethnology* 14:301–10.

Jones, D., and J. Hill-Burnett
1982 The political context of ethnogenesis: An Australian example. In *Aboriginal power in Australian society,* ed. M. Howard, pp. 214–46. Honolulu: University of Hawaii Press.

Joyce, J.
1937 Report on the Masarwa in the Bamangwato Reserve, Bechuanaland Proctectorate. Geneva, League of Nations Publication VI.B. Slavery, Annex 6:57–76.

Kahn, J., and J. Llobera
1981 Towards a new Marxism or a new anthropology? In *The anthropology of pre-capitalist societies,* ed. J. Kahn and J. Llobera, pp. 263–329. Atlantic Highlands, N.J.: Humanities Press.

Kandovazu, E.
1968 *Die Oruuano-Beweging.* Karibib: Rynse Sending-Drukkery.

Kann, U.
1984 Problems of equity in the education system: The provision of basic education in Botswana. In *Education for development,* ed. M. Crowder, pp. 85–100. Gaborone: Macmillan Botswana.

Katjavivi, P.
1988 *A history of resistance in Namibia.* London: John Currey.

Katz, R.
1976 Education for transcendence: !Kia-healing with the Kalahari !Kung. In *Kalahari hunter-gatherers,* ed. R. Lee and I. DeVore, pp. 281–301. Cambridge: Harvard University Press.

Keenan, J.
1977 The concept of the mode of production in hunter-gatherer societies. *African Studies* 36:57–69.

Kerven, C.
1977 Underdevelopment, migration, and class formation in North East District, Botswana. Ph.D. diss. (anthropology), University of Toronto.
1979a *Botswana mine labour migration to South Africa.* National Migration Study Issue Paper 3. Gaborone: Central Statistics Office.
1979b Urban and rural female-headed households' dependence on agriculture. Ministry of Agriculture, Botswana.
1980 *Rural-urban migration and agricultural productivity in Botswana.* National Migration Study Issue Paper 1. Gaborone: Central Statistics Office.
1982 Introduction. In *Migration in Botswana: Patterns, causes, and consequences,* ed. C. Kerven, pp. 7–88. Gaborone: Central Statistics Office.

Kienetz, A.
1976 Nineteenth century South West Africa as a German settlement colony. Ph.D. diss. (history), University of Minnesota.
1977 The key role of the Orlam migrations in the early Europeanization of South-West Africa (Namibia). *International Journal of African Historical Studies* 10:553–72.
Kinahan, J.
1984a On the relative homogeneity of a short Holocene sequence of stone tool assemblages from the central Namib Desert. *South African Journal of Science* 80:73–276.
1984b The stratigraphy and lithic assemblages of Falls Rock Shelter, western Damaraland, Namibia. *Cimbebasia* 4:13–27.
1986 Settlement patterns and regional exchange: Evidence from recent Iron Age sites on the Kavango River, northeastern Namibia. *Cimbebasia* 3:109–16.
Kinahan, J., and J. Kinahan
1984 An archaeological reconnaissance of Bushmanland and southern Kavango. Report to the South West Africa Department of Agriculture and Nature Conservation, Windhoek.
Kinsman, M.
1981 Notes on the southern Tswana social formation. In *Collected Papers*, ed. K. Gottschalk and C. Saunders, 2:167–94. Cape Town: Centre for African Studies, University of Cape Town, Africa Seminar.
Kiyaga-Mulindwa, D., ed.
1980 *Politics and society in Letswapo*. Tswapong Historical Texts 2. Gaborone: University College of Botswana.
Kjaer-Olsen, P.
1978 Ncojane Village area and Ncojane Farms. Rural Sociology Unit, Ministry of Agriculture, Botswana.
Köhler, O.
1971 Noun classes and grammatical agreement in !Xu (zu-|hoà dialect). *Annales de l'Université du Abidjan (Linguistique)*, pp. 489–522.
1975 Der Khoisan Sprachbereich. In *Die Völker Afrikas und ihre traditionellen Kulturen*, ed. H. Baumann, pp. 305–37. Wiesbaden: Fritz Steiner.
1986 Allgemeine und sprachliche Bemerkungen zum Feldbau nach oral Texten der Khoe-Buschleute. In Afrikanische Wildbeuter: Internationales Symposion, Tagungberichte, ed. F. Rottland and R. Vossen. *Sugia* 7, 1:205–72.
Koma, K.
1984 Education and class structure in Botswana. In *Education for development in Botswana*, ed. M. Crowder, pp. 114–23. Gaborone: Macmillan Botswana.
Konner, M., and M. Shostak
1986 Ethnographic romanticism and the idea of human nature: Parallels between Samoa and the !Kung San. In *The past and future of !Kung ethnography*, ed. M. Biesele, pp. 69–76. Hamburg: Helmut Buske.

Konner, M., and C. Worthman

1980 Nursing frequency, gonadal function, and birth spacing among !Kung hunter-gatherers. *Science* 207:788–91.

Krader, L.

1972 *The ethnological notebooks of Karl Marx.* Assen: Van Gorcum.

1973 Karl Marx as ethnologist. *Transactions of the New York Academy of Sciences,* ser. 2, 35:304–13.

1976 The ethnological notebooks of Karl Marx: A commentary. In *Toward a Marxist anthropology,* ed. S. Diamond, pp. 153–71. The Hague: Mouton.

Kreysler, J.

1978 *National nutritional surveillance.* Gaborone: Nutrition Unit, Ministry of Health.

Kriegskarte von Deutsch Südwestafrika

1987 *Archeia* 9. Archives Publication Series. Windhoek. Facsimile reprint of 1904 original.

Kuper, A.

1969 The Kgalagadi in the nineteenth century. *Botswana Notes and Records* 2:45–51.

1982 *Wives for cattle.* London: Routledge.

1987 The transformation of African marriage in southern Africa. In *South Africa and the anthropologist,* ed. A. Kuper, pp. 134–48. London: Routledge and Kegan Paul. Reprint of 1985, Sage Foundation.

Laclau, E.

1971 Feudalism and capitalism in Latin America. *New Left Review* 67: 19–38.

Lau, B.

1979 A critique of the historical sources and historiography relating to the "Damaras" in precolonial Namibia. B.A. thesis (honors), University of Cape Town.

1981 Thank God the Germans came: Vedder and Namibian historiography. In *Collected Seminar Papers,* ed. C. Saunders, pp. 24–53. Cape Town: University of Cape Town.

1982 The emergence of commando politics in Namaland, southern Namibia: 1800–1870. M.A. thesis (history), University of Cape Town.

1984 "Pre-colonial" Namibian historiography: "What is to be done? Conference on Research Priorities in Namibia, Institute of Commonwealth Studies, University of London.

Leacock, E.

1972 Introduction. In *The origin of the family, private property, and the state,* by F. Engels, pp. 7–67. New York: International.

Leacock, E., and R. Lee

1982 Introduction. In *Politics and history in band societies,* ed. E. Leacock and R. Lee, pp. 1–20. Cambridge: Cambridge University Press.

Lee, R.

1965 Subsistence ecology of !Kung Bushmen. Ph.D. diss. (anthropology), University of California, Berkeley.

1969 !Kung Bushmen subsistence: An input-output analysis. In *Environment and cultural behavior,* ed. A. Vayda, pp. 47–79. Garden City, N.Y.: Natural History Press.

1972a Population growth and the beginnings of sedentary life among the !Kung Bushman. In *Population growth: Anthropological implications,* ed. B. Spooner, pp. 330–42. Cambridge: MIT Press.

1972b !Kung spatial organization: An ecological and historical perspective. *Human Ecology* 1:125–47.

1974 Male female residence arrangement and political power in human hunter-gatherers. *Archives of Sexual Behavior* 3:167–73.

1976a Introduction. In *Kalahari hunter-gatherers,* ed. R. Lee and I. DeVore, pp. 3–24. Cambridge: Harvard University Press.

1976b The !Kung's new culture. In *Science year,* pp. 180–95. Chicago: World Book Encyclopedia.

1976c !Kung spatial organization: An ecological and historical perspective. In *Kalahari hunter-gatherers,* ed. R. Lee and I. DeVore, pp. 73–97. Cambridge: Harvard University Press.

1979 *The !Kung San: Men, women, and work in a foraging society.* Cambridge: Cambridge University Press.

1982 Politics, sexual and non-sexual in an egalitarian society. In *Politics and history in band societies,* ed. E. Leacock and R. Lee, pp. 37–59. Cambridge: Cambridge University Press.

1984 *The Dobe !Kung.* New York: Harcourt Brace.

1986 !Kung kin terms, the name relationship and the process of discovery. In *The past and future of !Kung ethnography,* ed. M. Biesele, pp. 77–102. Hamburg: Helmut Buske.

Lee, R., and I. DeVore, eds.

1968 *Man the hunter.* Chicago: Aldine.

1976 *Kalahari hunter-gatherers.* Cambridge: Harvard University Press.

Leepile, M.

1988 When manna falls from heaven. *Mmegi wa Dikang* 5 (18–24 June): 8–9.

Leutwein, T.

1906 *Elf Jahre Gouvernour in Deutsch-Südwestafrika.* Berlin: E. S. Mittler.

Lévi-Strauss, C.

1963 *Totemism.* Trans. from *Le totémisme aujourd'hui* (1962) by R. Needham. Boston: Beacon.

1966 *The savage mind.* Chicago: University of Chicago Press.

1967 *The scope of anthropology.* Trans. from *Leçon inaugural* (1960) by S. Ortner Paul and R. Paul. London: Jonathan Cape.

Lipton, M.

1978 *Employment and labour use in Botswana.* Gaborone: Government Printer.

Lister, M., ed.

1949 *Journals of Andrew Geddes Bain: Traveler, explorer, soldier, road engineer, geologist.* Cape Town: Van Riebeck Society.

Listowel, J.

1974 *The other Livingstone.* Cape Town: David Philip.

Livingstone, D.
1912 *Missionary travels and researches in South Africa*. London: John Murray. Facsimile reprint of 1857 original.
LMS. *See* London Missionary Society
London Missionary Society (LMS)
1935 *Report of an enquiry by the South Africa District Committee*. Alice: Lovedale.
Loomis, C., and J. McKinney
1957 Introduction. In *Gemeinschaft und Gesellschaft*, by F. Tönnies, trans. C. Loomis and J. McKinney, pp. 1–29. New York: Harper and Row.
Loth, H.
1963 *Die christliche Mission in Südwest-Afrika: Zur destruktiven Rolle der Rheinischen Mission beim Prozess der Staatsbildung in SWA*. Berlin: Akademie.
Lubbock, J.
1913 *Prehistoric times as illustrated by ancient remains and the manners and customs of modern savages*. New York: Henry Holt. Facsimile reprint of 1865 original.
Luttig, H.
1933 *The religious system and social organization of the Herero*. Utrecht: Kemink en Zoon.
MaCabe, J.
1855 Journal kept during a tour in the interior of South Africa to Lake Ngami and the country two hundred and fifty miles beyond. In *History of the colony of Natal, South Africa*, by W. Holden, pp. 413–34. London: Alexander Heylin.
MacCormick, G.
1983 Problems in the description of African systems of landholding. *Journal of Legal Pluralism and Unofficial Law* 21:1–14.
Mackenzie, J.
1871 *Ten years north of the Orange River*. Edinburgh: Edmonton and Douglas.
Maggs, T.
1977 Some recent radiocarbon dates from eastern and southern Africa. *Journal of African History* 18:161–91.
Malinowski, B.
1926 *Crime and custom in savage society*. London: Kegan Paul, Trench.
Marks, S.
1969 The traditions of the Natal Nguni: A second look at the work of A. T. Bryant. In *African societies in southern Africa*, ed. L. Thompson, pp. 126–44. London: Heinemann.
1972 Khoisan resistance to the Dutch in the seventeenth and eighteenth centuries. *Journal of African History* 8:55–80.
1982 Industrialization and social change: Some thoughts on class formation and political consciousness in South Africa, c. 1870–1920. Boston University African Studies Center, Walter Rodney Seminar.

Marks, S., and A. Atmore, eds.

1980 *Economy and society in pre-industrial South Africa.* London: Longman.

Marks, S., and S. Trapido, eds.

1987 *The politics of race, class, and nationalism in twentieth century South Africa.* London: Longman.

Marshall, L.

1957 The kin terminology system of the !Kung Bushmen. *Africa* 27:1–25.

1959 Marriage among !Kung Bushmen. *Africa* 29:333–65.

1960 !Kung Bushmen bands. *Africa* 30:325–55.

1961 Sharing, talking, and giving: Relief of social tensions among !Kung Bushmen. *Africa* 31:231–49.

1968 Discussion. In *Man the hunter,* ed. R. Lee and I. DeVore, p. 94. Chicago: Aldine.

1976 *The !Kung of Nyae Nyae.* Cambridge: Harvard University Press.

Martin, P.

1972 *The external trade of the Loango coast, 1576–1870.* Oxford: Clarendon Press.

Marx, K.

1906 *Capital.* New York: Kerr. Reprint of 1867 original.

1971 *A contribution to the critique of political economy.* London: Lawrence and Wishart. Reprint of 1859 original.

Marx, K., and F. Engels

1977 *The German ideology.* New York: International. Unpublished original dated 1846.

Massey, D.

1978 A case of colonial collaboration: The hut tax and migrant labour. *Botswana Notes and Records* 10:95–98.

1980 The development of a labor reserve: The impact of colonial rule in Botswana. Boston University African Studies Center, Working Paper 34.

Mattick, P., Jr.

1985 Review of M. Bloch, *Marxism and anthropology. Studies in Soviet Thought* 29:247–51.

1986 *Social knowledge: An essay on the nature and limits of social science.* Armonk, N.Y.: M. E. Sharpe.

Mautle, G.

1986 Bakgalagadi-Bakwena relationships: A case of slavery, c. 1840–c. 1930. *Botswana Notes and Records* 18:19–32.

Meillassoux, C.

1960 Essai d'interprétation du phénomène économique dans les société traditionelles d'auto-subsistance. *Cahiers d'Etudes Africaines* 1(4): 38–67.

1964 *Anthropologie économique des Gouro de la Côte d'Ivoire.* Paris: Mouton.

1967 Recherche d'un niveau de détermination dans la société cynegétique. *L'Homme et la Société* 1:95–106.

1972 From reproduction to production: A Marxist approach to economic anthropology. *Economy and Society* 1:93–105.

1973 On the mode of production of the hunting band. In *French perspectives in African studies*, ed. P. Alexandre, pp. 187–203. Oxford: Oxford University Press.

Miers, S.

1983 Botlhanka/Bolata under colonial rule. Seminar paper, Department of History, University of Botswana.

Miers, S., and M. Crowder

1988 Botlhanka/Bolata under colonial rule. In *The end of slavery in Africa*, ed. S. Miers and R. Roberts, pp. 172–200. Madison: University of Wisconsin Press.

Miller, J.

1976 *Kings and kinsmen: Early Mbundu states in Angola*. Oxford: Clarendon Press.

1983 The paradoxes of impoverishment in the Atlantic zone. In *History of Central Africa*, ed. D. Birmingham and P. Martin, pp. 118–59. Cambridge: Cambridge University Press.

Morgan, L.

1964 *Ancient society*. New York: Kerr. Facsimile reprint of 1877 original.

Moritz, W.

1980 Erkundungsreise ins Ovamboland 1857: Tagebuch Carl Hugo Hahn. *Aus alten Tagen in Südwest* 4, Schwäbisch Gmünd.

Mossop, E., ed.

1935 *The journal of Hendrik Jakob Wikar (1779), (English translation by A. van der Horst), and The journals of Jacobus Coetse Janz (1760) and Willem van Reenan (1791)*. Cape Town: Van Riebeck Society.

1947 *The journals of Brink and Rhenius*. Cape Town: Van Riebeck Society.

Motzafi, P.

1986 Whither the "True Bushmen": The dynamics of perpetual marginality. In Proceedings of the International Symposium on African Hunters and Gatherers, Sankt Augustin, ed. F. Rottland and R. Vossen, pp. 295–328. *Sprache und Geschichte in Afrika* 7.1.

Motzafi-Haller, P.

1987 Transformations in the Tswapong region, central Botswana: National policies and local realities. Ph.D. diss. (anthropology), Brandeis University.

Murdock, G.

1959 *Africa: Its peoples and their culture history*. New York: McGraw-Hill.

Murray, A.

1986 Social and economic history in Botswana. Joint History Departments Seminar (Regional), University of Zambia, Lusaka.

Murray, M.

1976 Present wildlife utilization in the Central Kalahari Game Reserve, Botswana. Department of Wildlife, National Parks, and Tourism, Gaborone.

Mushingeh, A.

n.d. *The political economy of disease and medicine in Botswana, 1820–1945*. Cambridge: Cambridge University Press. In press.

Myers, F.
1989 Burning the truck and holding the country. In *We are here: Politics of aboriginal land tenure*, ed. E. Wilmsen, pp. 15–42. Berkeley and Los Angeles: University of California Press.
Nangati, F.
1980 Constraints on precolonial economy: The Bakwena state c. 1820–1885. *Pula: Botswana Journal of African Studies* 2:125–38.
1982 Early capitalist penetration: The impact of precolonial trade in Kweneng (1840–1876). In *Settlement in Botswana*, ed. R. Hitchcock and M. Smith, pp. 140–47. Marshalltown: Heinemann.
Nash, J.
1981 Ethnographic aspects of the world capitalist system. *Annual Review of Anthropology* 10:393–423.
Naude, C.
1931 *Ongebaande Wee: Die geskiendenis van James Benjamin Bassingthwaighte*. Cape Town.
Ncgoncgo, L.
1977 Aspects of the history of the Bangwaketse to 1910. Ph.D. thesis (history), Dalhousie University.
1982a Impact of the difaqane on Tswana states. In *Settlement in Botswana*, ed. R. Hitchcock and M. Smith, pp. 161–71. Marshalltown: Heinemann.
1982b Precolonial migration in south-eastern Botswana. In *Settlement in Botswana*, ed. R. Hitchcock and M. Smith, pp. 23–30. Exeter, N.H.: Heinemann Educational Books.
NDP5
1980 *National development plan, 1979–85*. Gaborone: Government Printer.
NDP6
1985 *National development plan, 1985–91*. Gaborone: Government Printer.
Nettleton, G.
1934 History of the Ngamiland tribes up to 1926. *Bantu Studies* 8:343–60.
Nienaber, G.
1952 Die woord "Boesman." *Theoria* 4:36–40.
Nienaber, G., and P. Raper
1980 *Toponymica Hottentotica*. Pretoria: Suid-Afrikaanse Naamkundsentrum.
NMS (National Migration Study)
1982 *Migration in Botswana: Patterns, causes, and consequences*. Ed. C. Kerven. Gaborone: Central Statistics Office.
Noten, F. van
1982 *The archaeology of central Africa*. Graz: Akademische.
Nurse, G., and T. Jenkins
1977 *Health and the hunter-gatherer*. Basel: Karger.
O'Brien, J.
1986 Toward a reconstitution of ethnicity: Capitalist expansion and cultural dynamics in Sudan. *American Anthropologist* 88:898–907.

Okihiro, G.
1976 Hunters, herders, cultivators, and traders: Interaction and change in the Kalagadi, nineteenth century. Ph.D. diss. (history), University of California at Los Angeles.
Oswell, W., ed.
1900 *William Cotton Oswell.* London: Heinemann.
Palgrave, W.
1877 Report of W. Coates Palgrave, Esq., special commissioner to the tribes north of the Orange River, of his mission to Damaraland and Great Namaqualand in 1876. Pretoria, State Library.
Palmer, R., and N. Parsons, eds.
1977 *The roots of rural poverty in central and southern Africa.* Berkeley and Los Angeles: University of California Press.
Parkington, J.
1984 Soaqua and Bushman: Hunters and robbers. In *Past and present in hunter gatherer studies,* ed. C. Schrire, pp. 151–74. Orlando, Fla.: Academic Press.
Parkington, J., and M. Hall
1987 Patterning in recent radiocarbon dates from southern Africa as a reflection of prehistoric settlement and interaction. *Journal of African History* 28:1–25.
Parson, J.
1979 The political economy of Botswana: A case in the study of politics and social change in post-colonial societies. Ph.D. thesis (political science), University of Sussex.
1980 The "labor reserve" in historical perspective: A political economy of the Bechuanaland Protectorate. Paper read at African Studies Association annual meeting.
1981a Cattle, class, and the state in rural Botswana. *Journal of Southern African Studies* 7:236–55.
1981b Through the looking glass: Inequality in post-colonial Botswana. Paper read at the Southeast Regional Seminar on African Studies, Emory University, Atlanta.
1984 *Botswana: Liberal democracy and the labor reserve in southern Africa.* Boulder, Colo.: Westview Press.
Parsons, N.
1974a The economic history of Khama's country in southern Africa. *African Social Research* 18:643–75.
1974b Shots for a black republic? Simon Ratshosa and Botswana nationalism. *African Affairs* 73:449–58.
1977 The economic history of Khama's country in Botswana, 1844–1930. In *The roots of rural poverty in central and southern Africa,* ed. R. Palmer and N. Parsons, pp. 113–43. Berkeley and Los Angeles: University of California Press.
1983 *A new history of southern Africa.* Marshalltown: Heinemann.

Passarge, S.
1905 Die Grundlinien im ethnographischen Bilde der Kalahari-Region. *Zeitschrift der Gesellschaft für Erdkunde zu Berlin*. Berlin: E. S. Mittler.
1907 *Die Buschmänner der Kalahari*. Berlin: Dieter Reimer.
Perper, T., and C. Schrire
1977 The Nimrod connection: Myth and science in the hunting model. In *The chemical senses and nutrition*, ed. M. Kare and O. Maller, pp. 447–58. New York: Academic Press.
Petermanns geographische Mitteilungen
1859 Reise der Herrn Hugo Hahn und Rath im südwestlichen Afrika, Mai bis September 1857, 7:299
1860 Ladislaus Magyar's Erforschung, 6:227–31.
1867a Der Cunene-Strom von Fr. Green erreicht, 1:8–12.
1867b Neueste Deutsche Forschungen in Süd-Afrika: Von Karl Mauch, Hugo Hahn und Richard Brenner, 1866 und 1867, 8:281–98.
1878 Herero-Land, Land und Leute, 8:306–11.
Peters, M.
1972 Notes on the place names of Ngamiland. *Botswana Notes and Records* 4:219–33.
Peters, P.
1984 Struggles over water, struggles over meaning: Cattle, water, and the state in Botswana. Boston University African Studies Center, Working Paper 88.
Pfouts, A.
1983 Economy and society in precolonial Namibia: A linguistic approach (c. 500–1800 A.D.). Paper read at African Studies Association annual meeting.
Phillipson, D.
1969 Early iron using peoples of southern Africa. In *African societies in southern Africa*, ed. L. Thompson, pp. 24–49. London: Heinemann.
1977 *The later prehistory of eastern and southern Africa*. London: Heinemann.
Phillipson, D., and B. Fagen
1969 The date of the Ingombe Ilede burials. *Journal of African History* 10:199–204.
Pirio, G.
1982 The role of Garveyism in the making of the southern African working classes and Namibian nationalism. African Series, Marcus Garvey papers, University of California–Los Angeles.
Pitt-Rivers, A.
1906 *The evolution of culture and other essays*. Oxford: Clarendon Press.
Postma, D.
1897 *Eenige Schetsen voor eene Geschiedenis van die Trekboeren*. Amsterdam: Höveker and Wormser.
Pratt, M.
1985 Scratches on the face of the country; or, What Mr. Barrow saw in the

land of the Bushmen. In Race, writing, and difference, ed. H. Gates, Jr., pp. 119–43. *Critical Inquiry* 12.

1986 Fieldwork in common places. In *Writing culture: The poetics and politics of ethnography*, ed. J. Clifford and G. Marcus, pp. 27–50. Berkeley and Los Angeles: University of California Press.

Prinsloo, J., and J. Gauche
1933 *In die woeste Weste: Die Lydensgeskiedenis van die Dorslandtrekkers.* Pretoria: J. H. de Bussy.

Public Records Office, London
1895 C0417:141, 5 June.
1899 C0574:248, RC, Serowe to HC, Johannesburg, 12 April.

Radcliffe-Brown, A.
1923 The methods of ethnology and social anthropology. *South African Journal of Science* 20:142–43.

RADW (Remote Area Development Workshop)
1978 *Remote Area Development Workshop.* Gaborone: Government Printer.
1979 *Remote Area Development Workshop.* Gaborone: Government Printer.
1980 *Remote Area Development Workshop.* Gaborone: Government Printer.

Ramatokwane, L.
1987 When Namibia becomes a sanctuary. *Mmegi wa Dikang* 4 (12–18 December): 6–7.

Ranger, T.
1978 Growing from the roots: Reflections on peasant research in central and southern Africa. *Journal of Southern African Studies* 5:99–133.
1983 The invention of tradition in colonial Africa. In *The invention of tradition*, ed. E. Hobsbawm and T. Ranger, pp. 211–62. Cambridge: Cambridge University Press.

Rey, C.
1932 Ngamiland and the Kalahari. *Geographical Journal* 80:281–309.

Rey, P.-P.
1973 *Les alliances de classes.* Paris: Maspero.
1975 The lineage mode of production. *Critique of Anthropology* 3:27–79.

Richards, P.
1983 Ecological change and the politics of African land use. *African Studies Review* 26:1–72.

RIDS (Rural Income Distribution Survey)
1976 *The Rural Income Distribution Survey.* Gaborone: Central Statistics Office.

Robbins, L.
1984 Toteng, a Late Stone Age site along the Nghabe River, Ngamiland. *Botswana Notes and Records* 16:1–6.

Roberts, S.
1979 *Order and dispute.* Harmondsworth: Penguin.
1982 Arable land tenure and administrative change in the Kgatleng. *Journal of African Law* 24:117–30.

Robertshaw, P.
1978 The origin of pastoralism in the Cape. *South African Historical Journal* 10: 117–33.
Russell, M., and M. Russell
1975 *Afrikaners of the Kalahari*. Cambridge: Cambridge University Press.
Sahlins, M.
1965 On the sociology of primitive exchange. In *The relevance of models for social anthropology*, ed. M. Banton, pp. 139–236. ASA Monograph 1. London: Tavistock.
1972 *Stone Age economics*. Chicago: Aldine.
Sandelowsky, B.
1979 Kapako and VunguVungu: Iron Age sites on the Kavango River, *South African Archaeological Society, Goodwin Series* 3: 52–61.
Sandelowsky, B., J. van Rooyen, and J. Vogel
1979 Early evidence for herders in the Namib. *South African Archaeological Bulletin* 34: 15–32.
Schapera, I.
1930 *The Khoisan peoples of South Africa: Bushmen and Hottentots*. London: Routledge.
1938 *Handbook of Tswana law and custom*. Oxford: Oxford University Press.
1940 *Married life in an African tribe*. New York: Sheridan.
1942 A short history of the Bangwaketse. *African Studies* 1: 1–11.
1943 *Native land tenure in the Bechananland Protectorate*. Alice: Lovedale Press.
1945 Notes on some Mbanderu genealogies. *Communications from the School of African Studies* 14.
1947 *Migrant labour and tribal life*. Oxford: Oxford University Press.
1952 *The ethnic composition of Tswana tribes*. Monographs on Social Anthropology 11. London: London School of Economics.
1953 *The Tswana*: London: International African Institute.
1956 *Government and politics in tribal societies*. London: Schocken.
1963 Kinship and politics in Tswana history. *Journal of the Royal Institute of Anthropology* 9: 159–73.
1970 *Tribal innovators*. London: Athlone.
Schapera, I., ed.
1959 *David Livingstone: Family letters, 1841–1856*. London: Chatto and Windus.
1961 *Livingstone's missionary correspondence, 1841–1856*. London: Chatto and Windus.
Scheffler, H.
1986 The descent of rights and the descent of persons. *American Anthropologist* 88: 339–50.
Schinz, H.
1891 *Deutsch-Südwest-Afrika: Forschungreisen durch die deutschen Schutz-*

gebiete Gross-Nama-und Herereroland, nach dem Kunene, dem Ngami-See und der Kalaxari, 1884–1887. Oldenburg: Schulzesche Hof.

Schneider, J.
1977 Was there a precapitalist world system? *Journal of Peasant Studies* 6:20–28.

Schrire, C.
1980 An enquiry into the evolutionary status and apparent identity of San hunter-gatherers. *Human Ecology* 8:9–32.
1984 Wild surmises on savage thoughts. In *Past and present in hunter gatherer studies,* ed. C. Schrire, pp. 1–25. Orlando, Fla.: Academic Press.

Schwartz, S.
1977 Introduction. In *Naming, necessity, and natural kinds,* ed. S. Schwartz, pp. 9–41. Ithaca: Cornell University Press.

Sebolai, M.
1978 A history of the socio-political changes in the condition of the Masarwa (Bushmen) in the Bamangwato Reserve (c. 1700–1940). B.A. thesis (history), University of Botswana.

Serton, P., ed.
1954 *The narrative and journal of Gerald McKiernan in South West Africa (1874–1879).* Cape Town: Van Riebeck Society.

Service, E.
1962 *Primitive social organization.* New York: Random House.
1979 *The hunters.* Englewood Cliffs, N.J.: Prentice-Hall.

Shapiro, W.
1973 Residential groupings in northwest Arnhemland. *Man* 8:363–83.
1981 *Miwuyt marriages.* Philadelphia: Institute for the Study of Human Issues.

Sheller, P.
1977 The people of the Central Kalahari Game Reserve. Report to the Basarwa Development Officer.

Shostak, M.
1981 *Nisa: The life and words of a !Kung woman.* Cambridge: Harvard University Press.

Silberbauer, G.
1965 *Report to the Government of Bechuanaland on the Bushman Survey.* Gaborone: Bechuanaland Government.
1981 *Hunter and habitat in the central Kalahari Desert.* Cambridge: Cambridge University Press.
1982 Political process in G/wi Bands. In *Politics and history in band societies,* ed. E. Leacock and R. Lee, pp. 23–35. Cambridge: Cambridge University Press.

Silitshena, R.
1978 Notes on some characteristics of population that has migrated permanently to the lands in Kweneng District. *Botswana Notes and Records* 10:149–57.

1979 Changing settlement patterns in Botswana: The case of the eastern Kweneng. Ph.D. thesis (sociology), University of Sussex.
1982 Migration and permanent settlement in the lands area. In *Settlement in Botswana*, ed. R. Hitchcock and M. Smith, pp. 220–31. Exeter, N.H.: Heinemann Educational Books.
Sillery, A.
1952 *The Bechuanaland Protectorate*. Oxford: Oxford University Press.
Skocpol, T.
1975 Wallerstein's world capitalist system: A theoretical and historical critique. *American Journal of Sociology* 82:1075–90.
Smith, A.
1983 Prehistoric pastoralism in the southwestern Cape, South Africa. *World Archaeology* 15:79–89.
Smith, R.
1984 Some issues concerning families and their property in rural England, 1250–1800. In *Land, kinship, and life-cycle*, ed. R. Smith, pp. 1–86. Cambridge: Cambridge University Press.
Snyman, J.
1969 *An introduction to the !Xũ language*. Cape Town: Balkema.
1975 *Žu|'hõasi phonologie en woordeboek*. Cape Town: Balkema.
Solway, J.
1979 Socio-economic effects of labour migration in western Kweneng. In *National Migration Study workshop on migration research*, ed. C. Kerven, pp. 36–42. Gaborone: Central Statistics Office.
Sorokin, P.
1957 *Contemporary sociological theories*. New York: Harper and Row.
Sousa Dias, G.
1948 *Julgareis qual e mais excellente . . . figuras da historia Angolana*, pp. 199–209. Luanda: Ediçao de Museu de Angola.
Sousa Martins, R. de
1976 A estação arqueologica da antiqua Banza Quibaxe. *Contribuições para o Estudo da Antropologia Portuguesa*. Coimbra: Universidade de Coimbra.
Sperber, D.
1985 *On anthropological knowledge*. New York: Cambridge University Press.
Spohr, O., ed.
1973 *W. H. C. Lichtenstein: Foundation of the Cape and about the Bechuanas*. Cape Town: Balkema. Reprints of 1807 and 1811 originals.
State Archive Service, Windhoek
1922a SWAA A396/4. Statement made by David Ngxiki on 3 October 1922.
1922b SWAA A396/4 NC. Windhoek to Acting Secretary, 12 October.
n.d. D2.8-A30. The Andersson papers. Microfilm A(83)1.
Steward J.
1938 *Basin-plateau aboriginal socio-political groups*. Bulletin 120. Washington, D.C.: Smithsonian Institution, Bureau of American Ethnology.

Stocking, G.
1987 *Victorian anthropologists.* New York: Free Press.
Stow, G.
1905 *The native races of southern Africa.* Cape Town: Struik.
Sundermeier, T.
n.d. *The Mbanderu.* Trans. from *Die Mbanderu,* (Sankt Augustin: Antro-posinstitut, 1976) by A. Heywood, ed. B. Lau. Windhoek: n.p.
Syson, L.
1973 Some agricultural data from the Shoshong area, 1969–71. United Na-tions Development Programme, Gaborone.
Tabler, E.
1953 The life of Frederick J. Green. *Africana Notes and News* 11:41.
1957 The Walvis Bay road: Rietfontein to Lake Ngami. *Africana Notes and News* 12:123–29.
1963 *Trade and travel in early Barotseland: The diaries of George Westbeech, 1885–88 and Captain Norman MacLeod, 1875–76.* London: Chatto and Windus.
1973 *Pioneers of South West Africa and Ngamiland: 1738–1880.* Cape Town: Balkema.
Tagart, E.
1933 *Report on the conditions existing among the Masarwa in the Bamang-wato Reserve of the Bechuanaland Protectorate and certain other matters appertaining to the natives living therein.* Pretoria: Government Printer.
Tanaka, J.
1969 The ecology and social structure of central Kalahari Bushmen: A pre-liminary report. *Kyoto University African Studies* 3:1–26.
1980 *The San: Hunter-gatherers of the Kalahari.* Tokyo: University of Tokyo.
Taylor, J.
1978 Mine labour recruitment in the Bechuanaland Protectorate. *Botswana Notes and Records* 10:99–112.
Taylor, J. G.
1979 *From modernization to modes of production: A critique of the sociolo-gies of development and underdevelopment.* London: Macmillan.
Terray, E.
1972 *Marxism and "primitive" societies.* New York: Monthly Review Press.
1975 Class and class consciousness in an Abron Kingdom of Gyaman. In *Marxist analysis and social anthropology,* ed. M. Bloch, pp. 85–135. Lon-don and New York: Tavistock.
Thomas, E.
1959 *The harmless people.* New York: Alfred Knopf.
Thompson, L.
1969 Co-operation and conflict: The highveld. In *The Oxford history of South Africa,* ed. M. Wilson and L. Thompson, pp. 391–446. Oxford: Oxford University Press.
Thornton, R.
1980 The rise of the ethnographic monograph in eastern and southern Africa:

References 383

The moral motive and market for ideas. Paper read at American Anthropological Association annual meeting.

Tindall, B., ed.
1959 *The journal of Joseph Tindall, missionary in South West Africa*. Cape Town: Van Riebeck Society.

Tlou, T.
1972 A political history of northwestern Botswana to 1906. Ph.D. diss. (history), University of Wisconsin.
1974 The nature of Botswana states: Towards a theory of traditional Botswana government. *Botswana Notes and Records* 6:57–76.
1976 The peopling of the Okavango Delta, c. 1750–1906. In *Proceedings of the symposium on the Okavango Delta and its future utilization,* pp. 49–53. Gaborone: Botswana Society.
1979 Servility and political control: Botlhanka among the BaTawana of northwestern Botswana, ca. 1750–1906. In *Slavery in Africa*, ed. S. Miers and I. Kopytoff, pp. 367–90. Madison: University of Wisconsin Press.
1985 *A history of Ngamiland, 1750–1906: The formation of an African state*. Madison: University of Wisconsin Press.

Tobias, P.
1962 On the increasing stature of the Bushmen. *Anthropos* 57:801–10.
1964 Bushman hunter-gatherers: A study in human ecology. In *Ecological studies in southern Africa*, ed. D. Davis, pp. 67–86. The Hague: W. Junk.
1970 Puberty, growth, malnutrition, and the weaker sex. *Leech* 40:101–7.
1975 Anthropometry among disadvantaged peoples: Studies in southern Africa. In *Biosocial interrelations in population adaptations,* ed. E. Watts, F. Johnston, and G. Lasker, pp. 287–305. Paris: Mouton.

Tönnies, F.
1957 *Gemeinschaft und Gesellschaft*. Trans. C. Loomis and J. McKinney. New York: Harper and Row. Originally published 1887.

Traill, A.
1974 *The compleat guide to the Koon*. Communication 1. Johannesburg: African Studies Institute.

Trapido, S.
1978 Landlord and tenent in a colonial economy: The Transvaal, 1880–1910. *Journal of Southern African Studies* 5:26–58.

Truswell, A., and J. Hansen
1968 Medical and nutritional studies of !Kung Bushmen in northwest Botswana: A preliminary report. *South African Medical Journal* 42:1338.
1976 Medical research among the !Kung. In *Kalahari hunter-gatherers,* ed. R. Lee and I. DeVore, pp. 166–94. Cambridge: Harvard University Press.

Turner, V.
1957 *Schism and continuity in an African society: A study of Ndembu village life*. Manchester: Manchester University Press.

Tylor, E.
1909 *Anthropology*. New York: Appleton. Originally published 1881.

Vansina, J.
1985 Do Pygmys have a history? In Proceedings of the International Sym-

posium on African Hunters and Gatherers, Sankt Augustin, ed. F. Rottland and R. Vossen, pp. 431–46. *Sprache und Geschichte in Afrika* 7.1.

Van Der Post, L.
1958 *The lost world of the Kalahari*. New York: William Morrow.

Vedder, H.
1938 *South West Africa in early times: Being the story of South West Africa up to the time of Maharero's death in 1890*. London: Frank Cass.
1966 The Herero. In *The native tribes of South West Africa*, by C. Hahn, H. Vedder, and H. Fourie, pp. 151–211. London: Frank Cass. Reprint of 1928 original.

Viegas Guerreiro, M.
1968 *Bochimanes !Khu de Angola*. Lisbon: Junta de Invetigaçoes do Ultramar.

Vierich-Esch, H.
1982 Adaptive flexibility in a multi-ethnic setting: The Basarwa of the southern Kalahari. In *Politics and history in band societies*, ed. E. Leacock and R. Lee, pp. 213–22. Cambridge: Cambridge University Press.

Vogel, J.
1971 *Kumadzulo: An Early Iron Age village site in southern Zambia*. London: Oxford University Press.

Vossen, R.
1984 Studying the linguistic and ethno-history of the Khoe-speaking (central Khoisan) peoples of Botswana: Research in progress. *Botswana Notes and Records* 16:19–36.

Wagner, R.
1981 *The invention of culture*. Chicago: University of Chicago Press.

Walker, N.
1983 The significance of an early date for pottery and sheep in Zimbabwe. *South African Archaeological Bulletin* 38:88–92.

Wallerstein, I.
1974 *The modern world system*. New York: Academic Press.
1977 The task of historical social science. *Review* 1:3–7.
1979 *The capitalist world economy*. Cambridge: Cambridge University Press.

Watt, M.
1983 "Good try, Mr. Paul": Populism and the politics of African land use. *African Studies Review* 26:73–83.

Wehmeyer, A., R. Lee, and M. Whiting
1969 The nutrient composition and dietary importance of some vegetable foods eaten by the !Kung Bushmen. *South African Medical Journal* 95: 1529–30.

Werner, W.
1980 An exploratory investigation into the mode of production of the Herero in pre-colonial Namibia to ca. 1870. B. Soc. Sc. thesis (honors), University of Cape Town.

White, C.
1963 Terminological confusion in African land tenure. *Journal of African Administration* 10:124–30.

White, L.
1959 *The evolution of culture.* New York: McGraw-Hill.

Wiessner, P.
1977 Hxaro: A regional system of reciprocity for reducing risk in the !Kung Bushmen. Ph.D. diss. (anthropology), University of Michigan.
1980 History and continuity in !Kung San reciprocal relationships. Second International Conference on Hunting and Gathering Societies, Quebec City.
1982 Risk, reciprocity, and social influences on !Kung San economics. In *Politics and history in band societies,* ed. E. Leacock and R. Lee, pp. 61–84. Cambridge: Cambridge University Press.
1983a Social and ceremonial aspects of death among the !Kung. *Botswana Notes and Records* 15:1–6.
1983b "To walk softly": Style, exchange, and land tenure among the Kalahari San. Third International Conference on Hunting and Gathering Societies, Bad Homburg.
1984 Reconsidering the behavioral basis of style: A case study among the Kalahari San. *Journal of Anthropological Archaeology* 3:190–234.
1986 !Kung San networks in a generational perspective. In *The past and future of !Kung ethnography,* ed. M. Biesele, pp. 103–36. Hamburg: Helmut Buske.

Wiley, D.
1982 Migrants to freehold farms and to farms in South Africa. In *Migration in Botswana: Patterns, causes, and consequences,* ed. C. Kerven, pp. 377–441. Gaborone: Central Statistics Office.
1985 The center cannot hold. Ph.D. diss. (history), Yale University.

Willan, B.
1982 An African in Kimberley: Sol Plaatje, 1894–1898. In *Industrialisation and social change in South Africa: African class formation, culture, and consciousness 1870–1930,* ed. S. Marks and R. Rathbone, pp. 238–58. London: Longman.

Willoughby, W.
n.d. Papers of Prof. W. C. Willoughby, file 739. Shelly Oak College Library, Birmingham.

Wilmsen, E.
1973 Interaction, spacing behavior, and the organization of hunting bands. *Journal of Anthropological Research* 29:1–13.
1976 Summary report of research on Basarwa in western Ngamiland. Ministry of Local Government and Lands.
1978 Prehistoric and historic antecedents of an Ngamiland community. *Botswana Notes and Records* 10:5–18.
1982a Exchange, interaction, and settlement in northwestern Botswana. In *Settlement in Botswana,* ed. R. Hitchcock and M. Smith, pp. 98–109. Marshalltown: Heinemann.
1982b Migration patterns of Remote Area Dwellers. In *Migration in Botswana: Patterns, causes, and consequences,* ed. C. Kerven, pp. 337–76. Gaborone: Central Statistics Office.

1982c Studies in diet, nutrition, and fertility among a group of Kalahari Bushmen in Botswana. *Social Science Information* 21:95–126.
1983 The ecology of illusion: Anthropological foraging in the Kalahari. *Re-
views in Anthropology* 10:9–20.
1985a Biological determinates of fecundity and fecundability: An application
of Bongaart's model to forager fertility. In *Culture and reproduction,* ed.
P. Handwerker, pp. 59–89. Boulder, Colo.: Westview.
1985b Conversations with Mr. Tommy Kays of Maun. *Botswana Notes and
Records* 17:175–78.
1986 Historic process in the political economy of San. In Proceedings of
the International Symposium on African Hunters and Gatherers, Sankt
Augustin, ed. F. Rottland and R. Vossen, pp. 413–32. *Sprache und Geschichte in Afrika* 7.2.
1989 Those who have each other: Land tenure of San-speaking peoples. In
We are here: Politics of aboriginal land tenure, ed. E. Wilmsen pp. 43–67.
Berkeley and Los Angeles: University of California Press.
n.d.a The antecedents of contemporary pastoralism in western Ngamiland.
Botswana Notes and Records. In press.
n.d.b Journeys with flies. Manuscript.
Wilmsen, E., and D. Durham
1988 Food as a function of seasonal environment and social history. In
Coping with uncertainty, ed. G. Harrison and I. de Garine, pp. 52–87.
Cambridge: Cambridge University Press.
Wily, L.
1979 Official policy toward San (Bushmen) hunter-gatherers in modern
Botswana: 1966–1978. Gaborone: National Institute of Development
and Cultural Research.
Wolf, E.
1982 *Europe and the people without history.* Berkeley and Los Angeles: University of California Press.
Worby, E.
1982 Anthropology comes to "class": Concepts of social form and human history in contemporary social theory. B.A. thesis (honors), McGill University.
1984 The politics of dispossession: Livestock development policy and the
transformation of property relations in Botswana. M.A. thesis (anthropology), McGill University.
n.d. "Not to plow my master's field": Discourses of ethnicity and the production of inequality in Botswana. Manuscript.
Worsaae, P.
1849 *The primeval antiquities of Denmark.* Copenhagen: Royal Danish National Museum.
Worsley, P.
1984 *The three worlds.* Chicago: University of Chicago Press.
Wright, E.
1983 The status of the political in the concept of class structure. *Politics and
Society* 1:321–41.

Wright, J.
1986 Politics, ideology and the invention of 'Nguni. In *Resistance and ideology in settler societies*, ed. T. Lodge, pp. 96–118. Johannesburg: Raven Press.

Yellen, J.
1970 A report to the Botswana government on archaeological investigations in western Ngamiland. Manuscript in National Museum, Gaborone.

1973 Notes to accompany archaeological materials shipped to the National Museum, Botswana. National Museum.

1975 Archaeological research in Western Ngamiland. *Botswana Notes and Records* 3:276.

1976 Settlement patterns of the !Kung. In *Kalahari hunter-gatherers*, ed. R. Lee and I. DeVore, pp. 47–72. Cambridge: Harvard University Press.

1977 *Archaeological approaches to the present*. Orlando, Fla.: Academic Press.

1984 The integration of herding into prehistoric hunting and gathering economies. In *Frontiers: Southern African archaeology today*, ed. M. Hall and G. Avery, pp. 53–64. Cambridge: Cambridge University Press.

1985 The process of Basarwa assimilation in Botswana. *Botswana Notes and Records* 17:15–24.

n.d. The present and the future of hunter gatherer studies. In *Archaeology in the late eighties*, ed. C. Lamberg-Karlowsky, Cambridge: Cambridge University Press. In press.

Yellen, J., and A. Brooks
n.d. The Late Stone Age archaeology of the !Kangwa and |Xai |Xai Valleys, Ngamiland. *Botswana Notes and Records*. In press.

Yellen, J., and H. Harpending
1972 Hunter-gatherer populations and archaeological inference. *World Archaeology* 4:244–53.

Index

Index

397

Malata. *See* Serfs
Malinowski, B., 165
Mambari traders, 96
Manchatees, 91
Manima-Moubouha, A., 70
Man the Hunter, 33, 38, 40
Man the Hunter Conference, 6, 304
Mapongubwe, 58, 70
Maquainas. *See* Bakwena
Marenga, 146, 153
Marital distance, 184, 185
Marks, S., 11, 26, 151, 153, 259, 274
Marriage
  Basarwa-Bakglagadi, 189, 279
  CaeCae-Ghanzi, 199–209
  and choice, 42
  Gcwi, 160, 161, 187
  Gxanna, 187
  and haro, 185, 186, 261
  Herero, 189
  Kwa, 188
  Nharo, 188
  payment, 181–83, 188, 189, 190
  service, 42, 181–83
  Tsassi, 188
  Tswana, 190
  Zhu, 163, 177–80, 219–21
  Zhu-Herero, 279
Marshall, L., 8, 9, 29, 33, 34, 40, 42,
  134, 149, 164, 169, 170, 171, 174,
  175, 176, 177, 178, 179, 196, 211,
  218, 219, 229, 264, 278, 304, 312
Martin, P., 11, 75
Marx, K., 5, 18, 19, 20, 21, 40, 46, 47,
  48, 49–51, 55, 57, 63, 258, 266,
  282
Marxian models, 5, 43, 47, 50, 54, 61
Masarwa, 30, 97, 101, 102, 126, 137,
  154, 155, 181, 278, 286. *See also*
  Basarwa
Massey, D., 281, 286
Matabele. *See* Amandebele
Mathiba, Kgosi of Batawana, 148, 150,
  152, 268
Matlapaneng, 72, 74, 76
Mattick, P., 54, 57
Mautle, G., 7, 283, 285
Mbanderu. *See* Ovambanderu
Mbukushu. *see* Hambukushu
Mechanical solidarity, 34, 44, 47

Meillassoux, C., xvii, 5, 40, 41, 42, 43,
  46, 47, 50, 51, 54, 57, 160, 196,
  259
Mercantile capital, 80, 123, 127,
  130–34, 139, 205, 256, 274
Mfecane. *See* Difaqane
Miers, S., 7
Miller, J., 76, 88, 95
Mirabib, 65
Mode of production, 19, 39, 42, 46, 47,
  49, 56, 60, 61, 63
Moffat, J., 85, 278
Mogalakwe, Regent of Batawana, 101
Mokwele (betrothal) animal, 182
Molele family, 154, 286
Molopo farms, 292
Monomotapa, 58
Moorsom, R., 11
Morgan, L, 14, 16, 21, 22, 23, 34, 38,
  40, 43, 62
Moritz, W., 28
Mossop, E., 86, 88, 94
Motzafi. *See* Motzafi-Haller
Motzafi-Haller, P., 99, 268, 276, 277
Müller, F., 119, 125
Munyuku, 141
Murdock, G., 9
Murray, A., 104
Murray, M., 297
Mushingeh, A., 312
Mzilikazi, 91

Nama. *See also* Orlams
  cattle, 98, 126
  destitutes called Bushmen, 85
  ivory and feather hunting, 120
  kommando, 93, 103
  northern dispossessed by Orlams, 93
  precolonial trade, 88–96
  raiding, 93, 103, 116, 121
  Red Nation (Rooi Nasi, Ovaserandu),
    93
  Red People (Rooi Volk, northern
    KhoiKhoi), 93, 94, 106
  relations to land, 186, 188, 191
  sā root of San, 31, 328
  tariff on traders, 106
Namaqua, 85, 91, 94, 112, 280. *See also*
  Nama
Named groups, 163

WITHDRAWN

3 1542 00183 0128

WITHDRAWN

330.968 W743L
Land filled with flies : a
political economy of the
Kalahari

Trexler Library
Muhlenberg College
Allentown, PA 18104

DEMCO